Domestic Intimacies

EARLY AMERICAN STUDIES

Series Editors
Daniel K. Richter, Kathleen M. Brown,
Max Cavitch, and David Waldstreicher

Exploring neglected aspects of our colonial, revolutionary,
and early national history and culture, Early American Studies
reinterprets familiar themes and events in fresh ways.
Interdisciplinary in character, and with a special emphasis on
the period from about 1600 to 1850, the series is published in
partnership with the McNeil Center for Early American Studies.

A complete list of books in the series
is available from the publisher.

Domestic Intimacies

Incest and the Liberal Subject
in Nineteenth-Century America

Brian Connolly

UNIVERSITY OF PENNSYLVANIA PRESS

PHILADELPHIA

Published by
University of Pennsylvania Press
Philadelphia, Pennsylvania 19104-4112
www.upenn.edu/pennpress

Printed in the United States of America
on acid-free paper
10 9 8 7 6 5 4 3 2 1

Library of Congress Cataloging-in-Publication Data
Connolly, Brian.
   Domestic intimacies : incest and the liberal subject in nineteenth-century
America / Brian Connolly.—1st ed.
   p. cm.— (Early American studies)
   Includes bibliographical references and index.
   ISBN 978-0-8122-4621-6 (hardcover : alk. paper)
   1. Incest—United States—History—19th century. 2. Liberalism—United
States—History—19th century. 3. Individualism—United States—History—
19th century. 4. Domestic relations—United States—History—19th century.
I. Title. II. Series: Early American studies.
   HV6570.7.C65   2014
   306.8770973'09034—dc23

                                                              2013047826

Contents

Introduction

Liberalism's Incestuous Subject

In 1828, in the first edition of his dictionary, Noah Webster defined incest as "the crime of cohabitation or sexual commerce between persons related within the degrees wherein marriage is prohibited by the law of a country."[1] As definitions go, this one seems rather straightforward. Yet, as far as incest goes, it presents numerous questions. The one thing we think we know about incest is that its prohibition is universal and has been in existence since humans organized themselves into something resembling families. Of course, this one thing is an illusion, and Webster's definition gets at some of the problems with that illusion. First, this particular definition hitched incest to the system of criminal law rather than to biblical injunction. Second, Webster tied the prohibition to the legal systems of nations, which inspires the question: If the prohibition of incest was dependent on nationally bounded legal systems, was it possible that a nation could simply forego the prohibition of incest? Finally, in Webster's definition the crux of the prohibition was dependent on marriage, yet it was unclear if the prohibition of marriage between near kin was part of incest or something else altogether. What is clear is that, for a universal prohibition that, for several centuries, has been treated as one of the fundamental laws of human culture, Webster, perhaps unwittingly, introduced a great deal of ambiguity.

Perhaps aware of this, perhaps simply trying to cut words, Webster modified the definition in an abridged version of his dictionary in 1839. Gone was the ambiguity; the definition was shorter but more capacious and seemingly universal. Incest was now "cohabitation of persons within prohibited degrees of kindred."[2] Cohabitation did more work than enumerating sex and marriage had in the original definition. Cohabitation was a legal category in itself but was also frequently used to describe a man and woman living together outside of marriage. Implicit in the term was some degree of intimacy. In that, it incorporated sex and potentially gestured at marriage. But if marriage and sex were encompassed by cohabitation, crime was gone altogether. This definition passed no judgment, made no claims. Finally, the particularity of the original definition, which hinged on the inclusion of national laws, was gone. With this elision one could presume that there were "prohibited degrees of kindred" everywhere, that men and women potentially cohabited everywhere, and thus that the prohibition of incest was universal.

A history of the incest prohibition in nineteenth-century America entails excavating this space between the universal and the particular in various articulations of the prohibition. In this period, the incest prohibition was in flux. No matter how frequently or forcefully one invoked the fundamental nature of the prohibition, its universal and uniform character, the function of the prohibition, its parameters, and indeed, its meaning, were increasingly unclear. If the universal and seemingly self-evident character of the prohibition is, to a greater or lesser extent, an illusion in every age, that does not mean it is the same illusion or doing the same work across time. The question is thus why and to what end was the language of universalism deployed in relation to the prohibition of incest in nineteenth-century America. Put differently, if the incest prohibition was supposed to be a foundational law of human society, universal in nature, that inaugurated both kinship and culture, why were so many people in the nineteenth century so worried that the family was inherently incestuous and that one of the great sexual and marital dangers of the period was incest?

In the chapters that follow, I trace articulations of the incest threat and the incest prohibition in the nineteenth century as a problematic of liberalism and the liberal subject.[3] Society in the early republic and antebellum America was, without suggesting a totalizing interpretation, increasingly liberal.[4] To treat incest in the context of liberalism, or, conversely, to treat liberalism in the context of incest, demands that both, despite their various universal claims, have a history. The central figure of both liberalism and the nineteenth-century incest prohibition was the liberal subject, that autonomous, rational individual who acted on his own desires, was endowed with the capacity for consent, was not dependent on others, and had his choices and desires ratified in contracts. This subject enjoyed a life in public—in market exchanges and fraternal societies, in the institutions of representative democracy, and in an ever-expanding print culture. Yet, at the same time, the liberal subject was supposed to find his greatest comforts, warmest affections, and most intimate affairs in the private life of the bourgeois, sentimental family. The liberal subject, then, was fully realized in the constant movement between the public world of markets, politics, and sociality and the private life of the family.

Liberalism, *sentimentalism*, *consent*, and *affection* are not words commonly associated with incest. Rather, *force*, *domestic violence*, *pedophilia*, *rape*, and, in a different register, *reproduction* have had an overwhelming influence on historical and psychological accounts of incest. My aim is not to replace one set of terms with the other—one need only glance at the nineteenth-century discourse of incest to see that it was determined by force and violence as much as sentiment and consent. Nor is my aim to refute those accounts of marriage and the sentimental family that associated it with a discourse of stability amid the social and political disruptions of liberal democracy. In historicizing the discourse of incest in the nineteenth-century United States, I seek to demonstrate how the separation between consent and force, sentiment and domestic violence, love and rape became at once structural conditions of the discourse and ultimately impossible distinctions. Force and consent were implicated in one another, as were sentiment and violence, love and rape.[5] That these structural conditions and their partial undoing came together in writings on incest in this period illustrates the extent to which the supposedly private family and sexuality were both implicated in one another and were at the core of the deployment of liberalism as a way of life.

The aim of this book, then, is to treat the incest prohibition and thus incest as the subject of a genealogy. Genealogy, Michel Foucault has written, must "record the singularity of events outside of any monotonous finality; it must seek them in the most unpromising places, in what we tend to feel is without history—in sentiments, love, conscience, instincts; it must be sensitive to their recurrence, not in order to trace the gradual curve of their evolution, but to isolate the different scenes where they engaged in different roles." In other words, genealogy takes those categories that seem natural or self-evident or culturally necessary and demonstrates that things have not always been this way, that categories like incest have not always had the same meaning, that at specific moments these categories had very different meanings and functions, frequently having little to do with what they meant either before or after that moment. Moreover, genealogy is not interested in discovering the origins of this or that category; indeed, "it opposes itself to the search for 'origins.'"[6] In this, then, a genealogy of the incest

prohibition sets itself apart from much of the work on the incest prohibition—anthropological, sociological, psychoanalytic, and sociobiological—
which frequently concerns itself with the origins of the prohibition, instead
inquiring in to the category of incest itself in order to denaturalize it.

In contemporary parlance, incest is most commonly constituted by two
relatively unrelated components. On the one hand, domestic sexual violence, especially that between fathers and daughters, has been at the center
of much of the discourse of incest in the twentieth century, especially since
the 1970s.[7] On the other hand, reproduction and hereditary degeneration
(on the level of the population, or, less persuasively, the individual) have
lent a seemingly scientific, objective, and "natural" basis for the prohibition.[8] These two positions have made it impossible to imagine incest as
constituted by anything other than violent, abusive sexual relations between
fathers and daughters or by the fraught prospects of consanguine (relations
by blood) reproduction. Yet, in the nineteenth century, most salient in
understanding incest and its prohibition was not necessarily violence
(which was certainly an important part of the discourse) but sentiment,
marriage, affection, and desire. And while concerns with reproduction
emerged in the mid-nineteenth century, they were mostly confined to the
work of phrenologists and physiologists until later in the century. Others
writing on incest and its prohibition—especially theologians, jurists, novelists, and anti- and proslavery writers (those treated in more detail in the
chapters that follow)—rarely invoked the language of reproduction. It is
between the late eighteenth century and the mid-nineteenth century that
the seeming naturalness of our contemporary meaning of incest begins to
fall apart and become less tenable. This does not mean that incest was of
little importance in this period; indeed, if anything, it was inescapable—
everywhere someone looked someone else was worrying about the incestuous state of the nation.

At the heart of this concern over incest were the emergent figures of
liberalism and the liberal subject. There was, however, something else about
this period that makes it ripe for exploring the historical contingency of the
seemingly universal, transhistorical prohibition. In this period, unlike those
before and after, there was no clear referent for the prohibition of incest.
In other words, while there was a pervasive discourse of incest and multiple
articulations of the prohibition, there was no locus to this discourse.
Through the middle of the eighteenth century, despite myriad doctrinal
debates and interpretive battles, the origin of the incest prohibition, and

thus the authority behind it, was clear (in western Europe and the American colonies, at least): the book of Leviticus. The foundation of the prohibition, then, was biblical. Theologians might debate who exactly was prohibited, Protestants and Catholics might hurl insults at each other over the accuracy of their respective prohibitions, but in the end, they all knew which text they were to refer to. The incest laws in the British North American colonies—those colonies that included a law prohibiting incest, anyway—were all derived from Leviticus, or the Anglican interpretation of the Levitical prohibitions, the Table of Kindred and Affinity, which was codified in 1563 and published in 1603. Those colonies without explicit incest laws did not permit incest, they simply assumed that the force of the Levitical prohibitions was so clear that there was no need for direct reference to them. Without attributing an undue stability—there never was a golden age of the incest prohibition, with the invention of the table in the sixteenth century being one clear signifier of the various crises of meaning in the history of the prohibition[9]—in the period prior to the mid-eighteenth century, the incest prohibition was Christian and universal, and its roots were in the word of God.[10]

By the end of the nineteenth century, a new basis for the universality of the prohibition had emerged and could be found in the emerging disciplines of anthropology and psychoanalysis. While religious writings on the prohibition did not disappear, the prohibition was now of human origins, but in a deep, indeed, lost past. Ethnographers like Lewis Henry Morgan theorized an evolutionary system by which humans moved from what he and others called "promiscuous intercourse," a term for incest in the absence of the incest prohibition, through a series of kinship relations that included communal marriage and polygamy, and ended in lifetime monogamous marriage.[11] The prohibition of incest, first between parents and children and later between siblings, was the origin of kinship. Without the prohibition kinship, families and society would never have developed.[12] This system, rather obviously, worked to make the modern, liberal West the pinnacle of civilization. The production of this new, universal, ethnographic incest prohibition was a transatlantic affair and included not only Morgan, but also English interlocutors like John McLennan and John Lubbock in England and Émile Durkheim in France.[13] Indeed, Morgan's evolutionary system of kinship, including his understanding of the incest prohibition, was the basis of Friedrich Engels's *The Origins of the Family, Private Property, and the State* in 1884.[14] Psychoanalysis also drew on the ethnographic imagination of the incest prohibition. If the connection was not quite manifest in Freud's articulation of the Oedipus complex, ethnography was the foundation of the primal horde (in which the fraternally bound sons murder the father in order to gain sexual mastery over the women their father controlled, making the origins of culture both incestuous and parricidal) in *Totem and Taboo*.[15] Again, like the Levitical prohibition, there was much debate over the parameters of the prohibition, how exactly it came into being, and why it had universal force. Those debates notwithstanding, there was general assent to the origins of the prohibition, which were as decidedly fantastic as the Levitical law, but based their claims somewhere other than the Bible and the word of God.

In between these two periods, that is, from the late eighteenth through to the mid-nineteenth century, most writers on incest and the incest prohibition were no less certain that the prohibition of incest was a universal, foundational Law, but there was no agreed-upon touchstone for its origins or foundational, universal nature. Protestant theologians wrestled with the force and parameters of the Levitical prohibitions across the first half of the nineteenth century while jurists and legal treatise writers abandoned the Levitical tradition in favor of a natural law foundation that looked dramatically different than the Table of Kindred and Affinity. While theologians may have lamented the legal changes, they were rarely part of the legal discourse and had little interest, in their own debates over the meaning of incest, in engaging with jurists and their natural law theories of the incest prohibition. Indeed, it is safe to say that they were rarely even aware of each other's writings. This was even more acute when it came to the reproductive incest prohibition developed by phrenologists and physiologists in the mid-nineteenth century. While phrenologists may have occasionally mocked theologians and their concerns over marrying a deceased wife's sister—the phrenologist Orson Fowler once wrote that "to waste so much breath and ink [on it], and divide the churches on a point no way essential, is weak and wicked"—they were generally uninterested in legal and theological debates, even as they introduced a radical deviation from received understandings of the prohibition.[16] And for their part, theologians and jurists rarely invoked reproduction as a basis for the incest prohibition, and when they did they seemed wholly unaware that there was, by the 1840s, a growing body of literature on incestuous reproduction.

In other realms of print culture, similar disjunctures appeared. Writers of fictional stories of accidental incest—in which a long-separated brother and sister, for instance, met and either married or engaged in some kind of sexual relation only to find out afterward that they were kin—seemed unaware that, at the same time, antislavery writers were lamenting the incestuous effect of the domestic slave trade, which fractured enslaved families by selling slaves all over the South. This fracturing, according to abolitionists, created the conditions for incest in slavery as genealogies became impossible to trace. Both kinds of stories were concerned with the circulation of bodies and the familial and sexual disorder that followed from it but never spoke to one another. The mobility of the liberal individual, consenting to occupy a position in the market, was profoundly different from, and indeed, opposed to the circulation of persons as commodities in the slave trade. Yet both were represented as potentially incestuous. And neither evidenced any awareness that at the same time laws were being passed in several states that required knowledge of the relationship for someone to be charged with incest.

Perhaps most common across the antebellum archive of incest was the incestuous nature of sentimental affection in the family. Some theologians, writing on the controversy over marriage with a deceased wife's sister, worried that such marriages encouraged domestic affection to be consummated in incestuous marriages. Jurists, redefining the law of incest in the early nineteenth century, worried that familial affection would result in incestuous marriages that would upend hierarchical relations of dependency and obligation. Both seduction and sentimental fiction frequently recounted tales of excessive familial affection that ended in incestuous, or near incestuous, marriages and affairs. And phrenologists, certain that sexuality had its origins in familial relations, encouraged the cultivation of this quasi-incestuous eroticism. Yet none of these discrete communities seemed aware of what was going on outside its own domain. In short, the incest prohibition had no foundation and, having none, is spread across the archive of antebellum America.

If there was no single foundation to the incest prohibition in the antebellum period, these different discourses often spoke a similar language: their fears of incest and the failures of the prohibition were borne of similar anxieties. These anxieties were tied to the emergence of liberalism and the liberal subject in the late eighteenth and early nineteenth centuries.[17] It was, in the words of Ralph Waldo Emerson, "the age of the first person singular."[18] The autonomous individual, imbued with agency and natural rights, driven by desire but tempered by reason and rationality, voluntaristic, and a figure whose actions and choices were recognized and formalized in contract, was the normative subject of liberalism.[19] Alexis de Tocqueville distinguished the individualism of a democracy from an earlier egoism. "Egoism," Tocqueville wrote, "is a passionate and exaggerated love of self which leads a man to think of all things in terms of himself and to prefer himself to all." Individualism was something else—although it had the air of egoism, it was more desirable because less passionate and more tempered. It was "a calm and considered feeling which disposes each citizen to isolate himself from the mass of his fellows and withdraw into the circle of family and friends; with this little society formed to his taste, he gladly leaves the greater society to look after itself."[20]

Tocqueville's distinction between egoism and individualism was subtle, and many writers in the nineteenth century were constantly concerned that the liberty of individualism would easily slip into the licentiousness of egoism. This emphasis on individual liberty was always threatening social and national stability. If the liberal subject was the foundation of political sovereignty, then the desire of the liberal subject often figured as a threat to the nation, given the unpredictability of desire. This fragility can be discerned in the easy slide from liberty into libertinage and licentiousness that one finds in an early version of Noah Webster's dictionary. Webster defined liberty as "freedom, permission, privilege"; licentious as "unrestrained, loose"; licentiously as "with too great liberty"; licentiousness as "contempt of just restraint"; and libertinism as "licentious of life."[21] The circularity here suggests a broader social and political problem of the antebellum United States: liberty was always on the verge of licentiousness and libertinism. Moreover, if licentiousness and libertinism could lead to anarchy, they were frequently represented in sexual terms, especially in the seduction literature of the period. This was the nature of the liberal subject, who was animated by desire, and the question constantly haunting him was how to both solicit and regulate that animating desire.[22]

Always lurking around the liberty of the individual, then, was the specter of just restraint. How could the individual be restrained, and which institutions were legitimately able to do so? The nineteenth-century political economist Francis Lieber understood liberalism as a dialectic of liberty and constraint. If the individual was a sovereign subject, he was also supposed to be ruled by "civil fortitude—that virtue which is acquired by the habit of at once obeying and insisting upon the laws of a free country, and shows itself most elevated when it resists alluring excitement." Moreover, individuals should have a deep "abhorrence of all absolutism, whether it be individual or collective." Man, Lieber wrote, was "too feeble to wield unlimited power, and too noble to submit to it."[23] For Lieber, as for Tocqueville, the family (and marriage) were institutions of that necessary constraint. "We call marriage an institution in consideration of its pervading importance," Lieber wrote, "its extensive operation, the innumerable relations it affects, and the security which its continuance enjoys in the conviction of almost all men." Marriage, for Lieber, "was pretty much the institution of the family."[24]

While there were a variety of locations for restraint, from the legal system to the church to reform societies, they all, in one manner or another, referred back to the family as the ideal source of constraint because the family was most likely to cultivate virtue with that constraint. Indeed, both Tocqueville and Lieber invoked the family and marriage in just this capacity. In language more effusive than either Lieber or Tocqueville, the liberal evangelical Lyman Beecher praised the family for its capacity to constrain excess and instill order in both individuals and society. Concerned that atheism was threatening all order in society, Beecher enumerated what would be lost in the family.

> The family—the foundation of the political edifice, the methodizer of the world's business, and the mainspring of its industry—they would demolish. The family—the sanctuary of the pure and warm affections, where the helpless find protection, the wretched sympathy, and the wayward undying affection, while parental hearts live to love, and pray, and forgive—they would disband and desecrate. The family—that school of indelible early impression, and of unextinguished affection—that verdant spot in life's dreary waste, about which memory lingers—that centre of attraction, which holds back the heady and high-minded, and whose cords bring out of the vortex the shipwrecked mariner, after the last strand of every other cable is parted—these political Vandals would dismantle. The fire of its altars they would put out; the cold hand of death they would place on the warm beating of its heart; to substitute the vagrancy of desire, the rage of lust, and the solitude, and disease, and desolation, which follows the footsteps of unregulated nature, exhausted by excess.[25]

That "vagrancy of desire" was the threat the liberal subject posed to the society and the nation; the family—bourgeois, sentimental, affectionate—was the best hope for constraining that desire and making it virtuous, producing proper citizens for the democratic republic.

Tocqueville's, Lieber's, and Beecher's invocations of the sentimental family were just three of thousands of instances of this kind of language. Historians and literary critics have traced the production and contours of this family across the eighteenth and nineteenth centuries. A new source of a reconstituted virtue necessary to the republic, populated with moral mothers and virtuous wives, the family was both a source of order and an intimate site for the development of liberal freedom. Whether in marriage or the affectionate relations between parents and children, the family ordered the democratic republic, supplying its necessary virtues, serving metaphorically to pacify violent conflict, and functioning as a training ground for the regulation of desire and passion through both reason and benevolence. The family, protected by a newfound privacy, lent coherence to an increasingly cacophonous and chaotic public sphere at precisely the moment when the social relations of kinship were being severed from the political calculus of democracy. Private, virtuous, sentimental, affectionate, egalitarian, the nuclear family was the liberal democratic republic's last best hope, a bulwark against the easy slippage from liberty to licentiousness, democracy to anarchy.[26] Moreover, it was *the* disciplinary institution in antebellum America. If the law, prisons, and reform movements all offered their own forms of discipline, it was the family, more so than any other institution, that was called on to discipline the excesses of the liberal subject. The family became a potentially effective site of encumbrance and constraint as it formed the liberal subject.[27]

The discourse of incest, however, suggested something quite different. The bourgeois, sentimental family was also a site of affective and erotic excess, which meant that the liberal subject that emerged out of it was never fully moral, rational, or stable. The desire of the family and the desire of the individual could reinforce one another in incestuous, rather than virtuous, directions.[28] It was the highest ideals of the family and the liberal subject that were incestuous. Incest, in antebellum America, was consensual, affectionate, and marital, as well as sexual and, at times, violent. Incest was the constant possibility, the immanent danger of the complex and necessary relation between the bourgeois family and the liberal subject. The discourse of incest suggested, time and again, that the motive force of liberalism (and democracy) was not reason but desire.

That incest inhered in the sympathetic, even passionate, attachments of family relations can be seen perhaps most clearly in Herman Melville's critique of sentimental fiction, *Pierre; or, the Ambiguities.*[29] It is a tragic tale of incest, suicide, and authorship, and the destructive consequences of passionate kin attachments—the way in which they both subject and create the conditions for the possibility of agency, which in this case are the choices of incest and suicide—are clear. In the more idealized familial attachments of the early part of the novel, incestuous love still animates the most forceful filiation. In describing the relationship between Pierre and his mother (his father, importantly and unsurprisingly, was dead and thus the patronymic security of kinship was ruptured), Melville both shifted the lineal relation to a lateral one and then, in order to capture the force of attachment, writes of them as lovers. In the absence of the father, Pierre and his mother referred to each other as brother and sister, a lateral relation that was less threateningly eroticized, for it confused the familial and the sexual, but it did not necessarily challenge familial hierarchy. "In the playfulness of their unclouded love, and with that strange license which a perfect confidence and mutual understanding at all points, had long bred between them, they were wont to call each other brother and sister."[30] This did not make up for the absence of fraternal love, at least for Pierre, for this was a love fully eroticized. "He mourned that so delicious a feeling as fraternal love had been denied him. . . . He who is sisterless, is as a bachelor before his time. For much that goes to make up the deliciousness of a wife, already lies in the sister."[31] The sibling relationship, in all of its "deliciousness," revealed the eroticism of familial love. So too did Pierre's mother's choice to avoid suitors after the death of her husband. Translated into his sister, even if that translation did not "at all supply the absent reality," Mary Glendenning believed "a reverential and devoted son . . . lover enough."[32] That Pierre would go on to find his half sister, the offspring of his dead father's libertinage, and that he would be able to register that passionate attachment only to a no longer absent reality in erotic terms further instantiates the inherent eroticism of the sentimental family.[33]

If incest was a problem of life in the sentimental family, it was also an effect of disordered kinship. This disorder, I argue, was an effect of the circulation of bodies and things in markets. The general mobility of persons in antebellum America combined with the increasing emphasis on the nuclear family created conditions where the liberal subject was supposed to leave his natal family behind and make a new life of his own. This disorder, combined with a perceived decline in the authority of fathers, as in *Pierre*, led to a declining stability in the order of kinship. Indeed, we might think of these tales of incest, scattered throughout the antebellum archive, as some of the last acts in the transition from the patriarchal divine right of kings theorized by Robert Filmer to the consensual world of the social contract theorized by John Locke. These tales of incest suggest that, in the absence of absolute authority of fathers, a potential "kinship dystopia" awaited every marital or sexual relation.[34] The reconstitution of the incest prohibition for this liberal society was the perceived solution.

This disorder and excessive affection sometimes came together in one account. Indeed, nestled among tragic heroines, gothic lusts gone wrong, intemperate incestuous fathers, and sensational tales of incest, readers could even find humorous doggerel suggesting the complexities of kinship and the ever-present threat of incest. In 1805, readers of the *Miscellany*, for example, would have found just such an account of kinship and incest in "Paradoxical Wedding."

> A Wedding there was, and a dance there must be,
> And who should dance first, they all did agree:
> Old Grandpa and Grandma should lead the dance
>   down,
> Two fathers, two mothers should step the same
>   ground;
> Two uncles vouchsafed with nieces to dance,
> With nephews to jig it, it pleased two aunts.
> Two daughters there were, and danc'd with their
>   sires,
> The room was so warm they wanted no fires;
> Two sons there were, and danc'd with their mothers,
> Three sisters there were, and danc'd with three
>   brothers,
> Three husbands there were, and danc'd with their
>   wives,
> As bent so to do the rest of their lives;
> The granddaughter chose the jolly grandson,
> And bride she would dance with bridegroom or none,
> A company choice, their number to fix,
> I count them all o'er and find them but six;

All honest and good, from incest quite free,
Their marriages good; pray how can that be?[35]

No fires were needed, the room was warm, heated perhaps by amorous feelings circulating through a tangle of kin relations at a wedding. If disordered circulation was not at issue, kinship nonetheless was a series of confusions. Readers would wait nearly a month before the *Miscellany* published the solution.[36] But what they might have taken away, beyond (perhaps) being entertained by the riddle, was that by the early nineteenth century kinship was more an enigma than a source of stability, and, kinship being thus, incest was a persistent possibility. If this tangle of kin relations was not incestuous, incest nonetheless lingered at the end of the poem.

Figuring kinship as an enigma was not confined to northern literary magazines like the *Miscellany*. In 1806 readers of the *Mississippi Herald and Natchez Gazette* could find "A Lover of Riddles" attempting to solve a riddle of endogamy. In doing so, even as the author treated it as a problem of logic, its existence, like that in the *Miscellany* a year earlier, suggests that kinship, in either practice or discourse, was anything but stable in the early republic. The "Lover of Riddles" was responding to "an account of affinity, the singularity of which excited my curiosity."[37] The full account gives a sense of the convoluted nature of kinship knowledge. "The two men (Palmore and Westbrooks) were by the second marriage, fathers and sons to each other—& their wives were mothers and daughters to each other—the offspring of each party were sons and daughters, and also grandsons and grand-daughters interchangeably to the real parents of each other, and consequently were brothers and sisters, and first cousins interchangeably to each other."[38] The children of the children, here, according to the lover of riddles, "bore double the consanguinity to each other of that of ordinary first cousins."[39] It is difficult to make out what the point of this exercise is, but it is clear that kinship was again indecipherable, leading the author to call the second generation offspring "(if it is a proper term) double cousins to each other."[40] The redoubling of consanguinity here, which in an indirect way mirrored the increasing focus on consanguinity in antebellum descriptions of the family, required a new lexicon. The confusions of kinship, marriage, and desire were exceeding the limits of kinship.

Across the nineteenth-century archive, incest signified multiple types of sexual and marital relations: the violent abuse of a daughter by a father; the

intoxicated excess of siblings; the unregulated desire of religious enthusi-
asts; relations of affinity as well as consanguinity; the excess effusions of
sympathy and sentiment; marriage and/or sex. More than anything, incest
was a problem of affection and desire, sentiment and sensuality. It would,
by the mid-nineteenth century, become a problem of reproduction and
eroticism, as well. It was caught between force and consent, violence and
sentimentality. It was the condition and problematic limit of the liberal
subject, the bourgeois nuclear family, and the sexual subject. As kinship
was displaced by sexuality, it was remade as a site of instability and disorder,
thrown into chaos in its engagement with the wild desire of the liberal
subject.[41] In a world where the division between public and private both
animated social, political, and economic relations and was always being
transgressed, incest was a condition of both the public and the private lives
of the liberal subject. Indeed, the circulation of bodies in public, which
often occasioned the occlusion of natality, could create an unintended
incestuous return. This was the incestuous premise of both William Hill
Brown's 1789 novel *The Power of Sympathy* and Melville's *Pierre*. Incest
haunted the liberal subject, a danger to be avoided but also, simultaneously,
a danger cultivated.[42] The discourse of incest, as it cut across theology,
law, physiology and phrenology, ethnography, novels, and slavery produced
incest as an imminent threat to the actions of the liberal subject precisely
as it purported to represent that danger.

All of this suggested that the liberal subject was both the pivot on which
liberalism turned and its potential undoing; the family, the supposed source
of stability, was also rent by incestuous passions, and thus the incest prohibition needed to be rearticulated in order to manage both familial and
individual desire. Despite insistence to the contrary, the family was as dangerous as the liberal individual; the site of virtue was the site of vice; liberty
was always already licentious. Incest and the incest prohibition registered
this danger. And this persistent danger to the liberal subject and the bourgeois sentimental family created the conditions by which individuals could
be regulated and governed. There was no question that incest needed to be
avoided at all costs; at the same time, there was no question that incest
haunted both the family and sexuality in the nineteenth century.[43] Legists,
theologians, phrenologists, novelists, and others both produced this danger
and then attempted to rewrite the incest prohibition to govern both the
private family and the liberal subject.

The "liberal individual" is a common personage in histories of nineteenth-century America. I have chosen, however, to use the term "liberal subject" in this book. The reason is simple enough. The liberal individual, as I have noted, is often conjured as an autonomous figure endowed with reason and the capacity for self-government. All too frequently we take this figure as a given, and that discourses and institutions in nineteenth-century America were responding to the actions of this rights-bearing, consenting, autonomous individual. Yet this is only half-right. The discourses of the nineteenth century that presumed the existence of the liberal individual, precisely in that unstated presumption, also produced him. Subject captures this process in a way individual does not. The subject is both that figure who is subjected and as such has the capacity to act—autonomy and agency, hallmarks of the liberal individual, do not precede this act of subjection to power. As Judith Butler puts it, "subjection is, literally, the *making* of a subject, the principle of regulation according to which a subject is formulated or produced."[44]

The discourse of incest and the various articulations of the incest prohibition were one site of that subjection, that production of the liberal subject. Insofar as they presumed the liberal subject as a problem, these authors—in the pages that follow, novelists, theologians, jurists and legists, phrenologists and physiologists, anti- and proslavery writers, and ethnographers—produced that subject. Throughout this introduction, I have referred to the liberal subject with the masculine pronoun—this has not been an accident. Scholars have amply demonstrated over the past several decades the ways in which the supposedly abstract individual of liberalism was in fact highly particularized—for all of its universal language, the vast majority of persons were excluded from the rights and privileges of the liberal subject.[45] The liberal subject, more often than not, was white, male, property owning, and heterosexual. The discourse of incest and the articulations of the incest prohibition were central to the production of this subject. Indeed, if the prohibition was universal, there were constitutive assumptions built into that universality that made only certain persons fully capable of even potentially following the dictates of the prohibition.

Much of what follows argues that the family, as represented in much of the literature on incest in the nineteenth century, was conceived of as inherently incestuous. Michel Foucault makes a similar argument about sexuality, writing "that since the eighteenth century the family has become an obligatory locus of affects, feelings, love; that sexuality has its privileged point of development in the family; that for this reason sexuality is 'incestuous' from the start."[46] Yet, the family was not quite so abstract. It was not the family, but the increasingly private, bourgeois, sentimental family, that was the locus of such affection. If no one quite lived their lives in the manner represented in sentimental fiction or domestic advice manuals, this was nonetheless a discourse aimed at the middle class. If that was the case, then the insistent articulations of the incest prohibition by theologians, jurists, phrenologists, and others were prompted by the incestuous qualities of this middle-class family formation. These writers presumed families animated by effusive affection, loving relations, and a tempered sense of egalitarianism. Those outside of this family formation—the enslaved and the immigrant working class, for instance—were less likely to live up to the strictures of the new, liberal incest prohibition.

This was apparent in a report on tenement life in New York City from 1856. A committee convened by the state legislature investigated tenements all over Manhattan and Brooklyn to report on the living conditions of the poor. After chronicling buildings with dozens upon dozens of families, with eight to ten persons per family, living in one-room apartments, the committee devised suggestions on promoting some sense of public health and bourgeois morality. Despite investigators admitting to entering each building only for very short periods of time, one of the recommendations suggested, for "the prevention of prostitution and incest . . . that only a sufficient number of rooms, or a room properly divided in separate departments, shall be rented to families."[47] While it was unlikely that the reformers actually witnessed incest, given their short visits, the spatial organization of the apartments was such that there was no reasonable expectation of privacy. The families exhibited none of the signs of the sentimental family and thus were deemed incestuous. The committee did not recommend a material or economic solution such as higher wages; rather, they suggested a very limited implementation of the bourgeois home. If one were to remain in the conditions of the urban poor, there was little the incest prohibition could do to prevent incest. This population was not made up of liberal subjects.

If the incest prohibition had a class component, it was also profoundly gendered. Theorists of the prohibition, since at least Friedrich Engels and Sigmund Freud, through Claude Lévi-Strauss, Gayle Rubin, and Judith Butler, have either assumed or critiqued the relationship between the incest prohibition and sexual difference. In the archive of the nineteenth-century liberal incest prohibition, we see not only the production of sexual difference but also an asymmetry in the way in which men and women were treated by the prohibition. The discourse of incest was, with few exceptions, authored by men. If we find someone like Lydia Maria Child writing on incest and slavery, she was nonetheless an outlier. Moreover, the assumptions about who committed incest reinforced the fact that, no matter how transgressive the act, the liberal subject, that desiring individual, was a man.[48] Newspapers are littered with cases of father-daughter incest, and while there were certainly instances when the reports claimed that the daughter was seducing the father, this was a claim for the poor character of the father and his submission to the promiscuous desire of the daughter. The father either committed incest or had the capacity of reason to restrain himself from such action. Moreover, if incest was frequently represented as an effect of the disordered circulation of individuals as a result of market relations, it was men who circulated while women, encumbered by family, were less likely to enter into this public world of the market.

The discourse of incest was also a signal site in the history of nineteenth-century heterosexuality. In one of the most incisive works on the incest prohibition, Judith Butler has argued that the foundational nature of the incest prohibition masks the prior prohibition of homosexuality. In doing so, the incest prohibition produces a "heterosexual matrix"—a melancholy structure in which gender identity is constituted.[49] This is apparent in the nineteenth-century archive of the incest prohibition—for all its gregariousness on so many forms of incestuous relations, the discourse is silent on same-sex incest. Every iteration of incest in nineteenth-century America presumed, and in doing so produced, heterosexual subjects. This was most apparent in the midcentury rise of a reproductive incest prohibition, which eschewed any other explanation of incest beyond the hereditary health of future populations. Virtually unheard of in the late eighteenth century, it was an almost universal assumption by the late nineteenth century. Heterosexuality, then, was both a ground and effect of the liberal incest prohibition.

Finally, again despite its abstract, universal claims, incest and its prohibition were at the core of the racial formation of the liberal subject. As incest increasingly threatened both the sexual and marital choices of the liberal subject, it was increasingly racialized through an association with enslaved and potentially colonized populations. Antislavery writers, in critiquing the domestic slave trade and the licentiousness of the plantation, nonetheless associated incest almost exclusively with the enslaved, thus cordoning off the liberal subject, both racially and in terms of freedom. And by the mid-nineteenth century, ethnographers like Lewis Henry Morgan would associate the liberal subject with lifetime monogamy (a legacy of western European social practices), and incest with the indigenous populations of Pacific islands like Hawaii. In doing so, Morgan evacuated incest from the sentimental family and the liberal subject.

The discourse of incest in the nineteenth century was precisely this conditioning of the liberal subject. The family, erotically charged through the newfound valorization of affectionate relations, was a hotbed of incestuous passions. Protestant ministers feared that, in the absence of stringent moral governance, individuals would be compelled by fevered passions into incestuous marriages. Jurists justified penetration into the innermost recesses of the private family through regulating incest, the prohibition of which produced both sociality and dependency. The family, more commonly understood as a source of virtue and a haven from the competitive and vice-ridden world of the market and the public, was, in the discourse of liberalism, also incestuous.

In the chapters that follow, we approach incest and its prohibition from multiple perspectives. In doing so, we are able to discern both the commonalities between different domains and the manner in which the meaning of incest was almost hopelessly dispersed across a wide, interdisciplinary archive in the nineteenth century. Central to liberalism in the nineteenth century was a distinction between public and private. Incest, in a variety of fictional works spanning the late eighteenth and nineteenth centuries, was conceived of as a problem of both excessive privacy and excessive publicity, making liberal society incestuous. What made radical privacy incestuous? What made the public life of individuals, severed from natality, potentially incestuous? To begin to understand this, I suggest, we need to attend to the problem of circulation—of bodies and things—that animated liberalism in the antebellum United States. By attending to both public and private figurations of incest, we can discern the centrality of incest at the conjuncture of the liberal subject, family, and sexuality.

Not all writers were concerned with the circulation of people and disorder of kinship. Some were particularly concerned with the excessive desire of the sentimental family. This was readily apparent in the first postrevolutionary crisis of the incest prohibition in a theological controversy commonly referred to as "the marriage question." The prohibition of incest, legally and theologically, in western Europe and North American colonies had long been grounded in various readings of Leviticus. Expanded and codified in England in 1563 in the Table of Kindred and Affinity, this prohibition made no distinction between affinity and consanguinity. In the late eighteenth century, American theologians began to question the capaciousness of the prohibition by asking whether marriage with a deceased wife's sister ought to be prohibited as incest. This opened on to a much wider exploration of the force of foundational law, the legitimacy of theological interpretations, and the tensions between liberty, kinship and marriage. By the mid-nineteenth century most theologians had given up on the deceased wife's sister, signaling a formal contraction of the incest prohibition and an implicit blow to a foundational and transcendent prohibition of incest. This debate charted the tension between the incest prohibition and the liberty of the individual to choose his own marital and sexual partners.

Jurists and other legal writers addressed similar issues across the nineteenth century: issues of liberal desire in marriage and sex, the circulation of bodies around the nation, and, unlike either theological writings or the narratives of public and private incest, the problem of incestuous abuse. In the domain of the legal system, the incest prohibition took on a secular cast and replaced the biblical prohibition with one grounded in natural law. The legal system, in line with the increasing visibility of the sexual subject in antebellum America, defined incest in both marital and sexual terms. Moreover, symptomatic of the lack of a locus of the prohibition, the development of the law of incest was both profound and slower than some other domains, with many of the ideas of the new liberal law of incest emerging in the early nineteenth century but not being codified until the mid- to late nineteenth century.

Theologians and legal writers in the early nineteenth century only rarely addressed heredity and reproduction when writing of incest. By the mid-nineteenth century, however, a vigorous discourse of incestuous reproduction had emerged among phrenologists and physiologists. The emphases in the prohibition shifted from considerations of morality, marriage, and sociality (although these remained important) to population health, especially of the white imperial body. Incest needed to be prohibited to secure the health of an expanding population. At the same time, phrenologists, having confined incest to a problem of reproduction while articulating a

psychology of the sexual subject, began to argue for the necessary solicita-
tion of erotic relations between parents and children. The incestuous problems of the sentimental family were here normalized in the production of
the liberal subject as sexual subject.

The discourse of slavery engaged both the racial logic of the prohibition
in physiology and phrenology and the circulatory problems of public incest
in a field produced by both anti- and proslavery writers. If the liberal circulation of bodies and things created the conditions for incest insofar as individuals were severed from the encumbrance of family, how was this realized
when persons were transformed into commodities? How was the absence
of the sentimental family in slavery, a common image in abolitionist writings, a feature of the incestuous nature of slavery? And conversely, how
did proslavery writers invoke sympathy and sentiment in their paternalist
defenses of slavery? How was the incestuous family that followed from these
paternalist defenses rent by race, so that the slaveholding patriarch could
both uphold the (white) incest prohibition while transgressing the (black)
prohibition?

The book closes with a brief foray into the geopolitics of the incest
prohibition through a discussion of Lewis Henry Morgan's imperial ethnographic fantasies. Morgan was, in many ways, at the origins of the intellectual history of the incest prohibition. In his ethnographies of kinship he
developed an evolutionary scheme of kinship, which proceeded from "promiscuous intercourse" to lifetime monogamous marriage. This evolutionary scale indexed the civilizational status of various cultures and nations
and, in the process, produced a global map of incest. In this way, the liberal
subject was produced as an evolutionary product of the better regulation
of incest and promiscuity. In this global mapping Hawaii became the area
of the world closest to "promiscuous intercourse" at a moment when the
U.S. was entertaining imperial fantasies.

Linking all these discourses into one discourse of incest are variously
defined attempts to work out an incest prohibition and, concomitantly, a
notion of incest compatible with the dictates of liberal society and its key
figuration, the liberal subject. The family and the individual necessitated
one another, and both embodied certain kinds of freedom: the individual
was a source of desire and excess while the family was a source of encumbrance and constraint. The prohibition of incest claimed the status of
foundational law even as its liberal articulation eviscerated such universal
foundations. I argue that liberalism was and is at its core a system of

regulation and subjection, but one also marked, centrally, by the disorders of desire and the valorization of the individual. The rearticulation of the incest probation in antebellum America, in its moral, sexual, reproductive, racial, and imperial configurations, was not simply a part of regulation, it was regulation itself.

Chapter 1

Literature

Beginning in the mid-eighteenth century and reaching its apex in the mid-nineteenth century, a discourse of the private family came to dominate visions of social and political life in the United States. Where previously the family had been conceived as the central institution of social and economic life, serving as a "little commonwealth" analogous to the state, by the mid-nineteenth century, at least in prescriptive literature and sentimental novels, the family was private, increasingly cut off from economic production and political life. It did, however, retain a political function: the production and dissemination of virtue, morality, and chastity that ensured the political health of the nation precisely by abstaining from politics. As countless historians have told us, this made for a relatively clear, gendered distinction between public (male and masculine) and private (female and feminine).[1]

The public-private distinction, with the virtuous, sentimental family at its heart, was taken as the guarantee of stability for liberal democracy in nineteenth-century America. The social and political function of this family was to instill order in an increasingly disordered nation. Vice and licentiousness, keywords of the American Revolution, became only more prevalent with urbanization. In the discourse of the frontier, civilization was always on the verge of disintegrating. Democracy itself, once something to be feared, was becoming an object of desire, manifest in the expansion of universal white male suffrage, and later, in claims by women and the enslaved for liberty and full citizenship. Indeed, depending on the perspective, fear and desire emanated from the same things. While property-holding white men may have feared the force of democratic agency, marginalized populations lauded it. Mobs were frequent spectacles in urban metropolises, while the French Revolution served as a beacon call for a more radical democracy at the same time that the Terror increased democratic anxiety for others, especially Federalists. The wild popularity of seduction fiction was symptomatic of fears of the increasing visibility of women in public but also captured something of the increasing democratic (if still constrained) agency of white women. In this context, sovereignty (the location of political power) was becoming increasingly murky. The novelty of democracy was not that sovereignty disappeared, but that it was no longer localizable to any absolute authority. As the political theorist Claude Lefort has argued, "Democracy is instituted and sustained by the dissolution of markers of certainty. It inaugurates a history in which people experience a fundamental indeterminacy as to the basis of power, law, and knowledge . . . at every level of social life."[2] The sentimental family, naturally virtuous, would, ideally, work as a regulator of such indeterminacy.

But things were not as simple as this characterization, accepted by most historians of the family, suggests. For every idealized domestic scene, readers could also find families rent by incest, consensual or forceful. What are we to make of the emergence of a widespread discourse of incest in the same period? Sentimental fiction, the locus of the virtuous family, was littered with tales of incest. Theologians wrestled with the meaning of the incest prohibition. Reformers worried about the spread of incest, from urban tenements to the slave plantations of the South. Incest has generally been treated as a private transgression, hidden in the recesses of violent households. Yet, as I argue, incest was a problem, a condition even, for both private and public life in the nineteenth century. The distinction between public and private, frequently referred to as separate spheres, is a structuring fiction of liberal society. Yet, it is a figure that has been frequently (and persuasively) critiqued, primarily for the ways in which it is a misrepresentation of the gendered ordering of antebellum life.[3] Without claiming that the public-private distinction is reflective of lived reality (a wholly elusive and problematic category itself), it did animate much liberal discourse in the nineteenth century.[4] Indeed, as I demonstrate, despite claims to separation, the discourse of incest suggested that liberalism required the constant connection between public and private.

In this regard, incest constituted a limit to both private and public. To escape the vice-ridden, corrupting public by remaining exclusively within the family was to invite incestuous desire; but so too was its opposite, to become exclusively public, occluding one's natal family in the quest for democratic individualism.[5] The circulation of bodies and commodities, a condition of market capitalism, led to individuals, especially men, having the opportunity to leave their families behind. This public circulation diminished the capacity of kinship and family to regulate the liberal subject and made public incest possible. The structural condition of bourgeois liberalism, it seemed, was always on the verge of incest.

Private Incest

The increasing presence of incest in discourses of the family suggests that indeterminacy and vice were not easily expelled from the private sphere. The radically private, or solitary family, operated at the edge, neither inside nor fully outside society. From the late eighteenth century through the 1830s a mortifying tale of incest and cannibalism circulated through the periodical press and almanacs of the early republic, suggesting as it appeared time and again that, perhaps, the private family was not what it was imagined to be.

"The Life of Sawney Beane" recounted the robberies, murders, cannibalism, and incest of the eponymous patriarch's family. The tale first appeared in British chapbooks of the late seventeenth century and attained notoriety upon its inclusion in *The Newgate Calendar*, a compendium of criminal narratives published in England in 1760. In the United States, the tale could be found in any number of publications addressed to rural farmers, the working class, the emergent middle class, and the urban elite. It first appeared in America in 1783 in the first issue of the *Boston Magazine*, a periodical directed at elite, polite society. Its shocking depiction of murder, cannibalism, and incest was in decided contrast to the rest of the magazine, and its editor, the artisan William Billings, was immediately fired.[6] At the same time, however, the tale could also be found at the end of a publication like *Bickerstaff's New-England Almanack*, which was directed at a much wider swath of the literate population. As the nineteenth-century wore on, Sawney Beane became a staple of compilations of criminal narratives, such as *The Lives and Exploits of the Banditti and Robbers of all Nations*. The tale of Sawney Beane, then, was available in one form or another, to most of the literate population of the Northeast. While all versions generally conformed to the *Newgate* source material, there were occasional variations suggesting that the story was not always a simple reprinting, but was sometimes rewritten for American readers. So while not a new story, it nonetheless resonated with specific anxieties about privacy, the family, sexuality, and criminality prevalent in the postrevolutionary United States.[7]

The narrative spanned twenty-five years and was marked by a number of overdetermined scenes. Sawney Beane, the son of hardworking but poor parents, came of age in the Scottish county of East Lothian at the end of the sixteenth century, geographically, if not temporally, on the edge of the Scottish Enlightenment. Beane and his wife, "a woman as viciously inclined as himself," dwelled in a cave by the sea, where their family was "begotten in incest," entirely secluded from society.[8] While never exactly spelled out, the implication was that after having several children come of age, sex between parents and children and siblings was a common feature of the family. The family preyed on passersby, whom they assailed on the road outside their cave, which was sufficiently far enough from any town so as not to be easily known, but close enough to ensure a relatively high volume of traffic in the area. The Beane family, which ultimately included forty-eight people, would, over the course of a quarter century, rob, murder, and eat over one thousand people.

With murders and disappearances rising steadily, the surrounding society was finally alerted to the violence of the countryside but was unable to discover its source. In the midst of this uproar, body parts discarded by the Beane clan began washing up on shores throughout the region, confirming the worst fears of "civilized society." Finally, after twenty-five years, a husband and wife riding home from a fair were assailed by several members of the Beane family. While the woman "was carried to a little distance, and her entrails instantly taken out," the man, through much struggle, escaped when a larger party returning home from the fair came upon the scene of carnage.[9] Outnumbered, the Beane family retreated to their secluded cave.

This man, the only survivor of the Beane family attacks, was taken to a magistrate in Glasgow, who summoned James VI, then king of Scotland. With four hundred men James searched the area surrounding the site of the attack when, upon nearly retiring from another failed search, bloodhounds discovered the entrance to the cave, at which point "a great number of men penetrated through all the intricacies of the path, and at length arrived at the private residence of the horrible cannibals."[10] The entire family was apprehended and executed without trial, "it being deemed unnecessary to try those who were avowed enemies of all mankind, and of all social order."[11]

What significance does the repeated reprinting of this tale of an incestuous, cannibalistic family hold in an emergent liberal democracy fractured, as it was, by its own unstable social order?[12] We should begin with its peculiarity: *The Newgate Calendar* did not appear in the United States until well into the nineteenth century, so we cannot simply attribute its appearance to an effect of the *Calendar*. That is not to say that *The Newgate Calendar* was unknown in the United States; in the same period in which "Sawney Beane" circulated through the periodical press, crime literature in the United States was achieving a new, secular popularity.[13] In this context, I would suggest that the appeal of Sawney Beane, as opposed to the many other stories in the *Calendar*, was that it intersected with a number of anxieties in the early republic, namely the frontier; the increasingly private, bourgeois family; the circulation of goods and bodies in an increasingly market-oriented society; and the location of sovereign power in a liberal democratic republic. Despite its brief appearance in the narrative, I would argue that incest lies at the source of all these problems.

The most immediate resonances would have concerned the frontier. The tale's inclusion in *Bickerstaff's New-England Almanack* in 1787 suggested the potential dangers of travel on roads through relatively unpopulated areas, a practice increasingly common as commercial relations stretched further and further from the coast.[14] On the page immediately preceding the tale of Sawney Beane was a listing of the distances between towns in New England and Boston. The readers, in this case primarily rural farmers, would turn from this information, a common feature of most almanacs offered in order to facilitate movement between the rural hinterland and the urban center (and in that sense can be read as a guide to the circulation of bodies and goods) to a sensational story of incestuous cannibals whose barbaric domicile was hidden from the road, but in close enough proximity to ensure easy attack. In the story, the road, which on the preceding page was represented abstractly as a simple distance, is transformed into a site of grotesque violence.[15]

If the tale, in that specific instance, transformed abstract distances into figures of dismemberment, it would have, in any context, evoked common fears of the frontier. It is a well-worn trope of the early national United States that, as Thomas Jefferson famously noted, the republic needed "empire for liberty."[16] To put this logic into its narrowest political economic context, the phrase referred to the perpetual need for land acquisition in order to ensure the possibility of independent yeoman farmers and, at the same time, the neutralization of political heterogeneity through multiplication. If, however, the republic demanded imperial expansion to guarantee independence and liberty, then the frontier also threatened modernity. Both cannibalism and the grotesquely deformed family were common features of frontier tales.

The late eighteenth-century periodical press and popular captivity narratives presented cannibalism as an ever-present danger of the frontier. In most scenarios, frontier violence appeared in the form of Native American attacks on European American families, and these attacks sometimes led to cannibalism. As Carroll Smith-Rosenberg has pointed out, while Native Americans were said to perpetrate cannibalism in the early republic, by the mid-nineteenth century it had become a humorous pursuit of frontier whites, embodied by Davy Crockett's eating of Indians. The circulation of the Beane story occurred in the midst of this transition and signified the possibility of white savagery. The frontier cannibalism of Sawney Beane would have been compounded for the reader by a general belief that the family was a precarious institution on the frontier, a sentiment captured by J. Hector St. Jean de Crèvecoeur's claim that frontier families "exhibit the most hideous parts of our society." The tale of Sawney Beane, despite its formal setting in Scotland, would have strongly resonated with existing frontier anxieties.[17]

There is something about Crèvecoeur's phrase, that the frontier family is hideous but part of society, that resonates with the Beane family. The family, despite its privacy, was ideally always already oriented toward the public sphere, just as the public was always already oriented toward the family of the private sphere. It was in this complex, recursive loop between private and public that the family became the source of virtue and the model for national affection.[18] The shifting, porous boundaries between public and private, market/state and family, were a significant feature of the early national United States. If the separation of private and public was never complete, nor intended to be, then there was, nonetheless, an anxiety about the vice-ridden public world. "The Tale of Sawney Beane," however, served as a cautionary reminder of the dangers inherent not simply in the public—that is, in the liminal space of roads between towns (as well as markets and contracts), but, more importantly, in the confines of a wholly private family, the supposed salve to public wounds. If imperial expansion was necessary to secure liberty, then the fate of the nation rested on what were seen as increasingly secluded families, cut off from that recursive relationship.[19]

The Beanes were a private family without an orientation toward public life, or a public good; indeed, its only public, social orientation was predatory. It was thus a solitary family. The solitary individual was an ambivalent figure in the early republic, at once suspect because of his absence from civil society but also, for the same reason, less prone to corruption.[20] The solitary family, however, was of a different order—where the individual in solitude was alone, the solitary family retained a particular sociality, albeit in the absence of society, and in this instance the manifestation of intrafamilial sociality was the imperative to reproduce. Despite all of its perversions, the Beane family was still marked by one of the central imperatives of the heteronormative family—reproduction. But this was reproduction with a twist—reproduction in the absence of society. This not only made incest an option, but in fact secured it. The logic of the solitary but reproductive family, "The Tale of Sawney Beane" insisted, was incestuous.

Despite its perversions and violence, all versions of the tale insisted that this was a family. One version bore the title "Discovery of a Whole Family of Murderers"; another called them "so bloody and unnatural a family," but a family nonetheless.[21] The family was not inherently generative of virtue and moral purity, and the Beane family was testament to this. One can see this in the two competing notions of marriage in the tale. The conjugal couple, united in a consensually agreed-upon marriage, was the source of the virtuous family in nineteenth-century America. What is striking about Beane's "marriage" is that there was no sign of coercion. "Naturally idle and vicious," Beane "abandoned [his natal home] in company with a young woman equally idle and profligate, and retired to the deserts of Galloway, where they took up their habitation by the sea-side."[22] While the unnamed woman who lives in the cave with Sawney Beane is referred to as his wife, this was clearly a wife of circumstance, not a wife of legal, contractual marriage. Nonetheless, it was the seclusion, the absolute privacy of the marriage, that made it aberrant. Indeed, the absence of legal recognition of marriage was not uncommon in antebellum America, but it required local community recognition.[23] This, then, was the problem with the solitary family—Sawney Beane's wife could not be recognized at any level, as the couple existed outside of and in opposition to community. Thus the family following from the marriage was never recognized. Marriage was not only a contractual relation that structured kinship, but also a mechanism for the normalization of heterosexuality. The virtue of marriage in controlling fornication and other forms of illicit sexuality was absent in a fully private marriage. In contrast, the only person who escaped the Beanes, and alerted the state to the whereabouts of its predators, was with his presumably legal wife. All of this signified that they were part of the "humanity or civil society" that Beane and his wife had rejected.[24]

The sexual and reproductive logic of the wholly private family was incestuous. The private family, in this story, operated not only outside of but also against society, and the widespread destruction of society was made possible only through incest. Sawney Beane and his wife alone, or even with several children, could have threatened a small part of society, but not on a scale threatening the existence of society itself. Yet that was precisely the effect of the Beane family's reign of terror. In every version of the tale, "the country became depopulated."[25]

The specter of depopulation haunting civil society in the tale suggests that what was at issue was not the individual components but population in its entirety, which Michel Foucault has argued was in the domain created by the biopolitical, the object of liberal governmentality. Biopower, according to Foucault, denotes "the set of mechanisms through which the basic biological features of the human species became the object of a political strategy, of a general strategy of power."[26] Does not the tale of Sawney Beane deploy sexuality, food consumption, and life as problematics of governance? Does it not present a specific political problem insofar as the world surrounding the cave was being depopulated? Kinship was supposed to guarantee a social world—marital and sexual relations produced kinship out there, not in here. Sawney Beane, in contrast, constructs kinship as the limits of the social, not as one path into the social. In that sense, the solitary family was a threat to the biopolitical deployment of population.

In the eighteenth century, according to Foucault, "an absolutely new political personage" emerged, named "population."[27] Foucault's concern here is the moment in which population was understood as something to be managed, an object governed by its own internal logic, which could only be managed by the state, but not made obedient to sovereign power. Population took on a natural cast, manifested in desire. Put differently, while there is an unending proliferation of individual desires, each of which could be negated by the sovereign (or monarch), population desire cannot be controlled through negative laws, but only managed. And as Nicole Eustace notes, population included nearly everyone in the United States and was thus much more capacious than citizenship. If citizenship conferred a certain political identity, population included the resources of nearly everyone. As Eustace argues in regard to the War of 1812, if one could bear arms or children then they were a population resource that needed to be managed and protected.[28] In the case of the Beane family, the sovereign act was directed not at the population, whose movements—of bodies and things—

between towns was natural and could only be managed, but at that threat—
the Beane family—at the edge of society, or population.

This movement of bodies and things, on which the Beane family preys,
Foucault calls circulation and finds at the core of liberal governmentality.
It is in this circulation that government is able to expand on and manage
freedom. The apparatus of security that structures governmentality in relation to the population—in other words, the role of the state is not to protect the sovereign's territory, but rather to ensure the security of the
population—is concerned in large part, Foucault argues, with "the possibility of movement, change of place, and processes of circulation of both
people and things. . . . It is in terms of this option of circulation, that we
should understand the word freedom."[29]

If we think of freedom as the animating principle of liberalism, then
Foucault asks us to consider the circulation of bodies and things as central
to the meaning and practice of freedom. This should come as no surprise
to scholars of late eighteenth- and early nineteenth-century America. Shifts
in familial authority and the quest for independent landholding by young
men in the early republic were manifest in the move westward and the
imperial expansion of the nation. The expansion of market capitalism was
facilitated, in part by the state, through the construction and improvement
of internal transportation. One of the quotidian oppressions of slavery was
the strict regulation of moving bodies through a pass system, and thus one
of the first realizations of emancipation was the freedom of movement.
Circulation was of the utmost importance in the emergent liberal state that
was the United States.

At base, the appearance of Sawney Beane, in the context of late
eighteenth- and early nineteenth-century America, functioned as an allegory of the problem of circulation and freedom in liberal society. Moreover,
if the Beane family and the type of privacy it represented were an inherent
obstacle to the circulation of people and things, then the sovereign's act—
execution without trial—was an act of security in the domain of biopolitics.
At every point in the story the Beane family represents the constriction of
circulation. The incest was a rejection of the circulation, or exchange, of
persons constituting the structure of kinship; the murders and cannibalism
were obstacles to the circulation of bodies between towns; and the robberies, which resulted in the hoarding of wealth, disrupting the functioning of
the economy, were an interference with the natural circulation of goods. If
freedom was secured through the management of circulation, then the

private family operated apart from and against this freedom and, as such, was a threat to the public sphere of sociality.

If incest disrupted the circulation of bodies through marriage and extra-familial sex, then it also, quite explicitly, disrupted the circulation of social bodies and goods.[30] Every version of the tale included compilations of the accumulation of goods and body parts in the cave. After the bloodhounds discovered the cave "a great number of men penetrated through all the intricacies of the path, and at length arrived at the *private residence* of the horrible cannibals."[31] In another version of the story, the men "arrived at that *private recess from all the world*, which was the habitation of these monsters."[32] Both suggest that a private sphere fully severed from public, civil society can only be monstrous. What they found there, in addition to signifiers of the grotesque, was a profound disruption of circulation: "Legs, arms, thighs, hands, and feet of men, women, and children, were hung up in rows, like dried beef; a great many limbs lay in pickle, and a great mass of money, both gold and silver, with watches, rings, swords, pistols, and a large quantity of clothes, both linen and woolen, and an infinite number of other things which they had taken from those whom they had murdered, were thrown together in heaps, or hung up against the sides of the den."[33] In light of the invocations of privacy in the lead up to this description, this can be read as a rejection of the common conflation of privacy and domes-ticity. While this was privacy at its extreme limits, there was nothing domesticated about it: extreme disorder was compounded by the display of preserved body parts. Indeed, one might read this as a rejection of the continuation of domestic manufacture: here domestic labor was not only perverse and grotesque, it was a criminal act.

Not only were the bodies of those murdered on display, some of which had already been processed for consumption, but the accumulation of goods and money was clearly excessive. Most of the goods were useless, if we follow the logic of the story. Beane and his family never entered civil society, thus the gold and silver, the watches, rings, clothing and an "infinite number of other things" existed without use or exchange value. Indeed, even the dismembered bodies were accumulated in excess, since "they commonly had a superfluity of this their abominable food, so that in the night time they frequently threw legs and arms of the unhappy wretches they had murdered into the sea . . . the limbs were often cast up by the tide in several parts of the country to the astonishment and terror of all the beholders."[34] Even their main form of sustenance, human bodies, was accumulated in excess. This was the fantasy of desire fully unleashed and unregulated, with no limits. Desire, in and of itself, was useless and determinative—Beane accumulated to accumulate, with no utility in sight. Desire was what also led back to sex and incest; in its unregulated, limitless manifestation, desire deformed and destroyed reason, utility, and society.

Finally, we are left with the extrajuridical act of the sovereign. Upon their capture, after being housed in a jail overnight, the entire family was "executed without any process, it being thought needless to try creatures who were even professed enemies to mankind."[35] Why forego proper juridical form? What made the trial "needless"? And given this period, in which the United States was attempting to establish a stable, democratic society based in law, what would a tale that justifies an act of absolute sovereignty suggest? One answer could be the overwhelming attack on civil society and humanity, and clearly the murder and cannibalism were the manifest reasons. But I would argue, again, that incest was at the root of the sovereign act. The execution scenario suggests that sexuality—and in this case, all sexuality was incestuous—was at the core of sovereign understanding of the transgression. While all versions of the tale ended with an execution in which the men were dismembered and then bled to death in front of all the women, who were subsequently executed, the first American edition added castration. In the 1783 version published in the *Boston Magazine*, "The men had first their private members cut off, and thrown into the fire before their faces; then their hands and legs were severed from their bodies, by which amputation they bled to death in a few hours. The wife, daughters, and grand-children having been made spectators to this just punishment inflicted on the men, were afterwards burnt to death in three several fires."[36] In this manner, the conclusion to the tale offers a twist on older notions of spectacle punishment that were being displaced by the prison in this era. The men were treated as perpetrators and the women as spectators, presumably there to learn a lesson regarding the consequences of such criminality. Yet, the women as spectators were then summarily executed as well.

As I have argued, the scale of violence unleashed by this family was unimaginable in the absence of incestuous reproduction, and the recognition of incestuous sexuality as the generative transgression was suggested by the inclusion of castration in the first American version of the story. This also served to note the highly marginal position of the Beane family. While castration emphasized the centrality of reproductive sexuality—the castration was highly symbolic, given that everyone was subsequently executed—by the late eighteenth century, castration as a punishment for rape was mostly confined to African American men.[37] What this shows then, is that the private family, rather than a source of virtue, was a potential threat to the public, and that threat, generated in incestuous sexuality, demanded an act of absolute sovereign violence in order to secure the welfare of the public population.

Public Incest

Incest, then, marks the limits of the radically private, or solitary, family in the age of sexuality. If the tale had a multivalent story to tell, then it also had a relatively simple moral—the solitary family, especially on the frontier, was a locus of vice rather than virtue, precisely because the fundamental condition of subjectivity was sexuality, even if confined to the family. The lesson to be taken away was that a public orientation would serve as an antidote to incestuous families—the further one moved away from the private family, the less likely to engage in incest, even as virtue might be attenuated. But there was, perhaps paradoxically, an incestuous limit to radical publicity as well. Two texts from the mid-nineteenth century, Edgar Allan Poe's "The Spectacles" and a pseudonymously authored fictional memoir, *The Life of Dr. Richard Jennings, the Great Victimizer,* narrate the incestuous problem of radical publicity. In doing so, both stories track the ultimately disordered circulation of bodies in liberal market capitalism, both within the nation and internationally, and the unexpected return of the family and kinship in the midst of the public sphere.

Public incest tracks this circulation as the problem of disorder and indeterminacy. Is there any form in which certainty can be established, and what does this mean for the family? That is to say, if the sentimental family is offered as a regulator of desire and the indeterminacy of democracy and capitalism, in a word, liberal modernity (a proposition already undercut by the reappearance of Sawney Beane), then why does a discourse of incest expand in the late eighteenth and early nineteenth centuries? Elizabeth Maddock Dillon has argued that incest indexes "concern with the circulation of persons and relationships in the shifting terrain of the global economy."[38] If the incest of the Beane family was a result of withdrawing from circulation, then other stories registered incest as a direct result of participating in the circulation of the global economy. Anthropologist Elizabeth Povinelli has noted that what animated the subject of this society was "an expectation that the course of a man's life should be determined by *his* life, the life *he* made, rather than from his placement before his birth in a genealogical . . . grid."[39] But stories of public incest construct a scenario in which this is impossible— one's family or kin group always returns, despite all appearance of an absolute severing.

In 1844 Edgar Allan Poe published "The Spectacles," a comedic tale of incestuous marriage, in the *Philadelphia Dollar Newspaper*. It told the story of Napoleon Bonaparte Froissart Simpson, a proud member of a seemingly storied French lineage who had come to America with his father and was adopted, as an adult, by a distant American relative (Simpson) in order to receive an inheritance. Plagued with poor vision, which he refuses to correct with spectacles, Simpson meets a seemingly beautiful woman whom he courts briefly and then marries. After finally donning spectacles he realizes that the woman is eighty-two years old and his great-great-grandmother.[40]

What, specifically, we might ask, is Poe trying to tell us about desire and kinship in the liberal democracy of the United States? The possibility of Froissart becoming a liberal subject is premised on adoption, the contractual transformation of Froissart into Simpson, suggesting that one cannot become a liberal individual without severing oneself from natal origins. This severing, as both these tales and, as we shall see, the legal archive of incest suggest, was open only to men, making the status of liberal subject a masculine position. The process of adoption, in which Froissart becomes Simpson, registers as a traumatic rupture between the French genealogy and the prosaic world of liberal democracy in the United States.

> I assumed the name Simpson, with some reluctance, as in my true patronym, Froissart, I felt a very pardonable pride—believing that I could trace a descent from the immortal author of the "Chronicles." While on the subject of names, by the by, I may mention a singular coincidence of sound attending the names of some of my immediate predecessors. My father was Monsieur Froissart, of Paris. His wife—my mother, whom he married at fifteen—was a Mademoiselle Croissart, eldest daughter of Croissart the banker; whose wife, again, being only sixteen, was the eldest daughter of one Victor Voissart. Monsieur Voissart, very singularly, had married a lady of similar name—Mademoiselle Moissart. She, too, was quite a child when

married; and her mother, also Madame Moissart, was only fourteen when led to the altar. These early marriages are usual in France. Here, however, are Moissart, Voissart, Croissart, and Froissart, all in the direct line of descent. (688)

In this deployment kinship is the possibility of slippage along a chain of signifiers, whose force is redoubled through rhyme. Indeed, these perfectly rhyming patronyms suggest a nearly incestuous sameness, yet also offer stability located in intraclass breeding, where Froissart, Moissart, Croissart, and Voissart work, through repetition, to ensure his lineage. Simpson's French kinship offers the fantasy of stable, full knowledge of natal origins—rhyming surnames tell Froissart who constitutes his family and, importantly, who can be a legitimate object of desire. Moreover, the young age at marriage suggests that persons of a certain class in this fantasmatic France have their desire regulated by marriage and kinship before reaching an age of majority, at which point the unruliness of desire may take over.[41]

This French lineage is figured as loss in the act of adoption that initiates liberal kinship, and with it, Simpson's incestuous marriage. For Simpson kinship has become nothing more than a contractually organized social relation for the increase of property.

My name, at present, is a very usual and rather plebian one—Simpson. I say "at present"; for it is only lately that I have been so called—having legislatively adopted this surname within the last year, in order to receive a large inheritance left me by a distant male relative, Adolphus Simpson, Esq. The bequest was conditioned upon my taking the name of the testator. . . . My own name, though, as I say, became Simpson, by act of Legislature, and with so much repugnance on my part, that, at one period, I actually hesitated about accepting the legacy with the useless and annoying proviso attached. (688)

Contract has fractured and reconfigured kinship. Froissart has become Simpson, a "plebian," "useless and annoying proviso" that is the source of "much repugnance." Adoption appears as a leveling act through which Simpson becomes a member of the people, where, one might say, desire is undifferentiated. Yet, this leveling act was also the means to capital accumulation through the severing of lineage. Increasingly, property was disassociated from lineage and kinship, which is not to say that the antebellum

United States was an economic free-for-all where anyone could get ahead (the fantasy life of the liberal individual). Rather, it suggests that capital accumulation did not signify a location within a clearly delineated social structure. Froissart's aristocratic pretensions were not bolstered by the accumulation of capital; they were deflated. And indeed, it was this unruly, undifferentiated desire, a product of liberal kinship, that lead, inexorably, to incest.

Adoption, a mid-nineteenth-century novelty of U.S. domestic relations law, as the historian Michael Grossberg argues, "provided a legal mechanism for completely severing the bonds created by birth and replacing them with binding artificial ties. The new legal device allowed the formation of families brought together by choice and affection, not nature." The architecture for this type of adoption, however, where the child's ties to the natal family were fully severed in favor of those of the adoptive family, did not take shape until the passage of an 1851 Massachusetts law. Previously, adoption proceeded through private legislative acts, often producing ambiguously defined families in which the claims of both the adoptive and natal families had legal standing.[42] The transformation of Froissart into Simpson through "Legislative act" should be read as this type, as evidenced by the end of the story in which Simpson can make claims on both his Froissart and Simpson inheritances.

Simpson's adoption, however, was not simply about choice and affection. The language he uses to describe his new surname suggests anything but affection for his new relative. Simpson's adoption is not a moment in the expansion of affection and sentiment that Grossberg associates with nineteenth-century adoption. Rather, it is a moment in which choice reconfigures kinship in the service of increasing inheritance. Inheritance still moves through kinship, but kinship is no longer a system of consanguinity and affinity—adoption marks the entry of contract, and therefore, choice, into the architecture of kinship. That act of adoption makes kinship not the system of stability that Simpson summons in the rhyming surnames of his French lineage, but another site of the indeterminacy that Lefort identifies with democracy.[43]

Adoption creates a field of kinship in which indeterminacy is the norm and thus accidental incest is a possibility. "Love at first sight" names the desire that takes the individual through that indeterminate field, in this case to an incestuous marriage. In Poe's description of love, desire has an agency of its own, to which Simpson is subjected: "The most natural, and, consequently, the truest and most intense of the human affections are those which arise in the heart as if by electric sympathy—in a word, that the brightest and most enduring of the psychical fetters are those which are riveted by a glance" (688). Poe stresses the "anomalous . . . nature of the only true love" which is "so little really dependent . . . upon the external conditions which only seem to create and control it" (690). Simpson is thus subject to desire—the idea that one can control the magnetic force of "love at first sight" is simply an illusion. In this manner, Poe suggests that the sovereign subject, or autonomous individual of liberalism, who controls his desire through reason, is itself an illusion, too. The regulation of such a configuration of desire is the responsibility of one's genealogical past. Since one cannot escape this type of desire, the tragedy of the tale is not that desire leads to incest, but that the regulative force of kinship is lost in liberalism and thus public incest is made possible.[44]

Not only has adoption for inheritance created Simpson as the liberal individual subject to desire, it also forecloses his prior identity. Froissart is now the "plebian," democratic Simpson, potentially without an identity. When Simpson, upon his first (mis)recognition of Madame Lalande, asks his friend Talbot who she is, Talbot responds that Simpson must himself be unknown if he does not know her. "Why, in the name of all that is angelic, don't you *know* who she is? 'Not to know her argues yourself unknown.' She is the celebrated Madame Lalande—the beauty of the day par excellence, and the talk of the whole town. Immensely wealthy too—a widow—and a great match—has just arrived from Paris" (691). Simpson is now a man without knowledge or identity, a member of the democratic mass, who can no longer clearly see the distinctions of kinship. He does not know that he was already possessed of a great inheritance and that he is falling in love with his ancestor. The liberal individual, it seems, is without a past and therefore adrift in a sea of indeterminacy.

As the marriage approaches, Madame Lalande insists that Simpson wear glasses immediately after they marry. As she demands the correction of a physical infirmity, Lalande tells him that it is primarily a moral, rather than physical, flaw. "You shall conquer . . . for the sake of Eugénie whom you love . . . this weakness more moral than physical—and which, let me assure you, is so unbecoming of the nobility of your real nature" (701). In stressing the moral over the physical and the "nobility of . . . real nature," Lalande suggests that the transgression is the coming incest of the liberal individual. Simpson's weak vision, then, is not a physical

abnormality but a constitutive part of the liberal subject. His commitment to desire, to "love at first sight," and to liberty and choice is a
melancholic disavowal of his genealogical past.

It is perhaps fitting, then, that the return of knowledge and identity, as
well as a genealogical past, occurs in an incestuous marriage that, at least
on Simpson's part, was a result of a blind adherence to desire in the indeterminacy of liberal democracy. Once he finally dons his spectacles, the horror
of his marriage is revealed. His clear sight, resulting from the aid of both
the spectacles and his relative's insistence on correcting his vision, produced
a "horrific," "hideous" reaction (703). While this initial response corresponded to the intergenerational marriage, it is not until after Lalande
recounts her own lineage that Simpson discovers the incest. "Meantime I
sank aghast into the chair which she had vacated. 'Moissart and Voissart!' I
repeated, thoughtfully, as she cut one of her pigeon-wings, 'and Croissart
and Froissart!' as she completed another—'Moissart and Voissart and
Croissart and Napoleon Bonaparte Froissart!—why, you ineffable old ser-
pent, that's me—that's me—d'ye hear?—that's me'—here I screamed at the
top of my voice—'that's me-e-e! I am Napoleon Bonaparte Froissart! And
if I haven't married my great-great-grandmother, I wish I may be everlastingly confounded!'" (705).

It is in the recognition of his incestuous marriage that Simpson redis-
covers his identity and through which genealogical knowledge returns. That
is, the liberal subject finds his past in an incestuous marriage. But upon the
incestuous reclamation of genealogical identity, Madame Lalande unveils
the ruse—she knew who he was and married him as a "way of punishing
me for my impudence" (706). In the end, Simpson/Froissart finds that his
French lineage was what he imagined—immensely wealthy—and he is reinserted into the chain of rhyming signifiers—he becomes one again with
Croissart, Moissart, and Voissart—but with a difference—he marries Stephanie Lalande, Madame Lalande's beautiful relative through her second
husband. Madame Lalande names him her sole heir, guaranteeing a large
inheritance upon her death.

Or was it what Simpson imagined? If the Froissart lineage was so
impressive, then why did his father leave France for the United States? And
why would Froissart have been enticed by the prospect of an inheritance
through an adoption he despised? Lalande's reference to "the nobility" of
Simpson's "real nature" would seem to ratify his accounting of his genealogical past. But despite both Simpson's and Lalande's claims, their French

past seems to be at best an invented nobility. While "Froissart" and its rhyming kin suggest a deep genealogical past, "Napoleon Bonaparte," his common name, suggests something quite different: the invented peerage of the First Empire. Moreover, in his kinship claims to the medieval chronicler, Froissart, and a Parisian banker, there is nothing suggestive of nobility—the chronicler was of a middling background, and the Parisian banker, precisely by his profession, was not a member of the nobility. Even his derisive attitude toward his adoption was a ruse—adult adoption for matters of inheritance was a common practice in France, but less common in the United States.

Simpson's invention of a noble genealogy, lost in the democratic forms of kinship in the United States, is decidedly fantasmatic. Indeed, in this sense it recalls nothing so much as Freud's account of "family romances," in which the child substitutes more exalted, aristocratic parents, in fantasy, for his own parents, who have inevitably failed to satisfy his desire.[45] By undercutting Simpson's claims to nobility, and thus destabilizing his reliance on a certain genealogy, Poe suggests that in the age of transnational circulation of bodies, there may be no stable genealogical past to which one might refer, and thus incest is a constant possibility of liberal democracy, exacerbated by the porosity of national borders. To be sure, those individuals traveling across the Atlantic attempted to sustain family ties amid geographic fracture, especially through letter writing, but Poe's tale suggests that the inexorable logic of circulation was the severing of connections and the conditions of public incest.[46] We may take Simpson's final marriage, to a distant cousin arranged by Lalande, as proof of this: Simpson escapes an incestuous marriage, while still claiming both inheritances, through an endogamous, and potentially incestuous marriage.[47]

In wanting to be "everlastingly confounded" rather than recognizing his incestuous marriage, Simpson demands that the indeterminacy of liberal democracy protect him from the incestuous reality of his love. The incestuous marriage and its resolution operate at the social limit of democracy— the near-incestuous marriage insists on the continued relevance of kinship as a check on desire in liberal democracy while Simpson's gain of an inheritance and a wife from his original, French lineage both ratifies his desire and suggests that, in the end, there is no certain escape from incest.[48] The tale, which merges aristocratic wealth with contractual capitalist accumulation through adoption in the figure of Froissart Simpson, registers a certain ambivalence. If contracting wealth in the U.S. through adoption required severing natal ties and incurring the possibility of public incest, such a fortune was always tenuous, on the verge of being lost. If fortunes were made in antebellum America, they were just as frequently lost in speculative markets and financial panics.[49] The aristocratic inheritance can be read as an attempt to quell such indeterminacy, even if it took a near incestuous marriage to find it.

In the last analysis, "The Spectacles" demands a predemocratic form of kinship in the midst of a liberal democratic society but reveals such kinship to be a fantasy, a lost object that came into being only at the moment of its loss. Another story of accidental incest from the 1840s is a call for continued attachment not to the far reaches of transatlantic kinship but to the more immediate sentimental family. Together they suggest that by the mid-nineteenth century, there was no familial form that could finally foreclose the possibility of incest. *The Life of Dr. Richard Jennings, the Great Victimizer* (1848), a mid-nineteenth-century sensationalist novel, recounts the exploits of the eponymous criminal, as he seduces, robs, poisons, and murders his way through the United States. What finally stops him and sends him into a suicidal state is his accidental seduction of his sister. Like Simpson in "The Spectacles," Richard Jennings is unmoored from his family, but unlike Simpson, Jennings is a criminal. Where "The Spectacles" narrates the necessity of sovereign kinship to regulate and police individual desire in a liberal democracy, *The Life of Dr. Richard Jennings* suggests that the incestuous individual of liberalism is a product of the failed nuclear family. And in this sense, if incest is made possible by the unmooring of the liberal individual from his family, then the sovereignty of the family (or kinship) is never enough. In the end, Jennings submits to an ultimate sovereign—God—to atone for his incestuous transgression.

Richard Jennings (a pseudonym) was born in New York City in 1810, raised by a loving mother and an abusive, tyrannical father.[50] His father's abuse was the determinative factor in Jennings's family life, precipitating his move to Philadelphia to pursue a medical education, after which he established a medical practice. For a brief time, his independence and success lead him to believe that he had overcome the "unhealthy and pernicious passions to which my ill-treatment in early life had given birth."[51] However, after the failure of his medical practice, Jennings finds himself bankrupt and destitute, as both friends and family disavow knowledge of him. Vowing vengeance on father, friends, and society at large, Jennings turns to a life of crime.

He quickly becomes a criminal of uncommon genius, employing his professional training as a doctor and his savvy as a merchant/gambler to rob, poison, murder, and seduce—in a word, victimize—his way through American society. Jennings's criminality is marked by the telltale signs of liberal modernity—his crimes are sterile, rational executions of well-laid plans; he moves almost exclusively through urban metropolises (New York, Philadelphia, Baltimore, New Orleans, St. Louis); when not in a city, he is using modern transportation—steamboats and trains. All signify that Jennings is not an atavistic remnant of barbarism, but the embodiment of the modern individual.

After years of victimizing, having seduced countless women and amassed a fortune in excess of $700,000, Jennings's final transgression is the seduction of a young woman in St. Louis. After he seduces her, she recounts her life, at which point Jennings realizes that the woman is his youngest sister, whom he had not seen since she was three years old.[52] This incestuous seduction sends him into a downward spiral. He divides his fortune between his sister's family (none of whom ever found out he was her brother) and a prostitute in New Orleans who bore his only child. He then attempts suicide but, having lost all control over himself, or rather, having had such mastery revealed as an illusion, is unable to follow through with the act. He settles on removing himself from society and goes to a remote area in what is now the southwest United States, renting a shack from James Knight, a "professor of Christianity" (107). Here the atheist Jennings engages in daily discussions with Knight on the nature of God and belief. Ultimately he submits to the absolute sovereignty of God and dies in paroxysms of blood and penitence.

Richard Jennings, a criminal iteration of the liberal individual, was born of a failed family. One of the key transformations animating the late eighteenth and early nineteenth centuries was the displacement of the patriarchal family by the sentimental, affectionate family. Perhaps the signal event of this transformation was the replacement of corporeal punishment with disciplinary intimacy—the idea that parents met children's transgressions with love rather than violence. Corporeal punishment did not disappear nor did patriarchy diminish, even if it was transformed. Instead, the norm for middle-class, white families was loving intimacy, exemplified by the popularity of sentimental fiction in the antebellum United States. The sentimental family, however, was not necessarily a pure, virtuous institution, bereft of sexuality; often, the excess of affection was marked by eroticism, making incest both a condition and problem for the sentimental family.[53] Yet, as Jennings's narrative shows, incest also is a problem for the liberal individual in the absence of the disciplining function of the sentimental family.

Richard Jennings's early life, to which time and again he attributes his turn to crime, can be characterized as a failed sentimental family marked by an asymmetry along the lines of sexual difference. His mother was the epitome of sentimental governance: "Toward my mother, who never whipped, but always talked and reasoned so kindly with me when I had committed a fault, that I often wept bitterly, I had, and to this day retain, the strongest feelings of love and friendship; I . . . would hasten to do anything in my power to please her, always endeavoring to win from her the appellation of a 'good boy,' and a 'kind and dutiful son'" (4–5). Jennings's father is anything but sentimental: "I served as a species of *tenor drum* to my father, who, being a very passionate man, used to beat me severely for the most trifling faults" (4). Jennings's relationship to his father was one wholly inscribed within the register of violence; his father "took advantage of my helpless condition and my dependence upon him, and adopted another sort of logic with me, the *logique a la brute* [*sic*], such as he used to those non-reflecting, non-reasoning quadrupeds . . . thus placing his own child, his own flesh and blood, upon a level with the brute creation" (4). If Jennings's mother's treatment validated him as a feeling, reasonable human, then his father's treatment forced him to exist on a line between human and animal. These two countervailing styles of parental governance, however, did not cancel each other out; rather, Jennings became "the great victimizer" on account of his father's treatment. The force of motherhood, in this mid-nineteenth-century account, was less than sufficient to regulate the passions of man. The sentimental mother was not an antidote to the father's power.

Jennings's abuse at the hands of his father was coupled with his victimization at the hands of the market in the etiology of his criminality. Indeed, the problem of profit and market relations had their origins, like nearly everything else, in Jennings's father. "My father was a man whose almost every action or thought was devoted to that god of the world, money," Jennings wrote, and "the time devoted to the noble task of teaching and reasoning with me, was viewed as encroaching upon the dollar and cent time of business" (4). Despite, or perhaps because of this education in the complicity of violence and the market, Jennings's early career as a doctor was marked by benevolence and a resistance to the dictates of liberal market relations. The first years of his medical practice were successful and encouraged him "to subdue, if not finally overcome, those unhealthy and pernicious passions to which my ill-treatment in early life had given birth" (6). But Jennings found it impossible to collate the work of benevolence and the obligations of friendship with the demands of the market. This soon ruined him—Jennings became the picture of mid-nineteenth-century failure, destitute and alone. "It needed but little of this treatment, to render a mind, not yet divested of its early training, disposed to any evil," Jennings wrote, "and I now looked upon the whole human race as enemies" (7). It was, then, the violence of market liberalism and the absence of sentimentalism, commensurate principles that he had learned as a child, which produced "the great victimizer." Yet, if he was a criminal, then Jennings insisted that his criminality was a constitutive form of subjectivity in a liberal democracy.

The identification of criminality with liberal freedom is evident in the novel's first pages: "Untrammeled freedom is essential, highly essential, to the discovery of all and any truth—such freedom I have herein taken in its most extensive sense . . . I am not in the remotest degree accountable to any person, clique, party, or sect, and will not, therefore, so far descend from my true position, as to gratify them by foregoing the enjoyment of my rights, or by neglecting the fulfillment of my duties" (3). Like Poe, Richard Jennings is ultimately engaged in a critique of this fantasy, suggesting that the ideal of self-control and reason's capacity to control desire are simply illusions. At the moment when Jennings realizes that he has amassed sufficient wealth to retire from victimizing, he owns up to the fact that he cannot, that such an action is beyond his power: "The more I acquired, the more I desired, and it would not have gratified my revengeful and destructive passions to have stopped in the midst of my sanguinary glory . . . *there seemed an invisible, irresistible impelling power urging me onward in the road I had selected from myself*" (41–42, italics mine). Here Jennings begins to suggest that, despite his earlier claims to "untrammeled freedom," there is a force, a desire, compelling him otherwise.

This is, moreover, the central logic of the common, bourgeois citizen in the nineteenth century. The only thing separating Jennings from the professional classes was the latter's adherence to law and custom. "I think

I resemble the great mass of community," Jennings confides to his readers. "They act according to law and custom, overstepping them only occasionally, while I act according to will, feeling, and passion, respecting law and custom only inasmuch as they served to assist me in carrying out my grand designs" (8). The ubiquitous motive for men in the liberal society of mid-nineteenth-century America was a compelling desire, or will. Thus, Jennings realizes untrammeled freedom by rejecting and contravening the law. It is of great importance that the end of his victimization occurs when he contravenes the foundational law of sociality and the instigator of kinship—the incest prohibition. "Government and laws are all humbug," Jennings writes, "the rules of a dark, barbarous, and aristocratic age; the people of a free country ought to be able to govern themselves, without any other laws than those of *right*—without any other government than that of *mutual good*" (80). What does his incestuous end tell us about liberty? How does the family align itself with "mutual good" and the violation of one's own family, particularly the sympathetic attachment animating ideal familial relationships, transgress the desire for "untrammeled freedom"?

If that desire often manifested itself in an uncontrollable pursuit of wealth, it was, nonetheless, most prevalent, and ultimately most problematic, in the sexual domain. Seduction was not simply a secondary pleasure of victimizing; it was, rather, central to Jennings's construction of himself as both criminal and individual. Instances of seduction and rape (the distinction is rather arbitrary in Jennings's delineation) are guided by his "unhallowed passion" and "the excess of my love" (19, 21).[54] Perhaps most telling is Jennings's description of his time spent at a popular hotel in Saratoga Springs—a key signifier of middle-class comfort and leisure. Spending some of his time at a hotel aptly named the "United States," Jennings seduced a number of women. "I also made love to several of the beauties who graced the rooms of this last hotel, and I may say, that where I breakfasted and dined at my own hotel once, I repeated similar course at the United States several times, for it was at this place where I expected to meet another victim" (61). Here it is not difficult to see the hotel United States as a thinly veiled allegory for the nation as a site of constant seduction, with men moving through the country by passing from one woman to another, making sexuality a part of public life rather than private intimacy. Here the distinction between public and private collapses as a result of radical publicity. If the consummation of incest occurred in the private world of intimacy, it was facilitated by Jennings's public circulation through the nation in a kind of criminal commercialism. Intimacy was detached from the familial home and became a constitutive part of the public sphere.

Indeed, Jennings suggests as much in his critique of contemporary business practices and their effect on marriage and families: "This doing business in one town, and dwelling in another, particularly if the places are situated at a distance, where the husband cannot visit his wife oftener than once in every week or two, is a very reprehensible practice, one which most generally eventuates in the destruction of the peace and happiness of the family" (46). The problem with such a practice, central to market expansion and commercialization in antebellum America, was that husbands and wives continued to be animated by sexual desires that needed to be satisfied, thus making adultery a necessary companion of liberalism. "Husbands would always do better by [living and working in the same city], for I know many, very many instances, where the man has his wife at one place, and his cher ami [*sic*] at the other; and also, about as many more, where, in the absence of the husband, his loving spouse receives the visits of amorous gallants" (46–47). What is most interesting about Jennings's critique of market capitalism and sexuality is that this practice of doing business was not the cause of such sexual escapades but, rather, the result: "This separation plan . . . was originated by some old debauchees, who, not being able to sport in their licentiousness while their families were at hand, removed them out of the way, under the pretext of economy, comfort and fashion . . . at all events, those wives and husbands who really value domestic happiness, would do themselves no injury by attending to this matter" (47). The peripatetic life of modern business, of which Jennings is exemplary, if criminal, was simply a pretext to satisfy more fundamental sexual urges. Sexual desire, in the final instance, has a life of its own, to which the seemingly autonomous individual is subjected. For Jennings, this leads to incest.

After murdering and robbing his last victim aboard a steamboat traveling on the Mississippi, Jennings escapes and later boards one heading for St. Louis. It is here, in St. Louis, that Jennings commits the act of accidental, or public, incest with his sister, "the most awful" of all his crimes (102). Jennings's arrival in St. Louis registers the dislocation of his peripatetic life of crime and business. Jennings "took lodgings at the Planter's Hotel, intending, as I had accidentally or incidentally, I know not which, visited the place, I would remain there for a month or two" (102–3). His circulation through the nation, necessary not only to accumulate wealth in a market society, but also to escape prosecution, has left him unsure of where he is and, more importantly, why he is there. Nonetheless, he goes about his normal life, donning a disguise and seducing a woman almost immediately. This seduction, as we should come to expect at this point, was not simply an action driven by his own will. "Passing through the streets one day," Jennings writes, "I met a lady whose beauty, grace, and figure fascinated and captivated me at once" (103). That is, in a chance encounter in a city he was captivated by a beautiful woman, making his desire not his own, but the desire of the other. That this woman was his sister, a fact he would learn only after seducing her, is a testament to the dislocations of market circulation. His family returns in the figure of "that little, playful sister, of whom I was so fond—almost the only being in this world whom I truly loved!" (104). Jennings is led, almost inexorably, back to his family, but not the abusive family of his father. Rather, he returns to the sentimental, affectionate female fold embodied by his sister, his knowledge of whom had been lost, "for, not having seen her since she was a child, I had entirely forgotten her features" (104).

Jennings is beholden by "utter dismay" as it was "the only crime of my whole life which I regretted" (104). "It was the very sin I would not have been guilty of—and like a flash, it seemed to come upon me as a punishment for past deeds" (104). Jennings's life of crime is over. That it was the encumbrance of sentimental familial relations that had the capacity to regulate the actions of the individual is apparent in Jennings's response to his incestuous seduction. He spares his sister and her family the knowledge of the incest, leaving her simply as a seduced woman, with the advantage that her husband was none the wiser. Jennings then leaves half of his fortune to his sister's young son and instructs the parents that they may live off of the interest that accrues on the inheritance. While this may be read as an attempt to assuage his guilt, it is of greater significance given the source: Jennings's father's abuse. His father's violence and lack of sympathy for his children was a consequence of his desire for wealth—sentimental parenting interfered with the demands of the market. In leaving an immense fortune to his sister's family, Jennings obviated the cause of parental abuse.

After settling accounts with his sister's family—all of whom were overjoyed with the inheritance if somewhat perplexed by his actions—Jennings journeys to New Orleans to bequeath the other half of his fortune to a prostitute who is the mother of his only child. It is here that one can see the force of the sentimental family as an encumbrance on liberal forms of circulation and desire. Rather than simply bestowing the money on mother and child, Jennings marries the woman and takes on the role of temporary father. "I felt that I had done this young lady much injustice," Jennings writes, "and when I informed her that *I would endeavor to make all the reparation in my power for the past, by marrying her,* she appeared to be nearly delirious from joy" (105, italics mine). While the marriage was in part a mechanism by which to secure the transfer of his money, Jennings's formulation here suggests that the marriage—the institutionalization of conjugality—was also intended to atone for his entire past. Accordingly, he takes on the role of father and imparts to her the proper mode of raising their son, one that is antithetical to his own upbringing. Rather than imparting the *"logique a la brute,"* Jennings is the benevolent patriarch. While he leaves his new wife and child because he is no longer a legitimate member of society, he imparts the dictates of sympathetic parenting to his wife, so as to ensure the regulation of his son's desire. "Always be kind to him, and let him see that you are at all times, during right or in error, his best friend," Jennings advises his wife, "by this course, you need entertain no fears concerning him, when, having arrived at manhood, he enters the broad arena of life, to contend for honorable and manly distinction" (106).

If Jennings embodies liberal subjectivity—in a criminal form, but, as he argues throughout the text, the liberal subject of the mid-nineteenth century, beholden to the market, is a criminal—then we must take his incest as a serious comment on the desire of liberalism. Jennings's marriage and the sentimental child-rearing instructions he imparts to his new wife, coupled with his sympathetic feelings toward his mother and sister, suggest that it was the absence of the sentimental family and the unruly desire of market relations that made the incestuous seduction of his sister inevitable. But, at the same time, Jennings's narrative of his own family, as well as the plethora of dysfunctional families he comes across throughout his travels, suggests that this family, despite the burgeoning discourse praising it as an ideal, was rather elusive. Thus, to rest the stability of democracy on the shaky foundations of the sovereignty of the sentimental family was a risky proposition. Just as Jennings offers the sentimental family as the antidote to the incestuous logic of desire, he suggests, obliquely, that it is not up to the task.

These narratives of public incest cast the desire of the liberal individual as a problem of individual sovereignty and the occlusion of the family and kinship. Both Simpson and Jennings embody liberty and the mechanisms of liberal democracy only to be subsumed by a desire greater than themselves, which, in the end leads to incest. This incest is, I have argued, represented as a consequence of their public lives, which have severed their ties to natality. In both stories it is at the moment of incest that kinship and the family become idealized locales of sovereignty. Put differently, if Simpson and Jennings had made their forays into the public while simultaneously maintaining an attachment to their families, then they could have acted on their desires without the possibility of incest. In that sense, these stories suggest that kinship and the family are necessary, but ultimately less than satisfactory, sources of sovereignty in a liberal democracy where the individual man is enjoined to act on his desire and the location of sovereignty is indeterminate. Public incest figures that indeterminacy as the danger of unregulated desire.

What in the end, does incest signify for nineteenth-century liberal democracy in the United States? Accounts of private and public incest suggest that the family, so often trotted out as a solution to public problems, endowed with a certain amount of virtuous sovereignty, was no such thing. At the birth of liberal democracy in the United States, as political sovereignty is dispersed through the people, and a series of conflicts ensue over both who can exercise such sovereignty and how to regulate its excesses, the family and marriage are offered time and again as the regulative solution. The conjugal, heterosexual couple, legitimately united in marriage, was to be the private restraint on an excessive, public desire manifest in the autonomous individual man. Yet, sexuality in the form of incest continually disrupted this regulative fiction. Indeed, despite the differences between Beane, Simpson, and Jennings, all three are subjected to a desire that exceeds the autonomy of individual reason precisely in acts of love and sex. Put differently, the persistence of incest in liberal discourse registers sexual desire as a threat to the political function of the family. In the United States of the late eighteenth and early nineteenth centuries, even as incest constitutes the limit of both the private family and the public man, the liberal sexual subject—the exemplary subject of liberalism—also moves incessantly in its direction.

Richard Jennings's unexpected religious conversion and subsequent death point to a desire for a sovereign authority to regulate the liberal subject, one associated neither with the family nor the state or market. Religious belief seems to offer an inchoate atonement to Jennings. In the early nineteenth century mainstream religious denominations were attempting to articulate a prohibition of incest as a sovereign check on the desire of the liberal subject. Aligned neither with the private family nor the public market or state, the church could have, ostensibly, offered a prohibition of incest that was not riven by this division. Yet, the theological discourse of incest revealed that an otherworldly incest prohibition also ran up against a wall in attempting to regulate the liberal subject.

Chapter 2

Theology

In 1843 the Dutch Reformed minister Philip Milledoler asked, "Is it lawful for a man to marry his deceased wife's sister?" Noting this was "a question which may appear at first sight to be of minor importance," Milledoler argued that "the minor importance of this subject . . . is . . . not real; for if we view it in its bearing upon the happiness of individuals—upon the purity of the church and upon the best interests of the community at large, we shall see that it involves consequences of deep, if not of vital importance to mankind . . . for if such marriage be, as has been represented, INCEST, then they who enter into it, or in any way allow, encourage, or abet it, assume a position which no creature can assume without guilt and peril." As Milledoler suggests, and as many other theologians in the early republic attested, such marriages indexed anxieties over desire, marriage, family, and kinship, all of which, when unregulated, tended toward incest—a symptom and signifier of apocalyptic moral decay.[1]

Milledoler's text was published at the tail end of a seventy-year public theological discourse in the United States on marriage with a deceased wife's sister that was generally referred to as "the marriage question." The question was whether marriage with a deceased wife's sister was incest; however, the marriage question taken as a whole was a broad inquiry into the force and function of the Levitical incest prohibitions. While Presbyterians dominated the debate, most of the older denominations in the United States—Congregationalist, Dutch Reformed, and Episcopal—also contributed. The marriage question was not articulated along denominational lines, and it often manifested itself as an intradenominational quarrel. On the one hand, this was prompted by the growing disjunction between religious and civil incest laws. Once grounded in the Levitical prohibitions, state incest laws began to diverge from their biblical bases in the 1780s. On the other hand, the marriage question was an arcane exegesis on the force of Levitical law and the legitimacy of biblical interpretations. In this sense, the marriage question was often an abstract controversy over legal interpretation and acceptable translation of the Bible. Theologians and ministers like the Congregationalist Jonathan Edwards, Jr., the Presbyterian James Finley, and John Henry Livingston of the Dutch Reformed Church spilled a great deal of ink in an effort to prove or disprove the existence of a transhistorical, universal, moral law of incest, applicable at all times and in all places and derived from the word of God.

Stories like those of Sawney Beane, Richard Jennings, and Napoleon Bonaparte Froissart figured the incestuous subject of liberalism as operating outside the reaches of the law—Beane and Jennings, quite self-consciously, transgressed laws in following their own desires while Froissart's accidental incest revealed the limits of nationally circumscribed laws of kinship and incest to regulate the transnational circulation of bodies. Yet, much of the discourse of incest in this period articulated some form of the incest prohibition with both universal and contemporary force. If the narratives of the previous chapter staged the incestuous subject of liberalism as both criminal and perversely normative, this and the following chapter explore intertwined but distinct attempts to articulate an incest prohibition—theological or legal—that could regulate liberalism's incestuous subject.

The marriage question, then, was never simply an arcane doctrinal debate as participants to the controversy worked through the problematic conjunctions of kinship and sexuality, foundational laws and history. The marriage question leads us into a world where the meaning of incest and its prohibition were never clear, forcing a reconceptualization of incest. Normally figured as a violent transgression of either domestic order or heredity, incest in this case was consensual, affective, and, in the case of its titular object—the deceased wife's sister—affinal (between relations by marriage) rather than consanguine (between relations by blood). Indeed, as an exploration of the marriage question makes clear, an understanding of the social, cultural, and political functions of the incest prohibition, and the historical conditions of its construction, must exist independent of sociobiological claims that humans possess a natural instinct to avoid incest in order to perpetuate the species. Yet it also problematizes cultural explanations of the incest prohibition, which in their anthropological and psychoanalytic formations, tend to return to the fantasmatic origins of the taboo.[2] The marriage question, operating outside the logic of consanguinity and presenting a tortured origins narrative, forces a more historicized reading of the incest prohibition.

If the marriage question challenges theories of the incest prohibition, it also forces a reconsideration of the affectionate family and the virtues of love in the early republic. Central to the propagation of the sentimental family was the conjugal couple of consensual marriage, which carried social, cultural, and political force, particularly as an allegory of the nation. While that may be true, a growing incest anxiety, articulated in the marriage question, reveals that marriage, as much as it ideally ensured an affectionate, loving family, was also a vexing phenomenon given the unruly nature of familial desire. As multiple scholars have noted, the late eighteenth and early nineteenth centuries witnessed the rise to prominence of an affectionate family, structured, ideally at least, by egalitarian love rather than hierarchical subordination.[3] As Nancy Cott has argued, republican thought of the early republic "tied the institution of Christian-modeled monogamy to the kind of polity they envisioned; as a voluntary union based on consent, marriage paralleled the new government."[4] Yet, as the consensual nature of the marriage contract reinforced the centrality of a consensually governed people in the new nation, the prominence of consent in these incestuous marriages called its virtue into question.[5] If the ideal marriage produced a loving, affectionate family resulting in virtuous citizens of a republic, then that same affection and love, in the absence of a clearly articulated, codified incest prohibition, led more directly to vice and, in theological visions, the apocalyptic end of American society. Indeed, taken as a whole, the marriage question, as Julia Stern claims for fiction in the era of federalism, "gives voice to the otherwise imperceptible underside of republican culture in the age of reason."[6] Given the highly erotic family that animated the marriage question, marriage itself could be corrupted by the affections endemic to the family.

While theologians from various Reformed denominations, particularly Presbyterian, Congregational, and Dutch Reformed, occupied various positions in the debate, taken as a whole the marriage question produced a highly erotic sentimental family and desiring liberal subject, both marked by incest. In this, the church was not necessarily a conservative force of religious authority opposed to liberal reform of the incest prohibition, although some individuals in the church certainly were. Rather, both positions, an effort to transform the prohibition in order to facilitate the liberal subject and an effort to preserve the biblical prohibition to chastise the desiring individual and control the sentimental family, manifested them-selves in the marriage question. Taken as a whole, and despite language that invoked a transhistorical, universal incest prohibition, the theologians of the marriage question remade the incest prohibition for liberal society. The effect of the marriage question was a highly eroticized sentimental family and tense relation between the liberal subject and the prohibition of incest.

The discourse of the marriage question maps precisely the relation between kinship and sexuality, while, as a whole, problematizing the force of alliance as a site of the law—does kinship, clearly articulated and codi-fied, have the power to regulate sexuality? That is the subterranean question animating the marriage question. Insofar as it is the site of the interchange of kinship and sexuality, this deployment of the modern family can be excavated in the late eighteenth- and early nineteenth-century United States. The marriage question is one particularly robust site of excavation: it is here, in theological discussions of incest, that the juridical claims of kinship in the form of ecclesiastical law, and the power and pleasure of sexuality in the family, were worked out.

The pamphlet war that initiated the discourse on "the marriage ques-tion" and later spilled over into religious and secular newspapers was prompted by an anxiety over marriage with a deceased wife's sister. Such marriages provoked a number of lines of inquiry concerning familial affection, eroticism, and sibling relations in the United States. However, these marriages were often a pretext for theologians to offer wide-ranging explorations of incest and its place in U.S. culture. This was most apparent in the ecclesiastical history of the marriage question, especially its develop-ment in the Presbyterian Church. This ecclesiastical trajectory reveals a fun-damental uncertainty over the meaning of incest and kinship, producing an erotic specter haunting constructions of kinship in the early republic. This uncertainty was central to the conjunction of kinship, sexuality, and affection in the sentimental family, as that discourse structured part of the marriage question and helps explain why there was such an increase in concern over marriage with a deceased wife's sister. Following from this uncertainty in the prohibition was a concern with the liberal subject. The incestuous conjunction of liberty and marriage that transformed ecclesiasti-cal regulation of marriage reveals that the desire of the liberal subject was at odds with the regulatory regime of kinship and religious governance. The ultimate uncertainty in the parameters of incestuous marriage inscribed a dangerous eroticism in the effusive affections of the sentimental family.

The Ambiguities of Ecclesiastical History

The marriage question was, in part, an episode in the long and complicated history of the Levitical incest prohibitions. Understood throughout the debate as a transcendent moral law, the Levitical incest prohibitions were treated, in the early republic, as an exemplary, transhistorical system of kinship, which drew on a long European Protestant tradition. Yet, the Levitical prohibitions were nothing if not ambiguous and had, in fact, been constantly modified almost since their inception.[7] While this is a long and often arcane history, in the context of the nineteenth-century transformation of the incest prohibition, the major revision occurred in 1563 when Archbishop Matthew Parker issued the Table of Kindred and Affinity in the wake of Henry VIII's marital adventures. Henry VIII's first marriage was to his deceased brother's wife (Catherine of Aragon), a marriage explicitly forbidden in Leviticus (Lev. 18:16), but enjoined in Deuteronomy (Deut. 25:5–10).[8] After many years of marriage without a male heir, Henry VIII wanted a divorce and in 1530 convened major scholars from England and the Continent in order to determine the legitimacy of his first marriage. After much disagreement, the marriage was declared void for its initial violation of Leviticus. The Church of England came into existence, in part, as a result of this controversy. This controversy went on to influence the reigns of Mary Tudor and Elizabeth I, whose claims to power rested on the legitimacy or illegitimacy of Henry's first marriage. Henry furthered the controversy in 1540 when he married his cousin Catherine Howard. In order to legitimize this marriage, Henry legalized all first-cousin marriages, which were prohibited in the Catholic Church. Matthew Parker, whom Elizabeth had appointed archbishop, drew up his Table in 1563.

The Table, which was included in the Anglican Book of Common Prayer from 1603 onward, codified the interpretative model of parity of reason. First used by Calvin to claim that the Levitical prohibitions referred to degrees rather than specific persons, parity of reason was given a new, formal authority in Parker's table. In England, and then the larger British Atlantic, marriage with a deceased wife's sister explicitly became incest. Although the majority of participants in the marriage question in the early republic maintained that they relied on the Bible alone in defining the prohibition, their justifications for an expansive reading of the Levitical prohibitions mimicked the logic of the Table. Importantly, in the effort to rationalize the disordered Levitical prohibition, the Table addressed both men and women, with thirty relations prohibited for each.[9]

While incest is often viewed, inaccurately, as a subject widely considered unfit for public discussion, the marriage question existed almost exclusively in public discourse. In this configuration, incest, an ostensibly private transgression, was made eminently public. At the core of this public discourse was the irrepressible fact that the meaning of incest was anything but clear. As one author noted, "We can easily tell the adulterer, the fornicator . . . what law they have violated. . . . We are . . . directed to tell those who are charged with [incest], you have been guilty of transgression, by *implication* or *construction*."[10] As this author suggests, the marriage question was primarily an attempt to clarify a biblical law—the incest prohibition—which, in its foundational form in Leviticus, appeared without reason. The Levitical incest prohibitions, it seemed, were always in tension with social reality. In other words, the ambiguity at the center of the incest prohibition (despite the evil attached to it, we are never quite sure what constitutes incest) made incest itself a subject of public discourse.[11]

This ambiguity was at the core of Reformed theological discourse of the early republic. One can find pamphlets, books, and missives from Congregationalists, New Divinity preachers, Episcopalians, Dutch Reformed ministers, and others, but the bulk of the writings came from Presbyterians. While the Second Great Awakening led to a marked increase in church membership in the United States, particularly among Methodists and Baptists, Presbyterians and Congregationalists also witnessed growth. More importantly, in this era of emotional revival, Presbyterians and Congregationalists controlled theological discourse through their dominance of the seminaries and theological quarterlies. It was in these two institutions that theological teachers and students produced discourse. Moreover, as older denominations encompassing traditionalists and evangelicals, Presbyterians and Congregationalists were tied to the idea of a learned clergy interpreting biblical texts and disseminating knowledge, a feature that structured the marriage question. Presbyterians were the most prolific theological publishers in the nation, and, as the marriage question existed, to a great extent, in this emergent periodical press, Presbyterians were bound to offer the largest share of the writings. Such magazines and newspapers as the *Christian Advocate*, the *Christian Observer*, *Biblical Repertory and Princeton Review*, *Biblioteca Sacra*, *Spirit of the XIX Century*, and *New York Observer* were edited and published by Presbyterians and all contained extensive commentary on the marriage question. Finally, while

Presbyterians dominated the production and publishing of the works that made up the marriage question, it is important to note that one could find secular publishers like T. and J. Swords responsible for some of the longer books that contributed to the discourse.[12]

Allied with the centrality of Presbyterians to theological discourse was a sense, prevalent among many Presbyterian ministers and theologians, that social relations in the new nation were particularly profligate. Intemperance, antisabbatarian sentiment, the triumph of Jefferson and the decline of Federalism, the increasing saturation of life by market relations—all of these and more suggested a state of moral, political, and cultural panic. In order to combat increasing ungodliness, Presbyterians turned, more often than not, to reassertions of the authority of the Westminster Confession of Faith. In a society where, at least perceptually, authority was diffusing among the people, Presbyterian and other Reformed ministers attempted to reestablish clear authority in a religious text. In this sense, then, the marriage question, and the centrality of Presbyterians to it, is symptomatic of both these trends. It was not so much that Presbyterians opposed liberal democracy as it was an attempt to stabilize the incest prohibition in an era when the desire of the individual was increasingly privileged, lauded, and feared.[13]

Beginning in the early eighteenth century, a series of ecclesiastical trials concerning marriage with a deceased wife's sister (or an equivalently marginal kin relation) were tried in the Presbyterian Church. There are thirteen extant cases between 1717 and 1842 from a variety of synods and, after 1789, the General Assembly of the Presbyterian Church.[14] This does not include any cases that may have remained at the level of the church or presbytery. While the first trial occurred in 1717, the public discourse in the colonies began in 1695, in a published letter, signed by several prominent Boston ministers, condemning marriage with a deceased wife's sister.[15] Yet, it was not until the late eighteenth century that conflict over the legitimacy of such marriages hardened into the marriage question. In 1779, the Presbytery of New Castle, Delaware, referred the case of Anthony Duchane, who had married his former wife's sister, to the Synod of New York and Philadelphia. After three years of deliberation, the synod ruled that Duchane and his wife were not to be excluded from the church and should remain married. The decision, however, would last only one year. At the meeting of the synod in 1783, "remonstrances from sundry congregations" were filed demanding a reversal of the 1782 decision.[16] The synod ruled that Duchane and his wife would remain members of their congregation and that their marriage need not be annulled, but that they could not be received into communion without serious admonition. Moreover, all members of the Presbyterian Church were discouraged from such union and were to see it as their public duty to dissuade anyone from considering such marriages.[17]

The Duchane case was important for several reasons. First, it was the culmination of a series of less authoritative rulings tending toward the removal of marginal kin from the prohibitions. The synod continued to discourage these marriages but did not prohibit them. This was symptomatic of a general anxiety inherent even in defenses of an expansive reading of Leviticus—while opposed to such marriages, the church refused total sanction of them. Perhaps most important to the subsequent articulation of the marriage question, the case was the primary impetus behind the publication of James Finley's 1783 pamphlet inaugurating the public discourse on incest.

With the publication of Finley's polemic against the synod's decision, the Presbyterian Church, and then Reformed theology more generally, witnessed the blossoming of the deceased wife's sister controversy, or, the marriage question. By 1847 the controversy led one newspaper to worry that incest would cause another schism in the Presbyterian Church.[18] Between 1783 and 1847, a series of pamphlets and books were published representing various positions on incestuous marriage, all of which further destabilized any attempts at a coherent incest prohibition. The General Assembly furthered an already combustible situation by refusing to rule that any marriages before the court were clearly incestuous, even if they were "highly inexpedient and unfriendly to domestic purity."[19] Moreover, contemporary changes in the civil law furthered the instability in the incest prohibition. Beginning in 1785 in Massachusetts, with the removal of a wife's sister and niece from the list of prohibited relatives, individual states began contracting the list of relatives considered incestuous in marital and sexual relations. This excision from civil law heightened theological concern over the state of the American family.[20]

In the context of such civil and ecclesiastical confusion, the deceased wife's sister controversy reached its peak between 1824 and 1846. The number of pamphlets, books, and articles published was at its height, and the two highest-profile cases of the controversy also occurred in this period. In 1824 Donald McCrimmon, a ruling elder of Ottery's Church in Fayetteville, North Carolina, was suspended from his position for marrying his deceased wife's sister. And in 1842 the case of Reverend Archibald McQueen, also a member of the Fayetteville presbytery, was appealed to the General Assembly after he was suspended from his office for the same offense. These two cases elicited a great deal of ecclesiastical and public commentary inscribed in the broader themes of the discourse on incestuous marriage. In attempting to resolve these issues, both cases and the opinions that emerged from them revealed the difficulty of ordering incest and kinship, and by extension society and the nation, around the problematic distinction between consanguinity and affinity at a time when domestic affection was seen as the key to familial and national harmony.

In early 1824 the Ottery's church session of Fayetteville received a troubling report concerning Donald McCrimmon. McCrimmon, it was alleged, had committed incest by marrying his deceased wife's sister, an act "deeply injurious to the interests of the Redeemer's Kingdom."[21] The language of the charge against McCrimmon is revealing.

> COMMON FAME LOUDLY PROCLAIMS that Donald McCrimmon . . . forgetful of his obligations . . . to maintain a life of purity, is guilty of the crime of incest, in having, not more than five weeks after the death of his wife, the late Hannah McCrimmon, taken to himself, Mary Dunlap, the sister of his said deceased wife . . . McCrimmon, has continued, and does still continue, to live with the said Mary Dunlap, in the same state of intimacy and cohabitation, as if she were his lawful wife.[22]

The indictment pointed out that incestuous marriage was not a private but a public act; that intimacy and familial affection were potentially incestuous; and that this was evidenced by the short time that elapsed between the death of McCrimmon's first wife and his marriage to her sister. Given the short interval between death and remarriage, Colin McIver, the session's prosecutor, speculated about adultery as well, arguing that "it must be allowed to be, in general estimation, an offence against decency; and therefore, an aggravation of the principle offence." This concern with adultery suggests the eroticization of family relations, where unregulated affections may turn the family into a training ground for unregulated sexuality. Put differently, without a clear, strict incest prohibition, the family, rather than protecting one from illicit sexuality, would encourage adultery. Paradoxically, it was the law itself, rooted in Leviticus, that produced its own ambiguities.

In responding to the charge, McCrimmon admitted to the marriage but maintained that it was not incestuous. After the session pointed to the section of the Westminster Confession banning such marriages, McCrimmon admitted that he had transgressed the ecclesiastical rules of the Presbyterian Church, but that they were a misinterpretation of scripture. Employing parity of reason, the session then pointed to specific passages in Leviticus supposedly condemning McCrimmon's marriage and found him guilty of incest, suspending him from his office as a ruling elder until he severed ties with Mary Dunlap and repented for his transgression. McCrimmon, in turn, requested that his appeal be heard in front of the General Assembly, where he could challenge both the session decision and the Westminster Confession itself.[23]

The appeal was heard by the General Assembly in May of 1824. McCrimmon offered his appeal through a representative, a decision he justified based on his poverty—the large family he had to support would have made it impossible for him to afford the trip from North Carolina to Philadelphia. Proving adept at exegesis and critical interrogation of the confession, McCrimmon demonstrated that there was no express prohibition of marriage with a deceased wife's sister and that the problem lay in labeling such marriages incestuous. Because the session of Ottery's Church, in making such a judgment

> did not rest contented with considering and pronouncing the act which they so severely condemned, as merely a rash and inconsiderate act of indiscretion, or as a step unadvisedly and injudiciously taken; (all of which I freely, admit; and for which, I would, without appeal, have willingly submitted to their censure, admonition, rebuke, or suspension:) but they have proceeded so far as to adjudge me to be guilty of the crime of INCEST; and to determine it to be essential to my repentance for this crime, that I separate myself from the woman whom I have chosen as my wife.[24]

It was the separation, McCrimmon contended, that was the most severe crime. In order to end a marginally transgressive marriage, the session first named it incest, a transgression of a severity that no one disputed, and then insisted on separation or divorce.[25] For McCrimmon the session's decision, rather than his marriage, was evidence of man's fallibility.

Despite his criticism of both the Confession of Faith and ecclesiastical decisions, McCrimmon took the pragmatic route and cited previous decisions of the assembly (those of 1797, 1802, 1804, and 1821) that, while admittedly disapproving of such marriages, refused to annul them once they had been entered into. Rather than issuing a decision, the General Assembly formed a committee to consider the issue, which finally rendered a report in 1827. Like Anthony Duchane before him, McCrimmon remained suspended from communion throughout the deliberations. The committee recommended retention of the clause prohibiting such marriages and, with the assembly's support, upheld the discipline. Reflecting divisions within the Presbyterian Church as a whole, the presbyteries of New York and New Brunswick removed the clause from the confession, while those of Ohio and Pennsylvania retained it. As McCrimmon violated no civil law, he chose to remain married to his new wife and, fulfilling speculations by some of the central figures of the trial, became a Baptist, where such marriages were not explicitly prohibited.[26] The increasingly voluntaristic relation many Americans held toward religion exacerbated denominational distinctions in the incest prohibition, further undercutting its foundational authority.

While McCrimmon caused a stir within the confines of the Presbyterian Church, Archibald McQueen was at the center of the most notorious ecclesiastical incest trial in the nation. If McCrimmon's case was well known but generally confined to the pages of religious magazines and newspapers, McQueen's case, while generating a great deal of writing in religious circles, was also followed in the secular press. By the end of the affair McQueen was reinstated as minister of his Fayetteville church, and the controversy over marriage with a deceased wife's sister began to subside in the United States. But during the trial, all the contradictions and permutations of the marriage question appeared. Unlike McCrimmon, McQueen never admitted any wrongdoing and in fact pleaded with the editor of a Presbyterian newspaper to publish a series of articles in defense of his position. The whole controversy, McQueen felt, was "in some measures due to me, and by doing so, You will confer a favor of no ordinary character on a suffering Brethren."[27] On 5 January 1842, the presbytery charged, again, according to "common fame," that McQueen had married Mary McCloud, the sister of his deceased wife. He was convicted of incest and suspended from his ministerial duties.[28]

When McQueen's appeal reached the General Assembly a number of eminent ministers and theologians weighed in on the future of his tenure in the Presbyterian Church. Like McCrimmon, McQueen was unable to appear before the assembly, and his representative was appointed at the last minute. McQueen argued variously that the illegality of such marriages had not been uniformly sustained; that the members of the presbytery had relied on the Confession of Faith but had doubted its scriptural basis (a claim not supported by the records of the presbytery); and that his condemnation was "at variance with God's word." Extending the critique, McQueen argued "if affinity is made a ground of prohibiting marriages, the peace of many virtuous families will be disturbed."[29] This charge placed the burden of familial discord squarely on the shoulders of the church hierarchy. Moreover, virtue, still a relevant political and familial term in 1842, was threatened not by his marriage, but by the expansive circumference of the meaning of incest. If virtue was constituted in a loving, affectionate family, then the Levitical incest prohibition, broadly construed, was antagonistic to familial and national harmony.

McQueen, then, took up two familiar strains of argument: one, that the prohibition of marriage with a deceased wife's sister lacked any foundational authority in scripture, and the other, that the familiarity of the family was enough to justify the marriage in question. Initially, the most authoritative statement in the assembly came from Robert J. Breckenridge, a conservative minister and chairman of the General Assembly's Committee on Judicial Business. He took McQueen's claim that the prohibition was at variance with the word of God as the basis of the entire appeal and argued that this was of critical importance to the Presbyterian Church. "I liken the present case, not . . . to that of a suitor at the bar of a civil tribunal impeaching the very constitution of the land," wrote Breckenridge, "but rather to that of one trying the laws by the constitution itself, and invoking the court to look back to the sacred fountain of all law."[30] Breckenridge saw this as a profound and necessary critical intervention into the man-made laws of the church and their relation to foundational, divine law while simultaneously analogous to the relation between civil law and the Constitution in the young nation. Everyone involved in the case envisioned it as a final answer to the marriage question, which was attested to in the *New York Observer* in 1842. "The subject was approached with deep sensibility, and with a strong conviction of the necessity of settling the law of the church in reference to incestuous marriages . . . we never heard a debate in any deliberative body, conducted with more profound solemnity, with a greater apparent desire to know the mind and to do the will of the lord, and with more freedom from the excitement of human passion, wither for or against the accused."[31] This, then, was an act of reasoned judgment, one in which the individual transgressor was of little importance, and the authority of the law was the only consideration. Differently put, both Breckenridge and the *Observer* saw this case as a moment of the reasonable fixing of an incest law obscured by excessive passion.

Even though Breckenridge deployed the constitutional metaphor, he argued that the prohibition was foundationally sound and that McQueen's discipline should be upheld. The door to civil authority and liberal society, however, had been opened. Arguing against Breckenridge, "A Layman" wrote in Breckenridge's *Spirit of the XIX Century* that "law becomes oppressive, and the liberty of one is prostrated before the scruples of another."[32] Rather than turning to theological authorities, Layman argued for such marriages from the ground of liberty and invoked the jurists James P. Wilson and Joseph Story for support. Incest, it seems, was becoming more and more civil and secular, even in theological circles.

Ultimately, the General Assembly decided in McQueen's favor, finding the prohibition of marriage with a deceased wife's sister to be at variance with the foundational law of incest found in Leviticus. Tellingly, one commentator claimed in regard to the prohibition that "such statutes curtail our liberty as rational beings."[33] Over a century of theological debate and ecclesiastical trials were decided in McQueen's appeal, and the theological construction of the incest prohibition would, by this time, share claims to the foundational incest prohibition with liberalizing civil laws and the emergent discourse of hereditary degeneration.

McQueen's and McCrimmon's cases can be read as part of several larger trends in the early republic. First, there is a sectional element to both cases. While both were from the Fayetteville presbytery in North Carolina, northern ministers and theologians made the preponderance of decisions and produced nearly all the discourse. Moreover, even their representatives— the prominent Philadelphia Presbyterian Ezra Stiles Ely and the New York minster John Krebs, representing McCrimmon and McQueen, respectively—revealed the centrality of northern opinion in the Presbyterian Church. Indeed, as a letter in the *Christian Observer* argued, "this is one of the *sectional questions* which divides the North from the South."[34] The author, William Hill of Winchester, Virginia, claimed that in the South public opinion and the law opposed such marriages, evidence of which could be found in the Virginia marriage statutes. The North, according to

Hill, was marked by increasing acceptance of incestuous marriages. While others refuted this characterization, it is noteworthy that subsequent letters published in the *Christian Observer* were signed "A Northern Man" and "A Man of the Middle States."[35]

Another way of reading these cases is as representative of an assertion of clerical authority over marriage. While marital form in the United States followed generally from Christian practice, it was a decidedly civil institution. Indeed, as the editors of the *Christian Observer* speculated, "Is it certain that a *divine* law is necessary to prescribe to the Christian church *what* marriages are proper, and what are improper and sinful?"[36] While the editors tended toward a negative response, they were in a decided minority. As the civil law moved away from the Levitical basis of kin-based marriage restrictions, these trials and the wider marriage question were assertions, by theologians, of the profoundly religious, Christian foundation of marriage. "Are the good people of the State of New-York . . . aware that . . . it is lawful for a man to marry his aunt and niece by blood; as well as . . . his wife's sister," wrote Sereno E. Dwight. "Has the possession of the Bible carried us downward, on the scale of moral elevation . . . below that occupied by the more decent heathens?"[37] As Dwight suggests, the concern was that the transformation of the incest prohibition in statutory law was symptomatic of a decline in religious authority and an obscuring of biblical truth. In such a context, the inherent immorality of statutory marriages required the assertion of clerical authority to determine the legitimacy of marriages. Inadvertently, however, this led to an internal theological crisis over the meaning of incest.

Both McCrimmon and McQueen invoked the language of individual autonomy and consent when defending their marriages. This was also characteristic of the broader discourse of the marriage question, which was saturated with the liberal language of consent. As McCrimmon made clear, incest was the effect of the discursive ordering of social relations, and not a prediscursive act merely represented in language. He had chosen Mary Dunlap as his wife, a choice he had the right to make based on his status as a willing, autonomous individual, or liberal subject. So not only did the session, according to McCrimmon, misinterpret scripture, it also ruled contrary to the predominant understanding of marriage in the early nineteenth century. As Michael Grossberg has argued, the nineteenth-century vision of marriage served "to make the law of domestic relations an ally, not a competitor, in the creation of a society grounded as much as possible in the bourgeois ideal of unregulated private competition and individual choice."[38] McCrimmon was not arguing for historical contingency in the incest prohibition, but, nonetheless, his understanding of marriage was an iteration of an early republic idiom.

Here the marriage question took up the tension between a voluntaristic, liberal society and the transhistorical, universal incest prohibition. Consent in marriage suggested voluntaristic relations and seemed to privilege a happy union of reason and love. Consenting to marriage or sex without the tempering effect of reason could have disastrous consequences, especially for women. This was apparent in the volumes of seduction fiction that dominated the print public sphere in the early republic. Yet, love and reason, when combined, ideally lead to beneficent and long-lasting marriage. It should go without saying that this was a utopian longing for a world in which voluntary, loving familial relations purified the vice and disorder of liberal democracy. The incest prohibition, however, did not privilege consent. Rather, it privileged constraint and encumbrance. The theological incest prohibition, derived from Leviticus, claimed that, regardless of the union of consent, love, and reason, some unions were simply prohibited, no matter how beneficent and affectionate they might appear. The liberal subject and an attendant liberal incest prohibition were produced in this crucible of consent and constraint. Both McCrimmon and McQueen were censured and told that their marital choices needed to be constrained, but in the end they chose their affectionate union over the force of the incest prohibition. In this, the prohibition was slowly remade to account for the force of consent, in a manner that insisted whatever the logic of consent and individual choice, the liberal subject also required constraint.

If McCrimmon and McQueen used consent as a defense of their supposedly incestuous marriages, the larger discourse cast a pallor over the purity of consent in the new nation. Both marriages, by all accounts, were consensual and do not bear the iniquity of coercion. The concern of the marriage question was unimpeded male desire associated with consensual marriage. That is, in a discourse authored exclusively by men, the primary concern was not the sexual force of women, but rather the wild desires inherent in men. The underlying assumption of the marriage question as a whole was that without a clear prohibition restraining the husband's desire, the family would become an institution of illicit sexuality. While there was a concern with the "vulnerability of unmarried women" in the early republic, here women functioned almost exclusively as abstractions.[39] One can see this in the concern over Donald McCrimmon's potential adultery in 1824: Mary Dunlap served simply as an object of his sexual desire, an object that led to incest and adultery. Dunlap never took on the appearance of a subject, and this was representative of the position of women in the marriage question. Despite the appearance of gender parity in the ecclesiastical law, derived from the Table of Kindred and Affinity, in which the prohibition addressed both men and women with lists of prohibited kin that mirrored one another, the discourse itself always presumed that men acted. This problem of the conjunction of consensual marriage and incest was symptomatic of the key legacy of the marriage question: The sentimental family, marked by effusions of affection, was inherently erotic. The preceding ecclesiastical history is an instance in the production of conditions— ambiguous delimitations of incest—that would aid the development of erotic excess immanent to sentimental, familial affection.

The Eros of the Affectionate Family

This history of the marriage question reveals an uncertainty at the core of early republic constructions of the incest prohibition. But it still leaves the question of why that uncertainty was experienced as crisis in the postrevolutionary United States. The answer lies in the thickets of sexuality and the affectionate family. In the eighteenth century, according to Michel Foucault, sexuality, in which the relationship between sex and truth was solidified for the modern subject, emerged as the discourse that gave new meaning to the act of sex. Put differently, across the nineteenth century, in different registers, from theologians to phrenologists to moral reformers, a discourse developed presuming that the interior of the bourgeois liberal subject was manifest in sexuality. One's sexual life, in this discourse, revealed an inner truth that needed to be documented and regulated. Simultaneously, a discourse favoring affectionate familial relations emerged. This displaced older, patriarchal relations of discipline and authority that animated normative constructions of the family through the early eighteenth century and came to dominate familial discourse by the end of the eighteenth century. Central to this emergent discourse was the belief that the family was a refuge from the insidious desires of public life, and, with the exception of the conjugal couple, the family was, ideally, bereft of sexuality.[40]

The deployment of sexuality, according to Foucault, occurred in terms of the displacement of alliance, or kinship. In other words, with the emergence of sexuality as a discourse producing and regulating sexual acts, alliance receded in significance. We find a situation, then, where "the family is the interchange of sexuality and alliance: it conveys the law and the juridical dimension in the deployment of sexuality; and it conveys the economy of pleasure and the intensity of sensation in the regime of alliance."[41] In other words, the family should be understood as neither alliance nor sexuality exclusively, but rather the "interchange" of both—in the family alliance works to regulate sexuality, while sexuality infuses alliance with pleasure and affection. Foucault goes on to say that such an "interchange" or "interpenetration" makes the family "incestuous."[42] The marriage question registered just this incestuous tension.

The incestuous inner logic of the sentimental family in the early republic has not gone unnoticed by literary scholars of the period. Indeed, the sentimental novel of the nineteenth century was a key site of the articulation of familial affection, and from the late eighteenth century through to the mid nineteenth century, incest played a central role in fictional articulations of sentimentality. Anne Dalke has noted the presence of unintentional incest in early national novels as a symptom "of the dreadful condition incest symbolizes: the absence of a well defined social system."[43] Dalke's primary concern is with cross-class marital and sexual relations revealed to be incestuous, but, as she suggests, the ideal family is always already fragmented. These fictional families are ordered around a dead figure, usually the mother, and this fragmentation produces an incestuous return of kin. Conversely, Glenn Hendler notes the way in which the expansion of sentiment transformed social relations into kin relations. Both suggest a vexed relationship between kinship and sentiment, one in which the reconstruction of kinship in the context of consensual social and familial relations inscribed incest in sentimental relationships. It is in this context that the marriage question needs to be situated. The ecclesiastical record and periodical literature show the way in which kinship was being transformed around the figure of the deceased wife's sister—a transformation that highlighted instability in theological deployments of kinship and marriage, and this instability led to anxieties over the erotic force of the family.[44]

The sentimental family and its dangerous eroticism was a symptom of a perceived decline in patriarchal authority. Historians and literary critics have written of the overwhelming effects of the Revolution on patriarchal authority, and here the Presbyterian minister James Finley implies that it is the incest prohibition, as articulated in Leviticus, that instills "the order of nature" that preserves hierarchical relations and male authority. These scholars tend to overemphasize the decline of male authority because they ignore gender as a central category of analysis. The reassertion of the authority of the incest prohibition points both to the anxiety over hierarchical and patriarchal relations and the fact that there is an older law, with much more force, instilling natural, familial order and male authority: the law of incest. Indeed, the deployment of the Levitical prohibitions in the postrevolutionary United States can be understood, in part, as an attempt to reconstitute male authority in the family. That is, insofar as only men contributed to a discourse concerned with the regulation of male desire, the marriage question produced a crisis and an attempted resolution in the field of male sexual desire. The recodification of the Levitical prohibitions, deployed by men and subjecting men to their law, figured as an abstracted, juridical form of male authority in the family, one that would counter the disruptive tendencies of liberty and consent. In the discourse as a whole, then, we find a fraternal organization of male authority, and in instances like Finley's, we also see a competing patriarchal form, where some men—theologians—attempt to regulate their subordinate's sexual desire.[45]

An exchange between two writers in 1797 and 1798 exemplifies the articulation of kinship with sexuality, constituting a potentially erotic family. A letter published in 1797 and signed "A Citizen" opposed the prohibition on marriage with a deceased wife's sister. After substantial exegesis and commentary on translation, Citizen turned to the unencumbered good being withheld by the prohibition. A man and his deceased wife's sister were a perfect match because of the affection they had presumably already shared. "They pursue the blessings of the marriage-covenant in a way most likely to obtain the important object," Citizen wrote, "and, on account of the intimacy consequent on the marriage of the first sister, they must have been under special advantages to acquaint themselves with the qualifications each other possesses, in order to make the marriage state comfortable and happy."[46] This affection would produce not only conjugal bliss, but parental and filial affection as well. "A woman who takes the place of her deceased wife's sister by marriage . . . will be excited, not only by her matrimonial engagements, and her attachment to her husband, but by a consideration that those orphans, now committed to her care, are the offspring of her beloved sister, to a faithful discharge of the duties, not only of a wife, but also of a parent."[47] The bonds of affection, extended to those outside the conjugal family, had the potential to ameliorate the tragedy of death and perpetuate the family.

In 1798 the prominent Dutch Reformed minister John Henry Livingston delivered a polemical response to Citizen under the pseudonym "Eudoxius." Appalled by the "incoherent and sophistical reasoning" of the letter, Livingston had two objections to Citizen's account of affection.[48] First, to rely on the benevolence of domestic affection removed the authority of God from the law of incest and, as a result, essentially invalidated any part of the prohibition, which for Livingston rested on God's authority alone. "As you have put the law of God out of sight," wrote Livingston, "you throw off all restraint of *moral obligation*, and permit your candidate for marriage to rove at large, and to form what connection he pleases, provided he is only prudent enough to secure his *individual and domestic happiness*, and *the good of society*."[49] Simply to follow the pursuit of pleasure ultimately revoked any limitations or restraints on desire. Moreover, Livingston could not conceive an affectionate relation absent eroticism. This lead to Livingston's second objection—if domestic affection was the basis for marriage, why stop with a deceased wife's sister? "Suppose I should think my *own* sister best calculated to ensure these blessings . . . am I not, by your arguments authorised [sic] to enter into the *marriage-covenant* with her."[50] Sentimental affection was the involution of sexual desire—in the absence of a transcendent law of incest, sexual desire turned inward, devouring the family through the gentle language of sentiment. Where Citizen offered a seemingly pure, benevolent manifestation of familial affection, Livingston understood it as an insidious incursion of eroticism into the family.

The erotic family became a staple of the literature after 1800. If in 1792 Jonathan Edwards Jr., like Livingston, wrote that domestic affection would justify marriage not only with a deceased wife's sister, but with a man's own sister as well, and that "the whole question is not, who is most likely to be kind to the motherless children, but what is the law of God," after 1800 the problem of sex in the family would become much more explicit.[51] Benjamin Trumbull, the New Divinity pastor in North Haven, Connecticut, imagined a family whose desire was restrained only by the Levitical prohibitions, the constriction of which would have grave consequences. "These prohibitions are . . . to prevent the most horrible scenes of debauchery and incest in families and among near relatives; to preserve their purity and honor, and to prevent a general corruption of the human race."[52]

The Presbyterian minster J. J. Janeway, writing in response to Parsons Cooke's notorious *New-England Puritan* essays that had argued against the prohibition, concluded his book on the subject with similar images.[53] If marriage with a deceased wife's sister was permitted, "a delicate female . . . will feel that she cannot dwell in her sister's family with . . . ease and pleasure," wrote Janeway. "The purity of private life will be contaminated; public morals deteriorated and the commandment of the most High God disobeyed."[54] Henry Ustick Onderdonck, in a rare Episcopalian contribution to the marriage question, sounded a similar refrain. "The abhorrence of the intermarriage of near relations [is] a sentiment both natural and virtuous; but the extent of relationship to which this abhorrence shall prohibit marriage, can only be declared by positive institution."[55] A positive law of incest was necessary to govern those incestuous desires that exceeded the "natural sentiment" against incest. The Dutch Reformed minister Philip Milledoler expressed similar sentiment. "The law of incest is that barrier which God has set up to protect the laws of marriage, and especially to guard the moral purity of those who are in daily habits of domestic intercourse with each other."[56] The domestic space was always eroticized, but for Milledoler, in the absence of incest law there was nothing to police such desire. The law of incest was necessary "to prevent sinful familiarity between members of the same family . . . to promote domestic tranquility— and generally to enlarge the sphere of human benevolence and kind offices."[57] Here we find, cutting across three denominations (Presbyterian, Episcopal, Dutch Reformed), a similar sentiment concerning sexuality and kinship.

The erotic nature of the family, and the force with which it called families into being, was perhaps most apparent in John Henry Livingston's 1816 treatise on the marriage question. "God forbids incest and has mercifully implanted in the human heart an abhorrence of this crime," Livingston wrote, "and thereby banished every sexual propensity toward those who are near of kin."[58] Here Livingston makes incest almost irrelevant—God has imbued humans with an instinct to avoid incestuous connections, thus there should be no desire for kin. Yet, when approaching the current state of affairs in the United States, incest loomed large.

When the restraint of human laws is relaxed or removed, the influence of the divine law is frequently found, with the unprincipled, to be feeble and insufficient. To no other source can be ascribed the scandalous marriage with a sister in law . . . the impending evils of incestuous marriages may yet be suppressed. The defection is in its incipient state. . . . Resistance, prompt and unequivocal, is practicable, and will assuredly prove successful.[59]

The emergence of marriage with a deceased wife's sister upends Livingston's claim to a natural abhorrence. In this sense, the conditions of the sentimental family worked against the supposedly "natural abhorrence" all humans felt toward incest. Adopting metaphors of war and revolution, Livingston readied his followers to fight the "incipient" threat to domestic purity.

No one, however, took this argument further than the Presbyterian minister Alexander McClelland, known to his critics and supporters (a rarity) as "Domesticus." McClelland, who had been a professor at Dickinson College, Rutgers College, and the Reformed Dutch Theological Seminary, offered an iconoclastic view of the prohibition, arguing, even as he venerated the Levitical prohibitions, that they were not necessarily the final word on the subject. Instead, when deciding "how much should be followed," he argued "just so much as agrees with the physical, moral and political circumstances of modern society, and the rule in *General Expediency*, as apprehended by the common sense of mankind."[60] Contrary to nearly everyone, McClelland substituted man for God in determining the laws of incest. Presumably this would have aligned him with the changes occurring in the civil law, but just the opposite was the case. Given the state of society, the prohibitions required expansion. McClelland's historically minded interpretation of the prohibition lends credence to the idea that the deceased wife's sister and other marginal kin relations were in an ambiguous position. Indeed, if affectionate relations animated normative families, McClelland argued that those families often contained a wife's sister within the home. "If we cast our eyes over the land, what do we find more common, than one or more of a wife's sisters actually dwelling in her family."[61] Thus, to restrain desire in the family, she must be included in the prohibition. In the face of the affectionate, nuclear *family*, McClelland remained attached to the *household*.

Against the arcane exegesis common to the marriage question, McClelland offered a visceral, imagistic account.

Let us imagine a society constituted just as our families are; I mean a society containing many persons of different sexes and ages, having free and unrestrained access to each other, at all times,—sitting at the same table,—partaking in the same amusements,—sleeping under the same roof, perhaps in the same apartment; in one word living together as in a state of the most unreserved familiarity: Let us imagine such a Society, differing in no respect from ours, but in the circumstance, that these persons *are allowed to intermarry*, without the least opprobrium or criminality being attached to such a connection. That is to say, they are taught from earliest infancy to view each other in reference to the sensual appetite, exactly as they view *strangers* of a different sex, whom they are forbidden to touch indeed *now*,—before certain forms and *ceremonies* are passed through, called the "Marriage rite"; but after that, gratification is perfectly innocent and even praiseworthy. Would not every family become a school of abominable impurity, where the youthful mind would be initiated in the worst mysteries of vice, and long before it obtained years of discretion, turn out a giant in profligacy? What natural virtue could resist the constant, the ever pressing temptations of such a situation?[62]

McClelland invested the daily interactions of family members—not simply the affective discourse trumpeted in the periodical press, advice manuals, and novels, but the more mundane interactions too—with eroticism. Indeed, in the absence of prohibition, every familial interaction was laced with manifest erotic desire. The erotic family, it seems, was a construction of its critics.

Perhaps even more troubling, the incestuous family conjured by theologians had biblical roots. Theologians occasionally acknowledged specific instances of incest in the Bible, such as that between Lot and his daughters or the relations between Jacob, Rachel, and Leah. But the preponderance of the discourse was devoted to the law itself and ignored other countervailing and complicating evidence. The liberalization of legal marriage restrictions and the potential sexual anarchy in the family unleashed by affection explained the contemporary situation, but even the potential solution, the "Mosaic economy," as one anonymous author called the Levitical prohibitions in 1791, was unclear in terms of its scope and historical force.[63] If the ecclesiastical history of the marriage question suggested uncertainty about the force and parameters of Levitical prohibitions in the early republic, then the postlapsarian origins of the family and social life presented another problem: Humanity, it seemed, was born in incest. And it was this scene from Genesis, the specter of an originally incestuous humanity, that resonated most with those theologians concerned that the contemporary state of the nation portended a return to rampant incest. Was the United States an incest nation that would herald a catastrophe similar to Sodom and Gomorrah or the Flood?

Given the tendency to describe the Revolution as a filial revolt against a tyrannical parent, it is unsurprising that the Fall was a key allegory for the postrevolutionary United States. The optimism of the new nation, however, was at odds with the moral implications of the Fall. As Jan Lewis has noted, the Fall had to be remade in order to embody the revolutionary potential of these new Americans. If this variously was done through a focus on redemption, the invocation of fraternal society redolent with prelapsarian Adamic feeling, or the remaking of Eve as a virtuous woman, theologians still were anxious about the tendencies of unrestrained desire unleashed by the Revolution. If, as Lewis agues, "republican marriage represented Paradise," then, in the absence of clearly articulated laws of incest, it could also recapitulate the postlapsarian intermarriage and incest of the children of Adam.[64]

The marriage question, then, was intimately concerned with the consequences of original sin—expulsion from paradise and the incestuous marital and sexual relations of the children of Adam and Eve. The postlapsarian intermarriage of near kin and the ultimate installation of the law prohibiting incest and producing society served as allegories for postrevolutionary sex and marriage. With social relations established in the postlapsarian world, intrafamilial sex and marriage became incest, and thus both unnecessary and a transgression with potentially calamitous consequences. The power of affective discourse in the early republic would seem to mitigate reference to the destructive potential of familial relations. But the erotic family in the absence of an incest prohibition had already been deployed, so the postlapsarian world served as both an explanation of intrafamilial marriage and sex and a warning against its return. Focusing on Adam's children presented these writers with perhaps the most profound problem yet: Humanity was born in incest. If life after the Fall was incestuous, what was one to make of the return of incest as the internal logic of domestic life? This return to the postlapsarian family served as a fantasmatic staging of originary desire, at once masking the horror of incest and calling incest into being as the inherent logic of the family itself. As the young nation worked to establish a coherent, foundational law, the marriage question deployed the incestuous origins of humanity as a warning—even the source of virtue, the family, was at risk of devouring itself in the absence of law.[65] The tale of Sawney Beane, circulating through the print culture of the early republic, exemplified precisely this anxiety.

James Finley put the issue to rest in a manner that would come to dominate the exchange for the next fifty years. "Circumstances alter the very nature of the cases," Finley wrote, "so as to make a fact a great crime, a less crime, or no crime at all."[66] Incest, it would appear, was one of these cases. "Thus it was necessary for Adam's children to intermarry, God having for wise reasons so ordered that that they had none besides to join with, and yet commanded them to multiply. But this necessity being soon removed, so that all might have a choice among more remote relations, the tolerating marriages afterwards among those very nearly related would not have been proper; yea, it would have had bad consequences in our degenerate world."[67] Necessity was the mother of intermarriage between near kin; in the absence of necessity, that is, in the presence of society, such intermarriage was an abomination.

Finley, however, did not leave his reader to imagine the "bad consequences in our degenerate world." Instead, he articulated three of these consequences, all of which reflected a broader anxiety about the power of desire and the revision of familial and social authority in the revolutionary era. First, the absence of the incest prohibition "would have encouraged fallen men greatly addicted to lust"; that is, inhibiting the force of the incest prohibition, as some were advocating in the late eighteenth century, would have given license to those men already engaged in incest to move from kin to kin, making the family an endless repetition of sexual conquest after sexual conquest. In the absence of prohibition, every family member was a potential sexual partner.

Second, Finley worried that it "would have led to many instances whereby the order of nature would have been subverted, and the reverence and respect due from an inferior by nature to a superior destroyed."[68] Here Finley worked to preserve status in the increasingly sentimental, affectionate family. The preservation and maintenance of hierarchies and obligations, the fixing of statuses as ascriptive positions in the family, was a preoccupation of not only theologians, but of jurists too. While jurists would take a different path to a universal incest prohibition, theologians like Finley turned to the biblical prohibition to instill that order and protect the authority of the father and determine the dependency and subordination of his wife and children.

Third, and perhaps most importantly for Finley, the absence of the incest prohibition worked against the benevolent influence of society itself: "the allowing of persons very nearly related to marry," Finley wrote "would lead to the restricting and limiting our connections to a very narrow circle; so that every family would in a sort become a little world, disjoined from the rest of mankind through the want of a proper regard; which would be a very great evil."[69] This fear of deleterious social consequences animated nearly every discussion of incest in the early republic, the most morbid instance being the circulation of the tale of Sawney Beane.

John Henry Livingston carried the incestuous transgressions of the children of Adam and Eve to their logical consequences. As soon as women and men multiplied "impure lusts were imbibed, and incestuous connections were formed."[70] Where Finley saw necessity, Livingston saw transgression. "This enkindled the divine wrath and provoked the Lord to sweep such offenders from the *earth*, by an overwhelming flood."[71] In a similar sense, and serving as an even stronger warning to the postrevolutionary generation that the coming of incestuous marriages was a harbinger of greater destruction, Alexander McClelland explained that the deluge so soon after creation was a result of incest. "The Antediluvians had no determinate *law of Incest* . . . except for parent and child." McClelland continued with images that would shock even his most resistant readers.

> Children sucked in the seeds of pestilence, when lying on their mother's bosom. . . . Every family was a hotbed of pollution—Every woman had her Bastard. These bastards were thrown out like scum upon society,—under no restraints of paternal wisdom, wandered to and fro, increasing daily in numbers, and exhibiting all the energy and depravity of that wretched class of beings. . . . Monsters in activity and crime. . . . Such were the consequences of family impurity, and this family impurity was the necessary consequence of the want of a well-defined law of Incest.[72]

The affectionate family, for McClelland, Livingston, Finley, and a host of others was simply a prelude to incest, and the postlapsarian world was a warning. Without a clearly defined incest prohibition, and with it a clear meaning attached to kin relations regarding marriage and sex, incest was only a step away. Here origins evoked fear of unregulated desire—the biblical origins of humanity without an incest prohibition were analogous to the tension between social constraint and the autonomous, desiring individual of the new nation.

The postlapsarian discourse was part of a wider use of imagery of the Fall to describe the political and social conditions of the new nation. The marriage question and the incestuous anxieties it evoked were often tied to concerns about the consequences of liberty and consent that animated the political discourse of the new nation. The political context of the marriage question was not lost on Jonathan Edwards Jr. "In these times of revolution, some seem disposed to innovate in every thing, religious and moral, as well as political," Edwards wrote,

> or rather under the pretence of liberty . . . to throw off all restraint in morals and religion. Yet it is hoped, that our legislators, our churches, and the ministers . . . consider how far the general practice of marrying wives sisters . . . will tend to keep particular by themselves, and unconnected with their fellow citizens, and . . . promote narrowness, selfishness, mutual jealousy and enmity among fellow citizens, and aristocracy and civil broils in the state.

Implicit in Edwards's claim was that, in a nation where political power was located in the social, marriages that are antagonistic to the expansion of social relationships were politically problematic. He at once invoked the conditions of both Richard Jennings's and Sawney Beane's incests, for liberty, in some regard, animated both. This, for Edwards, was a problem for "republican government."[73]

The conjunction of liberty and incest was at the heart of a particularly contentious congregational dispute over an incestuous marriage in early nineteenth-century Connecticut. On 21 October 1810 Jabez Huntington, nephew of the Revolutionary War hero Jedidiah Huntington, married Sally Lanman, his deceased wife's sister, in Norwich, Connecticut. Although legal since 1795 in Connecticut, such marriages continued to be prohibited by Congregationalists. Having heard word of the proposed marriage, Walter King, the pastor of the congregation, attempted to persuade both Huntington and Lanman that their marriage would transgress God's law. King was unsuccessful but, believing that he could not sanction such overt transgression, refused either to perform the wedding ceremony or to administer communion to the incestuous couple. Huntington and Lanman persisted and were married in a nearby Episcopal church. After the marriage, Huntington, who served as foreman of a committee organized to dismiss King from his post, succeeded in this task. On 5 July 1811, King was dismissed from his duties as pastor of the Norwich congregation, a post he had held for twenty-five years. The congregation, with a fair degree of discord and cajoling by the powerful Huntington, implicitly validated what was once an incestuous marriage and dismissed the defender of a seemingly outdated interpretation of the Levitical prohibition.[74]

While the politics of the dismissal are of great interest, not least because the congregation viewed its relation King in terms of modern contract, what is of particular interest here are the competing notions of liberty and marriage advanced by Huntington and King. At stake was the justification of marital freedom for the liberal subject. When confronted by King concerning the incestuous nature of his proposed marriage, Huntington responded with a rousing call to individual liberty. King had sent Huntington a letter explaining why he was opposed to the marriage and the following day Huntington responded as follows:

> He was sorry that any measures on his part should cause an uneasiness in Mr. King's mind, in relation to their Christian connexion; but he knew not that *his liberty was to be judged of another man's conscience*: and as their relation to eternity was in the character of individuals, he endeavoured (if his heart did not greatly deceive him,) to hold this subject, as well as others, in reference to that time when *he expected to give account*.[75]

On the one hand, this is not the liberal subject as represented by Richard Jennings, who transgressed all laws and, until his incestuous encounter with his sister, rejected any sovereign God. Huntington acknowledged that he was a subject of God and that he would have to account for his actions. Yet, on the other hand, Huntington conceived of marriage and his relation to God as quintessentially voluntaristic: his liberty could not be regulated by the conscience of another man; his relation to God was individual, not collective. The subjects of God were radically atomized and would be judged by their individual actions, and his marital partner was to be determined by his individual liberty. Huntington conceived of marriage as an institution determined by individual liberty and his marriage to his deceased wife's sister as the realization of such freedom.

Walter King rejected this out of hand. For King, man was primarily the subject of God, and if the law of God prohibited such marriages then, regardless of any contemporary and individual desire, to engage in such a union was to sin. As King noted in a letter to Sally Lanman, "What God joins, man cannot put asunder; what God puts asunder, can no man join."[76] Such a conceptualization of marriage left no room for liberty, and this was precisely King's point. Indeed, King had provided Lanman with a copy of Jonathan Edwards's sermon, which railed against the presumptions of liberty in the question of incestuous marriages. King was concerned with the workings of liberty at any number of levels. The liberty that Huntington claimed was his alone; King identified it with "the fruits of an unsanctified heart . . . all polluted with selfishness, pride, and worldly vanity" for which "you must lie down in eternal sorrow."[77] Liberty was also associated with transgressive forms of novelty. "This marriage," King wrote, "would introduce a new practice, unknown before in this Church, one that was looked upon as criminal, when it was organized."[78] Liberty, in this instance, authorized criminality.

Man was, primarily, the subject of God, and King was concerned that this transgression of God's law was an instance of a too worldly imperative for marital action. As King wrote, "His [God's] will is the grand and sovereign law of the universe. Whatever he purposes shall be done; for, from the very nature of the divine perfections, he can neither err in his purposes, nor fail in their execution. We have, therefore, only to learn from Christ's own lips what his purpose is in this great concern, in order to have the fullest conviction that we shall all stand before his awful bar."[79] That the prohibition of marriage with a wife's sister was not part of Leviticus, and was articulated most forcefully in the Table of Kindred and Affinity, did not enter into King's calculations—he was certain that the rejection of this prohibition was a substitution of man's sovereignty for God's. Moreover, it was a carnal substitution that figured man as a sexual subject rather than a subject of God's law. "You must give account whether you have been *moved by the Holy Spirit, and a sincere desire to promote the glory of Christ, and the good of his cause,*" King wrote, "*or whether you have been moved by a worldly and carnal spirit, which could not endure the reproofs of divine truth.*"[80] If the prohibition of incest was a foundational law, as many theologians argued and King presupposed, then it was to be justified in biblical terms. Huntington and Lanman's marriage substituted carnal desire for the desire born of grace and thus shifted the location of sovereignty from the otherworldly to the worldly, threatening the order of the world, an order that was, in part at least, guaranteed by the prohibition of incest.

Whatever the controversy over King's dismissal, and Huntington seems clearly to have orchestrated it, King's position on incest and marriage was losing force. Huntington wanted the liberty to engage in marital choice as an autonomous individual, not to be judged by any other man's conscience, but acknowledged that there was a legitimate system of regulation and that, in the last analysis, he would be judged by it. Theological, and as we will see, legal articulations of the incest prohibition in the nineteenth century were increasingly concerned with producing a field of regulation in which the liberal subject had more room to move, especially in terms of marriage. Yet, this articulation of the liberal subject in terms of incest was inscribed within a field of regulatory imperatives. King was outmoded not in his demand for regulation but in his conceptualization of the subject—for him, sovereignty was not located in the individual but in God. As the eighteenth century passed into the nineteenth, the prohibition of incest was increasingly linked to the secular production of a subject of liberalism.

The invocations of postlapsarian cases of incest served as warnings to the rise of the affectionate family. Jonathan Edwards Jr.'s explicit relation of incestuous marriage to republican government made clear the stakes involved in the ambiguities of kinship and sentiment—incestuous marriages threatened the virtue of the nation. The feelings of love and affection between family members, in much literature regulating the relations between parents and children, were potentially erotic and, thus, incestuous. Moreover, the ratification of the liberal subject as a normative desiring subject whose freedom was realized in freely chosen marriage, as evidenced in the dismissal of Walter King, further cut away the authority of the theological incest prohibition. The only restraint on such desire was a clearly defined incest prohibition. The creation of a new world, or in the United States a new society, was rife with destructive potential. The making and remaking of kinship, marriage, love, and sex were potentially incestuous, or so believed the theologians of the early republic. The nation had a choice: a world of law, where the incest prohibition was in place and clearly defined, or a world without law, where desire was unrestrained, the family was a hotbed of sexuality and the postlapsarian condition awaited. Yet, inadvertently, in an effort to stabilize the law of incest and regulate desire in the sentimental family, these theologians collectively produced a family that was infused with a barely contained sexual desire. As theologians grappled with the consequences of liberal forms of sexuality and marriage, the secular law was reconstituting the law of incest in ways that diverged radically from its biblical foundations. The transcendental authority associated with Leviticus would be shorn away as the subject of law became increasingly the liberal sexual subject.

The church occupied an ambivalent position in the discourse of incest. Neither public nor private, its liminal position was an effect of increasing secularism. The place of the church in American life did not diminish—in fact, it expanded across the nineteenth century. Yet, what secularism meant was that there were now multiple choices from where to derive moral authority and foundational laws. In terms of incest, Leviticus and its various derivations were no longer the only source for a universal incest prohibition. The marriage question registered the liminal position of the church—neither on the side of the family nor the state, it was unclear why the church needed so forcefully to govern the prohibition of incest. Its concerns with incest in the sentimental family were taken up by novelists, temperance reformers, and phrenologists while its concern with articulating a universal incest prohibition was transformed in the state legal system. While the marriage question inaugurated the liberal discourse of incest, its concerns would spread throughout the entire discourse. It was in the increasingly secular legal system that a new universal incest prohibition, consonant with liberal society, would be produced.

Chapter 3

Law

In 1851, in response to a query concerning incestuous marriage from the London-based Marriage Law Reform Association (MLRA), Charles Mason, an Iowa Supreme Court justice, wrote, "our laws make no prohibitions what ever as to inter-marriages between kindred, nor has the crime of incest a place on our statute books."[1] This was likely more than the MLRA was looking for when they circulated a query to jurists, theologians, and other public figures in the United States, "where law and public opinion concur in making no distinction between a marriage [with a deceased wife's sister] and any other not prohibited in the Sacred Scriptures."[2] Mason further suggested that laws prohibiting incest were unnecessary and potentially detrimental to the force of the prohibition. "So far as my knowledge extends, no evil consequences have resulted from these omissions of law," Mason wrote. Furthermore, "our legislators seem to have acted under this belief, that the laws of nature on this subject needed no further sanction than normal feeling, fortified perhaps by public opinion; and that this sanction might rather be weakened than strengthened by superadding the penalties of the state."[3] In Mason's telling, the prohibition of incest was so strong that secular criminal laws would not only have been superfluous, they may have carried the unintended consequence of undercutting the more fundamental natural law that undergirded the prohibition.

Mason's assessment of both the law of incest and the prerogatives of Iowa legislators turned out to be wrong. Indeed, his mistaken account of the law in Iowa was rather perplexing: in 1844, as chief justice of the Iowa Supreme Court, Mason authored the opinion of the court in a case of brother-sister incest.[4] Nonetheless, his polemic was symptomatic of the transformation of incest law in the nineteenth century. By the middle of the nineteenth century, every state in the union had laws prohibiting incest.

However, in both content and justification they bore little resemblance to the biblically grounded laws of the eighteenth century. Colonial and early national laws were expansive, including both consanguineous and affinal relatives and, following from the Table of Kindred and Affinity (the codification of the Levitical prohibition by the Anglican Church in 1603), could include up to sixty persons. Across the nineteenth century, the religious foundation dissipated, and the list of prohibited kin was in nearly constant flux. In Mason's Iowa, for example, the 1843 territorial incest law made no reference to Christianity, prohibited only parent-child, stepparent-stepchild, and brother-sister, and referred to "sexual intercourse" rather than marriage.[5] Yet, in 1873 a new law in Iowa expanded the list of prohibited kin to include grandparents and grandchildren as well as uncle-niece and aunt-nephew.[6]

The import of Mason's response was in its seeming ignorance of the history of incest law in the colonies and early national period. In referring to natural law as the basis for the prohibition of incest, Mason registered the primary transformation of the incest prohibition in nineteenth-century law—its newfound, and frequently uncomfortable, secularity. The substitution of the law of nature for the law of God in the legal delimitation of incest replaced one foundational assumption with another, but the law of nature suggested the maintenance of obligations and duties in the family and encouraged the extrafamilial sociality of individuals and the use of reason. If the prohibition of incest was natural in the law it was also part of man's understanding of the world rather than the transcendent authority of Leviticus. While other respondents acknowledged the earlier sacred logic, even if they derisively dismissed it, as Horace Mann did in calling the prohibition of marriage with a deceased wife's sister "silly and superstitious," Mason abjured that history completely.[7] If eighteenth-century laws insistently referred to biblical justifications, whether Leviticus or derivative interpretations like the Table of Kindred and Affinity or canon law, by the mid-nineteenth century these references had mostly disappeared. In their place were natural law and the preservation of private, domestic accord.

While incest laws varied from state to state and changed rather significantly across the nineteenth century, there were commonalities across most of the statutes. Paradoxically, the variations across states constituted one of those commonalities—shorn of a foundational text (Leviticus), statutes varied widely without seeming to deviate from a transcendent norm. In the 1820s, legists and jurists began to present the natural law as a new universal

foundation of the prohibition. It privileged parent-child and sibling relationships, relied on a new notion of privacy, perpetuated and rearticulated
familial hierarchies and dependencies, and, finally, provided a means by
which the state, via the regulation of incest, could penetrate the sanctum of
the increasingly private family. In doing so, this new universalism aligned
the bourgeois nuclear family with the incest prohibition. Increasingly, the
more expansive prohibitions, like those derived from Leviticus, were seen,
in the law, as local variants, not universal prohibitions.

The law of incest was, in a sense, suspended between two domains of
law. On the one hand, it was part of domestic relations law, or what, in the
later nineteenth century would be called family law. Here, incest was linked
to marriage, divorce, polygamy, adultery, and parent-child relations. On
the other hand, it was part of emergent criminal sex laws, linking it with
laws prohibiting fornication, criminal connection, sodomy, and bestiality.
While this context is important, and forms one backdrop against which to
trace incest law in the nineteenth century, I have foregone much of it in
order to draw out the ways in which the law produced and was part of the
broader discourse of incest. If legists and jurists did not always refer to
theologians, phrenologists, ethnographers, and novelists, they nonetheless
frequently wrote in similar language. The disorder of the liberal incest prohibition, in which there was no agreed-upon locus of the prohibition,
meant that different discursive domains often hewed their own paths,
unaware that a similar language was being spoken elsewhere. To focus on
relations across legal categories would diminish the place of incest law in
the broader discourse of incest.

Where once the laws regulated kinship, with sex articulated within the
confines of alliance, in the nineteenth century incest laws increasingly regulated the emergent sexual subject, alongside continued, although transformed, regulation of marriage. More frequently incest laws bounced
between regulating sex and regulating marriage, which reinforced the plurality and disorder of the law from state to state. Indeed, a more generous
reading of Mason's response to the MLRA would be that it was precisely
this transition that structured his misprision. While he went as far as claiming that there were no incest statutes in Iowa, when he was more specific
he referred to "inter-marriages." His 1844 supreme court opinion made no
reference to marriage at all. "The statute," Mason wrote, "includes *any
brother and sister, who, being of the age of sixteen years, or upwards, shall
have sexual intercourse together, having knowledge of their consanguinity.*"[8]

The sexual subject, who was, not coincidentally, constituted as corollary to the liberal subject, was the new subject of the law. If the theological "marriage question" saw the family as infused with eroticism, the secular law presumed the subject of incest law to be a sexual subject. These were concurrent, indeed, overlapping discourses in the antebellum period—the secular did not so much replace the sacred as it emerged alongside it.

The legal incest prohibition was dispersed across statutes, legal writings, appellate case reports, newspaper reports, and pamphlets throughout the antebellum period. In this way, it trafficked more in the domain of legality than law.[9] In legality, the laws of incest are connected to other fields in the discourse of incest. It is no coincidence that the language of the law evoked not only the increasingly specialized lexicon of the professionalizing legal discipline but also the macabre specters of Sawney Beane and Richard Jennings. It is the unacknowledged assumptions and forms of subjectivity and truth, in a word, the *unthought* of the law of incest in the nineteenth century, that I excavate in this chapter. The incest prohibition as Law—theological, psychoanalytic, anthropological—has tended to resist historicization. Paradoxically, a turn to nineteenth-century law as legality contributes to the historicization of incest in terms of both law and Law.

Secular Law

Colonial and early national incest laws were derived from biblical incest prohibitions and often referred, explicitly, to Leviticus or the Table of Kindred and Affinity. By the end of the nineteenth century, the parameters of the legal prohibition privileged consanguinity over and against affinity, focused more specifically on those kin relations that made up the nuclear family, and rarely, if ever, referred to biblical foundations. Legal treatises and judicial opinions replaced the Levitical foundation of the law with a thoroughly anthropocentric natural law, oriented toward society and dependency rather than the sovereignty of God.

Accounts of nineteenth-century incest law tend to attribute a great deal of rationalization to the changes. This often takes the form of an emphasis on physiological issues (which were of little concern in the vast majority of antebellum laws and legal treatises) and the new focus on the nuclear family, both of which were taken to represent essential qualities of incest.[10] However, the secular transformations of the nineteenth century were uneven and ambivalent, not least because they produced rather than discovered a new essential and universal meaning that we still associate with incest today. Nineteenth-century law did not reveal true incest; it produced a new meaning of incest, one amenable to the social, cultural, and political context of liberalism.

Moreover, most historical accounts, whether articulated in terms of rationalization or not, privilege the changing parameters of the prohibition over the language of the law. As such, these accounts present a mostly linear, if occasionally uneven, constriction of the prohibition. Thus, the controversy over the deceased wife's sister has played an outsized role in the interpretation of incest law, which has privileged Massachusetts and Connecticut, the first two states to excise the deceased wife's sister.[11] Such an emphasis, while certainly important, nonetheless tends to read the law as a reflection of a prediscursive, demographic reality. Thus, the anthropologist Bernard Farber divides nineteenth-century incest laws into two categories: the "Biblical System" in the South and Northeast and a "Western American System" in the Middle and Far West. The legal categories, for Farber, reflected demographic realities, despite the fact that there is little evidence for this and it occludes the place of law in a broader discourse of incest.[12] By addressing the changing source of authority in the law of incest, we can discern the remaking of the incest prohibition for the production of the liberal subject. This entailed not only widening the field of marital and sexual partners by contracting the prohibition, but also making the location of sovereignty amenable to the production of a seemingly autonomous desiring individual.

This transformation might be best thought of as the increasing secularism of the incest prohibition in the legal domain. Secularism should not be confused with secularization, the mostly linear process whereby the modern secular—rational, profane, bureaucratic, capitalist, organized around the nation-state—replaces the sacred. Rather, secularism is a way of ordering knowledge, in which the religious became one mode among many others for apprehending the world. The religious, theological incest prohibition of the marriage question and the attendant concerns did not disappear. They continued to fester across the nineteenth century, and the incestuous anxieties theologians addressed to the sentimental family could be found in any number of places, from novels, to temperance and other reform movements, to phrenology, all of which had relations to that religious discourse. But, in the legal domain, the law of incest came to rest less and less, in its fundament, on the theological ground of Leviticus and the Table of Kindred and Affinity. This did not mean that the law never spoke to these concerns; instead, those theological definitions of the incest prohibition became one approach among many. In this, theology became localized, a matter of private belief. This liberal logic of the prohibition necessitated a new universal ground, and that emerged out of natural, rather than supernatural, law.[13]

Unlike the wealth of writing on the "marriage question," the diminishing religious authority in state law was not a particularly conscious process. Edward Mansfield, a professor of history at Cincinnati College, for instance, wrote that "the *holiness or unholiness* of the matrimonial contract, in reference to the ties of blood and other moral circumstances, is not considered by the law, but left entirely to the jurisdiction of ecclesiastical bodies, or the restraints of conscience. Nevertheless, for the sake of sound morals and public policy, the laws of nearly all Christian States do prescribe some limits of consanguinity, within which marriages may not be contracted."[14] By separating the law and ecclesiastical bodies, Mansfield obscured the long imbrication of the two in colonial and early national law, which he promptly acknowledged in the service of morals and the public good. Mansfield, like most authors of legal treatises in the nineteenth century, produced what he proposed to describe—the secularization of the law of incest.

The transformation and secularization of incest law that occupied antebellum America had its roots in an earlier and hardly secular era. It was the culmination of the uneasy transition of such laws to the British North American colonies in the seventeenth century. While all colonial incest laws were, like the metropolitan laws, unambiguously derived from the long tradition of Levitical exegesis, colonial laws were also marked by the uneasy transition of marriage laws to the colonies. In England the incest prohibition, like all marital regulations, was not part of the common law; rather, it was a subject of ecclesiastical regulation, to be ruled on by the "spiritual courts." Thus, there was a clear distinction between the sacred and secular, or spiritual and temporal laws, with the prohibition of incest falling on the side of the sacred and spiritual. William Blackstone, in his *Commentaries on the Laws of England*, made the relationship between the two orders of law clear. "In general," Blackstone wrote, "all persons are able to contract themselves in marriage, unless they labour under some particular disabilities, and incapacities."[15] These "disabilities" included "consanguinity, or relation by blood [and] affinity, or relation by marriage," which arose not

from the common law, but from the ecclesiastical.[16] "These canonical disabilities are either grounded upon the express words of the divine law, or
are consequences plainly deducible from them . . . they are properly the
object of the ecclesiastical magistrate's coercion; in order to separate the
offenders, and inflict penance for the offence."[17] Thus, the incest prohibition was not a part of the common law, even as it had effects therein.

Despite the juridical location of the law of incest, there were effects in
the common law. Marriages that violated the prohibition were voidable,
but not void, at the common law. Void marriages were illegitimate at all
times, meaning that even if they had been contracted somewhere, once
recognized by the common law courts, the marriage would be wiped
clean—it was never valid and would be treated as if it never existed.[18] Offspring of the marriage would be treated as illegitimate. Void marriages followed from civil encumbrances on the contracting parties, such as infancy,
mental incapacity, absence of consent, or previous marriages.[19] Voidable
marriages, on the other hand, would be treated as valid until separated, in
this case by the ecclesiastical court. Offspring from voidable marriages
would be treated, at the common law, as legitimate, even after the marriage
was terminated. Voidable marriages followed from canonical encumbrances
on the contracting parties, such as impotence, consanguinity, or affinity.[20]
So consanguineous and affinal—in a word, incestuous—marriages were
legitimate in the common law until terminated by the spiritual courts.

The distinction between ecclesiastical and common law, or spiritual and
temporal courts, did not survive the transatlantic journey to the North
American colonies.[21] Thus early colonial incest laws either bore the unmis-
takable imprint of the ecclesiastical laws or, as in some colonies, were
entirely absent from the statutory codes. Some colonies made the marriages
void, but most did not stipulate that as a consequence; regardless of the
punishments, the void/voidable distinction, as outlined by Blackstone
around the split between spiritual and temporal courts, did not survive in
the colonies. Colonial incest laws at times stated explicit prohibitions but
at other times simply invoked the Table of Kindred and Affinity; they were
most commonly concerned with marriage, yet several colonies explicitly
included sex; they all prescribed serious punishments.[22] Moreover, while
some colonies (Plymouth Plantation, Virginia, New York, Georgia, and
Delaware) had no statutes prohibiting incest in their original codes, the
remaining colonies exhibited no uniformity in where the prohibition was
located. Some passed specific laws prohibiting incest (Massachusetts, New

Haven, Pennsylvania, New Hampshire), others included the prohibition in broad acts concerning religious governance (Maryland and South Carolina), while still others included reference to incest in acts concerning rape (Rhode Island) or clandestine marriage (New Jersey).[23]

Despite these variations, indebtedness to the Table of Kindred and Affinity and Leviticus animated most of the colonial laws, an obvious inheritance from English ecclesiastical law, even if this derivation did not guarantee absolute uniformity. In some instances, such as Massachusetts and Pennsylvania, (re)productions of the Table were included, although neither was an exact replica, which may suggest the political and religious difference between Puritans and Quakers, respectively, and the Church of England.[24] The Massachusetts law, passed in 1695, generated controversy concerning the marriage of a deceased wife's sister. As the colonial jurist Samuel Sewall recorded in his diary, the act barely passed and was helped through by a letter written by several ministers, including Increase and Cotton Mather.[25] In Sewall's telling at least, the law was simply the codification of the law of God. After noting that much of the controversy emerged from the fact that "several [Deputies of the General Council] have married their wives sisters, and the Deputies thought it hard to part them," Sewall wrote "that not to part them, were to make the Law abortive, by begetting in people a conceipt [sic] that such Marriages were not against the Law of God."[26] The Pennsylvania law, passed in 1705 as "An Act against Incest," privileged marriage in its definition of incest and included a table, but one greatly reduced from the expansiveness of either the Massachusetts law or the Table of Kindred and Affinity (Figure 1).[27] This act, unlike most other colonial incest laws, did not refer directly to the authority of God.[28] Moreover, the Pennsylvania law, like that in Massachusetts, retained the gender parity found in the Table of Kindred and Affinity. While Leviticus was directed explicitly toward men, the Table had rationalized and balanced the Levitical prohibition. In this, as with most colonial incest laws, women were equally subjected to the law. Given that the statutes treated incest as a consensual act, gender parity in the law created the means by which both parties could be tried. The law, then, abstractly recognized women as equal partners with men, even if it was in a transgressive marriage.

By the early eighteenth century, colonial incest laws, despite some variation, had achieved a kind of uniformity, reflecting ecclesiastical law in England. They foregrounded marriage while disavowing incestuous sex and were, with the exception of Pennsylvania, explicitly biblically grounded.[29]

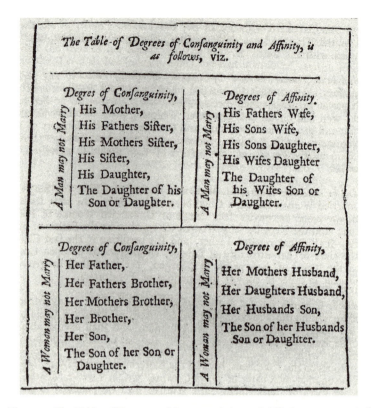

Figure 1. The Table of Degrees of Consanguinity and Affinity accompanied the Pennsylvania Act Against Incest (1705).

The colonial common law simply reproduced the biblical logic with the inconsistencies that accompanied the absence of spiritual courts. The force of incest laws emanated from the sovereignty of God regardless of the religiosity of each colony. Therefore, the existence of the laws required little justification. Despite variations from colony to colony in the specific parameters of each prohibition or the extent to which the law needed to enumerate prohibited relations, the source of the prohibition was absolutely foundational and followed from the transcendent sovereignty of God.

By the end of the eighteenth century, however, this reflexive source of authority, the edifice on which incest law was built, was beginning to crumble. Unlike the theological "marriage question," which occasioned much controversy, the shift in incest law from the sacred to the secular was subtler. This followed, in large part, from the fact that this shift occurred in the nominally secular domain of the law. This can be gleaned from the history of incest law in eighteenth- and nineteenth-century century Virginia. Virginia was one of the last colonies to enact a law prohibiting incest and one of the first states to register the shift from the sacred to the secular. Nonetheless, by 1850 Virginia was the only state still prohibiting marriage with a deceased wife's sister, a remnant of the theological prohibition. The coming of secular incest law was uneven, contradictory, and plural, even within individual states.

Like several other colonies in the seventeenth century, Virginia had no law prohibiting incest.[30] That changed in 1751, however, when an act prohibiting marriages "with in the Levitical Degrees" was passed. Despite referencing the Levitical degrees rather than the Church of England or the Table of Kindred and Affinity, the legal prohibition nonetheless deviated in several places from the kin enumerated in Leviticus.[31] Included in an omnibus statute covering vice, blasphemy, and "Incestuous Marriages and Copulations," the prohibition of incest was categorically a part of religious governance. Indeed, the prohibition made specific reference to Leviticus, and other parts of the law were dependent on "the Churchwarden or Churchwardens of the Parish."[32] Both the religious and marital context of mid-eighteenth-century Virginia help explain the timing of the law. In the 1740s, evangelical awakenings led by Presbyterians spread throughout Virginia. Such evangelical dissent occasioned a new assertion of power by the Anglican establishment, of which the 1751 law would have been a part, its discrepancies from the Table notwithstanding.[33] Moreover, in the mid-eighteenth century the Virginia gentry further consolidated its power as the younger generation of Virginians married amongst itself. The law would have provided a means by which near kin marriages contributing to class formation would also have been regulated to avoid incest and uphold a bulwark of Western civilization in the context of perceived enslaved African and Native American sexual and kinship practices.[34] Thus the law regulated near-kin sexual and marital relations in a social-class context where kinship was still a fundamental organizing principle.

In December 1788, the Virginia legislature repealed the earlier colonial law against incest, replacing it with "An Act concerning Incestuous Marriage." The transformation in the title alone was striking. The new law, which separated incest from other concerns of religious governance, replaced the unwieldy "An Act for the effectual Suppression of Vice, and

Restraint and Punishment of blasphemous, wicked, and dissolute Persons;
and for preventing incestuous Marriages and Copulations."[35] Explicit reference to Leviticus was gone; in its place was a list of prohibited marriages,
which was virtually the same, with one difference: where the colonial law,
like the Levitical prohibitions, did not explicitly note a prohibition of the
daughter, the 1788 law added the daughter to the prohibition. While copulation was excised and marriage privileged, this was most likely an effect of
the diminution of Leviticus. The culture of incest law in the eighteenth
century tended toward marriage, but Leviticus privileged sex. With the excision of Leviticus from the statute, Virginia fell in line with other states.
Despite similarities in the specific kin prohibited from marriage or sex, the
law was effectively severed from the authority of sacred sovereignty.

The transformation of the law from the sacred to the secular, as the
Virginia law demonstrates, was not simply a matter of who was prohibited.
This was also apparent in both Massachusetts and Connecticut, the first
two states to change their laws prohibiting incestuous marriage. In Massachusetts, the 1785 transformation of the law retained no reference to the
spiritual source of the prohibition.[36] Moreover, despite the fact that in theological circles the discourse was organized around the removal of the wife's
sister from the prohibition, the actual 1785 law went a great deal further,
removing a total of ten persons from the prohibition and adding two.
Importantly, the Massachusetts law now cleaved neither to the Table of
Kindred and Affinity, as, for the most part, the colonial law of Massachusetts had, nor to a strict adherence to the Levitical prohibitions. Connecticut revised the law in 1793 and also retained no direct reference to its earlier
religious source.[37]

From the 1780s onward, reliance on biblical justifications for the origins
of the incest prohibition diminished in the domain of the statutory law. This
is not to say that they had completely disappeared from legal discourse—
some nineteenth-century legal treatises, in part because of their engagement
with Blackstone, continued to invoke Leviticus or the Table of Kindred and
Affinity. But the ordering of the sacred and secular was changing, and the
ground of the incest prohibition shifted along with it. A late nineteenth-
century survey of incest laws across the nation, conducted by the U.S. com-
missioner of labor, unwittingly obscured the tension between sacred and
secular by focusing almost exclusively on which kin were prohibited from
marriage and sex. While there was a tendency toward including first cousins
in some states, and others focused in on lineal relatives and siblings, other

states included a number of collateral affinal relatives, as well.[38] Scholars have long relied on this compilation of incest laws and George Elliott Howard's early twentieth-century history of marriage as guides to nineteenth-century incest laws.[39] While both are indispensable, they reinforce the emphasis on who was prohibited rather than how they were prohibited and the logic of the laws. Paying closer attention to the language of the law shifts the emphasis from who was prohibited to the logic of the incest law itself, which in turn privileges a secular problematic.

The decline of religious justifications unmoored incest law. Coupled with the federalism of domestic relations laws—which created conditions for variegated laws of incest across the nation—a universal, rational standard for the prohibition of incest seemed neither possible, nor necessarily even desirable. As Hendrik Hartog has written of domestic relations law generally, "disorder may have been the rule in law and in many personal lives."[40] As territories formed and states entered the union, laws regulating marriage were often among the earliest enacted, including incest laws. Eastern states, in addition to realigning prohibited kin, tended to excise biblical references, while states and territories further west, most of which entered the union in the nineteenth century, tended to focus more narrowly on the nuclear family and found Leviticus and its biblical descendants of little relevance. Close attention to Ohio, Iowa, and Colorado illustrates the transformation further.[41] What becomes particularly clear is that there was little uniformity in the laws of incest, even within states, across the nineteenth century, shifting back and forth between marriage and sexuality, including more kin one year, less another, and still more another year. This variety and disorder was new, a result of the secular absence of any clear textual foundation. Indeed, if the law of incest retained some notion of a foundational law as its referent—and it most certainly did—its flexibility and variation, both from state to state and within states over time, created the conditions for the liberal subject. Caught between the regulation of foundational law and the disorder of incest statutes, the liberal subject could pursue its desire while being pursued by the law of incest itself.

The history of incest law in nineteenth-century Ohio was particularly vexed. The first state carved out of the Northwest Territory, Ohio passed its first incest law in 1803, the same year it was admitted to statehood. The law was in nearly constant flux across the nineteenth century, with sexuality coming to occupy a similar position to marriage; adding and subtracting prohibited kin with little logic or uniformity; addressing issues of consent and rape. Despite the persistence of change, all of this was rather common in regard to other states. However, Ohio law also had some rather peculiar features, chief among them a focus on seminal emission in charges of incest.

The Northwest Territory had no specific incest law, and territorial governance was at best ambiguous concerning incest across the nineteenth century, so the initial Ohio statute would serve as an important precedent for transforming a territory into a state. The 1803 statute read, "That male persons of the age of eighteen years, female persons of the age of fourteen years, and not nearer of kin than first cousins, may be joined in marriage."[42] While other western states did not exactly mimic Ohio, a trend in this direction across the nineteenth century was apparent. Yet, the brevity of the statute introduced a fair amount of ambiguity. Ohio was the first state to prohibit cousins from marrying. However, while the wording of the statute seemed to imply a focus on consanguinity, this was most likely not the case, since the phrase "not nearer of kin than first cousins" implied civil law reckoning of kin. By this logic, affinal kin would certainly be included if they were reckoned closer kin. In another way, however, the new law followed the marital emphasis that animated most other states in the union. Its great difference, then, in addition to including first cousins, was its brevity—one sentence in a broad statute regulating marriages. Its assumption of a self-evident quality of incestuous marriages was relatively novel, and, moreover, no punishment was specified for such a transgression.

In 1823 the law was radically revised, with the definition of incest shifting from marriage to sexuality and a distinction between consent and force being clearly articulated in the legal apparatus. The law of incest, which shifted from an act regulating marriages to an act for the punishment of crimes, or from domestic relations to criminal law, specified the prohibited kin. The earlier ambiguity was gone, replaced by a focus on the nuclear family, with relations between parents and children, stepparents and stepchildren, and siblings prohibited. All other relations were presumably permitted. As part of criminal law the act prohibited "sexual intercourse" rather than marriage.[43] And it prescribed a punishment of three to ten years of hard labor. Unlike contemporary significations of incest, which privilege sexual violence, the Ohio statute, like all other nineteenth-century statutes, treated both parties as guilty because incest was a consensual transgression. This did not mean that there was no manner in which to treat violent incest (although that was the case in several states). Rather, it signified a categorical distinction between incest and rape. This was clear in the statute, where

"Carnal knowledge of [a] daughter or sister, forcibly, and against her will ... shall be deemed guilty of rape."[44] The punishment illustrated that this was a more serious offense than rape, as the offender—father, brother, or stepfather—was sentenced to life in prison, whereas nonincestuous rape carried a sentence of seven to twenty years of hard labor.[45]

The transformation of incest law in Ohio, however, was not complete. By 1881, the focus on the nuclear family had disappeared, although the focus on sex remained and was amplified.[46] Incest was defined as "Persons nearer of kin by consanguinity or affinity than cousins, having knowledge of their relationship, who commit adultery or fornication together."[47] The law was essentially returned to its initial state (that of the 1803 statute), although the inclusion of consanguinity and affinity erased the earlier ambiguity, even as the lack of specification of "cousin" suggested an endless prohibition. The punishment had changed from hard labor to one to ten years in prison. The 1881 statute also repealed an 1835 act that treated each individual act of incest as a separate crime, now treating all acts as one crime.[48] As we will see below, this repeal combined with the 1881 statute's codification of the necessity of seminal emission for conviction of incest further entrenched the sexual subject as the object of the law. No longer could incest be treated as so many iterations of a criminal act; rather, those who committed repeated acts of incest were incestuous subjects. In this sense, then, incest was, in the eyes of the law, becoming something more than a criminal act or illicit marriage. As the desiring sexual subject became more prominent across the nineteenth century, incest law treated incest as a manifestation of that subject, part of his identity. The consolidation of incestuous acts into one crime suggested that these were the acts of an incestuous subject.[49]

These variations, symptomatic of the instability and lack of foundational ground of the law, were an effect of the secular logic—with no text, such as Leviticus or the Table of Kindred and Affinity to which to refer, a seemingly endless variety of incest laws marked the nation. Iowa, too, evinced a wholly secular law. The first incest law in Iowa, a territorial law passed in 1843, prohibited sex between parents and children, siblings, and stepparents and stepchildren. It required knowledge of the relationship, which was rendered as "consanguinity" even though it included stepparents and children. In 1873, the state passed a much-revised law, which included both affinal and consanguineous relatives, lineal through grandparent-grandchild, and collateral through uncle-niece and aunt-nephew. Moreover, it continued to address sex but also began to explicitly regulate marriages. After these changes, the 1879 criminal code included precedents from other states, including Ohio, Indiana, Missouri, Alabama, Michigan, Illinois, Vermont, and Mississippi, suggesting that the disorders of federalism did not foreclose precedents from other states. So in Iowa, the law moved from sex and the nuclear family to sex and marriage including extended kin. Still, like the other states, there was no reference to God.

The laws in Ohio and Iowa evidence several important changes in the nineteenth century. First, the secularization of the law, which, in contrast to the religiously grounded laws of the eighteenth century, marked the prohibition of incest with a kind of radical indeterminacy—it was less and less clear what, exactly, constituted incest. More importantly, it was less and less clear why incest remained prohibited in the absence of biblical law. Not only did laws change as one moved from state to state, a common enough feature of federalized domestic relations law, but they also changed within states, and with little sense of linearity or development. Despite this, most writers insisted that incest was one of the great crimes of humanity, a transgression of a fundamental law, however inchoate, the effect of which was precisely to occlude this indeterminacy. Second, despite this indeterminacy, sexuality was increasingly an object of incest law. It was not so much that sex displaced marriage as it was that they coexisted, awkwardly, in the same legal regime. The tension between marriage and sex in the law was symptomatic of the larger issue of the circulation of desire in the family—the threat of incestuous desire, especially through the excesses of sentimental affection, secured the possibility of state intervention into the private family. Whether the regulation of marriage, sex, or both was the most effective means of policing the incestuous family was unclear. Third, again, despite the indeterminacy of the secular law, the nuclear family was increasingly being singled out as an object of incest law, suggesting that the law apprehended a new configuration of the family. That this was the family most associated with the erotic dangers of excessive sentimental affection was not a coincidence.

The indeterminacy of the law, the absence of any uniformity, and ultimately the attenuated relationship between nineteenth-century incest statutes and a more universal, foundational prohibition, was nowhere more apparent than in Colorado. Colorado passed a statute prohibiting incest in 1876, the same year it was admitted to the union as a state, and it was similar to other western territories and states, in that it emphasized the nuclear family and limited collateral kin. While later in the nineteenth century, Colorado was both an anomaly and in many ways the culmination of

the indeterminacy of incest law in nineteenth-century America. The temporality of the transformation of incest law, across the nation, was uneven:
while many of the ideas animating liberal secular incest laws came into
being in the early nineteenth century, without an overarching regulatory
body, their implementation occurred haphazardly.

Unlike many other states, in Colorado incest was prohibited in two
separate statutes, one addressing marriage, the other sex. The former was
part of a statute regulating marriages and thus part of family law, while the
other was part of the criminal code. Both marriage and sex were included in
the criminal code, with only relations of consanguinity prohibited—parent-
child, grandparent-grandchild, brother-sister (including half siblings),
aunt-nephew, uncle-niece, and first cousins. Relations of affinity that were
common yet increasingly controversial in most eastern states were absent
in this prohibition. Those prohibited from marriage who "commit adultery
or fornication with each other, or . . . lewdly and lasciviously cohabit with
each other" could be punished with three months to two years in the penitentiary and/or a fifty- to five-hundred-dollar fine. Incest was, in this regard
and in all other statutes nationally, a crime of consent, and thus both parties
were charged. The consensual nature of legal definitions of incest was suspended, however, in one case. "If a father shall rudely and licentiously
cohabit with his own daughter," the statute read, he alone would be
charged and faced up to twenty years in a penitentiary.[50] This distinction in
the law of incest folded a portion of rape law into incest in the case of
the father, recognizing the asymmetries of power inherent in specific kin
relations. However, unlike rape law, this clause required no force.

The statute regulating incestuous marriages was distinct from that
found in the criminal code and was shot through with a racial logic. After
restating the list of prohibited kin it declared all such marriages to be "absolutely void," further noting that it "extended to illegitimate, as well as legitimate children."[51] Following the prohibition of incestuous marriage, the
statute then prohibited all marriages "between negroes and mulattoes, of
either sex . . . to be absolutely void." The contiguity of incest and interracial
marriage prohibitions in legal codes and the broader discourse was common in antebellum America.[52] Following these two prohibitions, the statute
then included a glaring exception: "nothing in this section shall be so construed as to prevent the people living in that portion of the state acquired
from Mexico from marrying according to the custom of that country."[53]
This exception referred to both incestuous and interracial marriages,

excluding part of the population of the state from these laws. On the one hand, this implicitly acknowledged the potential of different economies of both kinship and racial hierarchy. On the other hand, in designating Mexican marital regulations as "custom" rather than law, Mexico was implicitly situated in a lower position on the civilizational hierarchy.

The coexistence of Anglo-American common law traditions with European continental civil law regulations was not unheard of in this period. Louisiana and Texas, in particular, had strong civil law traditions inherited from colonial rule by the French and Spanish.[54] This hybrid civil-common law may have reflected the strong entrenchment of French or Spanish colonial rule, or possibly a powerful faction in the newly acquired U.S. territories. This may have been the case in Colorado, too, although by 1876 there was less likely to be a strong Mexican faction in Colorado. Viewed in this manner, the provision was pragmatic—too many people in this area were accustomed to the civil law reckoning of the incest prohibition.[55] Presumably, this would have obviated the need to void marriages contracted under the Mexican civil law statutes.

The law itself was quite ambiguous. Rather than referring to Mexican law, it referred to "marrying according to the custom of that country."[56] By substituting custom for law, the regulation of incest in that part of the state was effectively severed from the law. The Colorado statute clearly did not apply, but in designating custom there was no guarantee Mexican law would have jurisdiction, either. Indeed, one can read this as producing a static, premodern Mexico, organized around kinship customs rather than modern laws. If Mexican law did, in fact, guide interpretations of custom, would the incest law in this portion of the state continue to change with Mexican law; or, was the law tied to Mexican law circa 1848, the date of Mexican cession; or, did it refer to Mexican law circa 1876, the year in which Colorado was admitted to the union as a state and the laws of the state were passed? Moreover, to whom did this law apply? It marked a territory, not a population. Was it possible for U.S. Americans living in other parts of the state, or country, to enter this portion of Colorado and abide by Mexican incest custom? And if so, following the federal logic of American marriage law, would these marriages be recognized in other states? Or, was it limited to those persons who were living in the territory at the time of cession, or the admission to statehood? Rather than reading these as omissions or flaws in the law—they certainly were that, but such is a charge that could be leveled against nearly every state—they were symptomatic of the secular liberal incest prohibition itself. Instead of the family as source of social stability, even at the ideological level of the law, the family, constituted by the kin restriction on marriage and sexuality, was not even singular. The liberal subject, animated by his desire, could, in theory, choose which familial and sexual structure he wanted to inhabit, by deciding which incest prohibition to follow. In this regard, the social conditions—size of Mexican population, relative social and political power—seem less important than the fact that the incest prohibition, still regarded as a foundational law, could be so consciously fractured and plural.

This survey of Ohio, Iowa, and Colorado illustrates some of the constants in nineteenth century law as well as the instabilities, fractures, and federal disorder marking the law of incest. These were all secular, and thus the legal regulation and governance of incest was a matter of the modern liberal democratic state. All the laws treated incest as a consensual crime, meaning both parties were implicated in the transgression.[57] As we have seen, some states, like Ohio and Colorado, created rape-of-daughter laws that dealt with forcible incestuous sex, which was also, importantly, an effect of the continued unequal distribution of power in the bourgeois family. Reading these laws alongside incest laws suggests that there was an emergent logic setting the nuclear family apart from other relations in terms of incest. Even as there were a number of affinal and collateral kin included in the Ohio incest law, these persons, if raped, would be treated, at the law, as nonkin. If these constituted broad constants across the law, the differences across the states and internal to specific state histories were as important. While one could discern a shift to including sex alongside marriage in incest law, and from broad prohibitions including affinal and consanguineous kin, both lineal and collateral, to a narrower prohibition focused on the nuclear family, states like Ohio and Iowa demonstrated a contradictory logic, moving from broad to narrow and back to broad prohibitions. This instability, both a result of the decline of theological justifications and a condition of liberal democracy, was most clearly delimited in Colorado's dueling incest prohibitions. Yet, despite this instability and plurality, there was never a question in nineteenth-century legal discourse that the prohibition of incest remained a foundational rule of sociality. The question, then, was in the increasing absence of theological foundations, to what did that foundational certainty refer?

The New Universalism

With the pluralism of state incest laws and the loss of a relatively stable foundation, a new sense of uncertainty pervaded legal discussions of incest. Invoking marital "disqualifications of blood," the legal scholar James Schouler wrote "on no point have writers of all ages and countries been more united than in the conviction that nature abhors, as vile and unclean, all sexual intercourse between persons of near relationship. But on few subjects have they differed so widely as in the application of this conviction."[58] Schouler, writing at the relatively late date of 1872, highlighted precisely these tensions of uncertainty. A prohibition grounded in blood relations was a potentially new universal prohibition, but one not generally recognized in the law. Nature may have abhorred sex between near relations, but as Schouler noted, there was little but discord when it came to who and what nature abhorred *as* incest. Incest was, as one newspaper noted in 1837, a "Horrid Depravity," but what was universally horrid was less than clear.[59] In the absence of Levitical authority, the law of incest, in all of its pluralism, swirled uncomfortably in a liberal democratic breach between domestic relations and criminal law, searching for a new universalism.

The breach Schouler depicted, however, had been repaired in 1820 by the articulation of a new, natural law basis for the universality of the prohibition. This new universal prohibition included lineal kin (whether this included affinity in addition to consanguinity was often ambiguous) but limited collateral kin to siblings. Increasingly, it became the only iteration of a universal incest prohibition in the law of the early republic. The power to regulate marriage and sex between near kin came not from God or other theological precincts but from natural law. If incest statutes increasingly erased theological markers, at no point did any legal writers in the nineteenth century argue that theologically grounded incest rules had no place in the United States. Rather, those rules became increasingly privatized while the new incest prohibition became public, an object of universal state regulation through the law. Paradoxically, what was increasingly thought of as the archetypal private institution—the nuclear family—was the object of public regulation, while the regulation through prohibition of more extended kin relations, at least in terms of incest, was privatized by an association with religious or local moral systems. The question, then, was what made the marital and sexual relations between members of the family produced by this new, exceptional incest prohibition objects of state regulation through the law, while the marital and sexual relations of those other kin were regulated by increasingly private institutions like religion (or at least confined to state laws and thus varying from state to state)?

This new universalism was not part of any nineteenth-century statutes. Rather, it was articulated in the wider field of legality, especially in judicial opinions and legal treatises. Despite this, no nineteenth-century statute abrogated the prohibition on lineal relations in ascending and descending order and collateral relations through brother and sister.[60] The federalized structure of family law situated state incest laws within the interpretive purview of the conflict of laws. Briefly, in regard to marriage in particular, a state was required to recognize a marriage contracted in one state, even if it violated laws in the new state of residence. This was as true of marriage from state to state as it was from nation to nation. As Joseph Story wrote in 1834, in what was the locus classicus of the doctrine of conflict of laws in the United States, "the general principle certainly is . . . that between persons, *sui juris*, marriage is to be decided by the law of the place, where it is celebrated. If valid there, it is valid everywhere. It has a legal ubiquity of obligation." There were, according to Story, rare exceptions to this general principle. "The most prominent, if not the only known exceptions to the rule, are those respecting polygamy and incest."[61] Polygamy occasioned absolutely no comment in 1834; the incest exception, however, required a great deal of explication, which delved back into earlier legal opinions.

Where Story ended up was an 1820 opinion written by Chancellor James Kent, for the Court of Chancery in New York, in a case involving the marriage of a lunatic.[62] Kent had two aims in moving from the marriage at hand to a "hypothetically mentioned" incestuous marriage. First, he argued that the Court of Chancery had all jurisdictional authority over marriage because it filled a lacuna created by the absence of ecclesiastical courts in the colonies. Second, once he had invoked incestuous marriage, Kent claimed that there was a universal prohibition derived from natural law (rather than ecclesiastical law), which had to be recognized by the existing legal system whether or not an incest statute existed. This natural law not only shifted the sovereign authority of the incest prohibition away from the sacred to the natural; it imbued the natural with the sovereign, reasoning individual. No longer, according to Kent, did one need wonder about and then submit to the mysterious and opaque laws of God; rather, natural law would be in force insofar as it could be discerned through reason. Here the universal prohibition and natural law rested on the sovereignty of the reasonable liberal subject, governed by laws.

The absence of ecclesiastical courts in the colonies was one source of limited variety and ambiguity in colonial statutes and was certainly one of the causes behind Kent's own state of New York not passing an incest law until 1830. So in 1820 in New York, Kent invoked the prohibition of incestuous marriage in the absence of a law. "We are placed in a singular situation, in this state, and, probably, one unexampled in the christian [sic] world," Kent lamented, "since we have no statute regulating marriage, or prescribing the solemnities of it, or defining the forbidden degrees."[63] Despite the absence of positive laws, the power legally to regulate marriages and "forbidden degrees" had to reside somewhere in New York, and for Kent it was with the Chancery or nowhere. The Court of Chancery, or equity court, could be used to adjudicate cases, like an incestuous marriage, that were clearly illegitimate despite the fact that there was no positive statute referring to the transgression. For Kent the absence of incest law did not mean that there was no court that could prohibit incest.

Kent's expansion of the Court of Chancery's authority and his search for "sound and binding principles of common law" entailed a profound transformation of the legal definition of incest.[64] Kent distinguished between universal and particular incest prohibitions, making the one public by subjecting it to the state legal apparatus, and the other private (or at least local), aligning it with increasingly privatized religious and other moral codes. "Prohibitions of the natural law are of absolute, uniform, and universal obligation."[65] It worked to conserve specific affective and power relations within the emergent nuclear family. According to Kent such marriages, being between such near kin, if permitted, would be ruinous of both family and society. "Marriages among such near relations, would not only lead to domestic licentiousness, but by blending in one object, duties and feelings incompatible with each other, would perplex and confound the duties, habits and affections proceeding from the family state, impair the perceptions and corrupt the purity of moral taste, and do violence to the moral sentiments of mankind."[66] Kent was not alone, nor was he even the first, to suggest that incest in the nuclear family was perilous to both family hierarchies and the nation. Writing in 1795, Zephaniah Swift argued for an incest prohibition that applied to "all persons in the ascending and descending lines, to the remotest possible degree" because such marriages were "repugnant to the law of nature" and that "it destroys the natural duties between parents and children; for the parent could never maintain that authority, which is necessary for the education and government of the child, nor the child that reverence that is due to the parent, if such indecent familiarities were admitted."[67] Both Swift and Kent invoked familiarities and affections between parents and children but were sure to emphasize the need to preserve hierarchies within the family.

As Swift noted, in language that would have found a home in the theological "marriage question," sociality was insured by the incest prohibition. And even if it derived from natural law, it needed the clear force of law to secure the harmony of the house. Incestuous marriages "would open the door for such frequent and convenient opportunity for every species of lewdness and debauchery, that a universal corruption and depravity of manners would follow, and chastity and innocence be banished [sic] the world." Swift thus suggested the world-historical import of the incest prohibition, lest chastity and innocence be banished from the world. "Every family would be confined to itself in the exercise of licentiousness and wickedness; for such conduct would prevent the extension of family connections: a friendly intercourse which polishes and improves the manners of mankind, would cease to connect the different manners of the community, and the diffusion of love and charity, would no longer augment the happiness of mankind."[68] One might recall Sawney Beane in such a description— the incest prohibition guaranteed an imperative toward sociality, lest one remain within the family and become incestuous.

For Swift, however, the force of the law was biblical, since the statute was "copied from the Levitical law, prohibits all persons within certain degrees of propinquity, by blood or marriage, from intermarrying, declares void such marriages, bastardizes the issue, and punishes with great severity, such incestuous conduct."[69] For Kent, in contrast, the universality and uniformity was derived from a natural law effectively severed from biblical force. "That such a marriage is criminal and void by the Law of Nature," Kent wrote, "is a point universally conceded."[70] Natural law, as Jay Fliegelman has written, was "the dominant discourse of a liberal social utopianism," and Kent's articulation of it was exemplary in that regard.[71] In Kent's articulation it privileged both sociality and dependency. "By the law of nature," Kent wrote, "I understand those fit and just rules of conduct which the Creator has prescribed to man, as a dependent and social being; and which are to be ascertained from the deductions of right reason, though they may be more precisely known, and more explicitly declared by

Divine Revelation."[72] Despite references to the Creator and Divine Revelation, Kent offered a thoroughly secular and, indeed, anthropocentric authority governing the exception. Natural law may have been better known through "Divine Revelation," but Kent's concern was what could be deduced through "right reason." The incest prohibition was universal because it emanated from natural law, but apprehension of the universality of natural law rested on the use of reason. The natural law, that which made one both social and dependent, preceded humanity, yet it was only reason that granted access to natural law. Just as the incest prohibition gained a new foundation in natural law, Kent aligned it with the dictates of liberal reason—the prohibition extended only so far as "man" could discern. If natural law preceded the human and was the ground of reason, it was nonetheless subordinated to the capacity to reason out its existence. The incest prohibition, in its universal capacity, was reduced to human epistemological vision.

This new universalism, grounded as it was in natural law, produced and secured the minimal conditions for the circulation that stories like those of Richard Jennings and Edgar Allan Poe understood as potentially incestuous. If there was one universal effect of the prohibition of incest, in this natural law interpretation, it was the imperative to leave one's family of origin and move into the world, to circulate in public with the express object of attaining a new private family. This formulation of the incest prohibition presupposed marriage for all individuals and by deriving itself from natural law effectively naturalized the impulse to marriage. If we read Kent's opinion alongside the tales of accidental incest of Richard Jennings and Napoleon Bonaparte Froissart (Chapter 1), we can discern how the prohibition of incest created incest. As Jacques Derrida writes of the necessary but impossible incest prohibition, "before the prohibition, it is not incest; forbidden, it cannot become incest except through the recognition of the prohibition. . . . It is always *as if* I had committed incest."[73] The conjunction of Kent, Jennings, and Froissart captures the incestuous logics of sociality in the new universalism. Moreover, Kent's incest prohibition stands as the deep reality of the social, but a deep reality derived from sociality. Which is to say, just as it guides social life at a fundamental level, Kent's incest prohibition is conditioned by a prior assumption that man is fundamentally social and dependent.

Yet, as Kent noted, the universal incest prohibition also preserved and secured dependencies and obligations within the family. The distinctions in authority between parents and children, for instance, would have been sundered had the prohibition of incest been removed. For this reason, even as Kent's universalism constricted the prohibition in a manner that widened the field of marital and sexual partners, thus facilitating the liberal and sexual subject, it also secured the nuclear family as a site of social constraint and regulation. Indeed, in the age of contract, Kent outlined the natural conditions of status—there were specific familial positions that individuals occupied—father, mother, child, sibling—which, whatever the disorders of desire, contract, and circulation, could not be undone. The legal scholar Janet Halley has written of "family law exceptionalism," by which she means the peculiar articulation of marriage in the second half of the nineteenth century as status rather than contract. If liberalism generally entailed a shift from status to contract, then family law, and especially marriage, according to Halley, shifted from contract to status.[74] Duties and obligations derived from fixed statuses were necessary for the proper formation of subjects within the family but needed to be confined to the privacy of the family. The legal reconstitution of the incest prohibition in antebellum America provided a naturalized means to secure hierarchical statuses in the family, enshrining formal authority in the family as a necessary means of producing liberal subjects who would engage effectively in the public world of contracts.[75]

The new universalism was simply the minimal form of universal regulation of the liberal subject suspended between family and society, private and public. Other iterations of the prohibition, such as those from the Levitical tradition, were particular rather than universal, even if their foundations had provided the basis for an older universality. They proceeded from important sources, like religion and morality, but not from the law of nature. As Kent wrote, "the *Levitical* degrees are not binding, as a rule of municipal obedience; . . . this is stepping out of the family circle; and I cannot put the prohibition on any other ground than positive prohibition."[76] So religious prohibitions, and especially the Levitical prohibitions, were still legitimate, but they were no longer universal. Only the nuclear family (and the ascending and descending lineal line) was universal; all other degrees required statutory enumeration to be prohibited. Joseph Story, following from Kent, also found religion to be a slippery foundation. "In the diversity of religious opinions in Christian countries," Story wrote, "a large space must be allowed for interpretation as to religious duties, rights, and solemnities."[77] Or, as Joel Prentiss Bishop wrote in 1852, "an incestuous marriage, within the meaning of this exception, is not every marriage forbidden on account of consanguinity or affinity, by the legislative enactments of the country in which its validity is drawn in question; for a State may prohibit from motives of policy, or from religious considerations, matrimonial connections between relatives, which would not be held incestuous by natural law."[78]

Kent's opinion in *Wightman v. Wightman* transformed the legal discourse on incest. While it was cited as a precedent-setting case for the marriage of lunatics, and, in other instances, as a rather inexplicable expansion of the jurisdiction of the Court of Chancery, it was Kent's disquisition on incestuous marriages, and in particular his deployment of a new universal ground for the incest prohibition, that ended up being most influential.[79] It was cited in most of the major legal treatises of the nineteenth century in order to determine what it was, exactly, that constituted a universally incestuous marriage. Asa Kinne, for example, in a popular mid-nineteenth-century guide to legal knowledge, identified incest, along with polygamy, as "the most prominent exceptions" to the "rule of foreign marriages."[80] Or, as Joseph Story put it,

> Christianity is understood to prohibit polygamy and incest; and therefore no Christian country would recognize polygamy, or incestuous marriages. When we speak of incestuous marriages, care must be taken to confine the doctrine to such cases, as by the general consent of Christendom are deemed incestuous. It is difficult to ascertain exactly the point, at which the law of nature, or Christianity, ceases to prohibit marriage between kindred; and nations are by no means agreed on this subject.[81]

Even as Story and others derived a universal incest prohibition from Kent, the definition remained slippery, as Story's qualifications suggest. Kent's definition of the incest exception, combined with the prohibition of polygamy, attempted to universalize the nuclear family. By making all the other iterations of the incest prohibition localized, the universal incest prohibition had the consequence of making the nuclear family—relations between parents and children, brothers and sisters—the universal core of all kinship relations. As such, the sentimental family, with its duties and obligations configured in a lovingly disciplinary relation to the liberal subject, was universalized and naturalized as a legitimate encumbrance on the excesses of the individual in antebellum America.

We can discern these effects—the universalization of the nuclear family incest prohibition, the particularization of all other incest prohibitions, and the production of the nuclear family—as the basis of family and kin relations in an 1840 case involving an incestuous marriage in Massachusetts.[82] On 28 November 1834, in Duffield, England, Samuel Sutton married his mother's sister, Ann Hills. In England the marriage was forbidden by ecclesiastical law, so it was voidable but not void.[83] In 1835, the Suttons moved to Massachusetts, where their marriage violated the legal kin restrictions, which deemed such a marriage absolutely void.[84] Despite this, their marriage did not become the object of legal scrutiny until nearly ten years later. On 10 August 1840 Ann Sutton lent Thomas Warren $1,300, for which Warren signed a promissory note. After it became clear that Warren would not fulfill the terms of the note, Samuel Sutton sued for payment on behalf of his wife.[85] It was at this point that the incestuous marriage of Samuel Sutton and Ann Hills was implicated in the Massachusetts legal system. Warren did not dispute his debt to Ann Sutton—the note was evidence enough that he owed her the money; rather, he contested the legitimacy of their marriage. If the marriage was void under Massachusetts law, then neither Samuel nor Ann Sutton had any standing in court. For their part, the Suttons did not dispute their kinship and thus the legal precarity of their marriage. Ultimately, the case made its way to the Supreme Court of Massachusetts, which found that, though the marriage was absolutely void in Massachusetts, it was valid when contracted in England and so, following the *jus gentium*, or law of nations, was valid in Massachusetts as well. Warren was required to pay the $1,300 to Samuel Sutton.

Writing for the court, Justice Samuel Hubbard further instantiated the new universalism, defining the only marriages that escaped the general principles of the conflict of laws. "There is an exception, however, to this principle, in those cases where the marriage is considered as incestuous by the law of Christianity, and as against natural law. And these exceptions relate to marriages in the direct lineal line of consanguinity, and to those contracted between brothers and sisters."[86] Like other legal writers, Hubbard was not particularly committed to a process of secularization, nor was he necessarily conscious of the secular consequences of his decision. The law of Christianity and the law of nature, as defined by Kent, were at odds with one another, yet Hubbard's locution was deeply ambivalent, attempting to preserve the Christian logic of the law while advocating a natural law foundation. The "law of Christianity" had its own claims to universality, as we have seen, but they were not consistent with natural law. Moreover, Hubbard subsequently undercut the legal standing of Leviticus in articulating a universal law of incest. "I am not aware that these exceptions, by any general consent among writers upon natural law, have been extended further, or embraced other cases prohibited by the Levitical law."[87] Hubbard ruled decisively, concluding with the law of nature and no reference to Christian law. The marriage of Sutton and Hills "never was avoided, and though absolutely prohibited by our laws, yet not being within the exception, as against natural law, we do not feel warranted in saying the parties are no husband and wife."[88]

Finally, Hubbard offered a homologous justification of both the general principle of the law of nations regarding marriage and the new universalism. The general principle, whereby a marriage valid where contracted was valid everywhere, "has been adopted, as best calculated to protect the highest welfare of the community in the preservation of the purity and happiness of the most important domestic relation in life."[89] The exception of incest from this principle, which "rests on the ground, that such marriages are against the laws of God, are immoral, and destructive of the purity and happiness of domestic life," served nearly the same purpose.[90] The moral order of the nation was at stake—if marriage was so completely fluid and unstable as to be subjected to each and every state and national law, all hope for the national welfare would be lost. Families needed to know that their original marital status would survive the vexations of mobility. Yet, the autonomy of those families was not absolute—the intimate sphere needed to be regulated, and that was from where the incest prohibition derived its universality.

The natural law, despite its occasional and uneasy conflation with Christianity, was central to the secularization of incest law. It would be wrong, however, to take the trial as evidence of the linear progress of secularization through the particularization of religious and moral incest prohibitions. The secular-religious, public-private ambivalences were also incorporated into the corpus of midcentury legal treatises. The uneven character of secularization was especially apparent in the second edition of Tapping Reeve's treatise on domestic relations, *The Law of Baron and Femme*. Originally published in 1816, it reproduced Blackstone's taxonomy of the law of husband and wife, parent and child, guardian and ward, and master and apprentice, which occluded the jurisdictional issue that had prompted Chancellor Kent's opinion in 1820.[91] The legal prohibition "amounts to a declaration, that a marriage betwixt the parties who are so nearly related as to be within the Levitical degrees of kindred, is not a valid marriage. So, too, all marriages forbidden by the law of God."[92] Mirroring Blackstone and asserting Levitical authority just four years before Kent's opinion, Reeve's text is evidence of the fits and starts of secularization of the law of incest. This should come as no surprise if we treat the secular as a new ordering of knowledge rather than a linear, progressive process.

By 1846, Reeve's text was becoming anachronistic on the subject of incestuous marriages. Its adherence to Blackstone put it out of step with the emergent domestic relations law. Six years later Joel Prentiss Bishop would publish his *Commentaries on the Laws of Marriage and Divorce*, which would transform family law in the United States. Nevertheless, in 1846 it remained the only treatise written by an American jurist wholly devoted to domestic relations. Lucius Chittenden, the editor of the new edition (Reeve had died in 1823), recognized this tension, writing that *The Law of Baron and Femme* "continues to be the standard work on the subject of which it treats . . . and though subsequent legislation has, in many of the American states, changed the reciprocal rights and duties of the parties, yet . . . the author has in general correctly stated the principles upon which the common law has regulated those rights and duties."[93] To deal with the legal changes between 1816 and 1846, Chittenden limited his editorial work to appending notes, while leaving the text itself untouched. In the case of incestuous marriages, Chittenden's preservation of the conflict between Reeve's doctrine and subsequent legal decisions exposed the tensions in the ongoing emergence of the secular incest prohibition.

Chittenden appended a note to Reeve's discussion of incestuous marriages that invoked natural law and a fundamental uncertainty about the limits of the prohibition. "The precise limits, fixed by nature itself, within which the union should not take place, cannot, perhaps, be satisfactorily ascertained. . . . But the general tendency of all enlightened nations has been toward one certain limit, and in many of the states, where this is the subject of statute regulation, that limit has been fixed at the third degree of collateral relationship, and all marriages within that are void."[94] That he identified the natural parameters with those found in the Table of Kindred and Affinity went unremarked, as did the fact that the natural law reckoning of the prohibition, at least since Kent, served to dispel uncertainty in the law of incest—whatever else it may have been, across states and nations, the nuclear family was universal. Chittenden aligned natural law with uncertainty and subsequently attempted to paper over that uncertainty, writing, "Certainty is always most important in the law, and for this reason, it might be unwise to disturb these settled regulations, but were the law still unsettled, it would be better to place the limit one step further off, and prohibit all marriages between all relations standing within the fourth degree."[95] Chittenden's equivocations were not necessarily the result of poor reasoning, although they may have been that. Rather, they were compensatory, at once acknowledging the uncertainty in the antebellum law of incest shorn of its Levitical justifications and then disavowing that uncertainty. Whether one turned to legal treatises or case law, as the nuclear family became the basis for a new universalism, uncertainty and instability continued to mark the liberal incest prohibition.

Duties, Obligations, Violence, and Sex

The theological discourse of the "marriage question," for all its effects on the legality of incest, mostly conceived of the family in the absence of a clearly articulated incest prohibition as incestuous—the eroticism of the sentimental family as a unit elicited the sexual desire of its members. The law conceived its object as the sexual subject—an individual animated by sexual desire that needed regulation. This was apparent in the increase in criminal, as opposed to domestic relations, incest laws. And in Kent's new universalism, the preservation of duties and obligations in the family seemed, in theory, to regulate the emergent sexual subject. Yet, despite the legal discourse on incest emerging out of treatises, there was abundant legal evidence that these dependencies were just as likely to produce violence and abuse, often incestuous. As we have seen, the legal treatises, nearly without exception, treated incest as a legal problem of consensual marriage. Yet, many incest cases that made it to trial were often traumatically violent abuses of children. As such, the cases serve as an archive of foreclosed incestuous violence. Newspapers frequently reported on them and in some instances entire pamphlets circulated with trial narratives and execution sermons. Behind the legal language of marriage and consent was the violence and abuse of incest. The duties and obligations of the nuclear family, preserved by the new universal incest prohibition, were the same ones that produced the conditions for incestuous violence and abuse.

A counterarchive of incestuous violence complicates the prevalence of consensual incest and contributes to the emergence of incest as sex in the law. While the emergence and consolidation of the family as a private space in the nineteenth century was and is often associated with sentimentalism, affection, and domesticity, it was, just as much, a space of abuse, violence, inequalities, and hierarchies. What this discourse, broadly, and the legal field of incest suggests, however, is that the violence of the family was not simply an atavism, left over from an older age and destined to disappear. The hierarchies of dependency and obligation created and governed by the natural law incest prohibition were coeval with the production of the family as a sentimental, domestic, private space. As Ruth Bloch has recently written of the transformation of legal responses to wife beating between the colonial and postrevolutionary period, "newfound assertions of the family's institutional right to privacy worked to exacerbate inequalities between husbands and wives."[96] The history of the incest prohibition in the nineteenth century demonstrates the ways in which gendered inequalities between family members were exacerbated precisely through the mechanism of privacy so that incest as sexual violence rather than incest as marriage became a persistent feature of domestic life.

Cases of incest, especially father-daughter, abounded in newspapers throughout the nineteenth century.[97] In 1844, for instance, readers in New Hampshire learned of "one of the most brutal cases of incest," in which an older man was "living in incestuous intercourse with one if not two of his daughters."[98] The daughters had produced several offspring, and rumors spread that one of those children was also the victim of this incestuous grandfather. Privacy and dependency served as the father's defense. "The old man does not deny it; but says that, as he supports the offspring to which he stands in relation of father and grandfather, he thinks that no one has a right to interfere with the family arrangement!"[99] The tendency of the focus on marriage to assume that all intrafamilial desire needed to be prohibited because it would lead to a marriage that would upend the duties and obligations of the parent-child bond was circumvented here—the father claimed his incestuous right as a result of that hierarchy. It was illegal because he "carnally" knew his daughters—the violence and abuse may have been real, but New Hampshire law had no means of apprehending either within the confines of incest.[100]

Cases of incestuous fathers abounded in antebellum newspapers. In 1853, a man in Wethersfield, Connecticut, "fled from his home to avoid an arrest for the crime of incest with his only daughter, only fourteen years of age."[101] In 1860 the *New York Herald* reported a particularly violent episode. A Scottish shipwright, James Gathry, "made a diabolical attempt to ravish his daughter Catherine, a small, simple looking girl of fourteen. Failing in this attempt, he made unsuccessful attempts to kill her, and to end the tragedy."[102] In 1858, Jonathan Burroughs of Northampton, Massachusetts, "committed incest with one daughter and rape upon another."[103] The consensual nature of incest was upheld by the designation of rape of his other daughter. He was sentenced to life in prison. An 1833 case in Rhode Island made the relationship between incest and familial death clear. Jacob Insley, a middle-aged shoemaker, "was charged by his *daughter*, a girl now fifteen years of age, of having illicit intercourse with her during the two years past, threatening her with instant death if she made any disclosures of his atrocious practices."[104] The death of Insley's wife, who had been in poor health, was attributed to the incest, which had become public knowledge. "We are informed by a physician who attended her near her decease, that she often attempted to speak, and would point to her husband and cry 'wo! wo!' while her features expressed the deepest horror."[105] Insley had initiated the abuse "while the monster was excited by spirituous liquor," which had resulted first in his wife leaving the house to escape. This kind of temperance message could be found throughout the discourse of incest. In her absence he coerced his daughter into a sexual relationship. When the charges were issued, Insley escaped, possibly to Michigan, "and left a family of several young children penniless, on the charity of the public." Like the "old man" in New Hampshire, Insley's incestuous abuse of his daughter occurred within the patriarchal space of dependencies and obligations that the new natural law incest prohibition was ostensibly put in place to preserve.

Yet, if incest as sexuality seemed to emerge from newspaper reports of incestuous violence, it had long had a place in the legal archive, even if it was subordinated to the marital configurations. The terms of most laws were marital, and sex was addressed only as part of a progression that led to marriage. To be sure, some colonial statutes included references to carnality, but they were conflicted and anomalous. By the middle of the nineteenth century, however, the preoccupation of incest law with policing illicit sex produced the very object it sought. This was apparent in statutes, legal treatises, and the case record. The transformation was not simple and, in legal terms, had little to do with hereditary concerns of reproduction.

Rather, an excessively sexual subject, little concerned with marriage, needed to be controlled through incest law. In this scenario, the sexual parameters of incest came to sit alongside the marital laws in the legal domain.

By the middle of the nineteenth century this relationship would change as the sexual subject, a cognate of the liberal subject, increasingly became the object of the discourse. This transformation was already happening in the newspaper accounts, which never recognized incestuous marriage. Moreover, novels like *The Life of Dr. Richard Jennings* produced both the sexual subject and the incestuous result of unregulated sexuality. One can see this transition in select legal treatises as well. Timothy Walker, unlike most other legal writers on incest, was more concerned with incest as a carnal crime than a violation of kin restrictions on marriage. Incest was categorized among "Criminal Intercourse of the Sexes," which included "rape upon daughter or sister, rape upon any other woman, carnal knowledge of an insane woman, bigamy, incest, adultery, and fornication."[106]

Unlike earlier laws in the East, Walker defined incest as "Sexual intercourse between parent and child, or brother and sister, the parties knowing their relationship."[107] This mistake of fact defense—in which one could be acquitted on a charge of incest if they were unaware of the kin relation they had transgressed—would make sense given the broader discourse of incest in antebellum America. As we have already seen, there was a generalized anxiety concerning accidental incest in both the eighteenth and nineteenth centuries. Poe as well as the anonymous author of the *The Life of Dr. Richard Jennings* crafted stories of accidental incest. These resulted from moral failings and criminal activities, but more importantly from the potential for highly disordered circulation of bodies and the occlusion of natality through national and transnational market capitalism. William Hill Brown's 1789 novel *The Power of Sympathy* also staged potentially accidental incest, while the real horror of Melville's *Pierre* was that the relationship between Pierre and Isabel was at first occluded by unregistered paternity, but, when siblinghood was established, they nonetheless consummated their incestuous desire. As we will see later, part of the horror of Richard Hildreth's novel *Archy Moore; or, the White Slave* inhered in Archy's consummation of incest with his half sister without ever telling her who he was—the intent was one-directional in that case. While Walker was certainly not responding directly to any of these works of fiction, his invocation of the intent requirement was not simply a legal theory—it was part of a number of statues around the country, including those in Ohio and

Iowa. If the circulation of bodies and goods created the conditions of public incest, the intent requirement protected the liberal subject. Circulation was a central component of antebellum liberalism and market capitalism, and to restrict it threatened both. But it created the conditions for incest as well. The intent requirement was meant to prevent the bonds of family, kinship, and sexuality from impeding circulation. The liberal subject could circulate, as could the rest of his family; the guilt of incest inhered only in its knowing commission. Walker's text, as well as the intent requirements in most statutes across the nineteenth century, guaranteed that dislocations and the occlusion of knowledge that followed from social circulation need not carry the legal danger of public incest, so long as knowledge of the relationship was absent.

Here the law carried out the distinction between public and private incest that stories like those of Poe, Jennings, and Sawney Beane articulated in a different register. And the law was more punitive toward private incest, thus encouraging sociality, further bolstering the circulatory logic of liberal, market society enunciated in Kent's new universalism. The intent requirement made all incest within the confines of the private home incestuous since claiming not to know the relation of a family member within the household would be difficult to sustain. But the liberal individual, who went out and circulated through society, was protected from public incest by the law. In this manner, Napoleon Bonaparte Froissart and Richard Jennings would not have been legally guilty of incest because of a lack of knowledge. Moreover, this distinction between public and private incest in the intent requirement, at an ideological and discursive level, was more likely to protect white, middle-class men, those bourgeois liberal subjects most likely to leave the family behind as they circulated through the public world, from prosecution. Women, on the other hand, again ideologically and discursively, were more often aligned with the private, domestic family, and thus were more likely to be involved in a private incest in which the intent requirement, or mistake of fact defense, would be obsolete.[108]

The production of sexuality within the field of incest was perhaps no more evident than in a sensational trial for incest in Manhattan in 1846. On 11 April 1846 Daniel H. Burtnett, a "broker of Wall-street," entered the Lower Police Office in Manhattan with two of his sisters, Almira Burtnett and Jane Ann Waddell, to inform the police that their father, Daniel Burtnett, a wealthy butcher in the city, had sexually assaulted his two daughters. It was the father's "continuous brutality" toward the two women that "had at length compelled them, though reluctantly, to appeal to the protection of the law." Almira was accusing her father of aggravated assault and battery, of which the most recent occurrence had been just that morning. Yet, that was neither the only nor the most serious charge—"there were other more heinous offences that had been perpetrated" by the father. And it was Jane Waddell, the widowed eldest sister, who "at length, felt it to be her duty to expose, and among them would be found the unnatural and revolting *crime of incest with his daughters!*"[109]

In the end, after a month of testimony at the probable cause hearing, the judge, Justice Osborn, dismissed the case for lack of evidence and chastised Jane Ann Waddell and her siblings. I am less interested in the justice of this case as it was tried. As we have seen, the law was stacked against those who claimed men's rape as incest, and the place of consensual incest in this case was absent. While Daniel H. Burtnett brought the charges against his father on behalf of his sisters, the sisters were central to the charge, and thus, as was evident in the opening pages of the pamphlet, the entire case was framed as abuse. The charges against Burtnett were forcefully challenged, and the credibility of both Jane Waddell and Daniel H. Burtnett were thoroughly impugned by the defense. In this sensationalist, voyeuristic account of the trial, incest was a means of accessing and producing the sexual subject, in this case through the sexualization of the daughters, especially Jane Ann Waddell.

The case was reported almost exclusively by the *National Police Gazette*, an early tabloid that filled its pages with sensationalistic accounts drawn from police reports, primarily in New York City.[110] In fact, the Burtnett case set something of a tone for the *Gazette*, appearing as it did in the second year of the publication. It was certainly not the only case of incest reported in the *Gazette*. Over the years, one could find articles with titles like "Incest by a Clergyman Upon Three Daughters," or "Horrible Case of Incest and Child Murder; Shocking Immorality," or "Shocking Case of Incest," or "Investigation of the Charge of Incest, made by Lavinia Brown, against her Father, John J. Brown."[111] Incest was a staple of the sensationalist criminal erotic press.

The defense adopted two strategies in undercutting the charges. The first was to support the spotless reputation of Burtnett while impugning the chastity of his daughters, especially Waddell. The second was to suggest property-related motives underpinning the charges. In this way, the desire for property accumulation and sexuality were nearly reduced to one another, and what was ostensibly a trial for violent incestuous assault became a voyeuristic account of female sexuality. The invocation of property accumulation of women in a charge of incest was not confined to this trial. In 1846, in Yates County, New York, a father was charged with incest by two of his daughters. However, after his neighbors vouched for his "unblemished" character while calling one of his daughter "a loose woman," the father was acquitted. According to the *Barre Gazette*, the accusation "turns out to have been a conspiracy on the part of the old man's daughters to revenge themselves upon him for not bestowing his property as they wished."[112] Cases like these created cultural, legal narratives in which female property and sexuality were conflated and both were constrained. To own, or even desire property, as a woman, was to be promiscuous, and thus have no legal standing to oppose the desire of the male sexual subject, in these cases, fathers.[113]

Before the defense hypersexualized her and depicted her and her brother as avaricious manipulators, Waddell recounted the incestuous abuse. Waddell's claim in her initial examination was succinct and tells a particular story about the family. "Attempts were made upon me by my father when I was fifteen or sixteen years of age. It is impossible for me to tell how many; there were several. I married to relieve myself of that and other sufferings."[114] Waddell's testimony created a specific picture of antebellum marriage—not the result of love and agency, a site for the realization of freedom, as so many depicted this codification of intimacy; rather marriage was instrumentalized as a means of escape from incest. And the incest was a result of her father's uncontrolled desire. As Waddell stated, "He [Daniel Burtnett] succeeded in gratifying his passion, from the condition in which my clothes were left in—he never succeeded in having carnal intercourse with me—there never was penetration."[115] What is clear is that the entire account is about the pleasure that Daniel Burtnett derived from following his passions, even into a transgressive relationship with his daughter.

Yet, if Waddell depicted her father as overrun by incestuous passion, the defense deployed her as an archetypally desiring woman, out to ruin her father. The majority of the trial transcript was an accounting of Waddell's conniving passions and desires, elicited by the defense as a means by which her father was cleared of the charges of incest. One exchange with a witness stands out.

Q. How high did she pull her clothes?

A. Above her knees.

Q. For what purpose?

A. I don't know of any other, but to show her legs.

Q. Did she say anything?

A. No, sir, she laughed.

Q. Did she do anything besides laugh?

A. Yes, sir, she made gestures—commenced to throw her legs about.

Q. Is that all she did?

A. I believe it was sir.

Q. Did you see her naked legs above her knees?

A. She had stockings on; I saw her bare knees—yes, sir, I did on one occasion.

. . . .

A. On New Year's Day she requested me to send all the young men I was acquainted with to call on her.

. . . .

Q. How many times in all did you ever see Mrs. Waddell expose her naked bosom?

A. I have seen her once that I remember well of, and at other times that I don't remember well; once in particular I remember well.

This exchange was typical of the trial, in which witnesses testified to the licentious nature of Jane Ann Waddell, implying that her father's incestuous abuse was nearly impossible because she was too immoral to be a victim of his incestuous abuse. The predilection of the legal system to disbelieve the abusive nature of fathers was here borne out, as the judge would not even consider the lesser charge of consensual incest.

This kind of description was nothing out of the ordinary in the legal discourse of incest; only its sensationalist nature and detail distinguished it. In an 1846 case in which a Maine clergyman was accused of incest with three of his daughters, the charge shifted from rape to incest, in part as a result of the character of his daughter. "In defence, the prisoner relied upon proof of his own previous good character and of the bad character of his daughters for chastity and truth, as rendering them incredible witnesses."[116] This description, which resulted, at least in the newspaper account, in a shift from rape to incest, was premised on the promiscuity—an entirely discursive promiscuity—of the daughters. "After a short absence the jury returned a verdict of guilty of incest but not rape."[117] The discursive production of the daughters as transgressive sexual subjects was the condition of consent here, and thus the legal condition of the crime. Moses Goodhue, on trial in Andover, Massachusetts, in 1840 "for the crime of criminal connection, or rape upon his own daughter Olive Goodhue, under the most revolting circumstances," was also saved by the sexual nature of his daughter.[118] Despite the fact that "the evidence of the trial showed a state of moral degradation, such as we trust, for the honor of humanity, is seldom witnessed," Goodhue was convicted of incest rather than rape of his daughter.[119] The jury was out seven hours before returning their verdict. "This long deliberation was as to finding him guilty of the indictment which charged the crime of violence. . . . The bad character of the daughter probably saved her father's neck."[120]

Here we start to see the full effects of incest as a consensual act, one implicated in the discourses of desire and narratives of chastity. The consensual nature of the law, in which both man and woman were complicit in the act, constituted both as sexual subjects. This stretched back to the colonial laws, as we have seen in the gender parity of the 1705 Pennsylvania statute. But the abstraction of law produces a vision of society—it does not represent that society. The emergence in the nineteenth century of separate laws dealing with a father's rape of his daughter suggest that violent incest was creeping into the purview of the legal apparatus. But here, in these cases, the complicity of consent and violence in protecting the privilege of the father in the family is apparent. Rape was transformed into consensual incest, protecting the fathers from more serious punishment. The statutory archive is dominated by laws dealing with consensual incest while the trial archive is dominated by violent cases of incest, mostly between fathers and daughters. Read together, the legal logic of consensual incest had the capacity to facilitate violent incest, providing a means of escape for fathers from more serious punishments meted out for rape. As is evident in these cases, the means by which violent incestuous rape was transformed into consensual incest was through the narratives of promiscuous daughters with bad character. This complex scenario made up part of those rights, duties, and obligations that the new universal incest prohibition worked to invent and sustain.

The tense relations among consent and violence, and sex and marriage, came to a head in Ohio in the 1870s. The law in Ohio shifted back and forth between a narrow prohibition focused on the nuclear family and broader prohibitions that included multiple affinal relatives. The 1877 Ohio criminal code, which included a provision for *emissio seminis*, or seminal emission, calling it "an essential ingredient in the crime of incest," took the logic of incest as sexuality to its core and, like the newspaper reports, linked it to sexual violence.[121] Nationally, the law was an anomaly—no other state adopted emissio seminis in its incest law. In citing precedent for its own incest law, California, in 1872, confirmed both the centrality of the Ohio law and the anomalous character of its ejaculatory requirement. The Ohio criminal statute was cited as precedent, but the Ohio statute's precedence was qualified.[122] This is not to say that incest in California, by 1872, was any less about sex. "In California, the attempt must be manifested by acts which would end in consummation, but for the intervention of circumstance, independent of the will of the party."[123] Force and consent were evacuated from the statute, and it privileged sex, rather than marriage.

Emissio seminis as a condition of the crime of incest was derived from rape law, contributing to the recategorization of incest from domestic relations to carnal crime in the nineteenth century. Emissio seminis provided a great deal of protection to men in rape cases. In the history of rape law, which had long been influenced by Matthew Hale's dictum that rape was "an accusation easily to be made and hard to be proved, and harder to be defended by the party accused, tho never so innocent," this was not particularly surprising.[124] This instruction often bent juries in favor of the accused, and had a great deal of influence in the United States.

Seminal emission, as Sharon Block has noted, never enjoyed a clear legal consensus and raises some "fundamental questions about rape. Was rape a crime of ruined chastity, or of possible impregnation? Should it be determined by the immediate act done to the woman (penetration) or by a man's standards of sexual completion (emission)?"[125] In the case of rape the emission requirement inserted questions of male pleasure and reproduction into acts of violence and force. Incest, however, (legally) rested on consent and thus the probative value of ejaculation took on a different emphasis.

The requirement of seminal emission in the crime of incest did not emerge until 1872, and then it was through an appeal of an incest conviction. In December of 1872, the Ohio Supreme Court heard Harvey Noble's appeal of his indictment for incest with his stepdaughter, Adelia A. Hopkins. Noble appealed on two grounds, neither of which was denial that he had some sort of sexual relation with Hopkins. On the one hand, Noble's appeal disputed the legitimacy of his marriage to Adelia's mother, who had been married twice before and, according to Noble, lacked evidence that either marriage had been legally terminated. In this, Noble's appeal, like others in the nineteenth century, rested on the force of legitimate kinship— even if Noble and Hopkins's mother had lived as if married, the law, Noble claimed, could not recognize such cohabitation as legitimate marriage. He thus called into question whether there was either knowledge of the relationship or intent to commit incest. On the other hand, Noble claimed that seminal emission was "an essential ingredient of the crime of incest," thus privileging a logic that relied on determinations of sexual intercourse.

On the issue of emissio seminis, the justices disagreed. The initial judge "instructed the jury that *emission* was not a necessary element in the crime of incest."[126] Three of the justices took issue with this instruction. It was a rather circuitous route by which the justices arrived there. The justices agreed with Noble's attorney that "under Ohio statutes, in both incest and rape, coition must be complete, or the crime is not committed."[127] There was clear precedent for this in regard to rape, but in order to apply it to incest the justices followed the metonymic slippage introduced by Noble's attorney, Cooper K. Watson. "The terms 'carnal knowledge' [which was in the rape statute] and 'sexual intercourse' [which was in the incest statute] are synonymous. Hence, those decisions apply as well in case of incest."[128] This slippage was important, because this case was cited as precedent for the emissio seminis requirement in incest cases.

Both the attorney general of Ohio, F. B. Pond, and the prosecuting attorney, G. W. Knapp, rejected this metonymic slippage. Pond and Knapp argued that precisely because "the same minds" had authored both the rape and incest statutes, but chose different terms to describe the sexual act, it was improper to infer the emissio seminis requirement from the rape statute. Perhaps aware that the semantic distinction they were drawing was less than convincing, Pond and Knapp pointed to the definition of both "intercourse" and "sexual intercourse." They played on the centrality of commerce here, arguing "it is fair to presume that the legislative intent was to punish undue familiarity of 'commerce' between parties related."[129] In this, as in so much of incest law, Pond and Knapp were privileging the consensual over the violent in the delimitation of incestuous sex.

In responding to this, Justice Welch turned the commerce against the prosecution, noting that the issue was precisely the consent of incest. "That the same words are not employed in both cases probably arises from the fact that in one case the act is committed by a single person, while in the other it is the act of two. . . . For, it must be remembered the crime of incest is committed by two willing parties; and therefore, in ninety-nine cases out of a hundred, the act will be consummated. It must be remembered also, that in the hundredth case, as in all others, the fact in question will be *presumed* from the other necessary acts preceding it, and must be found to exist unless the contrary is shown by the evidence."[130] This conflation of consent and pleasure haunted incest prosecutions and was one of the particulars that distinguished incest from rape in the law. It also worked to occlude the links between violence, incest, and the private family.

The murky distinction between force and consent, so important in rape law, was of less concern, at least at the level of the law itself: incest was a consensual relation, as Justice Welch was at pains to demonstrate. In this case, the status of kinship was, of course, still central, but it was subordinated to the actions of the sexual subject. Noble's appeal was successful because it presumed that the law regulated the sexual subject and that the sex rested on the pleasure of the male subject. In the absence of ejaculation he had not fully occupied that position, so the law claimed, and thus had not realized himself fully as a sexual subject. All parties, in assuming that incest was consensual, evacuated violence and force from the law. In this, incest was upheld, at the level of the statutes, as a consensual crime. That the case record tells a different story, one in which incest and violence were imbricated in one another, ruptured the fantasy the law produced. Whether it was in newspaper reports, sensationalist accounts of incest like that of Daniel Burtnett, pamphlets like those pertaining to Ephraim Wheeler's trial and execution for raping his daughter, or the memoir of incestuous abuse kept by Abigail Abbott Bailey, the violence of incest in the wider legal discourse coexisted uneasily with the consensual language of statutory law.[131]

The legal archive tells multiple, conflicted stories about incest in antebellum America. Secularization was the overarching narrative and was organized around the emergence of natural law as the foundation of the prohibition. Leviticus and the Table of Kindred and Affinity did not disappear from the law. Direct references to God diminished while the law as derived from Leviticus became a particular, localized prohibition, an effect of positive statute, rather than universal. The secular incest prohibition that appeared in antebellum legality was not simply a linear development, even if it presented itself as such. Rather, the language of nature that came to pervade it marked it as something other than and contiguous with the religious.[132] From James Kent onward, most legal writers addressed the incest prohibition as if it self-evidently followed from natural law. That this was a radical transformation of the incest prohibition was never acknowledged. The universal incest prohibition, then, conjured a natural presence. The religious articulations of the prohibition became so many iterations of the local—religion could vary, natural law could not. The shift from Leviticus to natural law, religion to secularism, was profound. Moreover, the natural law emphasis produced the nuclear family as the universal core of all kinship—kinship configurations could vary, just like religions, but the nuclear family remained a constant. That the legal writers of the antebellum period produced this configuration rather than simply representing it went, like secularization, unnoted. Sociality generated by the universal prohibition was naturalized, making civil society and circulation of people outside of the private family a natural part of liberal democracy. But it also secured residual duties and obligations in the family that served as necessary encumbrances and sites of regulation on the liberal subject. That these duties and obligations also created the conditions for incestuous abuse, as is evident in a plethora of newspaper accounts and pamphlets, brought into relief the liberal democratic commitment to regulation.

Simultaneously, the law of incest became increasingly concerned with incest as sexuality. While marriage prohibitions remained in force all over the United States, terms like "carnal," "sexual intercourse," and "criminal connexion" crept into the legal lexicon of incest. This culminated, if that is the right term here, in Ohio's 1872 statute requiring seminal emission in cases of incest. The increasing focus on sexuality suspended incest between domestic relations and criminal law, highlighting incest as a tension between the dictates of sexuality and the encumbrance of the family. In this configuration, the sexual and the liberal subject appeared as coincident figures. The sexual subject, moreover, was produced in both the statutory field of consensual incest, in which both parties were complicit, and the legal field of newspapers and pamphlets, where incest was commonly a violent abuse of a daughter by her father. Both configurations emphasized the sexual over and against the marital, reversing the relationship between these two terms that had animated colonial incest law.

What was mostly absent, however, from the legal discourse was mention of incestuous reproduction. To be sure, there were offhand remarks made

here and there, but for the most part the reproductive and hereditary consequences of incest were not a concern of the law. Instead, they were left to
latecomers to the antebellum discourse of incest—phrenology and physiology. By the 1840s incest had become nearly exclusively an issue of reproduction and the population health of the United States. The moral, legal, and
theological considerations might have been important, but for these early
hereditarian thinkers they paled in comparison to the hereditary consequences of incestuous reproduction, which could mean the ruin of future
generations. By the 1840s, then, the incest prohibition took on a biopolitical
cast—as we shall see in the chapter that follows.

Chapter 4

Reproduction

As theologians and jurists multiplied novel justifications and explanations of the incest prohibition, one remained mostly submerged: incestuous reproduction and its hereditary consequences. To be sure, on occasion a jurist or theologian invoked its potential for degenerative hereditary consequences, but this was usually a minority voice. Indeed, even when it was invoked, it tended to bear little scrutiny and was often at odds with other explications. For example, in 1810 Benjamin Trumbull, pastor of North Haven Congregation in Connecticut, included a reference to reproduction at the end of his contribution to the "marriage question." "One view of the divine lawgiver in prohibiting intermarriages of near kindred," Trumbull wrote, "was doubtless to preserve the race of men in the most healthful, vigorous and useful condition, with respect to all their powers of body and mind: That they might not be imperfect, dwarfs, idiots, a debilitated and miserable race."[1] Yet this was simply an afterthought, an unattributed view to be found among an anonymous mass of theologians. Moreover, it contradicted much of the pamphlet itself, not least in its emphasis on consanguinity against affinity. Trumbull included this brief reference to reproduction but felt no compunction to assess or explain it.

By the middle of the nineteenth century the prohibition of incest had become linked to reproduction, particularly through concerns with hereditary degeneration. Theologians and legal writers continued, for the most part, to eschew reproduction, and thus the concern with incestuous reproduction was taken up by new entrants in the discourse of incest: phrenologists and physiologists. Both were concerned with the life of the body and mind: physiology addressed itself to the laws of life and the human (and occasionally animal) body, while phrenology was the antebellum science claiming that discrete mental faculties could be read on the surface of the skull. Incest was to be avoided, they argued, because it resulted in the physical and mental degeneration of the offspring. However, other physiologists, as well as animal breeders, rejected the degenerative assumption, arguing that incest either had no negative effects or might even result in superior offspring. While the former argument would become widely accepted by the early twentieth century, both positions, and those in between, shifted the discourse away from the concerns that had animated legal and theological renderings of incest and toward the biopolitics of the national body. As legal writers and jurists produced the natural law origins of the prohibition, physiologists and phrenologists shifted the prohibition to the bare life of the reproductive body.

Figuring incest as a reproductive transgression allowed for the regulation of the sexual subject at the level of life itself. As domestic relations law seemed increasingly to seclude the private life of the family, the regulation of incestuous reproduction created the means by which the sexual life of the body politic could be governed by other means. Physiologists and phrenologists, in order to insure bodily health at a time when the state and private charities were building asylums and humane societies to address the burdens of an apparently enfeebled population, aimed to regulate the reproductive habits of citizens. This was a political project, as much as a physiological and psychic one.

At the same time that phrenologists and physiologists shifted the discourse of incest toward reproduction, they also produced a new manifestation of the desiring sexual subject. Phrenologists, in delineating the psychic life of individuals into distinct faculties located in the brain, observable on the skull, and governing the individual, credited the first, fundamental faculty, "amativeness," with the essence of sexual desire. Humans foremost were sexually desiring subjects, something they shared with the "lower animals."[2] By making sexual desire the essence of modern individuals, phrenologists were confronted with how to regulate such desire, which, as we have seen, was both central to liberal democracy and its potential undoing. This regulation occurred primarily in the family through what appears, at first, to be the instrumental use of incest. Phrenologists, in America in particular, encouraged erotic relations between fathers and daughters and sons and mothers (the asymmetry is intentional) in order to facilitate the proper development of amativeness. So the modern sexual subject had its origins in a highly eroticized, sentimental family. What had been the dangerous excesses of the sentimental, affectionate family were transformed into a regulatory apparatus.

As incest was construed in narrow reproductive terms, the erotics of bourgeois family life were encouraged in a nonincestuous framework. While some scholars have read the writings of phrenologists as advocating incest, or creating a language by which the incestuous violence of domestic life was both rationalized and obscured, phrenologists themselves saw nothing of the sort.[3] Incest was confined to reproduction, and thus familial eroticism was acceptable, even necessary, so long as it did not result in offspring, which would then have crossed the line from appropriate amativeness to incest. The focus on incestuous reproduction allowed phrenologists to shift familial eroticism from dangerous excess to normative formation. It was a precarious site of emergence for the sexual subject. Psychic development demanded the proliferation of nonreproductive, intrafamilial eroticism; physical development demanded the extirpation of all incestuous reproduction. The modern sexual subject, a corollary to the liberal subject, existed in a rather precarious state, always on the verge of incest precisely because of the conditions of its development.

The physiological and phrenological discourse of incest aimed to avert, or at least regulate, the sexual excess of the liberal democratic citizen. By making birth the "anthropological minimum" of citizenship, as the liberal tradition seemed to have done, political identity then presumed reproduction as a central, if often unnamed, political practice.[4] Both phrenology and physiology entered the political domain in this manner. Hitching the prohibition of incest to reproduction, both eschewed the moral and social concerns of incest in favor of the reproductive, making proper reproduction a primary concern in the production of legitimate citizens. The regulation of incestuous reproduction aimed to insure the production of citizens who could exercise reason, as the most common degenerative effect of incestuous reproduction was idiocy, which enumerated a population legally excluded from full citizenship. Moreover, in phrenology's focus on amativeness and familial eroticism, there was the elaboration of pedagogic practices for the shaping of the proper sexual, liberal subject. The liberal subject, then, was the figure phrenologists and physiologists both presumed and produced. It was a fundamentally sexual subject, and incest was the mechanism of production and regulation.

Amativeness, or, the Desire of the Sexual Subject

Phrenology has its origins in the work of Franz Joseph Gall, who was trained in Vienna in the 1780s and by the 1790s had a flourishing medical practice in which he propounded the postulates of phrenology.[5] Gall divided the brain into discrete faculties and argued that character and intellect were the effect of the dynamic interaction of all the faculties.[6] Both Gall's student and then colleague, Johann Gaspar Spurzheim, and their most influential proselyte in England, George Combe, followed Gall in dividing the brain into discrete faculties. However, for Spurzheim and Gall the faculties were organized into a clear taxonomy, which, in its categorizations projected not only the organization of the mind but also the organization of ideal society.[7] There was, first, a fundamental division into "Affective" and "Intellectual" faculties. The affective were then subdivided into the "Propensities" and "Sentiments," while the intellectual were subdivided into the "Perceptive" and "Reflective" (Figure 2). "Amativeness" (sexual desire) was one of the affective propensities and, along with "Adhesiveness" (friendship) and "Philoprogenitiveness" (love of offspring) constituted the social faculties, or domestic affections.[8] The propensities, as a whole, were shared by both humans and "lower animals." According to Spurzheim, the propensities "produce only desires, inclinations or instincts . . . *propensities*, then, is only applied to indicate internal impulses which invite certain actions."[9] The propensities were what made humans animals; it was the harmonious, organic interaction with the other faculties that transcended animality and produced the human. Moreover, the propensities made desire *the* animating force of the human.

The affective and intellectual as general taxonomic categories of the mind, along with terms like "propensities," "sentiments," and "social" or "domestic" affections, organized the faculties into categories consonant with ideal liberal democratic society. They privileged the sentimental, sympathetic, and affective bonds between faculties that mirrored the bonds of society, governed by the rationalizing, human force of reason (intellectual).[10] These categories shed light on the appeal of phrenology in America, as the mind was naturally organized in a manner that reflected ideal sociality. Mind and society, ideally then, were mimetic replicas of one another. George Combe, the well-known British phrenologist, captured something of this mimesis, when he reflected on what it was that phrenology offered the world of critical analysis. Phrenology provided a

POWERS AND ORGANS OF THE MIND,

MARKED ON THE FRONTISPIECE.

AFFECTIVE.

I.—PROPENSITIES.

† Desire to live.

* Alimentiveness.

No. 1. Destructiveness.

2. Amativeness.

3. Philoprogenitiveness.

4. Adhesiveness.

5. Inhabitiveness.

6. Combativeness.

7. Secretiveness.

8. Acquisitiveness.

9. Constructiveness.

II.—SENTIMENTS.

10. Cautiousness.

11. Approbativeness.

12. Self-esteem.

13. Benevolence.

14. Reverence.

15. Firmness.

16. Conscientiousness.

17. Hope.

18. Marvellousness.

19. Ideality.

20. Mirthfulness.

21. Imitation.

INTELLECTUAL.

I.—PERCEPTIVE.

No. 22. Individuality.

23. Configuration.

24. Size.

25. Weight and Resistance.

26. Coloring.

27. Locality.

28. Order.

29. Calculation.

30. Eventuality.

31. Time.

32. Tune.

33. Language.

II.—REFLECTIVE.

34. Comparison.

35. Causality.

Figure 2. This taxonomy, titled "Powers and Organs of the Mind," was the frontispiece to J. G. Spurzheim, *Phrenology; or the Doctrine of the Mental Phenomena* (Boston: Marsh, Capen, and Lyon, 1838).

physiological, constitutional foundation to a philosophical inquiry into natural laws. As he put it in the preface to *The Constitution of Man*:

> *Physical laws* of nature, affecting our physical condition, as well as regulating the whole material system of the universe, are universally acknowledged to exist. . . . Physiologists, medical practitioners, and all who take medical aid, admit the existence of *organic laws:* And the sciences of government, legislation, education, indeed our whole train of conduct through life, proceed upon the admission of laws in morals . . . but, so far as I am aware, no author has hitherto attempted to point out, in a systematic form, the relations between those [natural] laws and the constitution of Man.[11]

Thus, for Combe and other phrenologists, the great contribution of phrenology was to determine that constitution and to determine its relations to itself and the world, relations reflected in the categorical organization of the discrete faculties.

In the United States, phrenology took off when Spurzheim and Combe arrived for a speaking tour in 1832. In major urban areas like Boston, New York, and Philadelphia, the principle of phrenology had spread among medical professionals and physiologists in the 1820s. But it was Spurzheim's speaking tour that greatly increased the visibility of phrenology in America. This was aided in a rather macabre fashion: after delivering eighteen lectures at the Boston Athenaeum, Spurzheim was taken ill in the middle of the tour and died in Boston in November 1832. His brain, skull ,and bodily organs were preserved at the Athenaeum and on the day of his funeral the Boston Phrenological Society was founded. Combe completed the speaking tour, often drawing crowds numbering in the thousands. By the mid-1830s phrenology was rapidly spreading through the United States, and Spurzheim's and Combe's works were being printed and distributed throughout America. Upon the American publication of Combe's *The Constitution of Man*, Horace Mann declared that it was "the greatest book that has been written for centuries."[12] Both Spurzheim and Combe deviated from Gall in a matter crucial to the reception of phrenology in America: where Gall believed in an innate propensity to evil, Spurzheim and Combe refused such an assertion. Instead, they presumed the possibility of perfectible harmony between the faculties, brought on by the insistent cultivation of the self. In an era that prized self-government and individual sovereignty, with

pretensions to expanding (white) democracy, this emphasis on the perfectible and progressive care of the self was particularly appealing.

Among those in the United State taken by phrenology were Orson and
Lorenzo Fowler, who along with their sister, Charlotte, and her husband,
Samuel R. Wells, would be responsible for what the literary critic Justine
Murison has called "the phrenological print empire of Fowler and Wells."[13]
This empire included not only their phrenological offices in New York and,
later, Boston, but also, and more importantly, the seemingly endless stream
of books and pamphlets they published, as well as the appearance, in 1838,
of the *American Phrenological Journal*. The Fowlers crafted their own style
of phrenology, one that was built on but frequently deviated from the work
of Spurzheim and Combe. Fowlerian phrenology, for instance, was made
up of thirty-seven faculties—in this they added several new faculties and
subtracted others (Figure 3). Like their European counterparts, the Fowlers
were committed to a system in which a deep interior of the subject was
legible on the surface of the body. In this, Fowlerian phrenology was central
to the production of modern interiority.[14] Mental character was signified
on and through the body.[15] Phrenology established a complex division
between the psychic and the physical while, at the same time, the physical
became a signifier of the psychic, thereby collapsing the distinction between
the two. This project, however, insistently cut at that interiority, or at least
at the idea that a deep interior, or human nature, preceded its reading on
the surface of the body. So as phrenologists produced interiority as they
discovered it, it was one that was always already legible on the surface of
the skull. Indeed, it was often reducible to that surface. The phrenological
method was all one needed to plumb the depths of the modern subject.[16]

For all these phrenologists, the essence of that interior, and thus one of
the keys to deciphering the signs on the skull, was amativeness and its
location in the cerebellum, at the base of the skull (Figure 4). The Fowlers
and other American phrenologists, especially through the 1840s and 1850s,
deviated from their European forebears in emphasizing the centrality of
amativeness. Where for Spurzheim and Combe amativeness was one of
several essential faculties, for Orson Fowler, especially, it bordered on an
obsession. Desire, unconscious but legible on the surface of the skull, was
inherently disruptive, and phrenologists and physiologists deployed their
sciences in a manner that linked desire and sexuality, making sex the means
through which the desire of the liberal subject could be managed.[17] This
unconscious desire was frequently constituted as a threat to the liberal

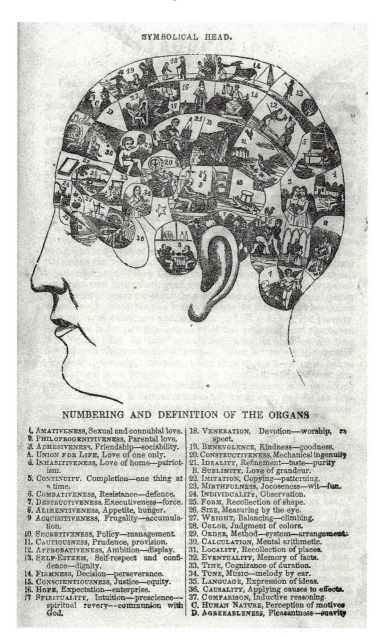

SYMBOLICAL HEAD.

NUMBERING AND DEFINITION OF THE ORGANS

1. AMATIVENESS, Sexual and connubial love.
2. PHILOPROGENITIVENESS, Parental love.
3. ADHESIVENESS, Friendship—sociability.
A. UNION FOR LIFE, Love of one only.
4. INHABITIVENESS, Love of home—patriotism.
5. CONTINUITY. Completion—one thing at a time.
6. COMBATIVENESS, Resistance—defence.
7. DESTRUCTIVENESS, Executiveness—force.
8. ALIMENTIVENESS, Appetite, hunger.
9 ACQUISITIVENESS, Frugality—accumulation.
10. SECRETIVENESS, Policy—management.
11. CAUTIOUSNESS, Prudence, provision.
12. APPROBATIVENESS, Ambition—display.
13. SELF-ESTEEM, Self-respect and confidence—dignity.
14. FIRMNESS, Decision—perseverance.
15. CONSCIENTIOUSNESS, Justice—equity.
16. HOPE, Expectation—enterprise.
17 SPIRITUALITY, Intuition—prescience—spiritual revery—communion with God.

18. VENERATION, Devotion—worship, respect.
19. BENEVOLENCE, Kindness—goodness.
20. CONSTRUCTIVENESS, Mechanical ingenuity
21. IDEALITY, Refinement—taste—purity
B. SUBLIMITY. Love of grandeur.
22. IMITATION, Copying—patterning.
23. MIRTHFULNESS, Jocoseness—wit—fun.
24. INDIVIDUALITY, Observation.
25. FORM, Recollection of shape.
26. SIZE, Measuring by the eye.
27. WEIGHT, Balancing—climbing.
28. COLOR, Judgment of colors.
29. ORDER, Method—system—arrangement.
30. CALCULATION, Mental arithmetic.
31. LOCALITY, Recollection of places.
32. EVENTUALITY, Memory of facts.
33. TIME, Cognizance of duration.
34. TUNE, MUSIC—melody by ear.
35. LANGUAGE, Expression of ideas.
36. CAUSALITY, Applying causes to effects.
37. COMPARISON, Inductive reasoning.
C. HUMAN NATURE, Perception of motives
D. AGREEABLENESS, Pleasantness—suavity

Figure 3. "Symbolical Head" depicts the faculties of the mind according to Orson Fowler. From *Love and Parentage: Applied to the Improvement of Offspring*, 13th ed. (New York: Fowlers and Wells, 1853), iv.

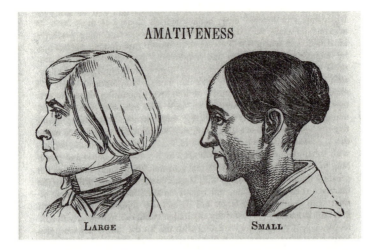

Figure 4. "Amativeness" depicts the difference in the size of the amative faculty in men and women. From Orson Fowler, *Love and Parentage: Applied to the Improvement of Offspring*, 13th ed. (New York: Fowlers and Wells, 1853), 51.

democratic order. Indeed, licentious threats to the stability of the republic had been represented in sexual terms in the seduction literature of the late eighteenth century.[18] As John Adams famously said, in a reference to Samuel Richardson's *Clarissa*, "Democracy is Lovelace, and the people are Clarissa. . . . The artful villain will pursue the innocent lovely girl to her ruin and death."[19] So as sexuality pervaded late eighteenth and nineteenth century culture, as a desire to be both cultivated and controlled, lest it destroy social and political bonds, phrenologists organized it into a discrete faulty in the mind and provided means by which to control it.[20]

The centrality of amativeness was, in some regards, a peculiarly American iteration of phrenology. As Spurzheim noted of Gall, he initially did not believe that there was an individual organ, or faculty devoted to sexuality, and he discovered it only by accident. In a manner uncannily prefiguring Freud in the late nineteenth century, Gall discovered amativeness while treating "a widow who was subject to violent hysterical fits."[21] Yet, in a manner distinctly different from Freud's later discovery of sexuality as the etiology of neurosis, Gall found the sexual faculty with his hand when supporting the woman's head during one of these hysterical fits. Gall "was astonished by the great thickness and heat of her neck. Acquainted with her peculiar character, he asked himself, whether the size of her neck, and consequent development of her cerebellum, might not have some relation to her inordinate passion?"[22] Following from this encounter, Gall determined the cerebellum as the seat of amativeness, a discovery that would link sexuality with the baser faculties that men shared with animals, as amativeness was at the base of the brain.

The seeds of intrafamilial desire that would blossom in Fowler's work were sown in Gall's and Spurzheim's early studies. Amativeness was inherently organized around heterosexual sex. As the organ that produced the desire necessary for reproduction, amativeness directed men toward women and women toward men. Same sex desire and masturbation were seen as primary perversions resulting from a degenerated or corrupted amative organ. Moreover, amativeness, and the larger cerebellum of which it was a part, needed to develop throughout youth and was not fully mature until adulthood. This was determined through the measurement of the skull, and Gall and Spurzheim claimed that between the ages of two and sixteen the cerebellum "is still imperfectly developed."[23] Indeed, only in adults, whose cerebellum had attained its full size, was amativeness fully developed, but even then the range of amative energies confounded any uniform development within the population. "It is well known that men feel in very different degrees the impulses of the sexual passion," wrote Spurzheim, "some individuals are almost or wholly deprived of it; others experience it moderately; whilst others again feel its ungovernable violence. In the first, the cerebellum is very small, in the second, it is of a middling size; and in the third class, it is very large and prominent."[24] If this varied from individual to individual, and man to woman, it also varied across race and ethnicity.

Curiously, the work most responsible for the initial popularization of phrenology in the United States, George Combe's *The Constitution of Man*, was relatively silent on amativeness. Combe considered amativeness as one of the propensities common to humans and animals and, more narrowly, when considered with the faculties philoprogenitiveness (love of one's children) and adhesiveness (a desire for friendship), as one of the "domestic affections." What was curious about the text is that Combe treated adhesiveness and philoprogenitiveness individually as, in fact, he does with nearly every other faculty that makes up the brain. Amativeness stood alone as the only faculty never fully addressed.

Amativeness, according to Spurzheim, "certainly is essential" to reproduction, "but it often acts without there being any intention to continue the species and is also satisfied in various ways incompatible with such purpose."[25] It was central to the propagation of humanity for its reproductive tendencies, but it was also of profound importance to society in both its reproductive and nonreproductive manifestations. "Its influence in society is immense, and has caused great disorder as well in civil as in other peculiar, especially religious institutions, where its activity has not been duly considered."[26] Not to satisfy amativeness, as Spurzheim noted was the chaste condition of some religious orders, could be disastrous; but so too could inappropriate satisfaction. "The disorderly satisfaction of the amative propensity undermines the health of individuals and even the species."[27]

An article on marriage in an early issue of the *American Phrenological Journal* provided as succinct a definition of amativeness as could be found among phrenological writings.

> From this faculty ["Amativeness"] the sexual feeling originates. The organ is generally larger in males than in females. Its size is known chiefly by the breadth of the neck from ear to ear; in new-born children it is the least developed of all the cerebral parts. It attains its full maturity between eighteen and twenty six years old, at which latter age it is about one-seventh of the whole brain. When its development is very large, it leads to libertinism and conjugal infidelity; but when under the guidance of the moral and reflecting faculties, it excites to mutual kindness, and the exercise of all the milder amenities between the sexes.[28]

A number of the most common features of amativeness were elaborated here. There was an asymmetry between men and women in regard to the faculty that reinforced common gendered assumptions. Amativeness was located at the base of the skull and thus among the baser faculties. The age of maturity, at which point amativeness was fully developed, coincided with the average period of marriage in the United States. Even though it was one of thirty-seven faculties, amativeness dominated the space of the brain, accounting for one quarter of the total brain. It was both destructive and beneficial, via libertinism or mutual kindness, respectively, when exercised in concert with other faculties.

As Helen Lefkowitz Horowitz notes, the Fowlers' increasing concern with amativeneness coincided with a "world of heightened sexual display."[29] Increasingly, middle-class Americans imagined themselves in sexual terms, and amativeness became the name for that sexual desire. Indeed, Walt Whitman, a well-known convert to the phrenological vision of mind and body, sang the praise of amativeness. "I know that amativeness is just as divine as spirituality—and this which I know I put freely in my poems."[30] Even those who disagreed with phrenologists tended to grant the interior presence of amativeness. One author, writing in the *Boston Medical and Surgical Journal*, argued that phrenology, which located amativeness in the cerebellum (the most inferior organ of the brain), simply misunderstood the relationship between the body and amativeness. Instead of the cerebellum, there was a connection "between what is called amativeness, and the general distribution of nervous excitement through the system. Phrenologists seem to have left unnoticed the consent and sympathy that prevails between the genito-urinary organs and the rectum, and the inference that may be derived from thence that they are often affected by one common cause."[31] If this author disagreed with the phrenological figuration of the nervous body, he nonetheless accepted amativeness as an organizing principle of the self, and one moreover, that rested on those liberal ideals of (bodily) consent and sympathy.

The centrality of amativeness, or sexual desire, to the emergent liberal democracy, and in particular its potentially destructive aspects, can be discerned in the antimasturbatory sex panic of the 1830s and 1840s. As scholars ranging from Michel Foucault to Thomas Laqueur to Helen Lefkowitz Horowitz and G. J. Barker Benfield have noted, at the center of bourgeois sexuality was a concern with the elimination of masturbation.[32] Orson Fowler had contributed to this with a pamphlet simply entitled *Amativeness, or, Evils and Remedies of Excessive and Perverted Sexuality*.[33] Masturbation, acknowledged as an evil endemic to both boys and girls (although writings on the masturbation of boys were much more voluminous), embodied the triumph of passion (or desire) over the control of reason. The world of the masturbator was one in which self-mastery had failed. An endless series of remedies were prescribed, among them useful work, which encompassed anything that militated against a sedentary lifestyle, and the constant surveillance of children. Masturbation, like incest, was linked to insanity, which according to many antimasturbation pamphlets of the 1840s and 1850s was a result of a decrease in semen, at the time understood to be stored in finite quantities.

As the solitary vice, masturbation portended a kind of radical individualism, antisocial from the beginning. In this respect, it could be grouped with other symptoms of the excesses of liberal individualism, like suicide.[34] If suicide represented excessive individualism and liberty as death, then masturbation, or "self-abuse," was often figured as slavery. "As white men surrendered to carnal impulses and lost control of their bodily flows," writes Russ Castronovo, "they became slaves."[35] Excessive sexual liberty, then, was not necessarily freedom, or even licentiousness, but rather death and slavery. Like the unencumbered liberal subject in *The Life of Dr. Richard Jennings, the Great Victimizer,* the social life so central to producing the liberal subject was, for the masturbator, foreshortened. Yet, masturbation, in addition to being a solitary vice signifying the failure of self-mastery, was a domestic vice. In a world of passionless, moral mothers and innocent children bereft of sin and sex, masturbation disrupted the domestic economy of desire. If children were inherently innocent, what was one to make of the universal abandon children, particularly boys, showed toward their own genitalia? The antimasturbation literature constructed a contradictory, ambivalent boy, at once innocent and inherently lustful. This ambivalence disappeared once the boy became a self-abuser, given over, in full, to desire. "It is a secret and solitary vice," Sylvester Graham wrote in his popular *A Lecture to Young Men on Chastity,* "which requires the consent of no second person,—and therefore the practice has little to prevent its frequency." Once begun, the desire represented by masturbation became overwhelming, "until it reaches the most ruinous excess, and acquires a power which irresistibly urges on the unhappy sufferer, in the voluntary course of self-destruction."[36] On the one hand, the potential liberal subject (children, as Holly Brewer and Caroline Levander have demonstrated, were excluded from such a personality)[37] was overtaken by desire that, in part, made him a subject of liberalism. Indeed, the child was subjected by desire. The masturbating boy was excluded from liberal rationality precisely through his rejection of consensual social relations. Yet, the passage closes with the "voluntary course of self-destruction." Graham thus suggested the fragility of the sexual liberal subject—to become a masturbator was not, initially, the subjection by and to desire; rather, it was a choice.[38]

The question, then, for the antimasturbation public, was how to encumber the masturbating boy? How, in other words, to contain and direct the amative, sexual child before desire took over entirely? The answer lay in the erotically dangerous environs of the family, an institution, as we have seen, that mixed obligations and duties with rights and choices. The familial encumbrance of antimasturbation literature rested on the stock figure of the moral, passionless mother. Antimasturbation literature was often directed at mothers who were instructed to curb the abuses of their sons. As the literary critic G. M. Goshgarian has noted, the mother, "a monitor as pure as masturbation was poisonous had . . . to be interposed between the young man and his penis."[39] It was in this sense, then, that the masturbation scare, firmly rooted in the bourgeois, domestic home, was structured by intrafamilial desire. The innocent/lustful boy was supposed to direct his desire either toward his mother as a substitute for himself or to his penis as a substitute for his mother. Unless, of course, his parents were pedagogic models, something Graham suggested was common. "The habit has in some instances been begun as early as the fifth or sixth year: and shocking as it may seem, nurses, and even parents, have been the teachers of this abominable vice!"[40] The erotic family, then, both incited masturbation and controlled it. Either way, the desire of the domestic scene was firmly bounded by the characters of the family.

In lecturing against masturbation the physiologist Thomas Low Nichols invoked intrafamilial desire as a positive weapon in the fight against the solitary vice. In a common rhetorical strategy, Nichols mentioned that masturbation was also detrimental to girls, but his main focus was boys. While this early manifestation of sexual desire was destructive if acted out on one's own body, it was another story altogether if acted out in a heterosexual relationship within the family. "The passion of love in our earlier years has what may be called a rudimentary development. In very young children we perceive signs of the sexual instinct. It is naturally shown in a gallant fondness which little boys have for their mothers, their older sisters, and generally for the female sex. At the same time, little girls have a peculiar tenderness for their fathers and male friends."[41] While Nichols generalized to the male and female sexes, the specific sexual objects of early childhood desire were mothers, fathers, and siblings.

The masturbation panic, a white, middle-class crisis in midcentury America, both demonstrated the pervasive character of amativeness as an individual, social, and national issue and the way in which familial desire would be the site of regulation of individual desire. Yet, as sexual desire, amativeness was split. It could lead to reproduction, but importantly, did not need to. It was in this manner, in which amativeness was insistently reproductive but also an animating desire of the subject that need not lead to reproductive ends, indeed could simply be articulated as pleasure, that the sexual subject was born and, in its heteronormative assumptions, disciplined. Both poles of amativeness could be destructive and thus needed to be disciplined: reproduction via a discourse of incestuous hereditary degeneration and nonreproduction through the erotic family.

Hereditary Descent and Incest

The linking of reproduction, heredity, and incest by phrenologists and physiologists was one of the mechanisms through which sexual desire was conditioned. As Nicole Eustace has recently written, "sexual reproduction took pride of place in the early republic's geopolitical imagination; . . . the 'natural' force of demography could fundamentally alter the shape of national geography."[42] Phrenological and physiological writings on incestuous reproduction produced a discourse by which this reproductive national expansion would be more likely to produce a healthy body politic. Moreover, phrenologists and physiologists shared in the imperial vision of reproduction, putting incestuous reproduction in the service of U.S. imperialism and white racial consolidation. Reproduction served as an increasingly prepolitical point of entry into governing the desire of liberalism.

If the articulation of incest with reproduction reached its height in the 1840s and 1850s, there were occasional voices in the late eighteenth century that insisted on the dire hereditary consequences of incestuous reproduction as either the only or primary reason for prohibition. Writing in 1790, Noah Webster argued that there were two reasons for prohibiting incest. First, incestuous marriages upended the "duties and rights of the natural relation."[43] In this, he sounded like any number of legists in the early nineteenth century. The second and more important reason was reproductive and hereditary. "It iz a law of nature that vegetables should degenerate, if planted continually on the same soil. . . . Animals degenerate on the same principle. . . . Consanguinity, and not affinity, iz the ground of the prohibition."[44] Unlike the theologians, or for that matter the moral philosophers and jurists of the period, Webster asserted the degenerative hereditary effects of intermarriage as the foundation of the incest prohibition.[45] Incestuous reproduction, Webster asserted, would produce "a race of pygmies" and "imperfect children" marked by "weakness, sickness and deformity."[46] Webster found little support for such an argument. Indeed, one reviewer found Webster's essay absurd. That incestuous reproduction caused hereditary degeneration was "unsupported by facts."[47] Furthermore, "as citizens of America . . . we shall rejoice to find Mr. Webster's principle verified by experience; for if, as he says, the marriage of relations has a tendency to make pigmies of the human race, surely we have reason to expect that a contrary cause will produce an opposite effect, and that from the heterogeneous mixture of our citizens, who are sprung from various nations, a mixt offspring will arise, strong and gigantic as the Patagonians themselves."[48] In the 1790s, Webster's talk of fears of hereditary degeneration was dismissed as a fable of pigmies and Patagonians.

If Webster's was a lonely voice in the early republic, phrenology's earliest practitioners, Gall and Spurzheim, were also reticent when it came to incest. Trumpeting the moral and physical influence of parentage in reproduction, the problem of incestuous reproduction was implicit in such writings; however, it was not addressed explicitly. As the historian Roger Cooter argues, the hereditarian concerns that suffused mid-nineteenth-century phrenology were, in fact, more prominent in America.[49] Indeed, for Spurzheim, incest remained, in some regards, a moral transgression. "Adultery and incest are not particular faculties," Spurzheim wrote, "they are abuses of the amative propensity."[50] It was George Combe who first broached the incest prohibition directly. After elaborating the multitude of faculties that made up the brain as well as the natural and organic laws to which man adhered, Combe turned to an analysis of the "miseries of mankind" and their relation to "infringements of the laws of nature."[51] It was here that Combe addressed the adverse effects of incestuous reproduction: "marriages between blood relations," Combe wrote, "tend decidedly to the deterioration of the physical and mental qualities of the offspring."[52] Combe's laws of nature were not those deployed in the legal domain. There the laws of nature preserved duties and rights in the family and encouraged sociality. Here the laws of nature were embodied and concerned with the physical health of offspring. Nature shifted from the moral and social concerns of reason to the bodily concerns of reproduction.

This opening paved the way for Orson Fowler's disquisition on incestuous reproduction. In his highly prolific career, Fowler addressed the reproductive and hereditary incest prohibition most fully in his 1848 work *Hereditary Descent*. Heredity, for Fowler, like many in the nineteenth century, including his phrenological forebears, was constituted by the transmission of both moral and physical characteristics. Physical deformities, diseases, and character flaws could all be transmitted to children based on the phrenological propensities of the parents. Likewise, positive traits were also transmitted to offspring from their parents. Fowler's phrenology was more practical than philosophical and, perhaps above all, a moral system.[53] Given the sexual subject at the center of phrenology, reproduction and heredity preoccupied many of its practitioners. The control of incest in its consanguineous form was central to this task.

Fowler was particularly concerned with elaborating abstract, universal laws of heredity that accounted for the particular propensities of different parents. In this, Fowler and most other American phrenologists simply reproduced the common understanding of heredity in antebellum America. As Charles Rosenberg notes, "heredity was hardly a subject for controversy. . . . 'Like' after all did 'beget like.' "[54] This simple assumption, according to Rosenberg, was marked by several subsidiary assumptions. These included the belief that acquired characteristics were inherited; heredity began with conception and continued through weaning; character, disease, and temperament were inherited as propensities; and sexual difference was central to heredity.[55] While phrenological conceptions of heredity were not wholly identical to these traits, they did fit generally within these parameters. Indeed, Rosenberg argues that it was phrenology that popularized this type of hereditarian thought.[56]

Despite these hereditarian assumptions, Fowler noted several exceptions to the rule of like begets like. "Though the correctness of this general law, that offspring inherit the mental and physical characteristics of their parents, is unquestionable, yet it is modified by several sub-laws, or other hereditary principles, one of which is that the children of near relatives either fall far below their parentage, or else are mal-formed or idiotic."[57] The incest prohibition seemed to disrupt this dominant hereditary framework, for a brother and sister, a parent and child, cousins, all of these may have formed a pair that, from a strictly phrenological standpoint, would have made a perfect conjugal couple. Yet, almost invariably, incest resulted in inferior offspring in relation to the qualities of the parents, whatever the seeming compatibility of the faculties. Like might beget like, but incestuous reproduction was an excessive similitude, an overidentification that would act as a check on excessive amativeness.

According to Fowler, incest violated the general principles of phrenology and supposedly proper, natural human development on two accounts. First, it disrupted the structure of kinship, which for Fowler was a mathematical principle.[58] In this manner, as the nuclear family became a site for the dense transfer of affection and sentiment that produced the liberal subject, kinship became a formal and neutral backdrop bereft of sentiment. Incest transgressed "nature's absolute requisition, that every human being should have two parents, four grandparents, eight great-grandparents, six- teen great-great grandparents, thirty-two of the next, and sixty-four of the next anterior generations, one hundred and twenty of the next, and two hundred and forty of the next, etc.—except where and as far as the off- spring of one common ancestor marry each other."[59] An article in the *American Phrenological Journal*, perhaps authored by Fowler, extended the equation by going back fifty generations, "amounting to the inconceivable number of two thousand three hundred and sixty-two billion, seven hun- dred and forty-nine thousand, nine hundred and fourteen million, two hundred and fourteen thousand and forty-six (2,362,749,914,214,046!)—a multitude verily! which no man can number, no mind conceive!"[60] This was of momentous significance, since "the blood of this vast host is running in the veins of every living mortal."[61]

Given over to mathematical formulas, Fowler's kinship was an abstract universal—everyone was related to one another via an originary blood. The idea of universal but deracinated kinship was not new and had been rejected before. It was precisely such kinship that William Blackstone had refuted in his first published work, *An Essay on Collateral Consanguinity*. As he put it in 1750, "the common Notions of Mankind will never teach us to look upon collateral Kindred as a Thing subsisting for ever. On the contrary, the Affection, the Remembrance, the very Name of Cousins ceases after a few Descents. . . . When we speak of *our Relations*, we only mean such as are within a few Degrees of us; nor do we pretend to argue, that because all Kinsmen are descended from one common Ancestor, therefore all who are descended from one common Ancestor are Kinsmen."[62] For Blackstone, then, kinship was a socially and affectively dense relation, whereas for Fowler, who invoked the abstractions of mathematics and reproduction, kinship was, at least in articulating a law of incest, universal and formal, but without affect.[63]

Putting aside possible mathematical errors, the recourse to a calculus of kinship as a barrier to incest was common in the antebellum period. Indeed, in 1840, John Lee, a mathematician, took it on himself to offer, in a letter to Joseph Story, a mathematical disproof of Blackstone's essay. In brief, Lee found the principles underlying Blackstone's genealogy to be spe- cious at best. Blackstone had presumed that the prohibition of "intermar- riage of relatives" would provide the necessary check on population growth, in order to make kinship and population finite rather than infinite. In this, Blackstone's kinship would have had the formal structure and order of which Fowler boasted. Lee pointed out that the prohibition was not a substantial check on population growth and thus Blackstone's entire theory needed to be discarded because of its mathematical absurdities. While Lee claimed that in the case of marriages of *"brother and sister*, [where] a field of horrors opens to view," these kinds of moral considerations were mostly absent.[64] What emerged from Lee's critique was kinship as an abstract principle, to which incest presented a formal, but not moral or social, problem.

Even in the debate over marriage with a deceased wife's sister, one finds a calculating turn. William Marshall criticized Sereno Dwight for his insistence on mathematical perfection in the Levitical prohibitions. "In each triad of relatives," Dwight wrote, "the first is a relative by the individual's own consanguinity: the second, by the individual's own affinity: the third by the consanguinity of the married partner. The law has thus a beautiful and truly mathematical simplicity."[65] Marshall was not convinced: "the difficulty with the author [Dwight] is, that if this list is complete, he cannot teach men their moral duties by mathematics. The ground over which the prohibitions extend will not form a circle."[66] While Marshall offered a geometry as opposed to Fowler's algebra, it nonetheless mirrored the belief that there was a mathematical principle to ordered kinship. Moreover, as Marshall suggested, the danger of a kinship calculus as the ground for an incest prohibition was that it potentially evacuated the moral imperative of the prohibition. Was it enough to prevent incest to know that one should have four grandparents and eight great grandparents?

This calculus of kinship had another, perhaps less obvious function as well. In making an abstract universal law of kinship, one that both explained the prohibition of incest and followed from it, Fowler conflated kinship with consanguinity. Blood relations and the nuclear family were at its core; the entire formula of kinship was ordered around the deracinated individual, the ego of systems of kinship that would become central to Lewis Henry Morgan's work on kinship several decades later. Kinship was not, as articulated here, a socially and affectively dense set of relations, as suggested by Blackstone; rather, it was a set of relations that followed from those of blood. And here, by positing it as an immutable law of heredity, the social and moral logics of kinship were obviated. Where the legal apparatus could acknowledge both a foundational incest prohibition and many varying iterations built on top of that foundation, and thus multiple kinships (at least in theory), physiology and phrenology knew no such flexibility. Such inflexibility was a more forceful basis for the expansion of the normative family and kinship.[67]

If incest transgressed a mathematical law, Fowler was ultimately more concerned with its reproductive effects. Detection required an empirical project, with effects demonstrated "especially by FACTS," rather than abstract theory.[68] Fowler was not alone in such a desire. Just a few years earlier, the physiologist Julius Steinau had complained that "we here find the subject [incestuous reproduction] so complicated with the dicta of authorities and the influence of ecclesiastical laws, which have produced so general and so strong a prejudice, that it is difficult to obtain a conclusion legitimately deduced from facts."[69] Theology and expert opinion were the enemies of a newfound empiricism. The abstraction of kinship was a theory; the hereditary effects of incest were written on the body and thus empirically observable. In demonstrating these effects, Fowler reported numerous instances of incestuous offspring, provided to him by Joshua Coffin, a Boston abolitionist. Coffin began his submission to Fowler with an effort to distinguish this reproductive imperative from its biblical counterpart. "Whatever may be the cause, the fact is undeniable, that those families who are so foolish as to intermarry with blood relations, very frequently, if not always, degenerate, both physically and mentally. Independently, therefore, of the divine inspiration of the laws of Moses, they are founded on strict physiological principles, which we should do well always to bear in mind, as they cannot be violated with impunity."[70] Thus, the physiological basis of the prohibition need not contradict the biblical basis; indeed, from Coffin's perspective they had little relation to one another. Incestuous reproduction was a site of intimate regulation quite apart from the moral considerations associated with the biblical law.

The proof of the problem of incest, then, was located not in theological niceties but in the physical and mental characteristics of the offspring. The incest of the parents was visibly inscribed on the body of the child. Coffin offered the "clump-footed," the "one-eyed," the "diminutive," one child with a head "shaped like a flat-iron," and another with "St. Vitus's dance" as evidence of sexual intercourse between cousins. Coffin's cousin, a Mr. Hale, provided Fowler with more evidence. Hale described cousin marriages that resulted in the birth of "cripples," "deaf," "mute," "nervous" children with feeble health, some of whom were "club-footed" and "wry-necked."[71] Indeed, bolstering this new scopic regime of incest, Hale reported that "the Bradstreets and Grants of G., Me., have intermarried, and I am told the children show it."[72] Incest became a transgression of hereditary laws, visibly inscribed on bodies, just as marriage and sex between cousins became a focus of reproductive incest. Long excluded in most American Protestant writings because it was associated with the excesses of papal authority in the Catholic Church, cousin marriage became a new object of the incest prohibition in the United States. However, the physiological and hereditary emphases inured phrenology from charges of incipient popery.

Of course, phrenology, like most hereditary thought of the period, posited that moral characteristics could also be transmitted hereditarily. By far the most common affliction said to result from incest was idiocy. Nearly all children with physical deformities attributed to incest were described as "idiots," "feeble-minded," "fools," "deranged," or of "weak intellect." The point here was to attribute mental degeneration to incestuous reproduction. The offspring did not necessarily have to be classified as idiots to deem incest a hereditary nightmare; as long as the children were of lesser intellect than their parents, incestuous reproduction proved detrimental to the progress of the race. Interestingly, incest's legacy, in particular idiocy, or mental degeneration, could affect both children and parents. Coffin's and Hale's compendium of incestuous offspring contained a number of situations in which the mother, father, or both parents became mentally unstable or died after an incestuous birth. Fowler commented, "These facts would seem to indicate that debility and sickness attended these parents as well as their children, an inference rendered probable, by that great law of harmony which pervades nature, and renders whatever is beneficial or injurious to offspring, equally so to parents."[73] It was the act, then, that created its debilitating effects. Here the children were explained by emergent hereditary ideas while the parents by earlier notions of punishment; both bore the marks of incest.

Fowler was not alone in his phrenological condemnation. Tales of incestuous corruption were fodder for a plethora of invectives against degenerative reproduction. One contributor to the *American Phrenological Journal* argued that "the incestuous propensity seems to be hereditary."[74] Linking incest to the propensities, this author further instantiated the incestuous nature of the desiring sexual, liberal subject. Recounting a trial in Portland, Maine, in which a thirteen-year-old boy was charged with "tying up and emasculating" another boy, incest was found to be causative of the crime.

The boy's grandfather had committed incest with his daughter, and the author argued that incest itself was a heritable malady. This was passed onto the next generation, as "her son committed incest with his mother, and the product of this double incest, was the lad who, at thirteen years old, was sent to the state prison for tying up another boy and emasculating him."[75] And, perhaps identifying the series of incestuous transgressions with the phallus, or literally with the genitals, the child's action was a displaced attempt to end the cycle of incest. Perhaps not incidentally, the castration that broke the incestuous conditions of this family recalls the extrajuridical castration of Sawney Beane and his sons at the hands of the state.

Fowler's concerns echoed through the hereditary discourse on incest in antebellum America. Incest as part of the scopic regime, the health of the future population, the focus on cousin marriage, the diminution of theological explanations of the incest prohibition—all found a prominent place around incest and reproduction. While for phrenologists and physiologists incest was essentially an issue of reproduction and heredity, it would be wrong to say that there was a linear movement from the moral considerations of early-nineteenth-century theologians to the reproductive concerns of phrenologists and physiologists in the mid-nineteenth century. Such an ascriptive narrative reproduces the logic of the phrenologists and physiologists, not to mention the juridical scholars, all of whom claimed to reveal a more accurate, or essential, incest prohibition. The new concern with reproduction and the hereditary effects of incest was, in certain respects, a radical and novel departure from previous accounts. But it was not a refinement of the incest prohibition. In the broader discourse—juridical, theological, ethnographic, moral (not to mention among phrenologists and physiologists)—incest remained tied to marriage and sexuality, neither of which could be reduced to a science of the mind or body (despite phrenologists' best attempts). Increasingly, medical professionals and phrenologists were concerned with incidences of blindness, deafness, idiocy, physical deformities, and the like. The concern with the future body shifted the gaze of the regulatory apparatus from the moral and legal present of courtship, marriage, and the erotics of family life to the future child.[76]

The association of physical deformity with incest was, in one sense, nothing new. However, the physical deformities associated with incest prior to the advent of hereditary explanations were examples of divine, or supernatural, punishment of a transgression of moral order. Claude Lévi-Strauss has noted the problem with interpreting monstrous offspring as a recognition of the potential hereditary defects of incestuous reproduction. "It is true that various monstrosities are threatened to the descendants of incestuous parents in the folklore of primitive peoples," Lévi-Strauss wrote; "it is sufficient to note that such punishments are, in primitive tradition, commonly expected for all those who break rules, and are in no way especially confined to reproduction."[77] Indeed, closer to the concerns of this book, Leviticus prescribed a variety of punishments for such transgressions, including death, expulsion, dying childless, and perhaps most relevantly here, that certain transgressions "shall bear their iniquity," which hints at the visible inscription of an incestuous transgression on the body. Yet Leviticus includes affinal and consanguineous relatives, thus confounding antebellum hereditary arguments. Monstrous births as punishment for incestuous transgression in earlier periods cannot be read continuously with the physical and mental disabilities that came to be associated with incest in the mid-nineteenth century.[78]

Humans in the Animal Kingdom

The monstrous birth, the visible inscription of incest on the body of the offspring, and the emphasis on reproduction shifted the discourse of incest into the commonalities between human and animals. For George Combe, for instance, the evidence for the degenerative tendency of incestuous reproduction was derived from the porosity of the boundary between humans, animals, and plants. Combe looked to an "organic law of the animal kingdom," thereby investing human reproductive and social institutions with the social and reproductive habits of animals, and later on in the text, plants.[79] To be sure, neither Combe, nor phrenologists more broadly, left humans in the natural world for all that long. The higher faculties were what separated humans from animals; the lower faculties, however, such as amativeness, or sexual desire, were shared across the human-animal boundary. Yet, if sexuality, or amativeness, was in part reserved to humans, the reproductive was shared with both flora and fauna. The need for breeding out, rather than in, followed from "a provision . . . made to prevent the male and female blossoms of the same plant from breeding together, this being found to hurt the breed of vegetables, just as breeding in and in does the breed of animals."[80] Combe moved directly from this logic to that of

European nobility and cousin marriage (in England, but the same could have been and was said about the United States), which exhibited all the telltale degenerative characteristics of breeding in and in. "In Spain kings marry their nieces, and in this country, first and second cousins marry without scruple; although every philosophical physiologist will declare that this is in direct opposition to the institutions of nature."[81] The prohibition of reproductive incest was the great leveler of the body politic.

In deriving the incest prohibition from reproductive laws of flora and fauna, Combe obviated what has been a central tenet of the intellectual history of the incest prohibition: namely, that the prohibition distinguished humans form the natural world. Georges Bataille, for instance, has written that the incest prohibition is what constitutes human, as opposed to animal, sexuality, "the passage from the simple sexuality of animals to the cerebral activity of man, which is implied in eroticism. I am referring to the associations and judgments that tend to qualify sexually objects, beings, places and moments that by themselves have nothing sexual about them, nor anything contrary to sexuality: the meaning attached to nudity, for example, and the prohibition of incest. In this sense, chastity itself is one of the aspects of eroticism, that is, of properly *human* sexuality."[82] The difference here is not that Combe believed that humans were entirely part of the natural world, whereas Bataille theorizes the mechanism by which humans distinguish themselves from nature—Combe would never have reduced the human to the purely natural. Rather, for Bataille it is sexuality produced through prohibition that distinguished the human from nature, or from the animal in nature. For Combe and other phrenologists, sexuality and the prohibition of incest, while foundational in the constitution of man, were, precisely because they were a foundational part of the natural world, shared with animals. It was the cultivation of amativeness in the erotic family that made for a properly human sexuality. If the evidence for the degenerative tendencies of incestuous reproduction collapsed the distinction between human and animal, the erotic family was nevertheless distinctly human.

Combe was not alone in this, and much of his support came from antebellum animal breeders. Discussions of incest in the breeding of plants and animals were relatively common in the period and sometimes took on an anthropomorphic cast. Indeed, as one doctor wrote, "however humiliating it may be to our pride . . . the rules which govern the procreation of species are not essentially different in man and domestic animals."[83] Such discussions appeared frequently in work devoted to agriculture and animal breeding, where there was no consensus on the efficacy or propriety of what was commonly referred to as "breeding in and in." Again, as in theology and law, incest was a conflicted category. In an 1836 essay on sheep, "A Wool Grower" cautioned against breeding in and in. "It is very important in crossing that the male be perfect in shape, and also what you want as it regards quantity and quality of his wool; and whether you cross on the other breeds, or attempt to raise the pure merino, most attention must be paid to the shape of the sire—also avoid breeding by incest as much as possible."[84] The use of incest in a discussion of breeding sheep suggests just the type of transformation occurring in phrenology and physiology. Both the theological and legal register articulated incest as a moral transgression of social and familial order, something that would have been impossible in the animal world. But here, with incest attached to breeding and reproduction, the permeability of the boundary between animal and human was plausible. Moreover, if terms like "perfection" and "pure" suggest antebellum constructions of race, "A Wool Grower" immediately clarified. "A black sheep and a white ram will most generally produce a white lamb, but that lamb will most generally produce black lambs, though connected with a white ram. Whatever animals we breed we must remember that there is a propensity to deteriorate; hence we must always breed from the best, and take the best of care too if we would expect to improve."[85]

An exchange between two breeders of racehorses between 1835 and 1836 further illustrated the links between incest, reproduction, and anthropomorphism. Here, if the animals, in this case racehorses, were anthropomorphized, the association also served to instantiate the reproductive incest prohibition, further eroding the incestuous line between human and animal. In 1835, a reader voiced concern about the arguments put forward by "Another Virginia Breeder" concerning the propitious effects of breeding in and in. "Another Virginia Breeder" had implied that, in the case of "a capital racer" called Janette, breeding in and in insured the highest quality racehorse. The reader disagreed and was rather surprised that someone would continue to advance such ideas. "She [Janette] was a capital racer, and is the best prop for this now, for the thousandth time exploded, notion [breeding in and in]. After her, *longo intervallo*, comes a numerous and rickety offspring of diversified incest, which have damned this theory to certain and irretrievable overthrow."[86] That one among the otherwise "rickety offspring" became a great racehorse "almost bid defiance to the laws of nature."[87] Like Combe, the laws of nature were here reproductive and hereditary.

In 1836, "Another Virginia Breeder" responded to his critic and in doing so provided a rather vigorous articulation of the anthropomorphized incest of racehorses. The author first claimed that he did not "advocate" such breeding; rather, he merely stated the fact that in a specific case, that of Janette, breeding in and in had produced a high-quality horse, which could be judged by its racing performance. Rather than being a theory "exploded," breeding in and in had merely become unfashionable, and, as he noted "this thing called *fashion* has a wonderful influence in all the concerns of human life."[88] Indirectly, at least, the prohibition of incest, which in other domains was articulated as transhistorical and foundational (even as it was being actively redefined), was here subject to the whims of fashion. "Another Virginia Breeder" then moved into a discussion of incestuous breeding that sounded awfully similar to some theologians and jurists.

> I wish that some knowing and *experienced* gentleman (I am sick of theories) would have the goodness to tell us how *near akin* we may vouchsafe (without committing "incest," or being in danger of having "a rickety and diversified offspring") to breed the blood horse. Shall we be excluded from the lineal line of descent, and confined to the collateral?—or shall we, in these very refined days, be excluded from both? I have, on a former occasion, shown that old Diomed and Castianira (who, between them, produced Sir Archy [the horse that "almost bid defiance to the laws of nature"]) were very nearly related in point of blood. I now add the famous Virginia bred horse HENRY, now of New York, whose mother was his aunt—both his sire and dam being got by old Diomed. But now, I suppose, it would be considered highly inexpedient, if not savouring of "incest," to permit two such near relations to cohabit! Better, far better, it is thought, to seek for some *remote foreign crosses!* The cry is—"*We have already too much of the Diomed stock.*" I understand all this perfectly, and so will the public in due season.[89]

"Another Virginia Breeder" was clearly referring to more than horse breeding here, especially in his concern with purity of stock and foreign crosses. Here he sounded like the wool grower above as well as proslavery partisans in the southern press. But he also imported the discourse of incest—near kin, lineal and collateral lines, expediency (recall Domesticus's incendiary remarks on the incest prohibition), near relations, cohabitation—into the world of domesticated animals. As incest was more frequently deployed in reproductive terms, the distinction between humans and animals was collapsing. Hereditary science and the science of animal breeding focused on the minimal conditions by which future population health could be secured. The emergence of the reproductive incest prohibition subjected humans to the disciplinary and epistemological regimes of the animal world.

In his emphasis on "foreign crosses," "Another Virginia Breeder" gestured at a well-known conflation that animated a number of texts on heredity and intermarriage, that of hybridity, or amalgamation, and incest. The relationship was metonymic, in that desire slipped along a chain of contiguous signifiers in a process of continual deferral. We might see these two fundamental transgressions of the nineteenth century as ways of articulating desire through prohibition. While endogamy and exogamy may seem radically opposed, they were linked by their frequent contiguity. If the desire of the liberal subject was to be satisfied, these two prohibitions made it possible both to govern the subject at the level of the reproductive body and sustain the continued deferral of desire.[90] To take but one example, Robert Newman, in a report for a committee convened in New York state to study the effects of consanguineous reproduction, moved to hybridity and immigration almost immediately. "Other investigators have not given sufficient attention to the effect of hybridity, or the commingling of different types, or distinct races, which nature seems to have determined upon, as a distinct governing law, through all her kingdoms. Again, many have mistaken changes incidental to emigration, or acclimation, for those occurring as the results of consanguineous marriage."[91] From incest to hybridity to geographic mobility (implicitly understood in a vein similar to Louis Agassiz), one slips metonymically along.[92]

Yet if hybridity was a concern for Newman, it was a strange, and often contradictory term, in the racial science of the day. Hybridity was often conflated with amalgamation and, later, miscegenation, but where both of those, with few exceptions, were transgressive and threats to the racial order (or at least conceived of as such; as we are well aware, they were also central to the sexual economy of the plantation), hybridity was flexible, a threat but also the potential strength of the nation. The hybrid was sterile and vigorous, normative and transgressive. This was clear in Samuel R. Wells's treatise *Wedlock; or, the Right Relations of the Sexes.* Wells had joined with the Fowlers in 1843 when he married Lorenzo and Orson's sister, Charlotte. Having had prior medical ambitions, Wells gave them up to pursue phrenology. Perhaps even more so than either of the Fowlers, Wells was responsible for the enormous publishing operation, since he recognized not only the scientific and reform impulses of phrenology, but also its commercial potential. By the time his book was published, however, Wells had separated from Orson Fowler, after a series of setbacks in the 1860s.[93] Like the Fowlers, Combe, Noah Webster, and various animal breeders before him, Wells opposed incest (in this case, specifically cousin marriage) on physiological grounds. However, unlike Orson Fowler, who posited the mathematical certainty of his calculus of kinship, Wells saw the problem in national terms, as he introduced a peculiarly America instability. "The evil effects of consanguineous marriages seem to be more strikingly manifested here than in Europe," Wells argued, "probably because we, as a people, are less evenly balanced in organization and character than our European congeners, and therefore more liable than they to transmit excesses or deficiencies disastrous in their results upon the bodies and the minds of offspring."[94] "Our statistics show, beyond all possibility of doubt," Wells wrote, "that the marriage of cousins is not here, as a rule, permissible on physiological grounds."[95] While Wells discouraged cousin marriage and incestuous reproduction, it was an acute problem in the United States, where the population was unbalanced and disorganized.

Wells's qualification of the prohibition in national terms—where European nations were associated with ethnic purity, the United States was problematically heterogeneous—reflected the divided opinions on incestuous reproduction on both continents. Wells acknowledged this in his turn to the authority of "European physiologists," who were admittedly "divided on this question." Symptomatic of this division, Wells cited the work of Julius Henry Steinau of the Royal Medical College in London, whose *A Pathological and Philosophical Essay on Hereditary Diseases*, published in 1843, contradicted Wells at nearly every turn. Steinau saw no correlation between Leviticus and contemporary physiological laws, was not opposed to cousin marriage, and more generally, argued against the association of hereditary degeneration and incestuous reproduction. Countering the assertion that the text was a divine revelation of physiological laws, Steinau rejected the assertion "that there is a divine command that near relations should not intermarry, to prevent diseases which prevail in a family from becoming strongly and for a long time established; and to cause that the race may be renewed, as it were, by members of different families intermarrying," for lack of scientific evidence.[96] If some physiological texts colonized Leviticus, Steinau simply discounted it—there was no relation between the moral strictures of Leviticus and reproductive sex.

In an appendix addressing the relationship between incestuous inter-marriage and hereditary descent, Steinau further argued against the degen-erative effects of incestuous reproduction. While acknowledging that "it is very certain that there exists in all an universal horror of marriage within a few of the nearest degrees," Steinau averred that this arose from theological and moral concerns, and that where physiology was concerned there was no evidence that such a universal horror was justified.[97] Steinau argued, contra Combe, that the relationship between the animal world and the human world was of only so much help in determining the extent of inbreeding degeneration. In fact, Steinau's turn toward the animal world, like the evidence offered by "Another Virginia Breeder" apropos race horses, proved that breeding with near relations actually tended toward healthier offspring. "The fact that some justly-valued and superior varieties of animals have been long preserved in well-merited estimation, though confined to a very few individuals," wrote Steinau, "seems to be conclusive against the necessarily deteriorating influence of close breeding."[98] Indeed, Steinau turned toward the "mongrel" as a "practical demonstration of the almost invariable degeneracy which results from the careless, inattentive deviation from this principle."[99] In the comparison between incest, pre-sumably imagined as racially bounded, and interracial sex, incest was pre-ferred, in both the animal and the human world.

Here, if to different ends, Wells and Steinau concurred on the problem of what, in the nineteenth century was often called amalgamation.[100] And in that concurrence they found themselves in the middle of a discourse of at least a century on hybridity, marked by a metonymic slippage between incest and miscegenation. Steinau's racial logic of incest, in which the purity of race could be maintained through intermarriage with near relations, was common in hereditarian discourse as well as among southern partisans of slavery. Writing in *DeBow's Review* in 1861, a proslavery writer argued that while incest and interracial sex were both to be condemned, a certain amount of endogamous intermarriage, within racial bounds, was necessary to improve the race. "We dislike all crossings of blood. Symmetry of form and character is only produced by breeding in-and-in. . . . The children of first cousins are always superior to their parents. Nature abhors incestuous marriages, but dictates the intermarriage of cousins."[101] Like Steinau, this author preferred a certain degree of endogamous reproduction for the maintenance of racial boundaries while simultaneously decrying incest and interracial sex. He also played on the ambiguous status of cousin marriage, desirable in the fantasmatic production of racial purity but also increasingly suspect in terms of hereditary degeneration. Nonetheless, the politics of proslavery dictated such a stance, as did the burgeoning racial science of the day, a field in which Steinau and other writers on heredity and incest trafficked.

Hybridity, like incest, was an ambivalent, conflicted category. Sources of both degeneration and vigor, depending on the author, incest and hybridity were at the center of hereditarian discourse as well as the reproductive incest prohibition. The racial dynamics and empiricism of the hereditary discourse reached their apogee in 1859, when S. M. Bemiss, a physician working in Louisville, Kentucky, compiled the most far-reaching statistical survey of incestuous offspring in the nineteenth century. Entitled "Report on the Influence of Marriages of Consanguinity upon Offspring," Bemiss's statistical compilation was published in *The Transactions of the American Medical Association*, hardly a bastion of phrenology. Bemiss was attempting to answer the question: "Is the offspring of marriages of consanguinity equal physically to the offspring of parents not connected by ties of blood—both classes being supposed to be similarly circumstanced in respect to all other causes affecting the integrity of their issue?"[102] Consanguinity and affinity were definitively severed from each other in this question, with incest taking on specifically reproductive connotations. After observing 873 marriages of consanguinity, Bemiss determined that there were clearly higher rates of degeneration among the offspring of incestuous marriages. It was, as one scholar wrote in 1912, "the largest single piece of direct statistical work on the subject. Unfortunately, however, his statistics have a strong, if unintentional, bias which seriously affects their value."[103] Regardless of its flaws or value, the import of Bemiss's statistical compilation lies not in its scope—it was symptomatic of the new positivism that inhered in the discourse of incestuous reproduction, and, more so than nearly any other text of the period, it figured the complicated relationship between race, incest, and reproduction.

Bemiss determined that incestuous reproduction was fairly widespread and thus, unlike others either at the time or since, did not (at least initially) ascribe incest to any particular social group.[104] "The neglect to accumulate statistical testimony as to the results of family intermarriage could not have proceeded from paucity of material," Bemiss wrote, "since, not only do the pages of history teem with instances of such marriage, but they are found in almost every social circle, and should receive the earnest scrutiny of physiologists."[105] Despite this relatively large sample size, Bemiss was cautious in his conclusions, as "the average fecundity and vital statistics of marriage in the United States" were unknown.[106] Moreover, Bemiss was cautious about deriving conclusions from maligned populations, particularly the practice of working backward from those individuals with hereditary defects to their parents. Writing of the doctors who supplied much of the information for his study, Bemiss remarked that "it is natural for contributors to overlook many of the more fortunate results of family intermarriage, and furnish those followed by defective offspring or sterility."[107] Nonetheless, the methodological assumptions, beginning with the maligned and working backward, inscribed conclusions in the study that would have been hard to obviate. The conclusion that incestuous reproduction led to inferior offspring was almost guaranteed by such a method.

As with most other accounts of incestuous reproduction, Bemiss's was weighted toward cousin marriage, which was morally ambiguous rather than clearly prohibited (like incest within the nuclear family), and thus this weighting made it easier to collect data. Cousin marriage, which included marriages up to the third degree, made up the vast majority (763 of 873 marriages, 630 of them being first cousins) of cases. Nonetheless, Bemiss did include other types of incest, including those within the nuclear family—there were ten cases of parent-child, twelve cases of sibling, and sixty-one cases of descendants of the same blood relations, which generally meant uncle-niece and aunt-nephew. In terms of tracking the hereditary effects of incest, however, Bemiss did not distinguish between these various incests. Indeed, in that sense the hereditarian discourse on incestuous reproduction, of which Bemiss's study was a central piece, contributed to the production of an abstract category of incest—unlike the theological and juridical discourses, which considered the differences between the nuclear family and more extended kin, the reproductive imperative flattened out these distinctions: consanguinity was consanguinity, from a hereditary standpoint. Moreover, by privileging consanguinity, affinity was not simply displaced; it was, at least in the hereditary domain, excised altogether, in a manner similar to what took place in phrenology.

Drawing on the reigning hereditary science of the day, Bemiss argued that the main reason for discouraging incestuous union was the possibility of a recessive, malignant trait appearing in the offspring of an incestuous union. "It will be perceived that parental infirmities are entailed with great certainty upon the offspring, and this . . . constitutes the strongest argument against the intermarriage of relatives; the fact that family peculiarities, tendencies, and infirmities, either of mind or body, which may be so slight on the part of the parents as to remain latent, become so exaggerated by this 'intensifying' of the same blood, that they are in the child prominent and ruinous defects."[108] By including all these illnesses under the heading "Marriages of Consanguinity," Bemiss, whether intentionally or not, conferred an incestuous etiology on a plethora of illnesses, thus making the regulation of marriage and reproduction central to the management of population.

While the diseases and defects were legion, Bemiss, like most public health advocates of the period, was primarily concerned with those maladies that had produced their own asylums, namely "deaf-dumbness, blindness, idiocy and insanity."[109] In these three categories, Bemiss determined that incest was the cause of over 10 percent of deaf-dumbness, over 5 percent of blindness, and nearly 15 percent of idiocy.[110] All of this led Bemiss to the conclusion "that multiplication of the same blood by in-and-in marrying does incontestably lead in the aggregate to the physical and mental depravation of the offspring."[111]

Bemiss had compiled the largest statistical survey of incestuous reproduction of the nineteenth century. It provided the reproductive incest prohibition with the veneer of scientific objectivity, as it seemed both to avoid the moral and social ambiguities of theology and law while providing a large sample as evidence to settle the hereditarian debates among physiologists and animal breeders. Its statistical bent helped achieve this. Of course, statistical surveys of incest could be put to nearly any use. Statistics were invoked, particularly in regard to incest, to prove myriad assumptions about moral decay and degenerative influences. One author, writing in the *Christian Register*, invoked the higher rates of insanity in Protestant nations to prove that Catholic prohibitions of intermarriage safeguarded the mental health of nations under Catholic influence. To take the extremes, in Connecticut the statistics purported to show that one in 425 persons were insane, while in Spain one in 7,181 were deemed insane. Working from the commonly held assumption that incestuous reproduction produced insanity, the conclusion was that Catholic prohibitions, which included cousins,

Table 1. S. M. Bemiss's Statistical Compilation of Illnesses
in Offspring of Consanguine and Nonrelated Marriages

Marriages of Consanguinity	Instances	Marriages of Nonrelated	Instances
Consumption	108	Consumption	6
Scrofulous Manifestations	55	Scrofulous Manifestations	2
Convulsions	44	Convulsions	6
Epilepsy	10	Epilepsy	0
Hydrocephalus	21	Hydrocephalus	1
Brain Affections	15	Brain Affections	3
Scarlet Fever	30	Scarlet Fever	4
Fever	22	Fever	10
Typhoid Fever	8	Typhoid Fever	0
Measles	1	Measles	2
"Acute Inflammatory Attacks"	6	"Acute Inflammatory Attacks"	8
Dysentery	14	Dysentery	2
Diarrhea	6	Diarrhea	3
Croup	8	Croup	2
Whooping Cough	4	Whooping Cough	1
"Asthma"	0	"Asthma"	2
Psoas Abscess	0	Psoas Abscess	1
"Exanthemata"	0	"Exanthemata"	6
Accidental	25	Accidental	2
Pneumonia	4	Pneumonia	2
Stillborn	37	Stillborn	6
Cholera Infantum	15		
Marasmus	12		
Dentition	6		
Anæmia	6		
Cyanosis	3		
Apoplexy	3		
Erysipelas	4		
Inanition	4		
Imperfect Development	1		
"Insanity"	3		

Source: S. M. Bemiss, "Report on the Influence of Marriages of Consanguinity upon Offspring," *Transactions of the American Medical Association* 11, no. 2 (1858), 329.

were more beneficent, in terms of population health, than the Protestant variety.[112]

Yet, in a speech delivered before the Louisville Medical Club prior to publication of his report, Bemiss offered a more speculative analysis that tied incest to the contours of national development. The neutral language of scientific objectivity was replaced with passionate claims about the constitutional vigor of Americans. Westward expansion, incest, and immigration were tied together into one problematic, purifying national project. Early communities in "the West . . . were separated from each other and from the older States, by miles of dangerous wilderness. It was natural that each community should be composed in a great degree of blood relations. . . . When in their new homes, a scarcity of marriageable material would often render unions between relations expedient, and afterward, these covenants, arising at first from necessity, became a habit, often convenient in some respects, since it preserved estates within the family circle."[113] As it was for southern planters, incest—or at least endogamy—was important to westerners for the consolidation of property into tightly knit kin groups that could claim clearly marked racial boundaries.

The small populations and geographical seclusion that led to frequent incest would presumably have lead to higher rates of hereditary degeneration, and such might have been the case, Bemiss claimed, for isolated populations in "the valleys of the Alps" and "in this country, the Jews." Bemiss, unlike either Samuel Wells or Julius Steinau, associated ethnic purity with a greater likelihood for degenerative incestuous reproduction. Yet miraculously, such was not the case in the West. There, "these pioneers were a hardy, robust people, living much in the open air, and undergoing vigorous exercise; having for their aliment wild game and the fresh products of a genial soil, and not addicted to any habits calculated to impair the integrity of their well-endowed constitutions. We would naturally expect conditions of life so favorable to the sound development of the bodily organism to overrule all counteracting influences."[114] And so, for Bemiss, they did. Despite his claims a year later, there was an antidote to incestuous reproduction—the sanguine environs of the West. The geographical blessings of the ever-expanding United States ameliorated the potentially degenerative effects of incest. If reproduction offered a new universalism for the incest prohibition, the United States, as a state of exception, could transcend the banality of the universal.[115]

If geography was one ameliorative, the constitution of the people was the other. Who were these intrepid, incestuous, robust pioneers of whom

Bemiss spoke? They were Americans, of course, whose, "extraordinary activity and energy" were "due to the composite nature of their blood."[116] The absence of racial purity in the United States, that is, "the ingrafting of nations differing in constitution and temperament from each other," produced "the most vigorous people."[117] Hybridity, that is, ethnic and national intermarriage and sex, produced a vigorous people, who flouted the hereditary rules of incest. This was, however, hybridity within limits. "I do not look upon mulattoes as hybrids," Bemiss wrote, "but think they exhibit less of vigor and vital force than are found in crosses where there is less contrast."[118] The racial characteristic of the nation—hybrid whiteness—in its "ingrafting of nations," worked against the usually degenerative effects of incest.

Bemiss mediated hybridity effectively—hybrid whiteness, as a national essence, tapped into the celebrations of hybridity by late eighteenth-century writers like Thomas Paine and J. Hector St. John de Crevecoeur but foreclosed the dangerous hybridity that crossed the race line. National or ethnic hybridity was central to the national imperial project of manifest destiny while racial hybridity was articulated as a threat to that project. Indeed, hybrid whiteness combined with the purifying environs of North America—all of which, many Americans imagined, would ultimately be encompassed by the United States—made the U.S. an incest nation. While others envisioned incest as symptomatic of moral decay, Bemiss saw it as a mark of transcendence. Indeed, the only comparisons to these pioneers that Bemiss could conjure were biblical—the children of Adam, Abraham, and Isaac. Thus U.S. imperialism was situated in sacred time, where incest was not only necessary but where the vigorous, hybrid whiteness of those people who engaged in it produced humanity.

The Normalization of the Erotic Family

One of the central tropes in the history of sexuality between the eighteenth and the twentieth centuries in the "West" is the severing of sex and reproduction. Indeed, some have maintained that it was precisely this decoupling that allowed for the production of myriad sexual identities in the late nineteenth and early twentieth centuries.[119] While such a trope has had a profound impact, in many ways deserved, on the history of sexuality, it also tends toward closing down avenues of investigation. In particular, the eroti-cization of the bourgeois family has been left relatively unexamined in favor of the proliferation of new sexual identities outside the family. Indeed, the trope's liberatory logic has sometimes tended toward an ignorance of the newly subjecting sexual positions that were created as part of such a history.

Amativeness split sexual desire into two component parts. The first, as we have seen, was reproductive and hereditary. The second was the erotic family. Primarily figured as an immanent danger to the bourgeois senti-mental family, it was what novelists, theologians, and jurists had worked to contain by reconfiguring the incest prohibition to facilitate and regulate the liberal subject. Phrenologists took a different tack. Rather than treating it as an incestuous danger, phrenologists, as we have seen, confined incest to reproduction and heredity. In doing so, they severed the erotic family from incest and made this family the regulative condition of amativeness and the sexual, liberal subject. Indeed, normal psychic development was condi-tioned by the cultivation of familial eroticism, especially that between par-ents and children. By emphasizing the importance of amativeness and the necessity of intrafamilial eroticism, phrenology both produced the sexual subject and made the eroticized family, but not incest, one of its conditions.

If we recall Thomas Low Nichols's antimasturbation admonition that unrestrained amativeness could be controlled by cultivating "the passion of love" between parents and children, in its "rudimentary development," we might think of him as encouraging incest to stop masturbation. Yet, Nichols would not have considered this incest. Indeed, the manifestation of intra-familial desire worked to curb other sexual abuses, primarily masturbation, but also sodomy and bestiality. Nichols, like others at midcentury, under-stood incest exclusively in terms of reproductive sex. "Incest, alas, is so common among the crowded populations of the very ignorant and very poor, that it is seldom punished. The marriages of near relations are also far too frequent; for there can be no doubt of their bad effect upon the bodily and mental organization of their offspring. In a true society there would be no marriages of interest or consanguinity. The law of love is like that of magnetism—the attraction of opposites."[120] The true society was one governed by the incest prohibition of natural law, thus gesturing toward the sociality derived from the incest prohibition and secured through the language of hereditary degeneration. Yet, just as others would associate incest with enslaved Africans or the indigenous populations of remote islands like Hawaii in order to exclude them from liberal modernity,

Nichols did the same with the "crowded populations," which in 1854 would have included the large population of Irish immigrants.

Nichols was not alone in such a view. Orson Fowler was also concerned with the production and regulation of sexual desire, especially in the family, which is where it would be normalized. His monumental 1859 work *The Family*, which collected and recycled material published in various forms over the previous decades, works well as a summary of his ideas. And in this work intrafamilial desire was central to the ordered and moral functioning of the family.

In a section entitled "Fathers and Daughters Loving Each Other," Fowler tells the story of a pair of women who came to see him professionally. "Finding Amativeness large, and all the indices of sexuality unusually apparent," Fowler wrote, "I described her as passionately fond of her father, and if married, of her husband."[121] His subject was astonished with the precision of his reading and confirmed his hypothesis. "In one part of your description you were singularly felicitous—my devotion to my father. For I do not believe daughter ever lived that loved father as I love mine. And always have. Nor would anything have tempted me to leave him, but that I love my husband still more. And now my whole soul is perfectly wrapped up in devoted affection for both."[122] While this may appear as yet another variation on domesticity and sentimentalism, the indicator of the woman's love for her father unveils the erotic content of such sentiments. Fowler determined that the woman was "passionately fond of her father" based on an observation and analysis of "amativeness" and other markers of sexuality. And the woman's response was that Fowler was indeed correct in his assumption about her devotion to her father and that, furthermore, her love, her sexual love, was caught in a hopeless bind between two objects of desire—her father and her husband. Whereas Freud would have understood this as an appropriate and complicated transfer of love from father to husband, the pre-Freudian logic of phrenology understood the husband as nothing more than a simple substitution. For Freud, this transference would have entailed complex psychic consequences, articulated beneath the veil of the unconscious. Phrenology's adherence to reading the psychological on the surface of the body did not allow for such complexities. Amativeness was amativeness, and the husband was simply a substitute for the original object of the woman's desire, her father. If psychoanalysis would plumb the depths of the unconscious to find the sexual etiology of the neuroses, phrenology found sexual desire at the root of interiority by measuring the surface of the skull.

Moreover, the attainment of heterosexuality, particularly for women, was one that was a debilitating and complex process that, for Freud, was brought on by the castration complex. As the pre-Oedipal child was bisexual, assumed everyone possessed the phallus, and directed its desire almost wholly toward the mother, the resolution of the Oedipus and castration complexes was of great significance and complexity. Not only would the girl, according to Freud, have to displace the phallic organization of her libido from the clitoris to the vagina, she would also have to renounce the mother as her love-object and replace her with the father. This was brought on by the castration complex, in which the girl realized that she did not have the phallus. From this followed the Oedipus complex and ended the pre-Oedipal bisexuality, replacing it with femininity.[123] Freud's work here, as Juliet Mitchell and others have noted, is a compelling description of the accession to gender identity in a patriarchal culture.[124] The complexity and crisis of this psychic account is nowhere to be found in phrenology. While psychoanalysis has heteronormative aspects to it, the construction of heterosexuality is complex, and the resolution of the Oedipal crisis by no means implies a heterosexual result.[125] Phrenology's entire sexual apparatus was predicated on an unproblematic psychic and physical heterosexuality. Amativeness existed, according to phrenology, in order to ensure reproduction, even though it could not be reduced to reproduction. Same-sex relations, like masturbation, could be conceived of only as perversions, and thus threats to the health of the organism (both individual and collective). The cultivation of the erotic family conditioned amativeness and the subjects thereof to find satisfaction of their desire in objects of the opposite sex. The heteronormative family produced heteronormative sexual subjects.

The scene described above, between Fowler and his female patient/client, would seem to imply that the supposedly innocent devotion of a daughter to her father was in fact an example of incestuous sexuality.[126] Yet, Fowler found the situation between father and daughter to be ideal, and, like many other phrenologists and physiologists, he was opposed to incest. This is a moment where it is imperative to read incest in relation to and as a product of the incest prohibition. As these writers narrowed the domain of incest to the world of reproduction, the erotics of the sentimental family emerged from their subterranean world. Intrafamilial desire was neither subversive nor transgressive in this telling: it was ideal and indeed critical to normal amative and psychic development.

For Fowler and practical phrenologists like him, it was not enough simply to acknowledge the erotic content of the domestic, familial scene; amativeness, as one of the faculties of the mind, needed to be exercised, lest it die off. "So the love element, unexercised, must die out of mere inanition. Action is a law of organism, of nature. And this love faculty being born in us, and forming an integral part and parcel of us, must either be exercised, or starve. And a practical unsexing ensue."[127] The desire that theologians had worked to control through the reification of laws of incest was the same one on which Fowler encouraged fathers and daughters to act. While amativeness led, in later life, to sexual intercourse and reproduction, its exercise in childhood and adolescence was that of chaste desire without intercourse.

Spurzheim, less inclined to sensationalism than Fowler, nonetheless also spoke of the familial nature of amativeness. "Fathers are commonly more attached to daughters, than to sons, and mothers are often prepossessed in favor of their sons. . . . The attraction of the sexes towards each other is involuntary, and society improves, if both sexes meet."[128] Spurzheim, writing on amativeness, easily moved from the relationship between parents and children to the general relations between the sexes: all were structured according to a heterosexual logic. Moreover, amativeness produced the subject and, in a sense, obviated the autonomy of the subject. The erotic family was necessary to regulate that involuntary characteristic lest it exceed social and familial limits. The liberal subject, a subject of desire, was always already heterosexual if the conditioning of the erotic family was effective.

The power of this argument inhered in the fact that while it was widely recognized that the bourgeois family was a site of potentially transgressive eroticism, phrenologists acknowledged such eroticism and encouraged its proliferation, within limits. Fowler understood the desire for a husband to be a mere displacement of the love for one's father:

> Amativeness has its express object. And that object is the opposite sex. And nothing else. Of course every female in exercising it must love some *masculine*. And all masculines some feminine. And what masculine can a daughter love as appropriately as her *father*? Between them there is hardly a possibility of its wrong exercise. She needs someone to love all along from infancy, through childhood

and womanhood, down to her grave. Her father should be her first love—should awaken and nurture this love element till old enough to be transferred to a husband. Nor will any girl who loves and is beloved by her father elope, or form a premature attachment, or indiscreet marriage.[129]

The necessity of acting on heterosexual intrafamilial erotic desire was manifest. Indeed, where Combe was loathe to deal with amative excess, Fowler claimed it was nearly impossible for love between father and daughter to follow the wrong path. Of course, Fowler's own body of work suggested otherwise. As Christopher Castiglia has argued, the domestic propensities, which included amativeness, were the most likely to be perverted. "Perversion begins with desire," Castiglia writes, "which can produce the heaven of normative domesticity, or the hell of promiscuous appetites."[130] The erotic family was the path to the heavenly state of domesticity. It is only in the context of the erotic family as a regulatory institution for amativeness that Fowler could have understood the exercise of amativeness as "a right exercise of the sexuality, which always, and in the very nature of things, improves."[131]

This was not simply a relation between father and daughter: mothers and sons were also supposed to recognize and follow their amative impulses toward one another. Amativeness, and phrenology in general, as we have seen, anticipated psychoanalysis in that it displaced individual autonomy precisely in the production of the liberal sexual subject. One was constituted by the development of individual faculties, or propensities, and these directed the life of the individual.[132] The ideological projections of domesticity, the pure, passionless mother and the masculine son whose passions were curbed by his mother, were at the forefront of this amative relation. "Her love to him is naturally pure and deep. Inexpressibly so. What true mother can depict the intensity of her love for her son? And his being loved by a female naturally calls out his love in response. And this enhances his manliness of body, of mind. Nor can any boy become a fully developed man without love for his mother, or some female who fills her place."[133] The excessive quality of the love seems to exceed the bounds of the passionless mother, and as it was a love derived from amativeness, the sexual content, which could be disavowed in other modes of domestic literature, was here unavoidable.

As Nancy Cott has persuasively argued, monogamous heterosexual marriage has been one of the cornerstones of political and public culture in the United States. It was inscribed in the republican political theory of the founders and worked through as the hegemonic form of familial relations in confrontations between the federal government and various groups in the nineteenth century, such as Indians, the enslaved and then freed people, and Mormons. Marriage set the terms for the heteronormative monogamous socialization carried out in familial relations.[134] However, such monogamous heteronormative relations, codified in marriage, originated, according to Fowler and the phrenologists, in the parent-child relation. "Hence, show me the son who loves or provides for mother, and I will show you the husband who loves and provides for wife and children. This sign is infallible. It has its cause, namely, loving mother develops that sexuality from which love of wife emanates."[135]

This was not, however, a simple liberatory act. Intrafamilial desire was articulated as part of a mid-nineteenth-century disciplinary apparatus wrapped up in love.[136] Fowler's effusive praise of intrafamilial desire through the exercise of amativeness was in the service of virtuous citizenship. As vices corrupted the individual so too was the republic corrupted. A healthy dose of amativeness between parents and children would work to purify the child and, by proxy, the nation.

> No mother ought ever to breathe one word of censure or even blame to her son. Nor any male to female. Nor female to male. This is not the way, the means, by which the sexes should influence each other. That way is by *love only*. Pure, simple, gushing love. This alone begets love in return. And this love gives you that power you desire, require. . . . I appeal whether the feelings between mothers and sons should not be on a plane infinitely above chastisement, or even chiding. Affection and chastisement are incompatible with, and fatal to, each other. Natural antagonisms. Only affection can ever beget affection. And thus secure obedience.[137]

Such relations inscribed discipline within the effusion of intrafamilial desire. Amativeness, in the conjugal relation, bred reproduction. In the filial relation, it bred obedience and discipline.[138] Such love and sexuality, rooting heterosexuality in the parent-child relation, held an ambivalent relationship to the radical critiques of marriage and sexuality prominent in the mid-nineteenth century. Whereas John Humphrey Noyes and the Oneida community advocated complex marriage, the Mormons advocated polygamy; the free love movement offered myriad critiques of marriage and monogamy; phrenology saw sexuality as a positive, because natural, characteristic but one necessarily subjugated to bourgeois domesticity. Fowler, when asking "whether promiscuity is Nature's law, and exclusiveness sheer prudery," claimed that "Nature has answered, '*One* love, incomparably.'"[139] And of course, nature spoke through the phrenological faculties of mind, and in particular amativeness.

Fowler was not content to settle on amativeness as narrowly consigned to the private world of domestic relations. Instead, the relationship between amativeness and conjugality was at the core of progress. In a series of articles published in the *American Phrenological Journal* in 1852, Fowler elaborated on the natural progress of mankind, a progress that was above all rooted in amativeness, or sexual desire. Fowler addressed the more quotidian and worldly pursuits, particularly the development of acquisitiveness, which manifested itself in the sixteenth century. In part as an antidote to sex, war, and bacchanalian pleasure, which had been the ruling passions of the previous two thousand years, but also as a marker of economic progress, acquisitiveness would be a foundation of future progress.[140] But he always returned to amativeness, for in Fowler's vision of progress, more than anything else, the world needed to be populated. In this Fowler theorized an imperial amativeness that recalls S. M. Bemiss's hybrid white, incestuously imperial American pioneers. Yet here, for amativeness to achieve its imperial aims, the erotic family needed to be disciplining it in every iteration.

The centrality of amativeness was set in the context of both biblical and cosmological visions. "The first command of God to man was, 'MULTIPLY and replenish the earth'—and this command was effectually written in the inner constitution of man. And the race obeyed this command. History, both sacred and profane, attests that the one great object of man, for the first two or three thousand years of human existence, was PROPAGATION."[141] Fowler goes on to give biblical examples, particularly those, such as Tamar, Lot, Abraham and Sarah, Jacob, and others who presented the most problematic figures in the Old Testament to those theologians attempting to stabilize the biblical injunction against incestuous marriages. But despite the sources from antiquity, or Fowler's invocation of acquisitiveness as a modern faculty, amativeness, that is sexual desire and its reproductive end, was to occupy the central place in progress well into the future. If, in other discourses, it was ostensibly the market that animated liberal desire, here sexual desire always preceded market desire.

After opening the entire series of articles with a discussion of astronomical and geological progress, thus situating man within larger natural forces, Fowler moved on to man. "But not to dwell on the application of this law to the lower forms of nature and of life, let us proceed at once to apply it to man—nature's great type—fully assured that whatever is true of man is equally true of universal nature, and also that whatever is true of nature, as a whole, is more significantly true of man."[142] Much like his articulations of hereditary descent and laws of kinship, where there was an algebraic certainty to kinship that would be disturbed by incest, Fowler begins his discussion of human progress with the "numerical." If wars and pestilence ceased, and in Fowler's vision they would fall by the wayside against the forward current of progress, then amativeness would be free to populate the earth until it was fully covered by humans. By the year 2033, Fowler estimated, the population of the earth would be over 583 billion. This would leave little time for anything but sexual intercourse and reproduction. For Fowler, it was certain "that this progressive law will go on steadily but effectually to fill the earth *completely full* of human beings, just as full as can live comfortably."[143] This was all a result of amativeness, and in the specific American case, was thus rendered within the context of the imperialism of westward expansion. "Judge from the way we are peopling California and Oregon," Fowler wrote, "as well as filling up our own borders, from Maine to Texas, and from the Atlantic to the Rocky Mountains."[144] Implicit in such a statement, tying sexuality to imperial expansion was that amativeness, as a progressive faculty, was inscribed in whiteness.

In such a utopian, progressive vision, sexuality dictated imperial expansion and the hope of a beneficent future. In its cosmological, propagative, and imperial vision, Fowler's text situated the United States and sexual desire in what Walter Benjamin has called "homogenous time." As Benjamin put it, "the concept of the historical progress of mankind cannot be sundered from the concept of its progression through a homogenous, empty time."[145] Fowler, in attributing to amativeness an essential quality, projected that as the one, unchanging logic of human history. Fowler had little to offer beyond the complete population of the world. But, returning to the small-scale discussions of amativeness that animated most of Fowler's writings, proper sexuality was inscribed within parent-child relations.

The progress of the race then, already inscribed in an imperial vision, had its origins in the domestic sphere.[146] Intrafamilial eroticism, encouraged by phrenologists and physiologists as they severed it from incest, narrowly understood by midcentury as reproductive sex only, thus underwrote national politics and the progress of race.

The emergence of a reproductive incest prohibition was one of the most radical transformations in the antebellum articulations of the prohibition. The moral and social concerns of law, theology, and fiction were largely absent from the reproductive discourse. Or, at least superficially absent. Incest became a problem of bodily and mental health, and thus the liberal subject was governed at the level of reproductive life. However, the eroticism of the sentimental family remained, and phrenologists encouraged the proliferation of desire between parents and children. As incest was recategorized, the eroticism of the sentimental, bourgeois family was normalized. As phrenologists and physiologists constructed a reproductive incest prohibition, they blurred the line between the human and the animal and began to speak much more explicitly of race and incest, particularly in the slippage between amalgamation and incest. Yet, phrenology and physiology were not the only domains in which incest was linked to the production of race. Incest figured prominently in the discourse of slavery, and it was there that race was in the nexus of incest and the circulation of bodies. But rather than to the liberal circulation of sociality, the discourse of slavery linked incest to the circulation of persons as commodities through chattel slavery. In the crucible of slavery and race, incest was increasingly racialized in a manner that protected the liberal subject from the danger of incest that was constantly haunting familial, sexual, and marital relations.

Chapter 5

Slavery

In the 1860 novel *Adela, the Octoroon*, H. L. Hosmer, an antislavery minister and supporter of colonization, painted a picture of the depravity of plantation life based in the incestuous actions of slaveholders. When George Tidbald, a southern patriarch and congressman, returned to his plantation from Washington, D.C., he found one of his slaves on her deathbed. Crissy, the slave, was also Tidbald's daughter, his lover, and the mother of his child. Disavowing this vexed web of relations, Tidbald assumed that it was the recent birth of a child and the physical difficulties of nursing that were at the root of Crissy's illness. He was correct in assuming that the child bore the etiology of the illness, even if it had little to do with the physical demands of childbirth and nursing. "What makes you feel so bad," Tidbald inquired, "when I speak to you about him?"[1] Tidbald, Crissy said, knew very well what upset her so and then she burst into tears.

As Tidbald walked back to the plantation house, he reflected on Crissy's situation and what she may have meant before she began to cry. "Can it be that Criss knows her origin? Has anyone informed her, and if so, does that knowledge cause this grief? Why should it? She is a slave, and there is nothing uncommon or at war with the privileges of the institution in this matter. If she does even, what of it? Why need I care, where my will is law?" (308). The affectionate "Criss," rather than Crissy, implied that Tidbald did not necessarily believe his own attempt at distancing their relationship. After Tidbald had left the slave quarters, Crissy was consoled and criticized by another slave, the motherly Aunt Christmas. What Christmas recognized in Crissy's grief was that it was not the incestuous abuse that paralyzed Crissy with melancholia, but rather that ties of family and love could not be recognized across the color line because of her status as a slave. Chastising Crissy for her reluctance to confront Tidbald, Christmas exclaimed, "I's sure I'd tell 'em. I's sure I'd let 'um know dat I knew I was his own chile. He know'd it all de while, de ole rascal" (307). While Crissy was dejected over the absence of expressed familial love, Christmas understood Tidbald's actions for what they were, incestuous abuse. And she demanded that Crissy, whom Tidbald imagined as nothing more than a mute commodity, speak her knowledge of kinship back to her owner father, thus disrupting the natal alienation that sustained the structure of slavery.

While Christmas found the relationship abhorrent, Crissy was more ambivalent, desiring paternal recognition while struggling to deal with the fact that her child was the product of incest. "'Yes, de ole villain!' said Aunt Christmas; 'and if dat was all, dere would be no use ob cryin', but he is de fader ob your chile, and dat's de berry reason dat I'd let 'um know it'" (307). For Christmas there was no utility in crying about incestuous rape, which was endemic to the life of enslaved women. Forcing acknowledgment of paternity, however, could have utility and might have brought advantage to mother or child or both. Crissy agreed, yet her solution was death, which in many ways could be associated with public knowledge of incest. To acknowledge openly her incestuous relation with Tidbald was to dramatize her own social death through literal biological demise.

Crissy did ultimately die, which further substantiated the intimate ties between incest and death. Yet before she died, she, along with Aunt Christmas, confronted Tidbald. Receiving Crissy's call just before her death, Tidbald "came, and as he gazed upon the shrunken features of the poor girl, a look of real concern seemed for a moment, to take possession of his naturally somber visage" (317). As Tidbald looked on the body of his dying daughter, he begged her not to die, or even speak of death. Crissy, for her part, just wanted to look upon her father one last time, but it was Aunt Christmas who could not bear the perversion of this scene, in which the daughter, victim of both slavery and incestuous violation, seemed only to want to reap the approval of her father/master one last time, while the father desired to see his slave/child live through her illness, brought on by the denial of fatherhood twice over. As she forced Crissy to reveal the secret, Christmas rebuked Tidbald just as Crissy finally received the recognition for which she was literally dying for. "My child—my beautiful, my dishonored child . . . all the blessing an erring father can bestow, shall be yours. Would to God I could recall the past and blot out its iniquities" (318). Receiving paternal recognition, at last, Crissy died. Her final words were for her father: "Oh, t'ank you! T'ank you! I'se so happy now" (318). Hosmer was quick to bring out the perverse logic of this deathbed reconciliation. "Her arm relaxed from his shoulder, she fell back heavily upon the pillow, and, with her eyes fixed fondly upon him, the father and seducer, she drew her last breath without a struggle" (318). Content in the knowledge that her seducer had finally acknowledged his status as her father, the struggle was over.

This vignette from Hosmer's novel raises a number of pertinent questions about the relationship between incest and the discourse of slavery. How, exactly, was incest imbricated with the discourse of slavery? How did a concern with incest disrupt dominant understandings of the family, race, sexuality, and slavery? And conversely, how did the incestuous logics of the discourse of slavery underwrite constructions of such categories? How did the confusions of kinship and paternity, in this case the dance of recognition between Crissy and Tidbald, transform sexuality and the family along the lines of incest? How did claims of the enslaved to kinship across color and property lines transform sexual and familial relations? At its base, as illustrated in Crissy's demand for Tidbald's recognition of his paternity and her knowledge of it, kinship became a question of competing epistemologies.

As much as the discourse of slavery transformed incest, this association was also a central part of racial formation in the United States. To put it simply, in the discourse of slavery, incest was aligned with blackness, and the incest prohibition was aligned with whiteness. If theologians, novelists, legal writers, and phrenologists presumed that the (white) liberal subject was constantly threatened by incest, writers on slavery, in particular, white antislavery writers, attempted to align incest with slavery and blackness. Antislavery writers contributed as much to the production of the sentimental affectionate family as anyone else in antebellum America, yet incestuous eroticism was not a feature of that family. It was, however, a feature of the plantation family. The sentimental family and liberal subject were thus cordoned off from blackness and incest. Except that, as with any site of racial formation in the United States, this was never absolute. The plantation was a site of disordered kinship and unbridled sex, and thus the racial order of incest was upset. If racial formation was figured on the ground of incest and the incest prohibition, and thus ordered populations, it was immediately transgressed as well.

The liberal circulation of bodies and things created the conditions for accidental incest, precisely through a kind of natal alienation necessary to the production of the liberal subject. The discourse of slavery treated that circulation at its most extreme—the point at which persons were transformed into commodities, and thus circulated seemingly without a trace of genealogical origins. This type of natal alienation underscored both the structure of slavery as well as abolitionist critiques of its domestic ravages. Yet, despite the foreclosure of access to origins, the enslaved could never be fully commodified. Antebellum slave narratives deployed alternative kinship epistemologies that challenged natal alienation and thus pointed to the incestuous quality of the plantation household. The imbrication of incest and slavery served to highlight the manner in which the incest prohibition and kinship more broadly were and are epistemological. Kinship and incest followed from regimes of knowledge, rather than reflecting prediscursive social relations. The discourse of slavery demonstrated and produced the racial structure of both kinship and incest and, more broadly, the antebellum United States. This imbrication also articulated a different sentimental family, one that, in antislavery writings, could never produce the moral, virtuous citizen of the liberal democracy because it was always subject to rupture by the domestic slave trade and in proslavery paternalism worked simultaneously to structure and mask the sexual violence at the core of slavery.

Taken together, the writings of northern abolitionists, southern proslavery ideologues, and slave narratives produced incest and the competing epistemologies of kinship as the core of both race and slavery in antebellum America. If this seems somewhat far afield from the precincts of the liberal subject, that is simply an illusion. We have traced the production of incest, the prohibition, and the liberal subject across the problems of circulation, public and private, theology, law, and physiology. All have suggested that, in pursuing freedom, the liberal subject was always running up against the threat of incest; and thus a new incest prohibition, commensurate with the dictates of the supposedly autonomous individual, was necessary. The discourse of slavery and incest marked the racial boundary of the liberal subject, as it implicitly consolidated the liberal subject via the exclusion of enslaved kinship and the black subject.

Vernacular Epistemologies of Kinship

The commodity is a mysterious thing, more so when the commodity is an enslaved person, fully ensnared in a system of alienation and exploitation in the capitalist world market. "It is . . . precisely this finished form of the world of commodities—the money form," Marx wrote, "which conceals the social character of private labour and the social relations between the individual workers, by making those relations appear as relations between material objects, instead of revealing them plainly."[2] This act of conceal-ment, which Marx called the fetishism of commodities, was even more acute in slavery. As Walter Johnson puts it, "in the traders' tables, human beings were fully fungible: any slave, anywhere, could be compared to any other, anywhere else. That was commodification: the distant and different translated into money value and resolved into a single scale of relative prices, prices that could be used to make even the most counter-intuitive comparisons—between the body of an old man and a little girl . . . or between the muscular arm of a field hand and the sharp eye of a seamstress, or, as many nineteenth-century critics of slavery noted, between a human being and a mule."[3]

This process, market based and seemingly material, was also, as Ste-phanie Smallwood argues, discursive, part of the order of knowledge. "Commodification's power resides in language, in discursive forms (led-gers, bills of sale) carefully crafted to define and imagine things in the terms that best facilitate their exchange and circulation."[4] The fetishism of the slave both avows and disavows natality.[5] The reproduction that structured North American slavery inhered in the slave and was repre-sented in his or her capacity to labor.[6] Yet, in this quality of abstraction and formal equivalence, the commodity disavowed natality by denying history and difference. As we will see, and as Marx suggests, this fetishistic foreclosure was never complete, as in the case of slavery; the commodity could speak back, offering alternative, vernacular epistemologies of kin-ship. Indeed, if the incest that marked anti- and proslavery texts was an effect of commodification, the registering of knowledge of incest was also a recognition that the genealogy of the enslaved was never fully occluded in the process of commodification.

The logic of commodification, as I have suggested, entailed specific effects in terms of kinship. Saidiya Hartman has called slavery the "ghost in the machine of kinship," an apt and menacing metaphor that encom-passes both this process of commodification and, relatedly, what the sociol-ogist Orlando Patterson has called "natal alienation."[7] For Patterson, natal alienation was a constitutive feature of the social death of slavery. As Patter-son puts it, the slave was "a socially dead person. Alienated from all 'rights' or claims of birth, he ceased to belong in his own right to any legitimate social order." The slave was "a genealogical isolate" insofar as the enslaved were "denied all claims on, and obligations to, his parents and living blood relations [and] all such claims and obligations on his more remote ancestors and on his descendants."[8] Patterson provides a useful and penetrating device for understanding the effects of commodification in terms of kinship and the force of both anti-and proslavery writing on kinship and incest. Yet, as we will see, the totalizing logics of natal alienation and social death foreclose the vernacular epistemologies of kinship that circulate in slave narratives. Thus, the social death and natal alienation of slavery were projections of slave owners (and, I would add, antislavery writers) to shore up their own kinship epistemologies and lives.[9] Indeed, these iterations of foreclosed paternity and the disruption of kinship served both to mark the perversion of slavery and secure paternity as the locus of kinship in an era of challenges to patriarchal authority in the form of consent and contract.

We might think of both anti- and proslavery discourses of incest and kinship as differentially articulated fantasies.[10] Fantasy, in the psychoanalytic sense, stages desire in a way that at once attempts to resolve the contradictions inherent in desire and allows for an articulation of desire that defends society from the excessive consequences of such desire. In this manner we might read both, and especially the antislavery iteration, as shoring-up the lineaments of the liberal subject and expelling its incestuous logic to the realm of slavery's chaos.[11] The abolitionist version of this fantasy functioned through a voyeuristic cataloguing of incestuous scenarios bounded by race and slavery. In that sense, the abolitionist fantasy functioned defensively through projection, as incest was associated with disordered kinship resulting from the domestic slave trade and interracial sex between masters and slaves. If incest perpetually threatened the liberal subject, the discourse of slavery was one site where that subject was racially bounded, with incest falling on the side of blackness and slavery, and the liberal subject falling on the side of whiteness and freedom.

Proslavery ideologues, more often than not reacting to abolitionist critique, frequently adopted the language of sentimentalism to the hierarchies, duties, and obligations of the plantation household and family and, in doing so, carried the erotic form of that family southward. Thus, the family was both incestuous and riven by racial difference. The enslaved were perpetual children, upholding the fantasy of the benevolent patriarch. Yet, these same writers frequently acknowledged the sexual violence between masters and slaves as endemic to the plantation South, even if they did not think of it in violent terms. The slaveholder's fantasy staged incestuous desire within the plantation family, which served the paradoxical function of at once prohibiting incest and allowing for the transgression of the prohibition. The racial disjuncture within the plantation family maintained the incest prohibition within the white family, as incestuous desire was acted out across the color line.[12] The proslavery fantasy also had its projective aspect, in which incest was made a common feature of family life under free labor. In this sense, then, the slaveholder's fantasy also had the double function of staging desire and defending against the incestuous consequences of such desire.[13] Both fantasmatic structures were ruptured by accounts of enslaved kinship, natal alienation, and incest. Antislavery images of disordered commodity circulation, trenchant as they were, discounted vernacular epistemologies of kinship, while they also ruptured the juridical foreclosure of paternity that animated the life of the slaveholder.

Historians occasionally have noted the possibility that incest marked slavery in general, and the fracturing of the enslaved family by the domestic slave trade in particular. Joanne Pope Melish, for instance, deftly addresses some of the contradictions of sex in the household across the color line and notes the way in which, to mark difference in the northern, slaveholding family, there was a "contradictory need to *incorporate* 'difference' in a quasi-kinship relationship invoked (again, in theory) the incest taboo against sex with slaves."[14] Yet, by the nineteenth century, incest was persistently associated with slavery, and thus the incest taboo was less forceful than her argument supposes. Writing of the sexual economy of the domestic slave trade, Edward Baptist has suggested that "the motifs of incest and/or oedipal competition" haunted it.[15] The haunting of incest occurred in a variety of places, from the absence of juridically recognized marriage to the rapacious process of capital accumulation that abolitionists referred to as "slave breeding."

Thomas Paine, in an early antislavery pamphlet, brought forth the specter of incest in slave society. "So monstrous is the making and keeping of them slaves at all, abstracted from the barbarous usage they suffer, and the many evils attending the practice," Paine wrote, "as selling husbands away from wives, children from parents, and from each other, in violation of sacred and natural ties; and opening the way for adulteries, incests, and many shocking consequences, for all of which guilty Masters must answer to the final judge."[16] Paine apprehended immediately what later antislavery writers would make a central part of their critique of slavery: that the buying and selling of human beings disrupted kinship in ways that would inevitably lead to incest. Indeed, Paine captured the legal foreclosure of slave marriages throughout the South, the circulation of the commodity, which functioned in part through and produced natal alienation, and, if natality was maintained, it was constantly threatened by the market.

One source of consternation for abolitionists was the absence of legally recognized marriage for slaves. As we have seen, marriage was treated as *the* institution of social and moral order, securing modern configurations of family and kinship, even as it was constantly figured as inherently incestuous. Its absence, for some abolitionists, guaranteed incest. William Lloyd Garrison, writing in the preface to Frederick Douglass's narrative, claimed that "when the marriage institution is abolished, concubinage, adultery, and incest must . . . necessarily abound."[17] Horace Mann agreed, writing, "the worst forms of all the crimes that a human being can commit—theft, robbery, murder, adultery, incest, sacrilege and whatever else there is that inflicts wide-wasting ruin upon society and brings the souls of men to perdition—the word slavery is the synonym of them all."[18] This indictment of slavery came at the end of a list of offenses perpetrated under slavery, including the absence of marriage, the sexual abuse of slaves at the hands of lustful masters, and the dissolution of all familial ties.

Similarly, after extolling the ravages done to the family as a result of slavery, another abolitionist wrote, "suppose, now, this system, all reeking with lust, incest, crime and cruelty, is brought out and placed under the blaze of Christianity. Whatsoever ye would that men should do unto you, do ye so even unto them; for this is the law. . . . Who has the hardihood to say that the practice of slaveholding is consistent with this injunction?"[19] And in reviewing the remarks of a Dr. Spring on slavery, an antislavery advocate quoted the doctor as writing the following: "Why the 'sin of Slavery' should embarrass human legislation more than other sins, remains to be shown. What if there are states in this Union . . . which legalize . . . incest or polygamy? Such Laws are sins; but it does not belong to the General Government to apply the remedy." Dr. Spring, of course, invoked the two marital or kinship systems that were uniformly prohibited in the United States. The reviewer, perhaps aware of this, found it utterly absurd, calling slavery, incest, and polygamy the "sum of all villainies."[20]

Many abolitionists and less radical antislavery writers found incest at the center of their vision of the relations between slavery and society, along with other originary violations such as murder and adultery. John G. Fee, an abolitionist, pointed this out in drawing a parallel between the incestuous act condemned by Paul in his letter to the Corinthians and slavery in the southern United States. "The laws of Corinth and the general practice of society, sanctioned the act of the incestuous person. But the way to correct these, was not for the church to shape her policy to suit corrupt laws and corrupt customs, but, by her practice, show what was right. It is a false love, not to discipline the deliberate offender."[21] Fee demanded that the South, in its violations of liberty and purity, be disciplined. The time for moral persuasion was over as fundamental transgressions had occurred. Another abolitionist concurred, forcefully arguing that the problem of slavery, like that of incest, was not a matter of opinion, but a matter of fact. "Slavery is not an Opinion. It is a hideous fact! A Fact as real as Murder or Incest, and infinitely more wicked, because a complication of all crimes; and an Opinion that it is right, is infinitely less tolerable than one in favor of the innocence of Murder or Incest, or of any of the single crimes which go to make it up."[22] What pushed slavery beyond the hideous transgressions of incest and murder was that it encompassed those transgressions. Slavery made transgression of fundamental prohibitions and laws a quotidian experience for all involved.

While incest was often invoked, it was less than clear what incest meant. Certainly the absence of legally sanctioned marriages was one source, but did this imply incest among slaves or incest between masters and slaves? The more frequent elaborations of incestuous scenarios depicted the sexual abuse and rape of enslaved women by their masters. Yet, the natal alienation and circulation of the enslaved as commodities in the domestic slave market, which ravaged slave families, suggested that incest was a problem internal to the slave community itself, as the tracing of genealogies became, in much antislavery writing, a near impossibility. To begin to understand the relationship between incest and slavery it is necessary first to turn to the legal definition of paternity in slave states and the rhetoric surrounding the domestic slave trade.

The legal structure of paternity in the slave South had been remade in the seventeenth century and continued to structure kinship under slavery. As historians such as Edmund Morgan and Kathleen Brown have argued, the laws developed in the 1660s and refined in the 1680s to regulate interracial and slave sexuality were central to the production of racial and sexual difference and the maintenance of the slave population.[23] These laws, which primarily focused on interracial sexuality and the status of children tied slavery and blackness together in the legal system, simultaneously engendering the growth of the slave population. A 1662 statute declared that all children of enslaved women would follow the status of the mother, not the father, as in traditional English common law constructions of paternity. "This act redefined slave motherhood and vitiated the legal foundation of slave paternity," writes Kathleen Brown, "thereby making distinctions between legitimacy and illegitimacy legally irrelevant for enslaved people."[24] Through the enactment of this law, not only were all children of enslaved women doomed to a life of slavery themselves, but also, as Brown points out, paternity became all but impossible to recognize legally, as the law severed paternity in slavery, thereby throwing notions of fatherhood, paternity, genealogy, and kinship into disarray.

The anthropologist Marilyn Strathern has argued that the positions of father and mother in Euro-American kinship systems are determined through two different conceptions of certainty. The mother was certainly a mother because of a biologically determined relation to the child. The materiality of motherhood in this conception of kin relations made motherhood axiomatic. Fatherhood, on the other hand, was paradigmatically uncertain in biological terms, becoming a social fact through a process of reduplication. A father is a father, according to Strathern, in so far as the identity of father in a kinship relation was performed repeatedly through specific socially and legally sanctioned actions.[25] Southern slave law protected the slaveholder from such reduplication while making it nearly impossible, in the register of the law, for slaves to establish paternity.

With the outlawing of the international slave trade in 1808, the development of the domestic slave trade ensured that the problems inherent in the transatlantic trade would not be eradicated and new abuses would emerge. The development of the domestic slave trade after 1790 resulted from a shift in southern agricultural production.[26] Northern slave states like Maryland and Virginia saw a decrease in production while states in the Deep South saw a sharp increase, especially cotton boom states of the mid-nineteenth century like Mississippi and Alabama. This shift in agricultural production produced a domestic slave trade, where slaves were sold from underproducing states like Virginia to states in the lower South with higher production. This development had a profound effect on slave culture. "The act of sale," writes Edward Baptist, "ruptured the old plantation districts' relationships of family, kinship, and community."[27] Abolitionists were quick to point this out. "If it is not just as profitable for the traders to sell them in families," wrote an abolitionist in the *Liberator*, "they hesitate not a moment to separate husband and wife—parents and children—and dispose of them to purchasers, residing in sections of the country, remote from each other."[28]

Not only were these families torn apart, disrupting kinship and family, as Baptist points out, but the domestic affections central to the sentimental, bourgeois family were also torn asunder through the workings of the domestic slave trade.[29] Amos Phelps, an antislavery minister from Boston, described the following scene at a slave auction. "There I saw the father looking with sullen contempt on the crowd, and expressing an indignation in his countenance that he dare not speak; and the mother, pressing her infants closer to her bosom with an involuntary grasp, and exclaiming in wild and simple earnestness, while the tears chased down her cheeks in quick succession—'I can't leff my children! I won't leff my children'! But on the hammer went, reckless alike whether it united or sundered forever."[30] While abolitionists like Phelps discoursed on the evils of the slave trade and the breakup of the slave family, they also projected the domestic affection of sentimentalism and domesticity southward in order to distance themselves from the incestuous structure of such visions. This is not to say that there was not affection in slave families, but rather that white antislavery discourse had a tendency to interpellate slave families as failed images of the ideal bourgeois family. Simultaneously, they painted pictures of slaveholders as unable to grasp the affective bonds that animated the slave family. This association of incest with disordered kinship served to substantiate claims to the moral and sexual purity of the sentimental family: if incest was associated with disordered kinship and the commodification of bodies, then the domestic scene of the northern middle class, an ideological haven from the excesses of the market, was exempt from the incestuous dangers of the family in antebellum America. A good liberal subject could still be produced there, free of the incestuous problems and their normalization in other discourses. Incest, in this discourse, was becoming black.

The legal foreclosure of paternity for the enslaved and the disruptive circulation of slaves as commodities in the domestic slave trade combined to create the conditions for the articulation of incest with slavery. Natal alienation was an effect of commodification and thus distinguished the more manageable alienation that produced the incestuous liberal subject. As one evangelical wrote in 1818, slavery in Kentucky "keeps up polygamy, incest, and adultery, in the church of Christ, for some of their owners, even professed Christians, make no conscience to receive their own or others' slaves into society, give them the right hand of fellowship, have them baptized, initiate them into the church of Christ, receive them to the Lord's table; then some will sell, buy swap, put them at inconvenient distances from each other, or prevent husbands from visiting their wives, which leads both parties into temptation."[31] Incest was linked to the buying and selling of slaves and the disruption of marriages as the rapacious nature of slavery vitiated even the blessings of Christianity.

In 1825, William Mack, the president of the Moral Religious Manumission Society of West Tennessee, made the link between the slave trade, natal alienation, and incest even more explicit. Recounting the abuses and violence of slavery, Mack included "the children torn from the parents, and parents from children, husbands from wives, and wives from husbands." Mack followed this fracturing of families with the sexual violence that was often the special burden of enslaved women. "We view, with horror, the female part of them subjected to brutal lust," Mack wrote, "without the least degree of legal redress, and even without liberty to use their physical powers for their own defence against their villainous abusers." This then slid into incest, which followed from natal alienation. "Still more are our minds agitated, when we know that the great mass of the slaves are made subject to the horrid crime of *incest*, by their not knowing their blood relations."[32] While this lack of knowledge was clearly related to the natal alienation of slavery, it also, in its language of subjection, suggested the rape that Mack had just invoked. In both scenarios, that of the disruption of kinship by the slave trade or the foreclosure of paternity that was the slaveholder's legal right, incest was the result.

Mack, of course, was not alone in such an assessment. The Declaration of Sentiment of the Clinton County Anti-Slavery Society also included a reference to incest. "We are the enemies of slavery, because it demands a traffic in the souls of men," the declaration read. The horrors of this traffic were primarily familial, including incest. Slavery "seizes and enslaves seventy thousand infants annually . . . robs the widow, the fatherless, and him that hath no helper—forbids the acquisition of knowledge . . . derides the sanctity and destroys the inviolability of the marriage institution—interferes with all parental and filial obligations, and cherishes a vast system of incest and pollution."[33] Incestuous pollution was the culmination to such disruptions to kinship and was certainly aided by the prohibition on knowledge. Natal alienation was as much an effect of the absence of knowledge of formal kin relations as anything else. This lack of knowledge stemmed from both the unimpeded circulation of the slave market as much as the slaveholder's control of knowledge. This was one of the primary criticisms of antislavery writers, despite proslavery ideologues' claims to keep the slave family together even through the market.[34]

Several fictional antislavery works dealt explicitly with the problem of slaveholding paternity and the complexities of incest. H. L. Hosmer's *Adela, the Octoroon*, which opened this chapter, pointed to the paradox of paternity in this system. Not only was there no recognition of Tidbald's paternity, he presumed there was no condition by which a slave, as a mute commodity, should be aware of her kinship. Yet, the unfolding of the scene suggested that despite the legal and property-based occlusion of paternity, it persisted as a social fact, especially among the enslaved. Indeed, we might think of this as a vernacular epistemology of kinship.[35]

Howard Meeks captured this ambivalence in his novel *The Fanatic, or, The Perils of Peter Pliant, the Poor Pedagogue*. After describing the great beauty of Hester, one of Charles Ashley's slaves, Meeks revealed that she was the object of desire of both her owner, Charles Ashley, and her brother, Freeman Morgan, who was Ashley's cousin. Here, however, the fracture of racial slavery haunted and, indeed, structured kinship and the scene of desire. Meeks pointed out the ambivalence in such a relationship, where Morgan and Hester were related through a white, slaveholding father, as well as the ambivalence in racial constructions of the period. Referring to Hester, Meeks asked, "was such a one a negro? We leave the reader to judge; she was the slave of Charles Ashley, and the sister of Freeman Morgan; at least she was the child of his father, and her mother was the child of his grandfather."[36] Not only does Meeks question the bifurcated racial caste system in America by questioning whether or not Hester, the product of interracial sex, was black, but he also points to the ambivalence in kinship in a slave society: while Hester was, according to blood, Morgan's sibling, it was less clear whether she was his sister. In both legal and physiological constructions of the incest prohibition in antebellum America, consanguinity and kinship were becoming equivalents. Here, in the context of slavery, consanguinity and kinship were severed by race and freedom. What was clear from Meeks's account was that interracial sex, because of the corruptions of the plantation, was inherently incestuous. Not only was Hester being seduced by her brother, she herself was the offspring of an incestuous relationship between her mother and father, who were themselves half brother and half sister. "Amalgamation is an idea abhorrent to southern sensibility," Meeks wrote, "but is the pill less bitter because gilded with incest and fornication?"[37]

This ambivalent construction of family and kinship coupled with the denial of paternity made up one of the key scenes of Lydia Maria Child's play *Stars and Stripes*. In a re-creation of Ellen and William Craft's narrative, Child inserted an incestuous scenario not present in their work, pointing to the fantasmatic structure of sexualized abolitionist discourse.[38] As we move through these antislavery scenarios of incestuous slavery, a result in large part of the disorders of commodity circulation, we should bear in mind that they associated incest with the circulation of bodies as commodities, thereby purifying the circulation of liberal society of its incestuous nature. As incest came to mark liberalism, it was racialized, in the discourse of slavery, physiology, and ethnography so that incest was the condition of nonwhite populations. Despite the intent to end slavery and the sympathetic identifications that animated antislavery discourse, this projection of incest into slave communities associated incest and disorder with blackness, assuming that slaves were unable to trace their own genealogies.

Child's plantation scenario was one of transgressive domestic affection, wherein the interracial structure of sex and family disrupted normative notions of domesticity while simultaneously distancing the ideal family from incestuous relations. While arguing over whether or not to attempt an escape, Ellen and William reflected on the great evils of the plantation, despite their owner Mr. Masters's claims that all of his slaves loved him and that "he couldn't *whip* 'em away from him, if he *tried*."[39] Child infused a perverse scene of domesticity with an intrinsic violence. While the idealized family of sentimentalism would have encouraged the perceived overflowing of love, the perversions of a slave society responded to such affection with violence. Ellen, having kept the information of Mr. Masters's sexual advances from William for fear of the trouble his anger may have brought, ultimately resolved to tell William of the situation. "When I am at the big house, sewing for missis, as sure as she goes out to ride, he comes into my room and asks me to sing, and tells me how pretty I am. And—and—I know by his ways that he don't mean any good. . . . Now massa says if I make him angry, he will sell you to the traders" (143). Here Child brought up two central concerns of antislavery. First, Mr. Masters maintained two families, one a secret object of his sexual advances, the other having left the plantation, apparently oblivious to the relationship between her husband

and Ellen. Abolitionists were quick to point to the relationship that many slaveholders held in relation to their slaves, a not-so-hidden secret of the plantation South. "What security for domestic purity and peace there can be where every man has had two connexions, one of which must be concealed," wrote Harriet Martineau, "and two families, whose existence must not be known to each other; where the conjugal relation begins in treachery, and must be carried with a secret in the husband's breast, no words are needed to explain."[40] The existence of two families, one of which was an open secret, was a fundamental disruption of kinship systems, one that led, as Child argued, directly to incest.

Second, Child addressed the omnipresence of sexual violence and of the market in slave families. Ellen suffered through the situation in order to keep her husband William on the plantation, in order, that is, to maintain family and kin. In this sense, then, the domestic slave trade worked to insure interracial rape/incest in order to avoid the separation of slave families. While most abolitionists saw the domestic slave trade as a disruption of ordered kinship and hence productive of incest, Child articulated a vision of incest as a transgression inherent to southern domesticity, and, therefore, satisfying the erotic desire of the owner also curbed his pecuniary desires, saving the slave family from the disruptions of the slave market. William, whose anger rose at just this moment, responded, "The old villain! And he knows all the while that you are his own daughter!" To which Ellen responded, pointing to the problems of the father-daughter relationship on the slave plantation: "I told him that, but he paid no attention to it. My poor, poor mother! I suppose she was afraid, too" (143). The denial of paternity vitiated the incest for Masters, while for Ellen that relationship could not be eradicated solely through refusal of recognition. For while denial of paternity and sexual access to his slaves may have in large part constituted Masters's identity as a slaveholder, for Ellen the assertion of her master's paternity constituted a recognition of the oppressive relations of paternalism.

Child, in writing *Stars and Stripes*, had been inspired by Richard Hildreth's novel *The White Slave; or, Memoirs of a Fugitive*, which was focused on plantation incest. She declared, "if I were a man, I would rather be the author of that work, than of anything ever published in America."[41] Mimicking a slave narrative, Hildreth told the tale of Archy Moore, the titular white slave, who escaped slavery because he could pass as white, and whose impetus to escape from the plantation on which he lived was, in large part, incest. Hildreth not only offered a searing critique of slavery and its disruption of common kinship patterns but also took on the incestuous overtones of domesticity, painting a picture of family life that was enveloped by incest. Again, like much of the discourse of slavery, incest was a consequence of the ambivalent foreclosure of genealogy, itself a consequence of the natal alienation of slavery. If we are to treat this as a part of the discourse of incest, we can discern the racialization of incest in a manner distinct from the incestuous disorder of liberal circulation and accidental incest. Unlike many antislavery writers, who included incest in positivist enumerations of slavery's various evils, Hildreth, like Howard Meeks, left his readers wondering what exactly constituted incest in a society structured by slavery and fractured kinship.

The sentimental family in slavery constituted Hildreth's first scene of incest. Archy, still young enough to be a playmate of one of Colonel Moore's children, was shielded from the ravages of slavery, due in part to that friendship, but also to the relatively comfortable status of his mother, one of Colonel Moore's concubines. In this sense, Archy experienced what would be a common feeling of middle-class domesticity: passionate love for his mother, infused with an element of the erotic. Archy, describing his mother's beauty in terms usually reserved for the language of courtship, not familial relations, realized the fine line between love for his mother and the desire for sexual relations with her.

> I describe her more like a lover than a son. But in truth, her beauty was so uncommon, as to draw my attention while I was yet a child; and many an hour have I watched her, almost with a lover's earnestness, while she fondled me on her lap, and tears and smiles chased each other alternately over a face, the expression of which was ever changing, yet always beautiful. She was the most affectionate of mothers; the mixture of tenderness, grief and pleasure, with which she always seemed to regard me, gave a new vivacity to her beauty; and it was probably this, which so early and so strongly fixed my attention.[42]

In painting a picture of early domestic bliss for Archy, Hildreth revealed the incestuous overtones of sentimental fiction and domestic rhetoric, in much the same way Herman Melville, in *Pierre*, depicted mother-son affection.[43] This mother-son affection, however, was melancholic. Indeed, it was structured by the "tenderness, grief, and pleasure" with which Archy's mother apprehended him—slavery could allow for only melancholic motherhood. For Archy this melancholy was rooted in ambiguous paternity. "Had I been allowed to choose my own paternity, could I possibly have selected a more desirable father?—But by the laws and customs of Virginia, it is not the father but the mother, whose rank and condition determine that of the child;—and alas! My mother was a concubine, and a slave!" (8). So the relationship to his father, his owner Colonel Moore, was at once the source of the domestic bliss that Archy remembered from his youth, and the cause of the grief, the melancholic state of Archy's family.

Hildreth, however, was not especially concerned with the eroticism of familial sentiment, except insofar as it was disrupted by slavery. Instead, Hildreth constructed an ambivalent account of incest in slavery that followed from the foreclosure of paternity across the color line. This foreclosure of paternity affected both lineal and lateral relations, as Hildreth accounted for both father-daughter incest across the color line in the rape of Cassy by her father/owner, Colonel Moore, and sibling incest between Archy and his half sister Cassy. Without a clear articulation of a paternal role the sexual relations conceived of between father and daughter and brother and sister could not be seen as simply incestuous. Yet, with the establishment of paternity such ambiguity could be displaced, as became evident in the relation between Cassy and Colonel Moore. If the prohibition of incest produced and secured kinship, the foreclosure of paternity across the color line in slavery made incest itself an ambivalent category. Rather than the positivist appraisals of incest in slavery that were so frequent in antislavery discourse, Hildreth's novel ultimately asks if incest is even possible in the ruptured kin system of the plantation. If paternity could be systematically foreclosed, then kin relations could not be acknowledged, or at least, they were bounded by whiteness. Could an incest prohibition exist in the plantation epistemology of kinship? And could incest exist in the absence of the prohibition?

Cassy, Archy's half sister and the daughter of an enslaved woman who Archy claimed was the rival of his own mother, became the victim of Colonel Moore's sexual advances at the same time that she and Archy fell in love with each other. Neither the lineal nor the lateral relation was fully acknowledged. While Cassy and Archy resolved to marry each other, a relationship approved of by Colonel Moore's wife, this was stopped immediately upon Colonel Moore's return to the plantation. The marriage was then performed clandestinely, Archy and Cassy relating to each other as if married, despite the absence of either legal or religious recognition. Having stopped the marriage, however, Colonel Moore revealed his own desires for Cassy through the giving of gifts, kind treatment, and comments on her beauty. Eventually Colonel Moore, after claiming to have tried to find a husband worthy of Cassy's status, claimed Cassy for himself, elevating her to the status of both her and Archy's mother. Cassy, however, could not submit, both because of her devotion to Archy and the incestuous nature of a relationship with her owner/father.

The nature of an affair with Colonel Moore was too much for Cassy to bear. "But she—the poor child—heard him with shame and dread; and was ready, she told me, to sink into the earth with terror and dismay. In relating it, she blushed—she hesitated—she shuddered—her breathing became short and quick—she clung to me, as if some visible image of horror were present before her, and bringing her lips close to my ear, she exclaimed in a trembling and scarcely audible whisper—'Oh Archy!—and he my father!'" (42). Colonel Moore's first rape attempt was interrupted by the return of Mrs. Moore and her daughter. The scene of seduction across the color line was ended by the reappearance of the visible family, pushing Colonel Moore's clandestine family to the netherworlds of slavery.[44] Again, as both Harriet Martineau and Lydia Maria Child had pointed out, incest was manifested in the fraught space between the two families of slave society. Moreover, the attempted consummation of incestuous rape rested on social death. Transgressing the dominant structure of kinship via the natal alienation of the enslaved woman as property, Colonel Moore figured Cassy as socially dead. She could not, in Moore's vision of her, speak her genealogy, precisely because the commodity masks its origins. This, then, gave the prohibition of incest a generative quality—to be subject to the prohibition designated humanity. The racial barrier seemed to obviate the incest prohibition and so gave license to Colonel Moore's seeming (non)incestuous rape.

This, however, was not the end of Colonel Moore's seduction of Cassy. After finding out that Cassy and Archy were married, Colonel Moore sold Archy, highlighting the threat the domestic slave trade presented to the tenuous slave marriage. Here Hildreth shifted the focus from the possibility of incestuous marriage to incestuous rape. After the sale of Archy, Colonel Moore kept Cassy in a well furnished cottage, away from the daily labors of the other slaves and known as the domicile of Colonel Moore's favored concubine. There Colonel Moore, who on first appearance was rather calm, yet haggard, visited Cassy with readily apparent intentions.[45] As he sat down next to Cassy on the bed "he smiled scornfully" throwing "one arm about her waist" (128). Moore, acting the role of benevolent patriarch, "plied her with flattery, soft words, and generous promises" (128). But as his promises turned to an explanation of his decision to sell Archy, his temper flared and he almost lost complete control of himself. The marriage of Cassy and Archy, incestuous on its face, angered Moore primarily because of its rejection of his patriarchal authority. This was an assertion of the patriarch as owner, not as biological father, as he was to both of them. Furthermore, as Michael Johnson has argued, the slaveholder's patriarchal authority over his white family rested on the control of his slaves.[46] Cassy and Archy subverted his authority not only through their marriage but also through an attempt at escape, which was what led to the revelation of their marriage.

Despite his impetuosity, Colonel Moore was able to control himself for the moment, explaining to Cassy that Archy was "much better than [he] deserved to be" and that once he had recovered would be sent to the slave market. In response Cassy begged to be sent to the market with him, claiming that she did not want to be separated from her husband. At this Colonel Moore lost all patience with Cassy. "That word, husband, put him into a violent passion. He told her that she had no husband and wanted none; for he would be better than a husband to her" (129). In the curious phrase "better than a husband to her," Hildreth suggested Colonel Moore's apprehension of the situation as one in which an impossibly incestuous transgression should exceed the pleasures of marriage.

With this move into violent rage Colonel Moore commenced the rape that had been interrupted on his first attempt. Cassy again resisted "his hateful embraces," but Moore persisted. In a final act of resistance, "summing up all her energies," Cassy forced the recognition of incest on Colonel Moore. "'Master,—Father!' she cried, 'What is it you would have of your own daughter?'" This was too much for Moore—the capacity for incestuous transgression with an enslaved woman was a mark of the slaveholder, but the slave's knowledge of kinship disrupted the natal alienation that structured slavery. Enslaved kinship was supposed to be effaced in the process of commodification, but here the commodity spoke that knowledge. It ended the attempted rape as Moore "staggered as if a bullet had struck him. . . . In an instant he recovered his self-possession, and without taking any notice of her last appeal, he merely said, that if she were really sick, he did not wish to trouble her" (129).

Throughout the conflict between Cassy, Archy, and Colonel Moore, the primary relation was one of master and slave. The role of father, through both law and custom, was occluded. However, Cassy did not let him out of his role so easily. Miscegenation and rape were offenses to which the slaveholding patriarch was entitled. Indeed, the sexual access to enslaved women in part constituted the slaveholder's identity. As Walter Johnson has argued, the fancy trade was one method of articulating a specific identity that placed the slaveholder within the bounds of acceptable sociability.[47] Yet incest, in this case, did not stand in the same relation to law and social custom. The naming of Colonel Moore as both master and father reduplicated paternity through a social action. Paternity unnamed was paternity unpracticed, and this made unnamed kinship irrelevant for Moore. The naming of him as father, however, was enough to stop his advances on Cassy, as kinship was established, however tenuously, between father and daughter.

Russ Castronovo has argued that the instability of genealogies was one of the hallmarks of the discourse of slavery. "The slave child followed no history of a father's rights and duties of citizenship," Castronovo writes; "instead, the slave issued forth not from a woman, but from a matrix of nonhistory, from a textual-sexual space that signified emptiness and absence, illegitimacy and silence."[48] Importantly, this textual-sexual space signified incest. The disrupted, confused genealogies of slavery, rooted in the denials of paternity inherent to the system, signified the emptiness and absence of the incest prohibition. The presence enacted through this absence was incest, the illegitimate sexual act par excellence. This scene, however, should not be read as a realist representation of sexual violence on the plantation. The establishment of kin relations was unlikely to ward off the systemic rape of enslaved women. Rather, Hildreth offered a critique of kinship, slavery, and incest. The foreclosure of the father-daughter relationship that undergirded the seduction and rape of Cassy rested on her status as a commodity, Cassy's naming of Moore as her father undercut the totalizing function of commodification of the enslaved. Cassy knew Moore was her father not because of legal recognition, or census, or plantation register, but because of the circulation of knowledge in the slave community. And the moment that she named that relationship the force of natal alienation and social death was ruptured. The socially dead, in Hildreth's imagining, could still speak the language of kinship, suggesting that if slavery rested on social death and natal alienation, the problem for the slaveholder was that the enslaved, the socially dead, this peculiar commodity, could speak, drawing on their own vernacular epistemologies of kinship. Indeed, the naming of the incestuous relations reasserted the incest prohibition across the color line.[49]

The force associated with Cassy's naming of incest as an assertion of the incest prohibition across the color line appeared in the legal record, as well. In 1830, four slaves were put on trial in Virginia for murdering their owner. The trial reveals the tension between the incestuous fantasy and public manifestations of incest between slaveholders and slaves. On 22 August 1830, two slaves, Peggy and Patrick, "moved and seduced by the instigation of the devil," entered the home of their master, John Francis, whereupon they assaulted him with a large stick and axe, and then killed him by setting the house on fire.[50] Two other slaves, Franky and Caroline, were accused of aiding and abetting the murder. All four were accused of murder, with Peggy, Patrick, and Franky found guilty, and Caroline innocent. Peggy and Patrick were sentenced to execution by hanging while the court begged the mercy of the governor to commute Franky's sentence to transportation, or at least stay the execution, as she was pregnant at the time of the trial.

The simple charge of murder, which was corroborated by both enslaved and white witnesses, was complicated by the fact that the murder of John Francis was, according to the witnesses, an act of vengeance, as Francis had attempted to rape Peggy, who was also his daughter. Jesse, one of the slave witnesses, claimed that Francis "had disagreed with Peggy and generally kept her confined by keeping her chained to a block" and that the reason he did this was because Peggy would not consent to his sexual advances.[51] Francis's response, according to Jesse, was to threaten "to beat her almost to death, that he would barely leave life in her, and would then send her to New Orleans."[52] Jesse then informed the court that Peggy would not yield to such requests and threats because Francis was her father. Two white witnesses who claimed that Francis's relation to Peggy and his attempts to rape her were common knowledge in the neighborhood supported this testimony.

Another slave, Hannah, who was not a witness to the murder of John Francis, testified to the importance of this information, even in the original trial. Testifying that she saw the house on fire only as she was returning from another plantation, Hannah claimed that Peggy was known to be

Francis's daughter. "I knew that Peggy was considered to be the child of the deceased[,] we had the same mother, and my mother always said the deceased was Peggy's father and Peggy considered him her father. I know the deceased wanted to cohabit with Peggy, to which she objected, and that was the cause of the difference between them."[53] The testimony of the two slaves and two white men of the community, out of which only one claimed to have witnessed the murder, highlighted the importance of publicly known incest for the trial and slave society. While the naming of incest here did not have the narrative resolution of Hildreth's novel, and did not seem to stave off Francis's attempts at rape, it carried a similar message. Incestuous desire sublimated, or in the case of proslavery discourse, staged in fantasy, was acceptable, and in fact necessary to the maintenance of social relations; its publicity made it a different story altogether. Furthermore, the knowledge of kinship, challenged by both abolitionists and proslavery ideologues, circulated on both sides of the color line. Not only did the slaves know that Peggy was Francis's daughter, but so too did the wider community of whites in the county. If Francis did not see incest or kinship as reason to stop raping his enslaved daughter, the wider community, black and white, slave and free, seemed to.

The blow to the incestuous fantasy was inherent in the white community's response to the trial. While none denied the horror of slaves murdering their owners, as a number of prominent men from the community attested to their "utmost abhorrence [of] the crime," nevertheless, Francis's incestuous infidelities were too much to ignore. One hundred of the leading white citizens of the county, including the sheriff and the justice of the peace, filed a petition with the governor to commute the sentences of the convicted from execution to transportation.[54] While sexual violence was endemic to the plantation South, the incest that structured such violence operated in veiled silence. This trial brought the incestuous nature of plantation sex to the fore and punctured the operation of the plantation fantasy, wherein the enslaved were both children in the "family black and white" and objects of sexual possession and violence. Not only were the custom and law of slaveholders' paternity subverted, the community at large repudiated not incest, as such, but its public knowledge.

While the assertion of paternity disrupted the natal alienation and social death that constituted the condition of incestuous rape, this was just one iteration of incest that followed from the foreclosure of paternity, for Cassy was married to her half brother. Archy's experience of Colonel Moore's paternity was different from Cassy's, and this made the intrafamilial sex and marriage between Cassy and Archy different as well. The childhood playmate of Moore's youngest son, Archy lost his favored status upon the early death of Master James. Being passed from James to his sadistic older brother William, Archy pleaded with Colonel Moore for reprieve from the abuse of his half brother. "Emboldened by the danger of becoming the slave of master William, I dared to hint—though distantly and obscurely—at the information which my mother had communicated on her death bed; and I even ventured something like a half appeal to Colonel Moore's paternal tenderness. At first he did not seem to understand me; but the moment he began to comprehend my meaning, his face grew black as a thunder cloud, then became pale, and immediately was suffused with a burning blush, in which shame and rage were equally commingled. I gave myself up for lost" (24). Hildreth staged a confrontation between the logic of natal alienation and the networks of enslaved knowledge regarding paternity. For Cassy, it transformed seduction and rape into incest, asserted her as more than property, and stopped the rape. For Archy, it led to paternal rage and the reassertion of natal alienation. In an act of repudiation, Archy chose to work in the field with the other slaves, rather than in the house as Master William's slave, which in effect consolidated natal alienation for Archy. It also enacted a rejection of whiteness in favor of the blackness of the slave that Archy had, prior to this point, always looked down on. Archy designated the color line and enslavement as a bar to kinship, an act of repudiation that, unintentionally, secured Moore's denial of paternity.

Archy and Cassy's intrafamilial sex and marriage were played out in this space of multiple rejections of paternity and ambiguous kinship, making its status as incest problematic. Immediately upon Cassy's return to the plantation, Archy was made aware of their relationship. "I learned from one of my fellow servants, that she was the daughter of colonel Moore, by a female slave, who for a year or two had shared my master's favor jointly with my mother, but who had died many years since. . . . Her mother was said to have been a great beauty, and a very dangerous rival of mine" (33). Again, enslaved kinship was constituted as part of an enslaved epistemology—Archy learned of his half sister through the networks of the slave community. "Cassy was one of nature's children. . . . We loved; and before long we talked of marriage" (34). "One of nature's children" should be read as an assertion of the enslaved living outside the bonds and structures of legal (white) kinship. In Hildreth's account, the enslaved might have been excluded from the rights derived from legal recognition of paternity and kinship, but that foreclosure also created the conditions for alternative kin relations. Archy reflected on this when he considered his owner/father's opposition to his marriage to Cassy. There were, for Archy, two possible motives for this opposition. The first, that Archy "could not think of" Colonial Moore sexual desire for Cassy "with the slightest patience," nor could he "bear to shock and distress poor Cassy by the mention of it." That Colonel Moore could desire incest with his own biological daughter was unimaginable to Archy. The second motive "was less discreditable" to Colonel Moore and "flattering to the pride of Cassy and myself." This credit to Colonel Moore, that, as father to both of them, he was opposed to their incestuous marriage, was, for Archy, also unmentionable, "without leading to disclosures, which I did not see fit to make" (38).

For Archy, it was possible that Colonel Moore objected to their relationship either to claim her as his sexual property or because he silently recognized the vexed kinship here and was opposed to the incest between Archy and Cassy. Archy ultimately rejected both explanations, just as he rejected his father's paternity. In doing so, he retained the enslaved epistemology of kinship as the reserve of men, leaving his relationship with Cassy in an ambiguous state. While Cassy was unaware of her relationship to Archy, he made sure that she stayed unaware, as it would surely disrupt their love. Furthermore, and in the context of paternity and incest much more importantly, Archy's rejection of Colonel Moore's paternity was also a rejection of any kin relations that resulted from it. Archy claimed natal alienation as a generative, productive moment, one that made possible the legitimacy of his marriage to Cassy. Therefore, just as his relationship to Colonel Moore's white family had ended when Archy chose the field over his half brother William, so too his relationship to Cassy as her brother could not be substantiated without the reduplication of Colonel Moore's paternity, something he refused.

Could a marriage be considered incestuous without the social rituals necessary to maintain genealogical certainty? The answer, as Archy points out, was yes and no. Even though he figured the marriage was based on the purest form of love, he could never bring himself to inform Cassy of their kin ties. And as Cassy was sure to invoke the paternity of Colonel Moore to stop his rape of her, she clearly would have viewed her marriage to Archy in a considerably different light had she known he was her half brother. Slavery's disruptions of genealogical certainty threw customary notions of incest into chaos. Werner Sollors finds the ambiguous status of Cassy and Archy's relation to be unconvincing. "On the one hand [Hildreth] expected the heavily represented theme of incest . . . to be . . . horribly shocking to his readers. . . . On the other hand, Archy rationalizes his own incest . . . with a very weak and sophistic turn, and, even worse, he never lets his own wife and sister know the truth."[55] Yet this discounts the critique of kinship and genealogy that Hildreth elaborated, as well as the fantasmatic qualities of racial formation within abolitionist discourse. To simply look at sex between close blood relations as incest discounts the primarily social and cultural relations of the incest prohibition. Hildreth's novel was less shocking exposé of the perversion of slavery (although it was that) than it was a sustained critique of the conjunction of slavery, race, and kinship, one that tracked the place of natal alienation, property, sex, and kinship across the color line in the ambiguous permutations of incest.

Hildreth, in tracking these permutations, made a strong case for the vernacular epistemology of enslaved kinship, where a kind of resistance was produced by the legal and cultural foreclosure of kinship and paternity in slavery. To know kinship was to claim a foreclosed knowledge, one that could produce a rupture of slavery's fantasmatic structure and allow for the elaboration of other kinships, and the maintenance of the incest prohibition both across the color line and within the slave community. In this sense, slave narratives tended to refute both the domination of the slaveholder via the denial of paternity and the antislavery fantasies of hopelessly disordered kinship that followed from commodification and natal alienation. What we find in slave narratives, however, was something of a vernacular epistemology of kinship, and the speech of the commodity form. Kinship and slavery, especially when we read abolitionist, proslavery, and slave narratives together, reveal the extent to which kinship is an epistemology that subjected people to its frameworks, not a representation of social reality.[56] For a number of ex-slaves and African American commentators, kinship was a system disrupted by slavery and race in antebellum America, but the experience of this disruption did not necessarily give license to intrafamilial sex and marriage. The African American response was much quicker to reveal the power invested in maintaining specific kinship arrangements and the incestuous implications of these arrangements.

William Wells Brown, a former slave, leading abolitionist, and black intellectual, revealed the cultural construction of kinship and the racialized authority implicit in such social arrangements in his narrative of 1848. The maintenance of marriage, birth, and death records was part of the white master's duty to instill order in social relations and maintain both commodification and natal alienation of the slave. In this manner, formal knowledge of kinship (articulated through such records) was coded white. Knowledge of kinship, both formal and folk, was never absolutely bounded by race, and this can be read as an unformulated subversion of both anti- and proslavery constructions of incestuous fantasies. In the preface to Brown's narrative, J. C. Hathaway, a white abolitionist, delineated the cruelties done to Brown as a slave, cruelties that went against the nature of the sentimental family. "The dearest ties of nature have been riven in his own person. A mother has been cruelly scourged before his own eyes. A father— alas! slaves have no father. A brother has been made the subject of its tender mercies. A sister has been given up to the irresponsible control of the pale-faced oppressor."[57] The violations of nature were violations of kinship.

While Hathaway articulated a common abolitionist construction of the family in slavery, and did this in the service of Brown's narrative, there was a contradiction between the white abolitionist account and the black ex-slave account. Brown opened his narrative with an origins story.

> I was born in Lexington, KY. The man who stole me as soon as I was born, recorded the births of all the infants which he claimed to be born on his property, in a book which he kept for that purpose. My mother's name was Elizabeth. She had seven children, viz.: Solomon, Leander, Benjamin, Joseph, Millford, Elizabeth, and myself. No two of us were children of the same father. My father's name, as I learned from my mother, was George Higgins. He was a white man, a relative of my master, and connected with some of the first families in Kentucky.[58]

Brown's genesis was one articulated within the confines of slaveholder rapacity and licentiousness, as Hathaway noted in his preface, yet it belied both anti- and proslavery fantasies of absent kinship and rampant incest. If enslaved kinship and genealogies were in part the province of the slave master, Brown's narrative suggested that this was never completely controlled. Brown's knowledge of kinship relations was possibly gleaned from furtive glances at the kinship ledger but was more an expression of experiential knowledge that exceeded the power structure of the ledger.[59] The ledger, signifier of the white control of kinship and family on both sides of the color line, was demonstrated to be, in part, a failure, as the experience of family and kinship always already exceeded the textual basis of white hegemony.

While there is a substantial body of work on black kinship and family within slavery, I am less concerned with the sexual relations that seem to constitute kinship than I am with kinship as competing and imbricated regimes of knowledge.[60] Indeed, in speaking of vernacular kinship and the incest prohibition, one would rightfully think first, perhaps, of Herbert Gutman's account of the rituals that prohibited incest in the slave community.[61] Yet, Brown's naming of his master's relative as father was more an epistemological claim than a practice. What does it mean for a slave to name his father across the color line? Put differently, what does it mean for a slave to name the unnamable (paternity) that upholds the fantasy? It goes without saying that, in Hortense Spillers's words, insofar as family and kinship refer to "the *vertical* transfer of a bloodline, of a patronymic, of titles and entitlements, of real estate and the prerogatives of 'cold cash,' from *fathers* to *sons* and in the supposedly free exchange of affectional ties between a male and a female of *his* choice," then family and kinship did not, for the most part, operate across the color line.[62] Yet, in deploying these vernacular epistemologies, the control of kinship and paternity, and thus the contours of incest, was not simply or only the province of white masters and legal systems.[63]

Brown's claim of kinship across the color line, no matter how constrained, was not an anomaly. Throughout the recollections of former slaves there are a plethora of claims to kinship, particularly paternity, across the color line. These claims, while never denying the abuse done to slave families through the domestic slave trade, disrupted the incestuous fantasy of proslavery ideologues, resting as it did on both denied paternity and the fiction of two families. Recognitions of paternity across the color line abounded, with one former slave recalling that his "mother was the daughter of a white man and a slave woman."[64] Another former slave recounted his origins: "I was born at Richmond, Virginia; my father was my first master; at the age of eleven months, myself, mother, and twin sister, were sold to my father's brother. . . . My mother and sister were resold, but to whom, or where taken I never could ascertain."[65] Yet another former slave recalled the selling of his half sister on the auction block, "a girl of seventeen, half-white, for she was the daughter of her deceased master!"[66]

Another former slave painted a similar picture of kinship and family across the color line. William Thompson, an escaped slave living in Canada, recalled a seemingly incestuous scenario he knew of from his days in slavery.

> I knew a man at the South who had six children by a colored slave. Then there was fuss between him and his wife, and he sold all the children but the oldest slave daughter. Afterward, he had a child by this daughter, and sold mother and child before the birth. . . . Such things are done frequently in the South. One brother sells the other: I have seen that done. True, I have not seen any barbarities, as some have.[67]

The reason for keeping one of the children, the oldest, hints at the incestuous desire that animated the plantation household. The oldest of his presumably young children was his primary sexual object, whom he raped, impregnated, and was forced to sell. The situation seems different from the perspective of the husband/father/master: why retain one of his slave daughters, as presumably there were other slave women to serve as his sexual object? Yet, perhaps the most revealing moment here is Thompson's perspective. There is a good deal of ambiguity in his conception of kinship and family. First, he modified the master's daughter with slave, making her, as was the case, not quite a daughter, but not simply a slave. It is this disruptive modifier that may account for Thompson's bizarre conclusion to this tale. Having just recounted what the average reader would assume to be an incestuous relationship between a slave master and his enslaved daughter, Thompson claimed that "such things are done frequently in the South," yet those things were not incest, but the selling of family members. Thompson at once claimed he had seen a brother sell a brother yet had never seen any barbarities. In this sense, then, it was ambiguous at best whether Thompson recounted a story of incest; instead, what is clear is that he recounted a story of interracial sex, the commodification of family members, and intrafamilial sex. Whether or not it constituted incest was the ambiguity that lay at the heart of the intersection between sexuality and family in the discourse of slavery.

Lewis Clarke, another former slave, writing in the *National Anti-Slavery Standard*, and recounting the intermixing of genealogies, revealed the incestuous logics of sexuality and family in slavery. "My grandmother was her master's daughter; and my mother was her master's daughter; and I was my master's son; so you see I han't got but one-eighth of the blood."[68]

While attempting to show that it was not right to enslave him since he was less black than white, Clarke in part based his claim to freedom on incest. Yet, this perverse claim to freedom was articulated in a language that denied the logics of the slaveholder's fantasy: writing in the language of sons and daughters demonstrated the vernacular knowledge of paternity and kinship across the color line.

While it may be unsurprising that former slaves' accounts of life in slavery would disrupt dominant slaveholding fantasies, they also disrupted the abolitionist fantasy, as they articulated different visions of the black family in slavery. While all the accounts describe the effect of the domestic slave trade in similar terms to white abolitionists, the consequences differ, showing the abolitionist discourse of slavery to have its own racial logics. Julia Brown, a former slave, recalled an incident of incest and the troubles it caused at the plantation on which she lived. Claiming that her owners, the Nashes, did not generally sell their slaves, Brown nonetheless recalled an instance when they sold a slave out of necessity. "They sold one once 'cause the other slaves said they would kill him 'cause he had a baby by his own daughter."[69] This recognition by both the slaves as well as their owners of family and kinship again belied the abolitionist fantasy of the racial ordering of kinship. Revealing a more complicated relation to the domestic slave trade, this account also revealed that the incest prohibition, seen by abolitionists as a casualty of slavery, functioned.

Perhaps most telling in regards to the abolitionist imagining of slave families was a comment made by Josiah Henson, an ex-slave made famous as the inspiration for Harriet Beecher Stowe's Uncle Tom. "Slavery had no power to eradicate the social ties that bound the different members of a family together, and though families were often torn asunder, yet memory generally kept the affections warm and abiding."[70] Indeed, it was precisely the eradication of affection by slavery, in addition to the legal constraints on marriage, natal alienation, and commodification, that seemed to render the slave family nonexistent and hence slave society incestuous. Henson's reliance on affection as a site of resistance to slavery challenged the abolitionist fantasy, as did the invocations of paternity across the color line.

The discourse of slavery presumed that the commodification of the slave entailed absolute natal alienation, compounded by the absence of legally recognized marriage and the disorderly circulation of slaves and rupturing of families by the domestic slave trade. All of these, taken together created the conditions for incest and the absence of an incest prohibition, a contradictory figuration. The discourse of incest linked processes of commodification to articulations of kinship and emphasized the epistemological form of kinship. In this manner, kinship was not a prediscursive reality represented by the language of kinship, but an effect of ledgers, plantation registers, birth and death records, and marriage certificates. The enslaved were either abstract commodities in these texts or excluded from them altogether. However, the enslaved produced vernacular epistemologies of kinship that drew on furtive glances at the documents of kinship and genealogy, articulated with the spread of information through slave networks. In doing so, they ruptured the racial boundaries of legitimate kinship, revealing the incestuous structure of slavery. This, however, was not the only configuration of incest in the discourse of slavery. Antislavery writers also envisioned a world of slave breeding where all prohibitions were transgressed in the rapacious pursuit of property and capital accumulation. In this process, race was made in the intersecting space of incest and interracial sex. This discourse, then, leads into the proslavery fantasy, in which the plantation household was both a sentimental, affectionate loving sphere and riven by sex across the color line.

Incest and the Plantation Family

The domestic slave trade, which increased the threat of disordered kinship and ruptured families, also invoked the specter of slave breeding. While the language of slave breeding was not new, it took on added force in the context of the domestic slave trade, which, according to many antislavery writers, produced the conditions incest.[71] Theodore Dwight Weld, in his study of the internal slave trade in the United States, divided the southern states into breeding and consuming states, where the northern states of Virginia and Maryland worked to increase the slave population through breeding in order to sell slaves to consuming states like Louisiana, Mississippi, and South Carolina.[72] Weld and others conceived of slave breeding as productive not only of growth in the slave population, but also, and primarily, of rampant sexuality transgressing all boundaries and prohibitions in order to gain profit. As the term breeding indicated, slaves were aligned with livestock rather than humanity, and since profit was the driving motive, rules of kinship were not ignored, but rather absent. "The pecuniary inducement to general pollution must be very strong," wrote Weld, "since the larger the slave increase, the greater the master's gains, and especially since the mixed blood demands a considerably higher price than the pure black."[73] Weld implicated the slaveholder and other white men associated with the plantation in slave breeding, as it was more profitable to sell mixed race slaves than "pure black" slaves. Quoting a Methodist minister from the South, Weld was able to draw what, in abolitionist discourse, would have been an authentic picture of southern plantations. "Planters have no objection to any white man or boy having free intercourse with all the females; and it has been the case that an overseer has been encouraged to make the whole posse his harem and has been paid for the issue. This causes a general corruption of morals."[74] Not only did it cause a corruption of morals, it also caused disruption of a supposedly ordered kinship system, as offspring were bred for the market with no intent of keeping the children in an organized kin community. Slave breeding, in Weld's telling, was a process of capital accumulation that knew no restraint, transgressing foundational rules of sexuality and kinship.

As James Oakes has argued, while slaveholders did not mean to imply interracial sex and abuse when they spoke of slave breeding, the value of the offspring and the power of the market often lead to such sexual abuse in practice.[75] And, as some abolitionists pointed out, the profit motive and the disordered licentiousness characteristic of slave breeding could very well lead to incest. Indeed, the confusion of genealogies inherent in the practice of slave breeding, if nothing else, at least did away with any of the basic structures of the incest prohibition, as people were conceived expressly to be sold away, leaving no manner in which incest could be prohibited.

George Bourne, an early abolitionist, painted a picture of incestuous slave breeding that followed directly from the unchecked lust of slaveholders. "On many plantations," wrote Bourne, "bribes are offered expressly to encourage the utmost licentiousness that children may be born; who are always for sale, provided rapacity can be satisfied; and thus all maternal and parental and pure domestic feelings wither and die."[76] In the context of this discussion of "breeding wenches," as Bourne described enslaved women, he invoked incestuous relations as the necessary result of such practices. Because of this breeding, Bourne explained, every plantation was to be found in the greatest degree of disorder and dissolution. "There may be some men, who will not degrade themselves by an actual participation in the fornication, adultery, and incest, which inhere to almost every slave quarter: but who ever heard of a man that would not connive at all these things, and reward the father and mother, if he had so promised, for so cheaply putting another 'fellow,' or another 'wench' within his grasp?"[77] Here, rather than incest being the anomaly, Bourne constructed a scenario in which the virtuous man, adhering to the strictures of the incest prohibition against the enticements of pecuniary gain, was the anomaly. In that manner, as with most of the abolitionist images, incest was intimately tied to the commodification of bodies and capital accumulation.

To illustrate the point, Bourne recounted a sojourn to the South in which he observed incestuous breeding firsthand. Meeting a Virginian on the road, Bourne rode a distance with him and had some of his curiosities about the South answered. Seeing Bourne distraught, the Virginian asked what was troubling him. With some hesitation, Bourne responded that he was "puzzling . . . to know how so many people of different colours could be collected together on one plantation." The Virginian, after uproarious laughter, explained that the plantation owner in question did not buy slaves but bred them. Bourne, however, was still confused about "how so many people of different colours could be . . . on one plantation." The Virginian then divulged "the major's process of multiplying and whitewashing his slaves," a process Bourne at first would "dare not publish."[78] However, the ambivalence of the incestuous fantasy played itself out in Bourne's text, as he followed the negation with a full delineation of incestuous breeding. After attesting to the high stature the plantation owner held in Virginian society, Bourne revealed the method of breeding and the gradations in skin color that he observed. "It is manifest, that there is scarcely a gradation in the crime of incest . . . which was not constantly and openly perpetrated, if not actually before the eyes, evidently within the knowledge of his wife and daughters."[79] The practice of slave breeding, central to the production of profit in the upper South, was in and of itself productive of and the product of incest. It was one of the primary places in the institution of slavery where the fundamental rules, laws, and prohibitions of American society broke down. Yet, while all of this served to disassociate northern ideal families from the perversions of slavery, Bourne could not completely sever the ties between this scene and broader American principles, as he described what he saw as an "unusual display of domestic purity and of American freedom."[80]

While Bourne was explicating the breakdown of the incest prohibition as a result of the profit motive, he also conflated incest with interracial sex,

Figure 5. "A Slave Plantation" depicts a slave coffle supposedly born of the incestuous lust of their master. From George Bourne, *Picture of Slavery in the United States of America* (Middletown, Conn.: E. Hunt, 1834), 94.

a trope common to antebellum America in both the North and the South. Bourne's initial confusion stemmed from the variety of skin colors he saw, which implied a great deal of interracial sex (see Figure 5). What he ended up with was a vision of incest, where gradations of color slipped into gradations of incest. This was not uncommon among abolitionist invocations of incest. Rejecting the criticisms of some, one abolitionist claimed he would rather be called an infidel and blasphemer than be associated with "child-stealers and man-hunters, and traders in their own flesh and blood, who bleach the complexion of their slaves by incest and adultery, to make them a more marketable commodity."[81] Where Richard Jennings (Chapter 1) had claimed that markets were established to facilitate sexual desire, here the profit motive prevailed over what Bourne considered normative sex.

Bourne was not the first to deploy this scenario, even if his had the added force of an act of authentic reportage. *The Adventures of Jonathan Corncob*, a late eighteenth-century picaresque that recounted the travails of a "Loyal American Refugee," also produced this vision of the sexual and racial economy of the plantation. Corncob, as his name implies, spent most of the novel moving from one sexual encounter to another. Yet, when he arrived in Barbados he was confronted with the incestuous life of the master and enslaved women on a plantation to which his friend had brought him. Corncob arrived at the plantation house with his friend while the master was out. Upon entering the house, Corncob remarks on the enslaved women he sees there: "at one end of [the apartment] was sitting an old negress, smoking her pipe. Near her was an elderly mulatto woman; at a little distance was a female still less tawny of complexion, called in the country, as I believe, a mestee; and at the other end of the room I observed a yellow quadroon giving suck to a child, which, though a little sallow, was as white as children in Europe generally are."[82] Corncob, like Bourne more than two decades later, commented on "this regular gradation of light and shade."[83] His friend informs him that these women are all part of the planter's family, and that the planter, Mr. Winter, "is the father of them all."[84] Corncob's friend then recounts the genealogy in a near biblical scene of begetting. "When he was very young he had the mulatto woman by the negress: when the mulatto was twelve years old, he took her for his mistress, and had by her the mestee. At about the same age his intimacy with the mestee produced the quadroon, who had by him a few months ago the white child you see in her arms."[85]

This incestuous genealogy was what both Bourne and Corncob's friend in Barbados called "whitewashing," and was a site where incest and inter-racial sex came together. Whitewashing has a rather long history that stretches back at least to William Byrd II in the early eighteenth century. In fact, Byrd's account of whitewashing, found in his commonplace book was peculiarly similar to Corncob's from the end of the eighteenth century. "A wicked West Indian," Byrd wrote, "boasted that he has washt the Black [. . .] White" through incest. The man "had an Intrigue with an Ethiopian Princess, by whome he had a Daughter that was a Mulatto. Her he lay with, believeing no man had so good a right to gather the Fruit as he who planted it." Carrying this on for several generations, the "wicked West Indian" ulti-mately had a "perfectly white" daughter.[86] Thomas Jefferson, in a letter from 1815, claimed that by the fifth generation of interracial sex the off-spring would be whitewashed, and thus a "free *white* man, and a citizen of the United States to all intents and purposes."[87] Significantly, Jefferson used the incestuous reproduction of a Merino ram as his example and a mathe-matical equation to prove his claim, blurring the line between human and animal in incestuous reproduction, much like animal breeders and phrenol-ogists. It also produced the racial dominance of whiteness, in a sense akin to the manner in which S. M. Bemiss had argued that American pioneers, because of their hybrid whiteness, could engage in incestuous reproduction and avoid hereditary degeneration (Chapter 4). Here, so the logic went, Winter's identity moved through each generation, as the incest produced a white descendant after several generations, at which point he had "washed himself white at a very early age, being at this time less than sixty years old."[88] For his part, Corncob was disturbed by both the incestuous practices and the quotidian manner in which his friend presented them. "This com-plicated incest, and the coolness with which my friend spoke of it, made me begin to think it no wonder that Barbados was subject to hurricanes."[89] Corncob linked the incestuous transgression of nature with the natural disasters to which Barbados was prone and about which he was worrying.

The Caribbean islands took on an incestuous quality in antebellum America, one associated with slavery. Orson Fowler, in his catalogue of incestuous maladies, singled out the Bahamas as a site of rampant incest and a disfigured population. And thus phrenology's suturing of incest, reproduction, and hereditary degeneration was (unsurprisingly) bound up in the production of racial difference and the hierarchies therein in antebel-lum America. One of Fowler's examples was quite telling in this regard.

> Dr. F. A. Pinckney, of Keywest, says he has seen many of the inhabi-tants of the Bahamas, and that all of them were deformed in body, and deficient and dull in intellect. He had never been there, but had understood that the specimens which he saw were but fair repre-sentations of the inhabitants of these islands. They generally are

employed in the meanest occupations, and have not capacity enough to take the lead in any pursuit. Dr. P. understood and supposed that the cause of their physical and mental infirmity was owing to intermarriage, and to that only.[90]

Island populations were frequently associated with incest in the nineteenth century. Missionaries and ethnographers often described Hawaii (or the Sandwich Islands) as incestuous, in part because of the isolation that island life bred in the past.[91] Yet, the Bahamas, and the Caribbean more generally, were certainly not isolated in the mid-nineteenth century and would not have been figured as such. Indeed, in the nineteenth-century American imaginary, the Bahamas would have conjured images of African slaves, and so Dr. Pinckney, via Hale, via a propagator of one brand of racial science, Orson Fowler, imagined an entire island populated by the offspring of incest. The enslaved were an incestuous lot in a certain American imaginary.[92]

While Fowler did not suggest a link between incest and interracial sex, he did secure the relationship between incest, slavery, and degeneration. The link between incest and interracial sex was not confined to abolitionist or satirical novels, nor was degeneration simply the province of phrenology. Henry Hughes, the southern sociologist and apologist for slavery, also saw the horrors of incest that lurked in the interracial sex of the plantation household. Hughes, the first intellectual to explicitly write a work of sociology in America, was responsible for one of the more infamous references to incest in the nineteenth century, one that also recalls the language of physiology and phrenology.[93] "Hybridism is heinous. Impurity of races is against the law of nature. Mulattoes are monsters. The law of nature is the law of God. The same law which forbids consanguinous amalgamation forbids ethnical amalgamation. Both are incestuous. Amalgamation is incest."[94] This passage has done a great deal of work in its career. Eugene Genovese, for instance, claimed that Hughes was "oblivious to the sport that later generations might make with his words."[95] Genovese's lack of interpretive work made his reference to Hughes accurate. Ranging from claims that it was contradictory in the sense that it forced someone like Hughes to acknowledge the common humanity of whites and blacks, to the claim that it was simply the confluence of taboos against too same and too different, invocations of this passage tend to treat it as an anomaly when in fact it was part of a much broader discourse on incest and slavery.[96] Its ambiguity, however, was key, compounded by Hughes's style, in which the words seem almost to precede the thoughts.

Hughes's conflation of incest and amalgamation recalls the writings of phrenologists, physiologists, and animal breeders and has a certain affinity with the antebellum slave codes. The codes tended to treat both incest and amalgamation in the same statute, making them formal equivalents. In Delaware, for example, incest and interracial marriage were in the same statute. "No man or woman shall intermarry within the degrees herein after named," the statute read, enumerating the prohibited relations, and then, "marriage shall be unlawful between a white person and a *negro or mulatto.*"[97] If it recalled the racial science of physiology and antebellum slave codes, Hughes's conflation of incest and amalgamation also trafficked in the same kinds of representations that Bourne deployed in his antislavery work.

Hughes's conflation of incest and interracial sex, when reinserted in its larger context, is both less mysterious and more far reaching, intersecting with questions of hygiene, ethics, and sovereignty:

> Races must progress. . . . They have hygienic duties. Hygiene is both ethnical and ethical; moral duties are coupled to the relation of the races. Races must not be wronged. Hygienic progress is a right. It is a right, because a duty. But hygienic progress forbids ethnical regress. Morality therefore, which commands general progress, prohibits this special regress. The preservation and progress of a race, is a moral duty of the races. Degeneration is evil. It is a sin. That sin is extreme. Hybridism is heinous. Impurity of races is against the law of nature. Mulattoes are monsters. The law of nature is the law of God. The same law which forbids consanguinous amalgamation forbids ethnical amalgamation. Both are incestuous. Amalgamation is incest. But the relation of the two races to each other, is moral: every relation has an ethical quality: *ethics is ethnic.* Moral hygienic duties must not be violated. . . . Polity therefore—the duty of the State— prohibits the sovereignty of the black race. Because, if the black race are sovereign, they must be co-sovereign. If not politically subordinate or superordinate; they must be politically coördinate. . . . They must be, the one subordinate, and the other, superordinate. They must not be aggregated; they must be segregated. . . . This is a

hygienic ethnical necessity. It is the duty of caste to prevent amalgamation; it is, caste for the purity of the races. For political amalgamation is ethnical amalgamation.[98]

Hughes here moved from the hygienic implications of amalgamation
through the moral and ethical, to the political rather rapidly. Following the
syllogistic logic Hughes deployed, if ethnical amalgamation was incestuous,
then so too was political amalgamation. And we might recall Jefferson's
whitewashing claims and the Merino ram—incestuous interracial sex
would, for Jefferson, produce a free white citizen by the fifth generation.

If at times contradictory, and at other times simply confusing, Hughes's
vision was a nomothetic one—he sought to elaborate unbending sociological laws, and thus this was a contribution to the antebellum articulation
of the incest prohibition. Among them from the passage above, were the
inexorable nature of progress—Hughes was delineating the obstacles to
what was, in itself, unavoidable and beyond human agency. His logic rested
on a series of equivalences, where hygiene was equated with racial purity,
preservation of race was equated with moral duty, degeneration was
equated with hybridism and sin, amalgamation was equated with incest,
and ethics with ethnics. The hygienic system, of which incest and amalgamation were primary violations, was, for Hughes, one of the primary systems
of an ordered society. The "body hygienic"—a state bureaucratic body—
had the power to "order hygienic statistics or censuses; to keep records of
births, deaths, and marriages; and to keep public hygienic registers," as well
as "to make laws for the conservation and progress of the race; and for
this to prevent degeneration, by prohibiting intermarriages manifestly and
perniciously degenerative."[99] It was the official genealogical record, from
which the natally alienated and commodified slave was excluded. Hygiene,
for Hughes, was racial purity and an effect of the link between legitimacy,
record keeping and paperwork.

At the center of Hughes's account was the incestuous amalgamation
between masters and enslaved women. Hughes could not imagine any other
type of incest or amalgamation, having evacuated the enslaved (as well as
free blacks) of any form of sovereignty; fully commodified, fully alienated,
they were, for Hughes without agency. Sovereignty, on the plantation,
inhered in the dependencies and obligations of the household as economic
matrix. Hughes systematically eliminated the sovereignty of individual families in favor of the larger family of dependencies. "In this system [warran-
teeism], the children of the laborer, are not dependent on the wages of their

father or mother. They are dependent on the capital of the association. That feeds, clothes, and houses them."[100] Hughes, for all intents and purposes, eliminated the functions of the slave family, as all became dependent on the capitalist, or warrantor. Hughes then asserted the patriarchal/paternal role of the capitalist/warrantor/master. "The capitalist is the economic head of the family. . . . He is the economic father of all the children."[101] All the orders of society—political, aesthetic, moral, hygienic, and religious—were rooted in capital, of which the warrantor was the representative.[102] And in this, it was the duty of caste, managed and secured by the father, to ensure hygiene. The father controlled the body hygienic and all the dependents on the plantation. He was the repository of sovereignty and controlled the ethical, ethnical, and hygienic. To engage in amalgamation, then, implied that it was instigated by sovereign authority. For the plantation father to engage in interracial sex on the plantation, in Hughes's scheme, was to engage in sex with his dependent children and thus incest. It was up to the plantation father/master to secure racial purity. And this, Hughes suggested, was a political consideration—sex across the color line, by masters with enslaved women, was both incest and amalgamation, a form of hybridism that violated racial purity and thus ethics, and lead to the degraded form of "political amalgamation."

Hughes's linking of interracial sex and incest also existed in the space of the paternalist familial metaphor common to most proslavery works. Paternalism was, in many respects, a moral justification for the exploitation of slavery. While some historians have argued that paternalism was accepted by both masters and slaves in order to protect both from the worst abuses of the system, others have criticized this line of thought, arguing that paternalism was simply a mask for the violence of slavery. Still other historians, led by James Oakes, have argued that because the majority of slaveholders were small holders oriented toward individualism, paternalism was, if effective at all, limited to a small proportion of slaveholders. Paternalism, however, is better understood as part of the flourishing of the discourse of domestic affection in the late eighteenth and nineteenth centuries. Rather than a form of atavism, paternalism animated the interpenetration of family and sexuality prominent in the antebellum period and in that sense was central to the incestuous articulations of the plantation household.[103] Central to the discourse of paternalism was a focus on the familial dimensions of the plantation.[104] While the pervasiveness of the discourse on the family aligned proslavery rhetoric with other versions of antebellum discourse, this focus on the family, as we have seen, had particularly incestuous connotations within the discourse of slavery. The familial rhetoric articulated an incestuous fantasy based on racial segregation, where the slaveholder, exerting his authority over a paternal institution, could simultaneously uphold and transgress the incest prohibition through the racial coding of his family.[105] As Susan Ryan notes, proslavery ideologues articulated "a particular theory of the family—one characterized by mutual obligations and responsibilities, by white benevolence on the one hand and black gratitude and dependency on the other."[106] Such a description, which neatly summarizes the organic vision of the paternalist family, also recalls the family produced and secured by the universal prohibition of incest in legal writings by James Kent and others, the difference, of course, being that slaves occupied the position children occupied in the legal scene.

The discourse of the family exerting affective ties between master and slave could be found in virtually any defense of slavery in the antebellum period. "It is a bondage from which springs relations, which, with few exceptions, bind the bondsman to his master by the dearest ties," wrote one defender of slavery, "*It is the bondage often of parent and child*, protector and protected: one which it neither offends moral feelings to encourage, nor the best purposes of society to promote."[107] Another defender of slavery was even more explicit about the familial love that existed between the master and slave. "We love our negroes. They form to us a more extended bond for human sympathies. We love our negroes; not as a miser loves his gold; but rather as a father loves his children. The tie, if not so close, is still of the same kind."[108] Here the enslaved peoples were explicitly distinguished from mere property and were made not only human, but part of the slaveholder's family. "As a larger family, associated in the same home interests, in the same hopes and the same fears, they are *of us*—a part of ourselves."[109]

George Fitzhugh, one of the most influential, iconoclastic, and vitriolic of the southern proslavery ideologues, also constructed a vision of the plantation as a family.

> Within the family circle, the law of love prevails, not that of selfishness. But, besides wife and children, brothers and sisters . . . slaves, also, belong to the family circle. Does their common humanity, their abject weakness and dependence, their great value, their ministering to our wants in childhood, manhood, sickness and old age, cut them

off from that affection which everything else in the family elicits? No; the interests of master and slave are bound up together, and each in his appropriate sphere naturally endeavors to promote the happiness of the other.[110]

Clearly the sense of dependence and paternal authority were present, but the ties of affection that served ideologically to mitigate the harshness of slavery were also there. There was an assumption of reciprocity between master and slave, common to most paternalist rhetoric, which Fitzhugh saw as the protection of the slave as well as the master. In some sense, then, these defenses of slavery constituted a "family black and white" that drew on both sentimental affection and the duties and obligations associated with the family by legal writers on the incest prohibition. As Jeffrey Sklansky has pointed out, Fitzhugh, "embraced the sentimental vision of domesticity as a model of hierarchical harmony, ostensibly founded upon familial affection rather than property and power."[111]

Yet, just as these apologists for slavery drew on the sentimental language of the family to demonstrate the benevolence of slavery as an institution, they were, surprisingly, slow to refute charges of sex between masters and enslaved women. Referring to Harriet Martineau's abhorrence of the licentious nature of the slaveholding male, William Gilmore Simms wrote, "it gives a collection of statements which are, no doubt, in too many cases, founded upon fact, of the illicit and foul conduct of some among us, who make their slaves the victims and the instruments alike, of the most licentious passions."[112] Chancellor Harper followed a similar logic, admitting the presence of sexual relations between master and slave. If one were to follow the representations found in some antislavery writing, Harper suggested, one might assume "that a slaveholding country was one wide stew for the indulgence of unbridled lust."[113] While he might have wanted to refute such a vision, Harper was at a loss. "Yet let us not deny or extenuate the truth. It is true that in this respect the morals of this class are very loose, (by no means as universally so as is often supposed,) *and that the passions of men of the superior caste, tempt and find gratification in the easy chastity of the females.*"[114] While others were slow to dismiss the abolitionist charges of unbridled lust but quick to move away from the problematic passions of the slaveholding class, Harper returned to it again and again. "He casts a shade upon the character of every individual of his fellow-citizens, and does every one of them a personal injury," Harper wrote. "So of him who indulges in any odious excess of intemperate or licentious passion."[115]

James Henry Hammond, in the same volume, took a more circuitous route than either Harper or Simms. Hammond was "of the opinion . . . that the public exposure of this vice, even to rebuke, invariable does more harm than good."[116] Hammond might have had a rather personal stake in such "public exposure" of vice, since he carried on incestuous, abusive affairs with several of his nieces.[117] Yet Hammond could not resist discussing the sexual relations of master and slave. He first claimed "that among our white population there are fewer cases of divorce, separation, crim. con., seduction, rape and bastardy, than among any other five millions of people on the civilized earth." However, as Hammond was well aware, it was not the sexual relations among whites that were being questioned by abolitionists.

> But it is said, that the licentiousness consists in the constant intercourse between white males and colored females. . . . I will not deny that some intercourse of the sort does take place. Its character and extent, however, are grossly and atrociously exaggerated. . . . Very few mulattoes are reared on our plantations. . . . If the truth be otherwise, then persons from abroad have stronger prejudices against the African race than we have. Be this as it may, it is well known, that this intercourse is regarded in our society as highly disreputable. If carried on habitually, it seriously affects a man's standing, so far as it is known; and he who takes a colored mistress—with rare and extraordinary exceptions—loses caste at once.[118]

Here was the problem that Hughes had identified—if the plantation was, indeed, a family, metaphoric or otherwise, then instances of "amalgamation" were incest, as the only figure with agency or sovereignty, the master, crossed the color line. Hughes, who serves as a pivot between the abolitionist discourse of slave breeding and the proslavery discourse of the sexualized plantation family, laid bare what these proslavery ideologues noted but never connected: if the plantation functioned as an organic, sentimental family, then sex with slaves was incest.

This discourse of incest also suggests why historians should, perhaps, avoid the antiseptic language of the household. Elizabeth Fox-Genovese has

argued that the use of the term *household* rather than *family* serves to divest
the social unit of the plantation of the emotional ties implied in the term
family.[119] Yet, it is misleading to eschew emotional and affective ties simply
because of the violence of the plantation household. The violence of plantation slavery was not anathema to the language of sentimental affection.
Proslavery ideologues, perhaps more so than any other southerners, lived
as if the slave was a family member enjoying similar privileges to the white
children of the plantation. As Fox-Genovese has pointed out "the metaphor
'my family, white and black' . . . captured the important, if elusive, vision
of an organic community."[120] This metaphor allowed slaveholders to live as
if their slaves were members of their family. Indeed, the incestuous logic of
slavery depended on it.

   The imbrication of incest and slavery was constituted around processes
of commodification and natal alienation. Yet, neither process was absolute.
Despite the frequent positivist enumerations of incest in antislavery lists of
slavery's abuses, the discourse of slavery, like the discourses of theology,
law, and physiology, put the stability and universal quality of the incest
prohibition into question. In this case, incest and its prohibition were
destabilized through race, freedom, and unfreedom. Both anti- and proslavery writings associated incest with slavery and blackness, thus implicitly
managing the immanence of incest to liberalism. If incest seemed to accom-
pany or haunt the circulation of bodies and things in liberal market society
and was a potential consequence of sentimental affection in bourgeois families, both of which in their dominant forms were white and middle class,
then the discourse of slavery attempted to cordon off the liberal subject.
Incest was not an effect of sentimentalism and exchange, but of commodification of persons and the impossibility of sentiment. Yet, even as both
white abolitionists and proslavery writers associated incest with slavery and
blackness, this was never absolute. The disordered genealogies that antislavery writers produced, effects of commodification and the domestic slave
trade, when combined with the acknowledgment of sex across the color
line on plantations, meant that the racialized incest prohibition was never
as effective as imagined. Thus, incest was a marker of blackness and slavery
while it also sat on the color line itself.
   Even as slave narratives produced a vernacular epistemology of kinship
and incest, it was one that, understandably, engaged both categories in the

space of slavery. This racialization of incest would be turned into a geopolitical distribution of incest around the globe as Lewis Henry Morgan crafted his ethnographies of global kinship. Thus the incest prohibition and kinship received sustained theorization in the emergent discipline of anthropology; incest, the persistent threat to and condition of the liberal subject, was relegated to "primitive" societies, especially those, like Hawaii, that were subject to American imperial visions. Morgan and other ethnographers thus accomplished the racial ordering of incest and liberalism begun by antislavery writers.

The Geopolitics of Incest

By the middle of the nineteenth century, the link between incest and the liberal subject had been fully established. Indeed, to think about the modernity of the liberal subject was to think about his relation to the incest prohibition, and his penchant for incest. The incest prohibition had been remade across the nineteenth century in order to both produce and regulate that liberal individual and the bourgeois, sentimental family. What had been primarily a theological, biblical prohibition had found a new foundation in natural law. That natural law, which made the nuclear family the only universal family formation by making only those relations prohibited from marriage and sex, was invoked in order both to preserve hierarchies of obligation and to encourage sociality by forcing children out of the family at some point in order to find marital and sexual partners. This conjugal assumption, that humans were inherently oriented toward coupling, further instantiated the heteronormative relation between incest and the liberal subject. This sociality, inaugurated and guaranteed by the prohibition of incest, implicated both the private and the public nature of liberalism in the discourse of incest. At precisely the moment that markets saturated social relations via the expansion of wage labor, the increase in commodity consumption, and the mobility of persons both to the West and to the rapidly growing urban metropolises of the Atlantic coast, the incest prohibition was articulated in a manner that explicitly encouraged wider sociality and shrunk the realm of kinship to the nuclear family. If the liberal subject needed to be both produced and governed in an age in which liberty was supposed to flourish relatively unimpeded, then the incest prohibition was one of the primary means of that production and governance. Once one is aware of how pervasive the discourse of incest was in the late eighteenth

and nineteenth centuries, it becomes impossible to understand the formation of the individual, the sentimental family, or sexuality without thinking
of incest and its prohibition.

Yet, at the same time that incest became central to the production and
governance of the liberal subject, mechanisms were emerging by which the
white liberal subject was increasingly protected from the danger of incest.
As physiologists and phrenologists articulated a reproductive incest prohibition in the mid-nineteenth century, race entered the picture in some surprising and some less surprising manners. Physiologists like S. M. Bemiss,
while developing a statistical account of the relationship between incest and
hereditary degeneration, claimed that, despite the evidence that incest led
to higher rates of hereditary degeneration, there were certain whites—hardy
pioneers constituting the vanguard of U.S. imperial expansion—who were
able to engage in incestuous reproduction because of their resilient racial
"stock." Phrenologists, who claimed that amativeness, or sexual desire, was
best developed by cultivating nonreproductive erotic relations between parents and children, consistently claimed that people of African descent were
constitutionally marked by excessive amativeness. Thus, the normalized
eroticism of the bourgeois sentimental family was apparently unavailable to
them, and incestuous reproduction was more likely among those of African
descent.

As antislavery writers associated incest with the domestic slave trade and
the natal alienation inherent in the circulation of persons as commodities in
slavery, incest was figured as endemic to slavery. Such an image, articulated
as a criticism of slavery, nonetheless associated incest with slavery and
blackness. If the mobility of persons across the nineteenth century had provoked fears of incestuous returns of alienated family members, abolitionists
made this more extreme form of the circulation of persons through unfreedom and commodification the basis of incest. In each of these developments, the liberal subject was becoming more and more inured to the threat
of incest. This coincided with the contract regime in both labor and marital
relations, demonstrating that the anxieties about how to govern and regulate the liberal subject were becoming less and less acute. Incest served less
as regulation on the liberal subject and bourgeois sentimental family and
instead was invoked to mark and police racial boundaries. Simultaneously,
a new locus of the incest prohibition was emerging in the half-formed discipline of ethnography. This new locus, which located the origins of the prohibition in a deep past accessible only through "primitive" societies, drew

on the racial and imperial visions of incest that had emerged in phrenology, physiology, and the discourse of slavery. Not only was incest becoming racially bounded, it would, in the ethnographic imagination, be projected outside the bounds of the United States and into locales that were being apprehended by the imperial gaze.

The conflicted diffuse incest prohibition of the antebellum period, which eschewed a universal, theological foundation for the prohibition, gradually found a new foundation in anthropology in the late nineteenth and early twentieth centuries. This new foundation, which imagined primitive societies without an incest prohibition and then theorized, based on rather hazy and fungible ethnographic knowledge, the manner in which the incest prohibition was established in order to organize society and culture. While there were debates over the precise mechanism, all iterations of this anthropological theory were compatible with the flourishing of the liberal subject. In the United States there was perhaps no more influential account of this process than the one found in the works of the Rochester lawyer turned ethnographer Lewis Henry Morgan.

Morgan was, without question, the most prominent ethnographer in nineteenth-century America and both his ethnographic work and his own biography intersected with nearly every major concern of the discourse of incest at mid-century.[1] Trained as a lawyer, Morgan spent his legal career particularly concerned with property law, capital accumulation, and later, indigenous property rights. His turn toward ethnography, which did not displace his career as a lawyer until later in his life, was also a result of his early fascination with indigenous Americans, especially the Iroquois, which was manifest in the fraternal societies he both formed and participated. In "playing Indian," to borrow Philip Deloria's apt phrase, Morgan attempted to construct an authentic American identity through a complex identification with Native Americans.[2] This process of identification moved from early literary fascinations to later ethnographic accounts, and from an incipient American nationalism to the staid language of ethnographic fact.[3]

If the literary, ethnographic, and legal structured much of Morgan's life, just as they did the contours of the incest prohibition, Morgan's life and work intersected with other aspects of the discourse of incest, as well. In 1851 Morgan married Mary Elizabeth Steele, his first cousin. Thus, just as Morgan embarked on his mapping of the evolutionary history of human kinship, he engaged in what was increasingly deemed an incestuous marriage. Compounding the situation, their first son, Lemuel, was born with a disability that was commonly attributed to the consanguinity of his parents (although there is no evidence that this was a factor).[4] Without suggesting that we travel down the problematic path of psychobiography, it is striking that Morgan's body of work evinced a tension between cultural and biological explanations of the incest prohibition. In this sense, precisely as he was mapping kinship and by extension the history of the incest prohibition, Morgan, in both his work and his life, was caught in the transformations wrought in the meaning of incest in antebellum America. Moreover, Steele, who prior to their marriage had planned to become a Presbyterian missionary, was a devout evangelical, while Morgan was, at best, disinterested, thus playing out the tensions of mid-century secularity. As John Lardas Modern has written in reference to Morgan's first published ethnographic work, *League of the Iroquois,* it "was part of the long transition from the study of a divinely sanctioned human society toward the investigation of human articulations of self and divinity as the relations between humans, determined, in part, by these articulations."[5] Sacred and secular, cultural and biological, legal and literary, Morgan's ethnography of kinship was thoroughly ensconced in all permutations of nineteenth-century liberal incest.

This is nowhere more apparent than in Morgan's first masterwork, *Systems of Consanguinity and Affinity in the Human Family,* which also furthered the imperial imagination of the incest prohibition articulated by phrenologists and physiologists.[6] In his classic critique of kinship studies, the anthropologist David Schneider wrote that "between the fieldwork and the monograph falls the shadow of translation."[7] In the imperial shadows of ethnography one finds a geopolitical distribution of kinship, one that managed, like the discourses of slavery, phrenology, and physiology, the incestuous threat to the liberal subject in antebellum America. Casting the longest shadow was one instance of ethnographic translation, a primal scene in the "invention" of kinship: Morgan's *Systems.* Doubly removed from the native informant (a notably problematic figure in her own right), Morgan's text relied on knowledge of kinship terms provided by Christian missionaries and U.S. diplomats.[8] At the center of Morgan's translations, which yielded nothing less than a global, comparative ethnography of kinship that also explained the progressive, evolutionary development of human history, was what Morgan called the "Hawaiian custom." A singular atavism that provided empirical ballast to Morgan's inevitable conjectures, Hawaii was represented as a nearly incestuous society that recalled the origins of humanity. By resting the entire edifice of kinship on Hawaii,

Morgan quite consciously located his ethnographic project within the American imperial imaginary of the nineteenth century. The conjunction of ethnography, kinship, incest, and Hawaii mapped a new world of national expansion across a globe divided by systems of kinship. In this mapping, Morgan was among the first to develop a new locus of the incest prohibition, one that would quell the disorder in the discourse of incest that had reigned in the preceding decades.

Morgan, and especially *Systems*, sits in a liminal position in the history of incest. While *Systems* bears some of the remnants of the incest discourse articulated across so many domains in antebellum America, Morgan's later and better-known work, *Ancient Society*, published just six years after *Systems*, bore none of this ambiguity.[9] Incest, or consanguine marriage, was to be avoided because of the deleterious effects on the offspring. Despite working out elaborate and complex kinship systems and their relation to the evolution of private property across human history, Morgan nonetheless associated the prohibition of incest with blood relations and reproduction. But prior to this, Morgan was less overtly concerned with reproduction as a basis for the incest prohibition.

Morgan published *Systems of Consanguinity and Affinity of the Human Family* in 1871 as part of the Smithsonian's Contributions to Knowledge series.[10] It was the first ethnographic, empirical, and comparative study of both Western and non-Western kinship structures, systematically linking them to descent, forms of marriage and family, property, and political organization. Despite the multiple microdivisions of world kinship, Morgan posited one great binary division between the classificatory and the descriptive systems.[11] The classificatory system worked on the principle of large, general categorizations that collapsed the distinction between collateral and lineal relatives (for example, the father's brother [uncle] and the father were both referred to as father). The descriptive system tended to describe each unique kin relation, usually through a combination of primary and secondary designations (for example, father and mother were primary, and then other relations would have secondary modifiers—father's brother, father's sister, mother's brother, mother's sister, etc.). Morgan located the classificatory throughout Asia, the Pacific, southern Africa, and the Americas; the descriptive throughout Europe and the Middle East. These two categories were then grafted onto a fifteen-stage evolutionary scale, which ranged from promiscuous intercourse (in which incest was not prohibited) to the "civilized family" (the monogamous conjugal couple). The classificatory was closer to the origin and the descriptive closer to the culmination of evolutionary development. Indeed, Morgan referred to the fifteenth and final stage as "The Overthrow of the Classificatory System of Relationship, and the Substitution of the Descriptive."[12] Despite the fact that all societies would ultimately evolve to the "civilized family," in the mid-nineteenth century human societies were distributed all along the evolutionary scale, suggesting that some societies developed at a more rapid pace than others. "Mankind, if one in origin, must have become subdivided at a very early period into independent nations," Morgan wrote. "Unequal progress has been made by their descendants from that day to the present; some of them still remaining in a condition not far removed from the primitive."[13] This type of historicism, as historian and critic Dipesh Chakrabarty has argued, "posited historical time as a measure of the cultural distance . . . that was assumed to exist between the West and the non-West. In the colonies, it legitimated the idea of civilization."[14]

Despite his insistence on an empirical and systematic program of research, the earliest stages in Morgan's evolutionary scale were entirely conjectural (a feature that has marked most writing on the incest prohibition both before and after Morgan). Morgan acknowledged as much, entitling an 1868 article "A Conjectural Solution of the Origin of the Classificatory System of Relationship."[15] Of the fifteen stages, the first three ("Promiscuous Intercourse," "Intermarriage or Cohabitation of Brothers and Sisters," and "Communal Family") were lost to the distant past.[16] Morgan, however, wanted more than conjecture to sustain his theoretical apparatus. "Although the universal prevalence of promiscuous intercourse in the primitive ages . . . rests, for the present, upon an assumption, evidence is not wanting in many barbarous nations of such a previous condition."[17] The fourth stage, which Morgan called the "Hawaiian custom," provided a glimpse of the deep past of promiscuous intercourse while meeting the empirical standards of Morgan's ethnography. In Hawaii, Morgan saw "a condition akin to that of inferior animals, and more intensely barbarous than we have been accustomed to regard as a possible state of man."[18] This was "neither a matter of conjecture nor assumption'" according to Morgan, since the ethnographic data had been compiled from missionary and diplomatic informants in Hawaii.[19]

In Morgan's account, Hawaiian kinship practices suggested that a visitor to Hawaii was traveling not only through space but also backward

through time. The Hawaiian custom, or what Morgan, through his informants, sometimes called the "Pinaluanic bond," was a form of communal
marriage. According to one of Morgan's informants, Lorrin Andrews, a
former missionary and at that time a justice on the Supreme Court of
Hawaii, *pinalua* was "rather amphibious."[20] All brothers held their wives in
common, just as all sisters held their husbands in common. Despite both
Andrews and Artemous Bishop, one of Morgan's missionary informants,
claiming that this was an ancient practice that had long since disappeared
and that "pinalua" now referred to a "dear friend or intimate companion,"
Morgan nonetheless rested his entire evolutionary scale on it. The anthropologist Thomas Trautmann has called the Hawaiian custom "a very
doubtful piece of goods" and "the creature of pure theorizing."[21] Morgan's
informants never claimed they had witnessed it nor that it existed in the
mid-nineteenth century, and few contemporary scholars believe that such
a practice ever existed.[22] Nonetheless, by the time Morgan came to summa-
rizing his contributions, the Hawaiian custom had moved from a "rather
amphibious" story, in part disavowed by his informants, to holding "a
material position in the [evolutionary] series, for the reason that it was an
existing and still prevalent custom in the Sandwich Islands at the epoch of
their discovery."[23] Its material position served as evidence of the preceding,
conjectural stages of human history. "It is promiscuous intercourse, within
limits. The existence of this custom necessarily implies an antecedent condition of promiscuous intercourse, involving the cohabitation of brothers
and sisters, and perhaps of parent and child; thus finding mankind in a
condition akin to that of the inferior animals, and more intensely barbarous
than we have been accustomed to regard as a possible state of man."[24]

Ultimately, I am not concerned with the veracity of the "Hawaiian custom." Rather, my concern is with its imperial implications, the expansionist
and civilizational fantasies it sustained through its claims to empiricism and
scientific veracity. Morgan's translation of ethnographic fact into mono-
graphic form made Hawaii the global exemplar of savagery and the origins
of the so-called human family; intellectually and systematically indispensable, Hawaii was "repulsive and distatsteful" insofar as it suggested promiscuous intercourse, which was "the lowest conceivable stage of barbarism"
in which "man could scarcely be distinguished from the brute; . . . ignorant
of marriage . . . of the family, except the communal . . . he was not only a
barbarian but a savage."[25] This description of Hawaii was not produced in

an ethnographic vacuum, and despite Morgan's concern with "the scientific acquisition of factual knowledge," the Hawaiian custom, the empirical pivot on which Morgan's conjectural history turned, was as indebted to missionary and imperial fantasies of the distribution of incestuous marital and sexual practices across the globe.[26] In its indebtedness to such representations, it also sustained them, lending scientific legitimacy to imperial fantasy.

Indeed, Morgan had already been producing a context in his ethnographic explorations of the indigenous population of continental North America. Morgan was an ambivalent imperialist—he produced ethnographic knowledge about the indigenous populations of North America, especially the Iroquois, which was often highly romanticized and tended to reify the indigenous population. While Morgan documented, or rather, produced representations of indigenous kinship systems, incest was not a central concern. Which is not to say that he did not find incest, or something like it. In notebooks Morgan kept on a journey through the western United States between 1859 and 1862, he recorded the marriage customs of the various Native American tribes he stayed with. In July of 1861, for example, Morgan constructed a fragment of Dakota "marriage customs." His informant told him that "they buy their wives, but that none of the kindred named on the schedule are allowed to intermarry, except those related by marriage. A man may marry his brother's widow, but is not obliged to do so."[27] Here there was the buying and selling of wives and a note that a man may marry his brother's widow, a relation, coincidentally, that was prohibited in Leviticus. Morgan traveled throughout the West for three years cataloguing kinship and marriage customs in order to fill out his evolutionary system. This process worked to confirm the modernity of liberal monogamous forms of marriage.[28]

As one can glean from the midcentury periodical press, the imperial road was seemingly paved with incest. Writing with concern for the "moral prospect" of Mexico in 1848, W. H. Norris noted that "the shocking crime of incest is common." This should not have come as a surprise, given Norris's sense that "in morals, the mass of the people are exceedingly depraved."[29] The quotidian quality of incest in Mexico (which, it should be noted, was just as quotidian in the United States, if one followed the newspapers) served as both a warning and a justification: a warning about the moral and sexual condition of the population in those areas ceded to the United States; and a justification of the imperial war that had just come to a close, locating the Mexican population among the savage rather than civilized nations.

Morgan, along with many missionary writers, located Hawaii outside of modernity and thus opened it to imperial expansion by noting the presence of incestuous practices and social relations fully enmeshed in kinship.[30] With incest indexing both political modernity and imperial opportunity, Hawaii was held up as a quintessentially incestuous society. This was, for Morgan, a consequence of its isolation. "From continental to island the change for the worse is very great with respect to opportunities and incite-ments to progress," wrote Morgan, "it would be expected that isolated pop-ulations would remain in a stationary condition through longer periods of time than the inhabitants of continents."[31] It is clear that Morgan drew his impressions of Hawaii from missionary writings, noting that "traces" of the Hawaiian custom "were found by American missionaries in the Sandwich Islands."[32] If isolation preserved these traces, their discovery was an effect of both global movement and imperial expansion, conditions that spelled the end of that isolation.

Missionary writings from the period exemplified this paradox. In *Poly-nesian Researches: Hawaii*, William Ellis, an English missionary who first arrived in the Polynesian islands in 1816, noted several features of marriage and kinship.[33] "The marriage tie is loose," wrote Ellis, "and the husband can dismiss his wife on any occasion."[34] Polygamy was permitted among all social ranks, according to Ellis, but was practiced only by "the chiefs, whose means enable them to maintain a plurality of wives."[35] The ease of separa-tion and legitimacy of polygamy would have worked to place Hawaiians beyond the pale of civilization, but these were not the end of transgressive marital practices. Where Morgan would posit a nearly incestuous practice in pinalua as evidence that a society without the incest prohibition had once existed, Ellis described loose marriage bonds, polygamy, and royal incest.

Incestuous brother-sister marriage, according to Ellis, was legitimate for only a small segment of Hawaiian society, "conducted on principals of political expediency, with a view to strengthen alliances and family influ-ence; and among the reigning family, brothers and sisters marry."[36] The implication was that such marriages, governed by political expediency and the consolidation of power in a kin group, would have been antidemocratic. Such marriages measured the distance between modernity and barbarism.

"This custom, so revolting to every idea or moral propriety, that the mind is shocked at the thought of its existence, appears to have been long in use."[37] Despite his revulsion, Ellis did not recount these perceived kinship practices simply to note their barbarism. Rather he was demonstrating the civilizingforce of Christianity.[38] With the same consequences, Morgan would refer to the "reformatory" power of evolution. Ellis recounted a brother-sister marriage proposed between a "young prince and princess, both the children of the same parents." Despite being a practice "long in use," the opinions of the council of chiefs and the Christian missionaries were sought regarding its propriety. The chiefs found the marriage favorable, arguing that "being the highest chiefs in the islands, they could not marry any others who were their equals, and ought not to form any alliances with inferiors, as it was desirable that the supreme rank they held should descend to their posterity."[39]

The missionaries were unimpressed with this justification, arguing "that such marriages were forbidden in the word of God, were held in abhorrence by all civilized and Christian lands, and had seldom been known to leave any descendants to wear the honour or sustain the rank the contracting parties desired thus to perpetuate."[40] Which is to say, such marriages transgressed the law of God, were met with civilized disgust, and, rather than perpetuating royal blood lines, were more likely to end in sterility. In the end, the reformatory power of Christianity was realized. "The marriage was postponed; and it appears to be the opinion of the chiefs in general, that it ought not to take place . . . and we view it as a happy circumstance, subversive of an evil custom, and tending to produce moral feelings highly advantageous, and illustrative of the collateral advantages arising from the influence of Christian missionaries."[41] Ellis does not bother to inform the reader how the chiefs' opinion was changed, but the implication, of course, is that the truly progressive nature of Christian forms of marriage and kinship was realized, thus liberating Hawaiian indigeneity of one of its barbarous encumbrances.

Morgan's disgust thus was aligned with more pervasive representations of imperialism in general, and Hawaii in particular. Ellis's tale would have served to bolster Morgan's claim that all societies would evolve toward the monogamous, conjugal couple, the hallmark of liberal modernity. In articulating the prohibition of incest as a marker of political modernity, Morgan was not alone. In the early eighteenth century, Lord Bolingbroke, for example, argued that the prohibition of incest was not a natural law, insisting rather that it was a mark of political society and the product of positive law, with the varying degrees to which incest was prohibited signifying the degree to which political society had matured. "The marriages of brothers and sisters . . . may be objected to, as they may be defended, by probable arguments drawn from political considerations; but no colour of an argument can be drawn against them from the constitution of nature, in which all her laws are contained, and by which they are all promulgated. . . . It is evident on the whole, that marriages, within certain degrees of consanguinity and affinity, are forbid by political institutions, and for political reasons."[42] In the late eighteenth century, Gilbert Stuart made a similar argument. "To the degrees of consanguinity and blood," Stuart wrote, "concerning which nature has dictated so little, and polity so much, it is not to be conceived that they paid a scrupulous attention to their marriages. It is a subject on which no infant communities are exact. They attended to it, when, having sallied from their woods, they grew refined by time, observation, and experience."[43] Put differently, the prohibition of incest was a political effect, which implicitly raised the question of whether or not the prohibition of incest was a necessity in a liberal society. As such, these accounts of the origins of the prohibition potentially opened the door to a society in which the incest prohibition was no longer politically expedient at precisely the moment of rising incestuous anxieties.

Morgan gave this developmental, political logic an evolutionary framework, making the prohibition of incest and the coming of the monogamous, conjugal couple makers of political modernity and, importantly, inevitable. The "civilized family" may have been the privilege of the West, but it was also a universal form to which the entire human family would ultimately accede. As such, it was the natural and teleological end, the realization of universality.

> As now constituted, the family is founded upon marriage between one man and one woman. A certain parentage was substituted for a doubtful one; and the family became organized and individualized by property rights and privileges. . . . Upon this family, as now constituted, modern civilized society is organized and reposes. The whole previous experience and progress of mankind culminated and crystallized in this one great institution. . . . The family, which in this view of the case is essentially modern, is the offspring of this vast and varied experience of the ages of barbarism.[44]

If this was the utopian end, Hawaii was the necessary origin, but one that needed to be overcome. It was both the intellectual and empirical lynchpin of Morgan's evolutionary system and an inevitably disappearing practice of kinship.

Morgan's recourse to universalism—we can all be the same in the future—relied on the presence of a geopolitical distribution of incest and kinship. His ethnography was descriptive and normative, and its normative prescriptions were imperial. It was incest that suggested a radical alterity, whether in Mexico or Hawaii, and Morgan's ethnography provided a scientific, evolutionary justification for the benevolent and inevitable eradication of the incestuous practices of a vanishing population. Morgan's ethnography created the evolutionary grounds for an imperial remaking of the world, one that moved through the field of kinship and marriage. And it was one that, in the last analysis, culminated in the liberal subject as the universal type. Antebellum America was the scene of the working-out of the modern incest prohibition, where incest constituted the immanent logic of the liberal subject. Constantly threatening the individual, the nineteenth century was witness to endless iterations of the incest prohibition, in forms that would cultivate the desire of liberal subject while also controlling the problem of incest. Morgan, who theorized the manner in which the liberal subject emerged out of genealogical society, accomplished this, ultimately, by banishing incest to the far-flung corners of the globe, corners that were always possible objects of imperialist expansion.[45] And in doing so, Morgan, more so than anyone else in nineteenth-century America, severed the link between incest and the liberal subject.

Appendix

The Theoretical Life of the Incest Prohibition

Early American history (and the discipline of history, more generally) has had a relatively anti-, or better, atheoretical orientation. The incest prohibition, however, has led a life of mostly theoretical abstraction. Both claims are potentially belied by some counterevidence, but on the whole these seem to be rather accurate descriptions. One aim of this book, however, has been to undermine both of these claims. At times this had the air of inevitability—my project was mostly genealogical; the archive as constituted was broader than the relatively narrow intellectual history of the prohibition. Yet, the prohibition, at least the versions of it that were both most useful and most persuasive, existed mostly in the domains of psychoanalysis and anthropology, which, of course, does not exhaust its theoretical abstractions. Nonetheless, there are useful theories and useless theories—sociobiology, for example, while it might be a particularly fruitful and complex symptom of our times, seems to fall into the latter category. In what follows, I'd like to explore, at greater length, the theoretical life of the incest prohibition, one that both informs the genealogy of the prohibition that structures this book and one that is challenged and critiqued by precisely that genealogy.[1]

In the nineteenth century the incest prohibition was rearticulated in order to govern the emergent liberal subject more effectively. Indeed, these articulations of the prohibition produced as well as governed the liberal subject. To say as much is to argue that the prohibition itself has a history and that there is an archive of the incest prohibition. Moreover, what follows from this is that the incest prohibition, in all of its supposed universality, is not simply a foundational law that orders kinship and culture; it is an effect of a long history of articulations of the prohibition. Put differently, the incest prohibition does not represent specific societies' sexual and marital taboos so much as it produces and orders those societies as an effect of anthropological or psychoanalytic apprehension. As the anthropologist David Schneider has argued apropos kinship, "the study of kinship derives directly and practically unaltered from the ethnoepistemology of European culture," which privileges blood relations as the basis of all kinship.[2] It is this reification of kinship, according to Schneider, that is so pernicious and orders other cultures and societies in a manner understandable in the European imagination. Theories of the incest prohibition have been at the center of this problem.

Theories of the incest prohibition have abounded since the late nineteenth century. All, in different ways, make claims to universality. Some, which we have explored in some detail already, are concerned with hereditary degeneration and reproduction. This is more properly understood as "inbreeding," and, while common sense suggests that the association between hereditary degeneration and incestuous reproduction has been conclusively proven, there is still much variability and debate on the point. Contemporary thought suggests that, at the level of population and across multiple generations, incestuous reproduction will lead to "inbreeding depression," in which fertility rates decline and certain disorders occur with greater frequency than in the general population. At the individual level, however, there seems to be no more genetic variation among the offspring of inbreeding than there is in the general population.[3]

Such theories operate in a discursive domain relatively isolated from cultural interpretations of the prohibition, largely because they are not concerned with relations of affinity or sexual abuse, or anything that is not reproductive. There is, however, a long tradition of writers who argue that humans develop an aversion to sex or marriage with those with whom they share their earliest years of life. This theory emerged in the late nineteenth century in the work of Edward Westermarck. As Westermarck argued, after a brief survey of ethnographic evidence, "among peoples in different parts of the world sexual modesty is especially strongly developed in relations between members of the same family circle."[4] For Westermarck, humans are almost naturally averse to incest. The question that begs to be answered is why societies, like the nineteenth-century United States, would need to expend so much energy defining the incest prohibition. In other words, if there is a natural aversion to incest, why articulate an incest prohibition in the first place? It is this that aligns Westermarck and his present-day epigones with those who treat incest as only a violation of genetic laws, as both obviate the manifest cultural concerns that have animated most writings on incest. While Westermarck's theories had fallen out of favor, they have been revised in recent years by sociobiologists.[5]

Other theories have postulated that there is an aversion to sharing similar bodily substances. These theories tend to make a more material argument about the body, which reduces cultural variation and history to the seeming ahistoricity of the body. The French anthropologist Françoise Hérritier, for instance, has argued that "the fundamental criterion of incest is the contact between identical bodily fluids; . . . what is universal (in the incest prohibition) is the methodical reflection on the placing into contact of identical or different bodies, or secretions, of identical or different substances, even if the solutions to the problem offered by various human groups vary in form and potency, in nature and intensity."[6] This all follows, for Hérritier, from the fundamental instance of identity and difference—sexual difference. Hérritier's essentializing and naturalizing account aligns the incest prohibition with bodily, anatomical difference, to the extent that she can account for even those prohibitions, such as marriage with a deceased wife's sister, in terms of bodily fluids. Such an account evacuates history from the prohibition and uses the prohibition to naturalize sexual difference.

Accounts like these tend to universalize in ways that efface the particularity in the archive of the incest prohibition. In that they are mere iterations of the productive power of the incest prohibition—whether a near-natural incest aversion, a concern with genetics and reproduction, or deduction of the centrality of bodily fluids to the incest prohibition in order to naturalize sexual difference—they all posit a universal prohibition that affirms a common humanity. For contemporary genetic arguments, we are all the same reproductively; for Westermarck the sexual modesty that followed from the incest prohibition could be found in Morocco, India, and the islands of the Pacific Ocean; for Hérritier, the entire ethnography of incest could be reduced to the concern with identical bodily fluids. The desire for this universality in these texts is best captured in Herritier's closing words: "The incontestable and irreducible character of sexual difference is at the origin of the various reflections and directions each society has taken."[7] No matter how different we may seem, Hérritier implies, we are all ultimately the same—we abhor incest in order to maintain sexual difference.

If this kind of bodily materiality was one avenue of universality, one that insistently upheld hierarchies of sexual difference (this continues through to the present day), then the concern with the origins of the prohibition is another. The incapacity to deal with the prohibition historically over the past century, I would argue, follows as much from the fascination with fantasmatic origins among anthropologists and psychoanalysts, which in themselves were, at least in part, a product of the universalizing tendencies immanent to liberalism. As I have argued throughout this book, simply because we can discern a long history of universal language for the incest prohibition does not mean that each invocation of universality was the same. The fact that we have not been able to apprehend something like a liberal incest prohibition, and thus liberal forms of incest, is an effect of the success of liberalism in defining our fields and categories of inquiry.[8] A genealogy of the incest prohibition, then, requires that we pass through the universal claims born of anthropology and psychoanalysis in the late nineteenth and early twentieth centuries and developed across the twentieth century. This does not mean, however, that we can simply dismiss these theoretical elaborations of the prohibition because of their seemingly false universalism.[9] Rather, genealogy demands that we read these theories— those of Morgan and Durkheim, Freud and Lévi-Strauss—critically. When we read them so, they all become more useful, but we might just discover what was lost when we began assuming that all these theorists argued for a simple universalism. Indeed, the universalism of psychoanalysis and anthropology exists ambivalently with particularity, just as in the liberal incest prohibition of nineteenth-century America.

Historians, insofar as they engage with incest at all, have tended to write histories of incest rather than of the incest prohibition. In this, they are distinguished from both the anthropological and psychoanalytic traditions, which have, as John Borneman has noted in regards to anthropology, "been much more fascinated with the incest taboo than with real incest."[10] This has resulted in an unfortunate unwillingness to interrogate the category of incest itself. Frequently, historians have treated incest as a transhistorical category that, whatever variations may have appeared across historical time, is essentially either an abusive relationship, primarily between fathers (or father substitutes) and daughters, or primarily organized around the consanguineous relations of the nuclear family or both. In addition, concerns with reproduction have been read into the prohibition as the underlying biological explanation for the prohibition. All of these have worked to foreclose critical engagement with the category of incest and, with the exception of the last, have tended to focus on incest at the expense of the prohibition.

If we are to historicize the incest prohibition and write a genealogy of incest, we need to engage with those universal accounts of the incest prohibition. In order to do this, I have chosen "representative" (by which I mean influential) accounts, in those of Claude Lévi-Strauss, Sigmund Freud, Jacques Lacan, and Judith Butler. This is in part because the incest prohibitions articulated by Lévi-Strauss and Freud have been the most frequently accused of foreclosing the possibility of incest precisely through their totalizing claims to universality. The intellectual history of the incest prohibition has been, in large part, the history of various theorizations of the universality of the incest prohibition. Indeed, much of this book is devoted to thinking through the reasons liberalism required a universal incest prohibition in the face of individual sovereignty and desire. Much of the literature on the incest prohibition in the late twentieth century and early twenty-first century continues to engage, even if critically, with Lévi-Strauss's structural account of the prohibition or Freud's dual account of the Oedipus complex and the primal horde. To pretend that we can get back to an unvarnished, prepsychoanalytic or structural incest prohibition sustains the illusion that has underwritten much historical writing on incest. Moreover, the liberal incest prohibition that emerged in the late eighteenth century and early nineteenth century fed the psychoanalytic and anthropological accounts of the nineteenth and twentieth centuries.

Lévi-Strauss famously theorized the incest prohibition as the foundational rule that inaugurated the shift from nature to culture via the exchange of women and the exogamic order of kinship. The rule, according to Lévi-Strauss, was neither natural nor cultural; rather it was a threshold. "The rule is at once social, in that it is a rule, and pre-social, in its universality and the type of relationships upon which it imposes its norm."[11] It is universal because fundamental. "The prohibition of incest is in origin neither purely cultural nor purely natural, nor is it a composite mixture of elements from both nature and culture," wrote Lévi-Strauss. "It is the fundamental step because of which, by which, but above all in which, the transition from nature to culture is accomplished. . . . Before it, culture is still non-existent; with it, nature's sovereignty over man is ended. The prohibition of incest is where nature transcends itself."[12] If the temporality of the prohibition is complex, its universality and foundational qualities seem to be unambiguous. Moreover, if Lévi-Strauss offers what remains a sophisticated, if problematic, theorization of the prohibition, it nonetheless sits in a long line of work that presumes the transcendent importance of the prohibition of incest to culture and society.[13]

Freud, of course, also theorized a seemingly universal prohibition in the form of the Oedipus complex. "The barrier against incest" effected social ends, insofar as "the child can erect . . . the barrier against incest, and can thus take up into himself the moral precepts which expressly exclude from his object-choice, as being blood relations, the persons whom he has loved in his childhood."[14] A necessary and fundamental moment in sexual development, incest was nonetheless reduced by Freud, as most theorists had reduced it by the turn of the century, to consanguinity. Yet, there was a certain ambivalence, as Freud seemed to equate blood relatives and those loved in childhood. Quickly, Freud shifted from blood to culture. "Respect for the barrier," he continued, " is essentially a cultural demand made by society."[15] Society, as many antebellum writers would argue in the United States, necessitated the prohibition of incest, or else the "establishment of higher social units may be swallowed up by the family."[16] To have culture and society (universal institutions), for both Lévi-Strauss and Freud, was to have a prior prohibition of incest. Freud further instantiated the universality of the prohibition in his quasi-ethnographic work of 1913, *Totem and Taboo*, in which, writing of "poor, naked cannibals," who would presumably share no morals with modern, civilized societies, nonetheless "set before themselves with the most scrupulous care and the most painful severity the aim of avoiding incestuous sexual relations."[17] Even those who, to Freud's and most modernist eyes, fell almost entirely beyond the pale of "civilization," recognized the prohibition. Indeed, one might say that the modern European norms Freud was investigating were articulated on the backs of the "primitive," a maneuver that was also central to earlier ethnographic accounts of the incest prohibition in America.[18]

This universality, however important to both Lévi-Strauss and Freud, is also something of an illusion. Lévi-Strauss repeatedly refers to the "ambiguity" of the prohibition, suggesting anything but a totalizing universality. Freud, of course, in his famous definition of the taboo in *Totem and Taboo*, writes, "the meaning of 'taboo' . . . diverges in two contrary directions. To us it means, on the one hand, 'sacred', 'consecrated', and on the other 'uncanny,' 'dangerous,' 'forbidden,' 'unclean.'"[19] This captures the central point of Freud's prohibition, that the prohibition forecloses the mother as an object of desire, instituting a never fulfilled desire for an incestuous return.[20] For Lévi-Strauss the prohibition was inherently ambiguous; for Freud it prohibited object-choice while producing incestuous desire. Jacques Lacan, who in some sense merged Freud's psychoanalysis with Lévi-Strauss's structural anthropology, also noted the fundamental ambivalence of the prohibition. Lacan points to the universality of the prohibition: "The law only operates in the realm of culture. And the result of the law is *always to exclude incest in its fundamental form*, son/mother incest, which is the kind Freud emphasizes."[21] Yet he does so only then to mark the fundamental ambiguity, the breach in the foundation of the moral law, where there is no "Sovereign Good" because the mother, who symbolizes such a Good, is "a forbidden good." [22] Thus the moral law, which follows from the incest prohibition, inculcates a desire for its transgression. What Lacan, Freud, and Lévi-Strauss demonstrate is that at the core of that universality is something like a breach; many criticisms to the contrary, they all suggest something more (or, perhaps less) than a totalizing, monolithic law of culture, even as they sometimes suggest precisely that. Such an unstable universalism attached to the incest prohibition is an inheritance, however indirect, from more widespread, liberal definitions of the incest prohibition in nineteenth-century America.

This instability, or irresolution, at the core of the prohibition invokes what Joan Scott has recently argued, apropos sexual difference, makes psychoanalysis so useful for the writing of history and critically engaging gender. "Gender consists of the historically specific and finally uncontrollable articulations that aim to settle the confusions associated with sexual difference by directing fantasy to some political or social end: group mobilization, nation building, support for a specific family structure, ethnic consolidation, or religious practice."[23] Gender and its histories, then, are so many attempts to resolve the fundamentally irresolvable problem of sexual difference. Of course, the incest prohibition has long been constructed as the foundation of sexual difference. This ambiguity, irresolution, and instability at the core of what appears to be a universal law prohibiting incest and instituting sexual difference can begin to account for the multiple iterations of the incest prohibition as universal. It also helps us account for the kernel of the incest prohibition that might resist historicization even as the majority of its iterations can be subject to genealogy.

In another vein, Judith Butler has noted the ways in which the language of universality that pervades the incest prohibition has the tendency and

institutional necessity of foreclosing genealogical inquiry. Moreover, Butler's influential critique notes not only the problem of universality but also
the problem with fantasmatic origins that haunts the accounts we find in
Lévi-Strauss, Freud, and Lacan. Butler, noting what Lewis Henry Morgan
would have called, more than a century earlier, the "conjectural history" of
the origins of kinship, and thus humanity, writes, "the foundational
moment in which the paternal law institutes the subject seems to function
as a metahistory which not only can but ought to tell, even though the
founding moments of the subject, the institution of the law, is as equally
prior to the speaking subject as the unconscious itself."[24] Butler exposes the
fantasy of the knowledge of origins that marks these accounts of the universal prohibition.[25] In exposing this fantasy, these theorizations of the incest
prohibition as the founding moment of culture presume a "heterosexual
matrix" and thus foreclose a prior prohibition of homosexuality. Despite
the fact that Butler, in theorizing prohibition remains in the hazy world of
psychic and cultural origins, the implications of her critical project cannot
be limited to originary fantasies: the incest prohibition and foundational
laws more broadly are open to genealogical inquiry.

Two things follow from this, according to Butler, both of which are
important for thinking about the consequences of treating both incest and
the prohibition genealogically. First, the function of this insistent universality, even if there is the acknowledgment of irresolution, is that it operates
to "disguise its own genealogy."[26] As Butler goes on to argue, "this configuration of the law forecloses the possibility of a more radical genealogy into
the cultural origins of sexuality and power relations."[27] While I am not
interested in origins in this book, Butler's genealogy of the prohibition creates the critical means by which to engage the universal articulations of the
incest prohibition in antebellum America. Second, the historicity of the
prohibition suggests a plurality of meanings in specific historical moments.
"Although the universality of the paternal law may be contested within
anthropological circles," Butler writes, "it seems important to consider that
the *meaning* that the law sustains in any given historical context is less
univocal and less deterministically efficacious" than universal accounts
might suggest.[28]

So incest is never simply incest. Contemporary theorizations of a universal incest prohibition note an immanent breach or instability in the law,
which thus opens up the possibility of history *and* the acknowledgment
that perhaps something continues to resist historicization. Universalism

works to foreclose genealogy, naturalizing normative configurations of family, kinship, and sexuality. Following from these assumptions, the critical demand on the historian of incest is a genealogy of incest and the prohibition. The genealogy of the incest prohibition, in the end, demands that we open up the political stakes of the universal prohibition to see what kinds of power relations are being secured at each historical moment, but also that we learn from the universal claims of the prohibition, and that we not sacrifice one to the other.

Notes

Introduction

1. Noah Webster, "Incest, n.," *An American Dictionary of the English Language* (New York: S. Converse, 1828).

2. Noah Webster, "Incest, n.," *A Dictionary of the English Language: Abridged from the American Dictionary* (New York: F. J. Huntington, 1839), 216.

3. I use the term "problematic" here advisedly. A central, if ambiguous, concept in the work of Michel Foucault, the term is frequently used loosely, too often simply a synonym for problem. Yet, as Michael Warner has usefully pointed out, problematic is more than a problem and has a much richer meaning. As Warner writes, Foucault "treats a problematic not just as an intellectual tangle, but as the practical horizon of intelligibility within which problems come to matter for people. It stands for both the conditions that make thinking possible and for the way thinking, under certain circumstances, can reflect back on its own conditions. Problematization is more than arguing; it is a practical context for thinking." The discourse of incest in nineteenth-century America was this horizon of intelligibility for understanding the liberal subject and for the occasional critically reflexive moment. Michael Warner, "Styles of Intellectual Publics," in *Publics and Counterpublics* (New York: Zone Books, 2002), 154–55.

4. Calling the period between the Revolution and the Civil War "liberal" necessarily implicates this book in the decades-old, and now relatively stale, historiographical debates over whether the Revolution was liberal or republican. I am interested not so much in this debate as I am in the production of the rights-bearing, consenting, contractual, autonomous individual, a figure that despite the tensions between liberalism and republicanism had a central place in both. In terms of the Revolution and the historiographical debate, Joyce Appleby has been the most fervent advocate of the liberal tradition; see, for example, *Capitalism and a New Social Order* (New York: New York University Press, 1984); and *Liberalism and Republicanism in the Historical Imagination* (Cambridge, Mass.: Harvard University Press, 1992). See also Jay Fliegelman, *Prodigals and Pilgrims: The American Revolution Against Patriarchal Authority* (New York: Cambridge University Press, 1985), and Gillian Brown, *The Consent of the Governed: The Lockean Legacy in Early American Culture* (Cambridge, Mass.: Harvard University Press, 2001), both of whom privilege Lockean conceptions of society. Some historians, like Gordon Wood, treat republicanism and liberalism diachronically, with

liberalism emerging out of the breakdown of republicanism circa 1800; Wood, *The Radicalism of the American Revolution* (New York: Vintage, 1991). J. M. Opal, in a different register, makes a similarly diachronic argument in *Beyond the Farm: National Ambitions in Rural New England* (Philadelphia: University of Pennsylvania Press, 2008). The liberal subject, however, cannot be reduced to these two political frames. For an approach that situates the liberal individual among a plethora of competing, overlapping, and reinforcing discourses, including evangelical Protestantism, see Carroll Smith-Rosenberg, *This Violent Empire: The Birth of an American National Identity* (Chapel Hill: University of North Carolina Press, 2010). As Bruce Burgett puts it, "liberalism and republicanism name two antithetical *and* inseparable possibilities inscribed within the larger idea of democratic self-government." Burgett, *Sentimental Bodies: Sex, Gender, and Citizenship in the Early Republic* (Princeton, N.J.: Princeton University Press, 1998), 20. The liberal subject was the subject of democratic self-government and moved in and out of various discourses across the late eighteenth and nineteenth centuries.

5. On these relations, to begin with, see Pamela Haag, *Consent: Sexual Rights and the Transformation of American Liberalism* (Ithaca, N.Y.: Cornell University Press, 1999), chapters 1 and 2; Sharon Block, *Rape and Sexual Power in Early America* (Chapel Hill: University of North Carolina Press, 2006); Elizabeth Barnes, *Love's Whipping Boy: Violence and Sentimentality in the American Imagination* (Chapel Hill: University of North Carolina Press, 2011).

6. Michel Foucault, "Nietzsche, Genealogy, History," *in Language, Counter-Memory, Practice: Selected Essays and Interviews*, ed. Donald F. Bouchard (Ithaca, N.Y.: Cornell University Press, 1977), 139–40.

7. Among other works, see Gillian Harkins's incisive account of incest and neoliberalism in *Everybody's Family Romance: Reading Incest in Neoliberal America* (Minneapolis: University of Minnesota Press, 2009); Judith Lewis Herman, with Lisa Hirschman, *Father-Daughter Incest* (Cambridge, Mass.: Harvard University Press, 2000).

8. See, for example, Arthur P. Wolf and William H. Durham, eds., *Inbreeding, Incest, and the Incest Taboo: The State of Knowledge at the Turn of the Century* (Stanford, Calif.: Stanford University Press, 2005).

9. The Table of Kindred and Affinity was a list of all kin relations considered to be near enough that marriage was prohibited. A hugely influential instance of the incest prohibition, it was born out of Henry VIII's various marriages and was implicated in both the legitimacy of succession and the origins of the Anglican Church. This is addressed in more detail in Chapter 2.

10. Leviticus and the Table of Kindred and Affinity, as well as the theological discourse on the incest prohibition more broadly, are treated in detail in Chapter 2.

11. I treat Morgan in more detail in the Epilogue.

12. On the history and uses of primitive society, see Adam Kuper, *The Invention of Primitive Society: Transformations of an Illusion* (London: Routledge, 1988).

13. See John Ferguson McLennan, *Primitive Marriage: An Inquiry into the Origin of the Form of Capture in Marriage Ceremonies* (1865; repr., Chicago: University of Chicago Press, 1970); John Lubbock, *The Origin of Civilisation and the Primitive Condition of Man, Mental and Social Condition of Savages*, 4th ed. (London: Longmans, Green, 1870); Émile Durkheim, *Incest: The Nature and the Origin of the Taboo*, trans. Edward Sagarin (New York: Lyle Stuart, 1963). On Morgan in light of this transatlantic production of kinship, see Thomas R. Trautmann, *Lewis Henry Morgan and the Invention of Kinship* (Berkeley: University of California Press, 1987), 1–17. On Durkheim, who both built on and rejected Morgan, see Judith Surkis, *Sexing the Citizen: Morality and Masculinity in France, 1870–1920* (Ithaca, N.Y.: Cornell University Press, 2006), 169–76.

14. Frederick Engels, *The Origin of the Family, Private Property, and the State, in the Light of the Researches of Lewis H. Morgan*, ed. Eleanor Burke Leacock (London: Pathfinder Press, 1972).

15. Sigmund Freud, *Totem and Taboo: Some Points of Agreement Between the Mental Lives of Savages and Neurotics* (New York: W. W. Norton, 1989), 175–81.

16. Orson Fowler, *Hereditary Descent: Its Laws and Facts Applied to Human Improvement* (New York: Fowlers and Wells, 1857), 234.

17. Joyce Appleby, "Liberalism and the American Revolution," *New England Quarterly* 49, no. 1 (March 1976), 7. Smith-Rosenberg, *This Violent Empire*, 74–75. For a particular account of liberalism and discipline that informs this book, see Michael Meranze, *Laboratories of Virtue: Punishment, Revolution and Authority in Philadelphia, 1760–1835* (Chapel Hill: University of North Carolina Press, 1996), 14. See also Richard Bell, *We Shall Be No More: Suicide and Self-Government in the Newly United States* (Cambridge, Mass.: Harvard University Press, 2012).

18. Ralph Waldo Emerson, *Journals, 1824–1832*, ed. Edward Waldo Emerson and Waldo Emerson Forbes (Boston: Houghton Mifflin, 1909), 164.

19. Haag, *Consent*, 25–26; Amy Dru Stanley, *From Bondage to Contract: Wage Labor, Marriage, and the Market in the Age of Slave Emancipation* (New York: Cambridge University Press, 1998). For competing overviews of the period, both of which privilege transformations in the market, see Charles Sellers, *The Market Revolution: Jacksonian America, 1815–1846* (New York: Oxford University Press, 1991); Daniel Walker Howe, *What Hath God Wrought: The Transformation of America, 1815–1848* (New York: Oxford University Press, 2007). For an incisive and lucid account of the emergence of the modern self, the individual with a deep interiority, in eighteenth-century England that informs this book, see Dror Wahrman, *The Making of the Modern Self: Identity and Culture in Eighteenth-Century England* (New Haven, Conn.: Yale University Press, 2006).

20. Alexis de Tocqueville, *Democracy in America*, trans. George Lawrence, ed. J. P. Mayer (New York: Harper Perennial, 1969), 506.

21. Noah Webster, *A Dictionary of the English Language; Compiled for the Use of Common Schools in the United States* (Hartford, Conn.: George Goodwin and Sons, 1817), 189.

22. As Wendy Brown has written, "liberty, which denotes the sovereignty of the liberal subject, marks the freedom to *do* what one *desires*, the freedom to discover and pursue one's interests where the law does not interfere." Brown, *States of Injury: Power and Freedom in Late Modernity* (Princeton, N.J.: Princeton University Press, 1995), 154.

23. Francis Lieber, *On Civil Liberty and Self-Government* (London: Richard Bentley, 1853), xi.

24. Ibid., 255. On Lieber, liberalism, and institutional life, see Christopher Castiglia, *Interior States: Institutional Consciousness and the Inner Life of Democracy in the Antebellum United States* (Durham, N.C.: Duke University Press, 2008), 77–88.

25. Lyman Beecher, *Lectures on Political Atheism and Kindred Subjects* (Boston: John P. Jewett, 1853), 98–99.

26. Historians who have presented such a family in this period include Fliegelman, *Prodigals and Pilgrims*; Jan Lewis, "The Republican Wife: Virtue and Seduction in the Early Republic," *William and Mary Quarterly* 44, no. 4 (October 1987), 689–721; Nancy Cott, *The Bonds of Womanhood: "Woman's Sphere" in New England, 1780–1835* (New Haven, Conn.: Yale University Press, 1997); Linda Kerber, *Women of the Republic: Intellect and Ideology in Revolutionary America* (Chapel Hill: University of North Carolina Press, 1980), chapter 9; Ruth Bloch, *Gender and Morality in Anglo-American Culture, 1650–1800* (Berkeley: University of California Press, 2006); Anya Jabour, *Marriage in the Early Republic: Elizabeth and William Wirt and the Companionate Ideal* (Baltimore: Johns Hopkins University Press, 2002); Sarah M. S. Pearsall, *Atlantic Families: Lives and Letters in the Later Eighteenth Century* (New York: Oxford University Press, 2008); Cindy Weinstein, *Family, Kinship, and Sympathy in Nineteenth-Century American Literature* (New York: Cambridge University Press, 2004); Steven Mintz and Susan Kellogg, *Domestic Revolutions: A Social History of American Family Life* (New York: Free Press, 1989); Stephanie Coontz, *Social Origins of Private Life: A History of American Families, 1600–1900* (London: Verso, 1989). This is a partial list, and other references appear throughout the text. The surveys by Mintz and Kellogg and Coontz are the closest to simply recapitulating early republic discourses. It is certainly worth noting that some of the earliest work, organized around separate spheres, has been critically engaged with by many of the authors themselves. See, for instance, Linda K. Kerber, Nancy F. Cott, Robert Gross, Lynn Hunt, Carroll Smith-Rosenberg, and Christine M. Stansell, "Beyond Roles, Beyond Spheres: Thinking About Gender in the Early Republic," *William and Mary Quarterly* 46, no. 3 (July 1989), 565–85; Linda K. Kerber, "Separate Spheres, Female Worlds, Woman's Place: The Rhetoric of Women's History," *Journal of American History* 75, no. 1 (June 1988), 9–39; and Cathy N. Davidson and Jessamyn Hatcher, eds., *No More Separate Spheres!* (Durham, N.C.: Duke University Press, 2002). I should be clear, however, that none of these scholars completely recapitulates the early republic discourse of the family as an empirical fact. Rather, they all, in different, and often compelling ways, treat this as *the* discourse of the family, and then read it critically, for the way it structures the politics of the period, the way it masks various power relations, the way it produces a kind of limited social

and cultural authority for women, the way it was bounded by race and class, etc. Indeed, this book is profoundly indebted to all these works. My point is simply that they treat the kind of representations of the family one finds in Beecher to be entirely paradigmatic, where I want to offer, initially, a counter strain, one that suggests that the same discourse of the family in antebellum America that represented it as a stabilizing, moral, and virtuous institution that formed proper republican and liberal democratic subjects also constituted that family as dangerously incestuous.

27. Elizabeth Maddock Dillon has provided the most sophisticated account of desire in liberalism, regulation, and freedom, structured around the public/private divide. Dillon maps a "recursive loop of desire" that makes the family the site of both freedom and constraint and finds the subject oriented always to both public and private. See Dillon, *The Gender of Freedom: Fictions of Liberalism and the Literary Public Sphere* (Stanford, Calif.: Stanford University Press, 2004), chapter 1.

28. Both Elizabeth Barnes and Karen Sanchez-Eppler have traced the incestuous problems of the sentimental family. Elizabeth Barnes, *States of Sympathy: Seduction and Democracy in the American Novel* (New York: Columbia University Press, 1997), chapter 1; Karen Sanchez-Eppler, "Temperance in the Bed of a Child: Incest and Social Order in Nineteenth-Century America," *American Quarterly* 47, no. 1 (March 1995), 1–33.

29. Passionate attachments may be more appropriate here in terms of the excessive force of sympathy and sentiment and its capacity to subordinate and subject. See Judith Butler, *The Psychic Life of Power: Theories in Subjection* (Stanford, Calif.: Stanford University Press, 1997), 7–10. As Butler writes, "Let us consider that a subject is not only formed in subordination, but that this subordination provides the subject's continuing condition of possibility . . . there is no possibility of not loving, where love is bound up with the requirements of life. . . . No subject can emerge without this attachment, formed in dependency, but no subject, in the course of its formation, can ever afford fully to 'see' it" (8). Sympathy and sentiment named this type of passionate attachment and held out the possibility that there was a degree of autonomy in the choice to be sympathetic.

30. Herman Melville, *Pierre; or, the Ambiguities* (1853; repr., Evanston, Ill.: Northwestern University Press, 1995), 5.

31. Ibid., 7.

32. Ibid., 5.

33. I have chosen to avoid extended engagement with *Pierre*, despite its centrality to an inquiry into incest in antebellum America. First, *Pierre* and its incestuous problems have been engaged with extensively. Second, this entire book might be treated as an archaeology of the incestuous problematic *Pierre* presents to its readers. The body of critical work on Pierre is enormous, but for some that have influenced this study, see Weinstein, *Family, Kinship, and Sympathy*; Nancy Bentley, "Creole Kinship: Privacy and the Novel in the New World," in Russ Castronovo, ed., *The Oxford Handbook of Nineteenth-Century American Literature* (New York: Oxford University Press, 2012),

97–114; Wai Chee Dimock, *Empire for Liberty: Melville and the Poetics of Individualism* (Princeton, N.J.: Princeton University Press, 1986); Gillian Silverman, "Textual Sentimentalism: Incest and Authorship in Melville's *Pierre*," *American Literature* 74, no. 2 (June 2002), 345–72; Michael Paul Rogin, *Subversive Genealogy: The Politics and Art of Herman Melville* (Berkeley: University of California Press, 2983), chapter 5.

34. I borrow the phrase "kinship dystopia" from Bentley, "Creole Kinship," 98.

35. "Paradoxical Wedding," *Miscellany*, 11 November 1805, 91.

36. The solution, which in a sense is immaterial to the concerns of this book, was nearly as confusing as the paradox itself. "The grandfather's wife was the son's wife's Sister. /Her sister again was the grandson's wife./Three sisters, three brothers in these you will find,/Three husbands three wives to each other kind /Two fathers, two mothers, you'll also see,/Two uncles, two aunts, in turn will agree,/Two nieces, two nephews, three husbands three wives/Resolved to live all the days of their lives." That the solution points to the fact that six individuals, three men and three women, can occupy multiple positions within an economy of kinship is both the most banal and profound component of kinship under liberalism. As we will see, it was ultimately the tensions between the structures of kinship and the disorders of circulation under both liberalism and capitalism that produced kinship as riddle rather than order. "Solution of the Paradoxical Wedding," *Miscellany*, 12 February 1805, 103.

37. *Mississippi Herald and Natchez Gazette*, 21 October 1806, 4. A similar story appeared in the same newspaper in 1807: *Mississippi Herald and Natchez Gazette*, 22 July 1807, 1. Thanks to Dawn Peterson for alerting me to these.

38. *Mississippi Herald and Natchez Gazette*, 21 October 1806, 4.

39. Ibid.

40. Ibid.

41. On the remaking of kinship, see Bentley, "Creole Kinship." On the displacement of kinship (or alliance) by sexuality, see Foucault, *History of Sexuality*, vol. 1, *An Introduction*, trans. Robert Hurley (New York: Vintage, 1978), 106–12; Elizabeth Povinelli, *The Empire of Love: Toward a Theory of Intimacy, Genealogy, and Carnality* (Durham, N.C.: Duke University Press, 2006), 175–236.

42. This paradoxical articulation gestures toward Freud's account of taboo: "To us it means, on the one hand, 'sacred,' 'consecrated,' and on the other 'uncanny,' 'dangerous,' 'forbidden,' 'unclean.'" Freud, *Totem and Taboo*, 24–25.

43. The cultivation of danger was central to the governmentality of liberalism. See Michel Foucault, *The Birth of Biopolitics: Lectures at the College de France, 1978–1979*, trans. Graham Burchell, ed. Michel Snellart (New York: Picador, 2008), 66, 319.

44. Butler, *The Psychic Life of Power*, 84. Saidiya Hartman offers an incisive account of this process in regard to slavery in nineteenth-century America. Hartman, *Scenes of Subjection: Terror, Slavery, and Self-Making in Nineteenth-Century America* (New York: Oxford University Press, 1997), especially chapter 4, "The Burdened Individuality of Freedom."

45. On the particularity of this supposedly abstract subject, see in particular, Joan Wallach Scott, *Only Paradoxes to Offer: French Feminists and the Rights of Man* (Cambridge, Mass.: Harvard University Press, 1996).

46. Foucault, *The History of Sexuality*, 1:108–9.

47. "Circular," *New York Journal of Medicine and Collateral Sickness*, May 1856, 425.

48. See Nancy Isenberg, *Sex and Citizenship in Antebellum America* (Chapel Hill: University of North Carolina Press, 1998).

49. Judith Butler, *Gender Trouble: Feminism and the Subversion of Identity* (New York: Routledge, 1990), chapter 2. For a particular relation to the nineteenth-century individual, and the relation between gender and sexuality, see Michael Warner, "Homo-Narcissism; or, Heterosexuality," in *Engendering Men: The Question of Male Feminist Criticism*, ed. Joseph A. Boone and Michael Cadden (New York: Routledge, 1990), 190–206.

Chapter 1. Literature

1. See Steven Mintz and Susan Kellogg, *Domestic Revolutions: A Social History of American Family Life* (New York: Free Press, 1988), chapter 3; Jay Fliegelman, *Prodigals and Pilgrims: The American Revolution Against Patriarchal Authority, 1750–1800* (New York: Cambridge University Press, 1982); Linda K. Kerber, *Women of the Republic: Intellect and Ideology in Revolutionary America* (Chapel Hill: University of North Carolina Press, 1980); Jan E. Lewis, "The Republican Wife: Virtue and Seduction in the Early Republic," *William and Mary Quarterly* 44, no. 4 (October 1987), 689–721; Ruth H. Bloch, *Gender and Morality in Anglo-American Culture, 1650–1800* (Berkeley: University of California Press, 2003). For works that challenge, or at least complicate this view, see Elizabeth Maddock Dillon, *The Gender of Freedom: Fictions of Liberalism and the Literary Public Sphere* (Stanford, Calif.: Stanford University Press, 2004); Ruth Bloch, "The American Revolution, Wife Beating, and the Emergent Value of Privacy," *Early American Studies* 5, no. 2 (Fall 2007), 223–51; Carroll Smith-Rosenberg, *This Violent Empire: The Birth of an American National Identity* (Chapel Hill: University of North Carolina Press, 2010).

2. Claude Lefort, *Democracy and Political Theory*, trans. David Macey (Minneapolis: University of Minnesota Press, 1988), 19.

3. See, for instance, the essays included in Cathy N. Davidson and Jessamyn Hatcher, eds., *No More Separate Spheres!* (Durham, N.C.: Duke University Press, 2002); Lora Romero, *Home Fronts: Domesticity and Its Critics in the Antebellum United States* (Durham, N.C.: Duke University Press, 1997); Jeanne Boydston, *Home and Work: Housewok, Wages, and the Ideology of Labor in the Early Republic* (New York: Oxford University Press, 1990).

4. Recent work that critically reimagined Jurgen Habermas's theorization of the bourgeois public sphere by paying closer attention to the intimate sphere has given

new life the private/public distinction. See, for example, Dillon, *The Gender of Freedom*. See also Habermas, *The Structural Transformation of the Public Sphere: An Inquiry into a Category of Bourgeois Society*, trans. Thomas Burger (Cambridge, Mass.: MIT Press, 1991), 43–50, 141–50.

5. On the discourse of incest and its relation to sentimentalism, see Glenn Hendler, *Public Sentiments: Structures of Feeling in Nineteenth-Century American Literature* (Chapel Hill, N.C.: University of North Carolina Press, 2001), 124–27; Karen Sánchez-Eppler, "Temperance in the Bed of a Child: Incest and Social Order in Nineteenth-Century America," *American Quarterly* 47, no. 1 (March 1995), 1–33; Elizabeth Barnes, *States of Sympathy: Seduction and Democracy in the American Novel* (New York: Columbia University Press, 1997), chapter 2.

6. Steven C. Bullock, *Revolutionary Brotherhood: Freemasonry and the Transformation of the American Social Order, 1730–1840* (Chapel Hill, N.C.: University of North Carolina Press, 1998), 94–95.

7. While each version has minor differences, it seems that most, if not all, versions in the United States were derived from *The Newgate Calendar*, that compendium of noteworthy criminals in Britain prior to 1700.See *The Complete Newgate Calendar* (London: Navarre Society, 1926).

8. "The Life of Sawney Beane," *Boston Magazine*, October 1783, 23.

9. *Lives and Exploits of the Most Noted Highwaymen, Robbers, and Murderers of all Nations . . .* (Hartford, Conn.: Ezra Strong, 1836), 16.

10. Ibid., 17.

11. Ibid., 18.

12. The period in which the tale circulated was particularly fractious, along social, political, and economic lines. Slavery rent the nation and was becoming an increasingly significant problem; the Articles of Confederation failed, and the new Constitution was a source of constant strife, embodied in the political struggles between Federalists and Republicans and then Whigs and Democrats; and the nation witnessed the full emergence of a liberal market society that began in the 1780s and reached its full embodiment in the 1820s.

13. See Karen Halttunen, *Murder Most Foul: The Killer and the American Gothic Imagination* (Cambridge, Mass.: Harvard University Press, 1998), 10, 35.

14. "The Life of Sauney Beane," *Bickerstaff's New-England Almanack for the Year of Our Lord, 1787* (Norwich, Conn.: John Trumbull, 1787).

15. This would serve also as an iteration of the original context of the story, which could be read as a tale of atavistic obstacles to political modernity and market capitalism represented by clannish social organization in Scotland. See Linda Colley, *The Britons: Forging the Nation, 1707–1837* (New Haven, Conn.: Yale University Press, 1992), 101–31.

16. Jefferson used the phrase, or the similar "empire of liberty," on several occasions, and it has become something of a mantra for historians and literary critics of

the early republic. On the imperial logic of the nation, see David Kazanjian, *The Colonizing Trick: National Culture and Imperial Citizenship in Early America* (Minneapolis: University of Minnesota Press, 2003); Amy Greenberg, *Manifest Manhood and the Antebellum American Empire* (New York: Cambridge University Press, 2005).

17. Smith-Rosenberg, *This Violent Empire*, 225–26, and also her *Disorderly Conduct: Images of Gender in Victorian America* (New York: Oxford University Press, 1986), 90–108; J. Hector St. Jean de Crèvecoeur, *Letters from an American Farmer and Sketches of Eighteenth-Century America* (1782; repr., New York: Penguin, 1981), 72.

18. On the recursive loop of desire structuring public and private, see Dillon, *The Gender of Freedom*.

19. This configuration of public and private, while generalizable up to a point, should also be understood as historically situated in the early republic. See Shirley Samuels, *Romances of the Republic: Women, the Family, and Violence in the Literature of the Early American Nation* (New York: Oxford University Press, 1996), 15.

20. Eric Slauter, "Being Alone in the Age of the Social Contract," *William and Mary Quarterly* 62, no. 1 (January 2005), 31–66.

21. "Discovery of a Whole Family of Murderers," *American Magazine of Wonders and Marvellous Chronicle* 1 (1809), 14; *Lives and Exploits of the Most Noted Highwaymen*, 17.

22. *Lives and Exploits of the Most Noted Highwaymen*, 14.

23. Nancy Cott, *Public Vows: A History of Marriage and the Nation* (Cambridge, Mass.: Harvard University Press, 2000), chapter 2.

24. "Discovery of a Whole Family of Murderers," 17.

25. "The Life and Atrocities of Sawney Beane," *Anglo American: A Journal of Literature, News, Politics, the Drama, Fine Arts, Etc.*, 17 August 1844, 400. A reference to "depopulation" appeared in every version of the story.

26. Michel Foucault, *Security, Territory, Population: Lectures at the Collège de France, 1977–1978*, ed. Michel Senellart, trans. Graham Burchell (New York: Picador, 2007), 1.

27. Ibid., 67.

28. Nicole Eustace, *1812: War and the Passions of Patriotism* (Philadelphia: University of Pennsylvania Press, 2012), 28–31, 252 n. 71.

29. Foucault, *Security*, 48–49.

30. This interpretation of the incest prohibition is, of course, indebted to both Lévi-Strauss and Gayle Rubin. See Claude Lévi-Strauss, *The Elementary Structures of Kinship*, trans. James Harle Bell, John Richard von Sturmer, and Rodney Needham (Boston: Beacon Press, 1969); Gayle Rubin, "The Traffic in Women: Notes on the 'Political Economy' of Sex," in *Toward an Anthropology of Women*, ed. Rayna Reiter (New York: Monthly Review Press, 1975), 157–210. Leonard Tennenhouse argues that the exchange of women continues its centrality through antebellum America; "Libertine America," *differences: A Journal of Feminist Cultural Studies* 11, no. 3 (1999–2000), 1–28.

31. *Lives and Exploits of the Most Noted Highwaymen*, 17. Italics mine.

32. "Discovery of a Whole Family of Murderers," 17. Italics mine.

33. Ibid.

34. "The Life of Sauney Beane."

35. Ibid.

36. "The Life and Atrocities of Sawney Beane," 400.

37. Sharon Block, *Rape and Sexual Power in Early America* (Chapel Hill: University of North Carolina Press, 2006), 150–51.

38. Elizabeth Maddock Dillon, "The Original American Novel, or, The American Origin of the Novel," in *A Companion to the Eighteenth-Century English Novel and Culture*, ed. Paula Backscheider and Catherine Ingrassia (London: Blackwell, 2009), 236.

39. Elizabeth Povinelli, *The Empire of Love: Toward a Theory of Intimacy, Genealogy, Carnality* (Durham, N.C.: Duke University Press, 2006), 185.

40. Edgar Allan Poe, "The Spectacles," in *The Complete Tales and Poems of Edgar Allan Poe* (New York: Vintage, 1975), 689, 688. Hereafter all page references will be in the text.

41. The focus on the young age of marriage also suggests the momentous shift from "status to contract," in which one's social and political position, once determined by birthright, became, in the course of the eighteenth and early nineteenth centuries, determined by the use of reason and volition implicit in contract. See Holly Brewer, *By Birth or Consent: Children, Law, and the Anglo-American Revolution in Authority* (Chapel Hill: University of North Carolina Press, 2005), 4.

42. Michael Grossberg, *Governing the Hearth: Law and the Family in Nineteenth-Century America* (Chapel Hill: University of North Carolina Press, 1985), 268.

43. Lawrence M. Friedman, *A History of Law in America*, 2nd ed. (New York: Touchstone, 1985), 212.

44. In some sense Poe seems to anticipate Lacanian notions of the unconscious and desire. "The unconscious is that part of the concrete discourse, in so far as it is transindividual, that is not at the disposal of the subject in re-establishing the continuity of his conscious discourse." See Jacques Lacan, *Écrits: A Selection*, trans. Alan Sheridan (New York: W. W. Norton, 1977), 49. Poe's description of love at first sight repeatedly discounts mere external appearances, like physical beauty, yet the love, the overwhelming desire, never simply springs from Simpson's interior alone; rather it is "sympathy of soul for soul" (690).

45. Sigmund Freud, "Family Romances," in *The Standard Edition of the Complete Psychological Works of Sigmund Freud*, Volume 9, trans. James Strachey (London: Hogarth Press, 1959), 237–41.

46. On transatlantic letter writing and family relations, see Sarah M. S. Pearsall, *Atlantic Families: Lives and Letters in the Later Eighteenth Century* (New York: Oxford University Press, 2008).

47. Cousin marriage in the United States, once perfectly acceptable, was, in the mid-nineteenth century, becoming more closely associated with incest. See Martin Ottenheimer, *Forbidden Relatives: The American Myth of Cousin Marriage* (Urbana: University of Illinois Press, 1996).

48. Here we might recall the literary critic Jonathan Elmer's gloss on Lefort in the context of his work on Poe: "Democratic, mass society both constitutes and reproduces itself by repeated encounters with the social limit in all its opacity." Elmer, *Reading at the Social Limit: Affect, Mass Culture, and Edgar Allan Poe* (Stanford, Calif.: Stanford University Press, 1995), 154.

49. Scott A. Sandage, *Born Losers: A History of Failure in America* (Cambridge, Mass.: Harvard University Press, 2006).

50. The novel is written in the first person and there is a disclaimer that "Richard Jennings" is a pseudonym. The title page identifies James Knight as the author; however, he is actually the preacher who appears at the end of the novel, writing a conclusion after he found the manuscript. The publishers concocted a foreword to the novel in which a stranger entered their bookstore in Cincinnati selling the manuscript, which they bought and published.

51. *The Life of Dr. Richard Jennings, the Great Victimizer* (Cincinnati: Stratton and Barnard, 1848), 6. All page references hereafter in the text.

52. This recalls Simpson's experience—the revelation of incest occurs in the woman's narration of her life. The difference is that Lalande—the matriarch of Simpson's lineage—is aware of and, indeed, controls the incestuous marriage, whereas Jennings's sister is unaware she is in an affair with her brother.

53. Hendler, *Public Sentiments*, 125–27; Sánchez-Eppler, "Temperance"; Barnes, *States of Sympathy*, chapter 2.

54. As both Sharon Block and Pamela Haag have noted, the line between seduction and rape, consent and force, was blurry well into the nineteenth century, in both law and custom. See Block, *Rape and Sexual Power*; Haag, *Consent: Sexual Rights and the Transformation of American Liberalism* (Ithaca, N.Y.: Cornell University Press, 1999), 3–60.

Chapter 2. Theology

1. Philip Milledoler, *Dissertation on Incestuous Marriage* (New York: H. Ludwig, 1843), 5.

2. By fantasmatic origins I mean those anthropological and psychoanalytic accounts that presume the origins of the incest prohibition in a deep past that must be entirely imagined. This vein of thought, so influential across the nineteenth century, has as one of its sources eighteenth-century conjectural history and nineteenth-century ethnography. I turn to the ethnography explicitly in the Epilogue. But fantasmatic should conjure the psychoanalytic concept of fantasy (or phantasy). In this sense, fantasy works to stage desire and resolve contradictions into a clear, linear narrative. In that sense, incest is prohibited in a fantasmatic past and is perpetually refined. The

genealogy that this book undertakes critically unpacks this fantasy. On fantasy, see Jean Laplanche and Jean-Bertrand Pontalis, "Fantasy and the Origins of Sexuality," in *Formations of Fantasy*, ed. Victor Burgin, James Donald, and Cora Kaplan (London: Methuen, 1986), 5–34; Slavoj Žižek, *The Plague of Fantasies* (London: Verso 1997); Joan W. Scott, "Fantasy Echo: History and the Construction of Identity," *Critical Inquiry* 27, no. 2 (Winter 2001), 284–304.

3. Jan Lewis, "The Republican Wife: Virtue and Seduction in the Early Republic," *William and Mary Quarterly* 44, no. 4 (October 1987), 689; Jay Fliegelman, *Prodigals and Pilgrims: The American Revolution Against Patriarchal Authority, 1750–1800* (Cambridge, UK: Cambridge University Press, 1982).

4. Nancy F. Cott, *Public Vows: A History of Marriage and the Nation* (Cambridge, Mass.: Harvard University Press, 2000), 10.

5. On the fragility of consent in marriage, see Nancy Bentley, "Marriage as Treason: Polygamy, Nation, and the Novel," in *The Futures of American Studies*, ed. Donald E. Pease and Robyn Wiegman (Durham, N.C.: Duke University Press, 2002), 341–70.

6. Julia A. Stern, *The Plight of Feeling: Sympathy and Dissent in the Early American Novel* (Chicago: University of Chicago Press, 1997), 2.

7. The biblical scholar Calum Carmichael chastises those who attempt to find transcendent reason in the Levitical incest prohibitions; see *Law, Legend, and Incest in the Bible: Leviticus, 18–20* (Ithaca, N.Y.: Cornell University Press, 1997). See also Marc Shell, "The Want of Incest in the Human Family: Or, Kin and Kind in Christian Thought," *Journal of the American Academy of Religion* 62, no. 3 (Autumn 1994), 625 50.

8. This discrepancy, whose contours lie outside the scope of this book, was the source of much consternation throughout the long history of the biblical injunction against incestuous marriages and made its appearance in the early republic.

9. On the table, see Sybil Wolfram, *In-Laws and Outlaws: Kinship and Marriage in England* (New York: Palgrave Macmillan, 1987), 21–30; Jack Goody, *The Development of the Family and Marriage in Europe* (Cambridge, UK: Cambridge University Press, 1983), 168–82.

10. Veritas [William Plumer], *Remarks on the Letter of Domesticus* (New York, 1827), 13.

11. This uncertainty was a hallmark of the history of the Levitical prohibitions. See Ellen Pollak, *Incest and the English Novel, 1684–1814* (Baltimore: Johns Hopkins University Press, 2003), 27–35.

12. The literature on the transformation of Christianity in the United States in the early republic is vast. For recent interpretations focusing on theology, see Mark A. Noll, *America's God: From Jonathan Edwards to Abraham Lincoln* (New York: Oxford University Press, 2002); E. Brooks Holifield, *Theology in America: Christian Thought from the Age of the Puritans to the Civil War* (New Haven, Conn.: Yale University Press, 2003); Paul Keith Conkin, *The Uneasy Center: Reformed Christianity in Antebellum*

America (Chapel Hill: University of North Carolina Press, 1995). For opposing inter-pretations set in the context of the broader transformations of the period, see Charles Sellers, *The Market Revolution: Jacksonian America, 1815–1846* (New York: Oxford University Press, 1990); Daniel Walker Howe, *What Hath God Wrought: The Transformation of America, 1815–1848* (New York: Oxford University Press, 2007). On the tumult of nineteenth-century Presbyterianism, see George M. Marsden, *The Evangelical Mind and the New School Presbyterian Experience: A Case Study of Thought and Theology in Nineteenth-Century America* (New Haven, Conn.: Yale University Press, 1970). On the transformation of clerical authority in New England, see Donald M. Scott, *From Office to Profession: The New England Ministry, 1750–1850* (Philadelphia: University of Pennsylvania Press, 1978). On the expansion of religious print culture, see Candy Gunther Brown, *The Word in the World: Evangelical Writing, Publishing, and Reading in America, 1789–1880* (Chapel Hill: University of North Carolina Press, 2004); David Paul Nord, *Faith in Reading: Religious Publishing and the Birth of Mass Media in America* (New York: Oxford University Press, 2007).

13. Noll, *America's God*, 257.

14. This brief history is drawn from William Marshall, *An Inquiry Concerning the Lawfulness of Marriage Between Parties Previously Related by Consanguinity or Affinity* (New York: Mark H. Newman, 1843), 64–77. In 1789, the various synods of the Presbyterian church linked themselves to one another in the General Assembly, which provided a modicum of centralized authority.

15. On the 1695 controversy, see Increase Mather, et. al., *The Answer of Several Ministers in and near Boston to that case of Conscience, Whether it is Lawful for a Man to Marry his Wives own Sister?* (Boston: Bartholomew Green, 1695); M. Halsey Thomas, ed., *The Diary of Samuel Sewall*, vol. 1, *1674–1708* (New York: Farrar, Straus and Giroux, 1973), 333–34.

16. Marshall, *An Inquiry Concerning the Lawfulness of Marriage*, 71.

17. The ambiguity of the Duchane decision was indicative of the earlier synodical decisions and, moreover, of the Presbyterian response to matters sexual. See Clare A. Lyons, *Sex Among the Rabble: An Intimate History of Gender and Power in the Age of Revolution, Philadelphia, 1730–1830* (Chapel Hill: University of North Carolina Press, 2006), 85–87.

18. A Pastor, "'Another Schism' Threatened," *Christian Observer* (Philadelphia), 7 May 1847, 73. On the original schism between New School and Old School Presbyterians, see Marsden, *Evangelical Mind*, 59–87.

19. Marshall, *Lawfulness of Marriage*, 73.

20. For a brief overview see Martin Ottenheimer, *Forbidden Relatives: The American Myth of Cousin Marriage* (Urbana: University of Illinois Press, 1996), 19–41; and Chapter 3 below.

21. Colin McIver, *Ecclesiastical Proceedings in the case of Mr. Donald McCrimmon, a Ruling Elder of the Presbyterian Church, who was suspended from sealing ordinances, and from the exercise of his office, by the session of Ottery's Church, for marrying the*

sister of his deceased wife . . . (Fayetteville, N.C., 1827), 11. The following discussion of McCrimmon's trial is drawn from this record, which despite McIver's obvious predilections against such marriages (he was the prosecutor in both the session and General Assembly), are accurate accounts of the proceedings drawn from the session and assembly records.

22. Ibid., 40.

23. The meaning of the Westminster Confession of Faith, according to George Marsden, "was the oldest controversy in American Presbyterianism." *Evangelical Mind*, 68.

24. McIver, *Ecclesiastical Proceedings*, 15–16.

25. On the social and legal ambiguities of separation, see Hendrik Hartog, *Man and Wife in America: A History* (Cambridge, Mass.: Harvard University Press, 2000), 29–38.

26. The Second London Confession of Faith of 1689 reads as follows: "Marriage ought not to be within the degrees of consanguinity or affinity, forbidden in the Word; nor can such incestuous marriages ever be made lawful, by any law of man or consent of parties, so as those persons may live together as man and wife." The confession was printed widely in America; see, for example, *A Confession of Faith, put Forth by the Elders and Brethren of Many Congregations of Christians, (Baptized upon Profession of their Faith), in London and the Country. Adopted by the Baptist Association of Philadelphia, September 25, 1742. And by the Charleston, in 1767* (Charleston, S.C., 1813), 53–54. The Westminster Confession, to which Presbyterians subscribed, was much more specific, explicitly including the deceased wife's sister. On the split among presbyteries, see "Marriage of a Wife's Sister," *Norwich (Conn.) Courier*, 7 November 1827.

27. Archibald McQueen to William Engles, 29 July 1842, Presbyterian Historical Society (Philadelphia).

28. "Archibald McQueen, Appellant from a Decision of the Presbytery of Fayetteville, Before the General Assembly of the Presbyterian Church, In a Case of Incest," *Spirit of the XIXth Century*, July 1842, 320. McQueen's case was reported on in a variety of secular newspapers. While this list is not exhaustive, I have found reporting of the case in the *New Hampshire Sentinel*, *Macon* (Ga.) *Weekly Telegraph*, *Constitution* (Conn.), *Daily Atlas* (Boston), *Newport* (R.I.) *Mercury*, *Farmer's Cabinet* (N.H.), *Berkshire County (Mass.)Whig*, *Hudson River Chronicle* (N.Y.), *Emancipator* (N.Y.), *Southern Patriot* (S.C.), and *New York Herald*. Seven years prior to McQueen's trial, this same controversy had just begun in England with the passing of Lord Lyndhurst's Act of 1835. In some sense addressing different issues, the British affair has generated more scholarly interest. See, for example, Wolfram, *In-Laws and Outlaws*, 30–40; Elisabeth Rose Gruner, "Born and Made: Sisters, Brothers and the Deceased Wife's Sister Bill," *Signs* 24 (Spring 1999), 423–47; Margaret Morganroth Gullette, "The Puzzling Case of the Deceased Wife's Sister: Nineteenth-Century England Deals with a Second-Chance Plot," *Representations* 31 (Summer 1990), 142–66; Nancy Fix Anderson, "The 'Marriage with a Deceased Wife's Sister Bill' Controversy: Incest Anxiety and the Defense of

Family Purity in Victorian England," *Journal of British Studies* 21, no. 2 (Spring 1982), 67–86. It is worth noting that even as the controversy quieted down in the United States, newspapers frequently reported the annual English parliamentary debates through the 1860s. Indeed, a revival of the controversy in the 1880s owed more to the English context than the antebellum marriage question.

29. "Archibald McQueen, Appellant from a Decision," 321.

30. Ibid., 322

31. *New York Observer*, 11 June 1842.

32. A Layman, "McQueen's Case—Marriage with a Deceased Wife's Sister," *Spirit of the XIX Century*, August 1842, 362.

33. "The General Assembly of 1842," *Biblical Repertory and Princeton Review* (Philadelphia, 1842), 502.

34. William Hill, "Letter," *Christian Observer* (Philadelphia), 8 July 1842.

35. A Northern Man, "The Marriage Question," *Christian Observer* (Philadelphia) 14 October1842, 164.

36. "Marriage of a Deceased Wife's Sister," *Christian Observer*, 15 July 1842.

37. S. E. Dwight, *The Hebrew Wife: or, The Law of Marriage Examined in Relation to The Lawfulness of Polygamy, and to the Extent of the Law of Incest* (New York: Leavitt, Lord, 1836), 71.

38. Michael Grossberg, *Governing the Hearth: Law and the Family in Nineteenth-Century America* (Chapel Hill: University of North Carolina Press, 1985), 20. On the relation between religious and civil marriage in the United States, see Cott, *Public Vows*, 5–6.

39. Ruth H. Bloch, "Changing Conceptions of Sexuality and Romance in Eighteenth-Century America," *William and Mary Quarterly* 60 (January 2003), 13–42, http://www.historycooperative.org/journals/wm/60.1/bloch.html (accessed 16 October 2008).

40. On the rise of the sentimental family, see Fliegelman, *Prodigals and Pilgrims*; Nancy F. Cott, *The Bonds of Womanhood: "Woman's Sphere" in New England, 1780–1835* (New Haven, Conn.: Yale University Press, 1977); Lewis, "Republican Wife"; Ruth H. Bloch, *Gender and Morality in Anglo-American Culture, 1650–1800* (Berkeley: University of California Press, 2003); Elizabeth Barnes, *States of Sympathy: Seduction and Democracy in the American Novel* (New York: Columbia University Press, 1997).

41. Michel Foucault, *The History of Sexuality*, vol. 1, *An Introduction*, trans. Robert Hurley (New York: Vintage, 1978), 108.

42. See also the important work done on this subject by Elizabeth A. Povinelli, "Notes on Gridlock: Genealogy, Intimacy, Sexuality," *Public Culture* 14 (Winter 2002), 215–38; and Povinelli, *The Empire of Love: Toward a Theory of Intimacy, Genealogy, and Carnality* (Durham, N.C.: Duke University Press, 2006),especially 175–236.

43. Anne Dalke, "Original Vice: The Political Implications of Incest in the Early American Novel," *Early American Literature* 23, no. 2 (1988), 188.

44. Glenn Hendler, *Public Sentiments: Structures of Feeling in Nineteenth-Century American Literature* (Chapel Hill: University of North Carolina Press, 2001), 124–125. On incest, sexuality, and sentimentality, see also Karen Sánchez-Eppler, "Temperance in the Bed of a Child: Incest and Social Order in Nineteenth-Century America," *American Quarterly* 47 (March 1995), 1–33; Barnes, *States of Sympathy*, 19–39; G. M. Goshgarian, *To Kiss the Chastening Rod: Domestic Fiction and Sexual Ideology in the American Renaissance* (Ithaca, N.Y.: Cornell University Press, 1992). Richard Godbeer has referred to the second half of the eighteenth century as one of sexual revolution, and while I would resist such a label, the eroticization of familial feeling was part of the constellation of ideas he discusses. See Godbeer, *Sexual Revolution in Early America* (Baltimore: Johns Hopkins University Press, 2002), part 3.

45. Gordon Wood, *The Radicalism of the American Revolution* (New York: Vintage, 1992), 145–68. On the transformation, rather than decline, of patriarchal authority, see Dana D. Nelson, *National Manhood: Capitalist Citizenship and the Imagined Fraternity of White Men* (Durham, N.C.: Duke University Press, 1998), 29–61. Nelson argues that male authority was organized fraternally after the Revolution. On the centrality of fraternal power in liberalism, see Carole Pateman, *The Sexual Contract* (Stanford, Calif.: Stanford University Press, 1988). On the installation of the incest prohibition and asymmetries in the power of men and women, see Gayle Rubin, "Traffic in Women: Notes on the 'Political Economy' of Sex," in Rayna Reiter, ed. *Toward an Anthropology of Women* (New York: Monthly Review Press, 1974), 157–209.

46. A Citizen, *The Marriage of a Deceased Wife's Sister Vindicated* (New York, 1797), 25.

47. Ibid., 26.

48. Eudoxius [John Henry Livingston], *The Marriage of a Deceased Wife's Sister Incestuous* (New York, 1798), 57–58.

49. Ibid.

50. Ibid.

51. Jonathan Edwards, *The Marriage of a Wife's Sister Considered in a Sermon, Delivered in the Chapel of Yale-College on the Evening of the Commencement, September 23, A.D. 1792* (New Haven, Conn., 1792), 23.

52. Benjamin Trumbull, *An Appeal to the Public Relative to the Unlawfulness of Marrying a Wife's Sister* (New Haven, Conn., 1810), 6.

53. Parsons Cooke, *The Marriage Question; or the Lawfulness of Marrying the Sister of a Deceased Wife* (Boston: Samuel N. Dickinson, 1842).

54. J. J. Janeway, *Unlawful Marriage: An Answer to "The Puritan" and "Omicron"* (New York: Robert Carter, 1844), 214–15.

55. Henry Ustick Onderdonk, *Considerations on Marriages Prohibited by the Law of God* (Philadelphia: Jesper Harding, 1841), 5–6.

56. Milledoler, *Dissertation on Incestuous Marriages*, 13.

57. Ibid., 14.

58. John Henry Livingston, *A Dissertation on the Marriage of a Man with his Sister in Law* (New Brunswick, N.J.: Deare and Myer, 1816), 35.

59. Ibid., 52–53.

60. Domesticus, *The Doctrine of Incest Stated* (New York: G. and C. Carvill, 1827), 7.

61. Ibid., 29.

62. Ibid., 12–13.

63. Anonymous, "The Mosaic Economy," *Christian's, Scholar's, and Farmer's Magazine* (Elizabethtown, N.J.), February–March 1791, 626–29.

64. Lewis, "Republican Wife," 706; Fliegelman, *Prodigals*, 83–89.

65. In this sense, Genesis 5–6 can be read, in part, as the production of kinship and culture. The incestuous origins of humanity are at Genesis 6:2."That the sons of God saw the daughters of men that they *were* fair; and they took them wives of all which they chose." This problem would be taken up by ethnography at midcentury and renamed promiscuous intercourse. On the psychoanalytic concept of fantasy, see Žižek, *The Plague of Fantasies*; Scott, "Fantasy Echo."

66. James Finley, *A Brief Attempt to set the Prohibition the XXIIIth and XXth Chapters of the Book of Leviticus in a Proper Light* (Wilmington, Del.: James Adams, 1783), 7–8.

67. Ibid.

68. Ibid., 8.

69. Finley, *Brief Attempt*, 8.

70. Eudoxius, *Marriage*, 22–23.

71. Ibid., 23.

72. Domesticus, *Doctrine*, 15–16.

73. Edwards, *The Marriage of a Wife's Sister Considered in a Sermon*, 25–26.

74. The account of Walter King's dismissal and the marriage of Jabez Huntington and Sally Lanman is derived from Walter King, *A Farewell Discourse, Delivered to the Congregational Church and Society of Chelsea, in Norwich, Connecticut, August 18, 1811, Together with an Appendix, Giving Some Account of the Ground of Difficulty between the Pastor and Society* (New York: J. Seymour, 1811). For a sentimental defense of the marriage, see also Edward William Hooker, *The Memoir of Mrs. Sarah L. Smith* (Boston: Perkins and Marvin, 1840). Smith was the daughter of the woman Huntington had married.

75. King, *A Farewell Discourse*, 28.

76. Ibid., 29.

77. Ibid., 19.

78. Ibid., 26.

79. Ibid., 6–7.

80. Ibid., 18.

Chapter 3. Law

1. Charles Mason, in *Marriage with a Deceased Wife's Sister. Letters from the Right Rev. Bishop McIlvaine, of Ohio, and other Eminent Persons in the United States of America, in Favour of Marriage with a Deceased Wife's Sister*, Marriage Law Reform Association (London, 1852), 15.

2. Marriage Law Reform Association, "Preface," in *Marriage with a Deceased Wife's Sister*, iii.The MLRA was attempting to reverse Lord Lyndhurst's Act, which was passed by Parliament in 1835, and made marriage with a deceased wife's sister, among other affinal marriages, void if contracted after that date.

3. Charles Mason, in *Marriage with a Deceased Wife's Sister*, 15.

4. *U.S. v. Martin Hiller, impleaded with Elizabeth Hiller* (1 Iowa 330) (1847). The Iowa Territory passed a law defining and punishing incest in 1843. *Revised Statutes of the Territory of Iowa* (Iowa City: E. H. English, 1843), 122.

5. *Revised Statutes of the Territory of Iowa*, 122.

6. J. C. Davis, *Iowa Criminal Code and Digest* (Des Moines: Mills, 1879), 146.

7. Horace Mann, in *Marriage with a Deceased Wife's Sister*, 7.

8. *U.S. v. Hiller and Hiller*.

9. On legality, see Christopher L. Tomlins, "The Many Legalities of Colonization: A Manifesto for Early American Legal History," in *The Many Legalities of Early America*, ed. Christopher L. Tomlins and Bruce H. Mann (Chapel Hill: University of North Carolina Press, 2001), 2. For a complementary, cultural studies approach to the law, see Austin Sarat and Jonathan Simon, "Cultural Analysis, Cultural Studies, and the Situation of Legal Scholarship," in *Cultural Analysis, Cultural Studies, and the Law: Moving Beyond Legal Realism*, ed. Sarat and Simon (Durham, N.C.: Duke University Press, 2003), 1–34. As they write, law is dependent "on a series of unacknowledged aesthetic, psychological, historical, and cultural assumptions. . . . The power of law [produces] forms of subjectivity and moments of truth" (24).

10. This is what animates the legal historian Michael Grossberg's account of nineteenth-century incest law. This assessment, which certainly possesses more than a kernel of truth, nonetheless reifies the category of incest itself. Michael Grossberg, *Governing the Hearth: Law and Family in Nineteenth-Century America* (Chapel Hill: University of North Carolina Press, 1985), 110–13.

11. See, for example, Grossberg, *Governing the Hearth*, 110–13; Martin Ottenheimer, *Forbidden Relatives: The American Myth of Cousin Marriage* (Urbana: University of Illinois Press, 1996), 19–41. For an exception to this, see Leigh B. Bienen, "Defining Incest," *Northwestern University Law Review* 92, no. 4 (1998), 1501–1639.

12. Bernard Farber, *Kinship and Class: A Midwestern Study* (New York: Basic Books, 1971), 39–48.

13. Secularization has undergone significant criticism over the past several decades. My approach here draws on more recent critical engagements with secularism, which have been lumped together under the unwieldy and problematic moniker postsecular. See Janet R. Jakobsen and Ann Pellegrini, "Introduction: Times Like These,"

in *Secularisms*, ed. Pellegrini and Jakobsen (Durham, N.C.: Duke University Press, 2008), 1–38; Talal Asad, *Formations of the Secular: Christianity, Islam, Modernity* (Stanford, Calif.: Stanford University Press, 2003); John Lardas Modern, *Secularism in Antebellum America* (Chicago: University of Chicago Press, 2011); Joan Wallach Scott, "Sexularism: On Secularism and Gender Equality," in *The Fantasy of Feminist History* (Durham, N.C.: Duke University Press, 2011), 91–116.

14. Edward D. Mansfield, *The Legal Rights, Liabilities and Duties of Women; with an Introductory History of Their Legal Condition in the Hebrew, Roman and Feudal Civil Systems* (Cincinnati: William H. Moore, 1845), 236.

15. William Blackstone, *Commentaries on the Laws of England*, vol. 1 ([1765]; repr., Chicago: University of Chicago Press, 1979), 422.

16. Ibid.

17. Ibid.

18. As Blackstone wrote, "they do not put asunder those who are joined together, but they previously hinder the junction. And, if any persons under these legal incapacities come together, it is a meretricious, and not a matrimonial, union." Blackstone, *Commentaries*, 424.

19. Ibid., 424–27.

20. Ibid., 422.

21. Lawrence M. Friedman, *A History of American Law*, 2nd ed. (New York: Touchstone, 1985), 202. See also Joel Prentiss Bishop, *Commentaries on the Law of Marriage and Divorce* (Boston: Little, Brown, 1852), 16. On jurisdictional difficulties inherent in the transition of the common law to the colonies, see Nan Goodman, "Banishment, Jurisdiction, and Identity in Seventeenth-Century New England: The Case of Roger Williams," *Early American Studies* 7, no. 1 (Spring 2009), 109–39.

22. None followed the Levitical penal prescriptions, which included "the land itself vomiteth out her inhabitants" (Lev. 18:25). Nonetheless, the punishments were often severe, including death in several colonies.

23. Colonial incest laws changed across the eighteenth century; this paragraph refers to the earliest colonial laws, passed in the seventeenth or early eighteenth centuries. For these laws, see the following: "An Act to Prevent Incestuous Marriages," *Massachusetts Province Laws, 1692–1699*, ed. John D. Cushing (Wilmington, Del.: Michael Glazier, 1978), 78–80; "An Act to Prevent Incestuous Marriages," *Acts and Laws of New Hampshire, 1680–1726*, ed. John D. Cushing (Wilmington, Del.: Michael Glazier, 1978), 39–40; "An Act Against Incest," *The Earliest Printed Laws of Pennsylvania*, ed. John D. Cushing (Wilmington, Del.: Michael Glazier, 1978), 37–38; "Incest," *The Earliest Laws of the New Haven and Connecticut Colonies, 1639–1673* (Wilmington, Del.: Michael Glazier, 1978), 35; "An Act for the Establishment of Religious Worship," *Laws of the Province of Maryland, 1692–1718*, ed. John D. Cushing, (Wilmington, Del.: Michael Glazier, 1978), 17–18; "An Act for the establishment of Religious Worship in this Province, according to the Church of England . . .," *The Earliest Printed Laws of South Carolina, 1692–1734*, vol. 1, ed. John D. Cushing (Wilmington, Del.: Michael

Glazier, 1978), 208; "Rape," *The Earliest Acts and Laws of the Colony of Rhode Island and Providence Plantations, 1647–1719*, ed. John D. Cushing (Wilmington, Del.: Michael Glazier, 1978), 29; "An Act to Prevent Clandestine Marriages," *The Earliest Printed Laws of New Jersey, 1703–1722* (Wilmington, Del.: Michael Glazier, 1978), 108. Rhode Island did not necessarily prohibit incest in any statute. In the statute concerning rape, a long footnote referred to John Cotton's "fundamental laws," which were printed in 1641 under the title "An Abstract of the Laws of New England as they are now Established."

24. The only discrepancy between the Table and the Massachusetts law, other than that of sexual difference, was that the Massachusetts law did not include mother. However, it was commonly assumed that such persons were included in the phrase "near kin" and were thus prohibited.

25. *The Answer of Several Ministers in and near Boston, to that Case of Conscience, Whether it is Lawful for a Man to Marry his Wives own Sister?* (Boston: Bartholomew Green, 1695).

26. M. Halsey Thomas, ed. *The Diary of Samuel Sewall, 1674–1729*, 2 vols. (New York, Farrar, Strauss, and Giroux, 1973), vol. 1:333. C. Dallett Hemphill has followed Sewall's suggestion that such marriages were common, and thus made the law and its enforcement ambivalent. See Hemphill, *Siblings: Brothers and Sisters in American History* (New York: Oxford University Press, 2011), 41–46. Hemphill's observations concerning the tension between varying degrees of religiosity and the social conditions that promoted, or at least tolerated, such marriages, is persuasive. My concern is different —where did the authority, or the force of the law, emanate from in this colonial period?

27. "An Act against Incest," in *The Laws of the Province of Pennsylvania, Collected into One Volumn* [sic], *by Order of the Governour and Assembly of the said Province* (Philadelphia, 1714), 38–39.

28. The Pennsylvania statute, perhaps marking the distinction between the regulation of the colonial legislature and the meeting, did not mimic the prohibition promulgated at Quaker meetings, which often included cousins. J. William Frost, *The Quaker Family in America: A Portrait of the Society of Friends* (New York: St. Martin's Press, 1973), 160–61; Barry Levy, *Quakers and the American Family: British Settlement in the Delaware Valley* (New York: Oxford University Press, 1988), 244.

29. The two carnal outliers to this uniformity were New Haven and the first Pennsylvania incest law. In 1700, William Penn passed "An Act against Incest, Sodomy, and Bestiality." The inclusion of incest with sodomy and bestiality, acts of carnal copulation that would not have been confused with marriage, located incest in the files of carnal crime rather than domestic relations. It was repealed and replaced in 1705. See James T. Mitchell and Henry Flanders, *The Statutes at Large of Pennsylvania, 1682–1801*, vol. 2 (Pennsylvania: Clarence M. Busch, 1896), 8. In the New Haven colony, alone among the earliest British colonies, the statutory definition of incest eschewed marriage in favor of sex. New Haven invoked chapter and verse from Leviticus and used

the phrase "wickedly defile," suggesting carnality rather than marriage. The law disappeared in 1665, when New Haven was absorbed by Connecticut. "Incest," 35. As Cornelia Hughes Dayton suggests, incest was associated with the violent lust of fathers and was universally condemned, as "incest was the *only* sexual crime for which white men pleaded not guilty in vain." Cornelia Hughes Dayton, *Women Before the Bar: Gender, Law, and Society in Connecticut, 1639–1789* (Chapel Hill: University of North Carolina Press, 1995), 274.

30. It is safe to assume that none of these colonies countenanced incest; only New York would persist in this absence into the postrevolutionary period, not enacting a statute until 1830.

31. The Virginia law invoked Leviticus and then named those prohibited kin. Like Leviticus it was directed to men only, and it was a close replica of the Levitical prohibitions. It did not, however, include either a mother's daughter (stepsister) or a father's wife's daughter (half sister). It added wife's daughter, wife's son's daughter and wife's daughter's daughter (stepgrandchildren). However, from its explicit reference to Leviticus one could assume that the omissions would still be prohibited.

32. "An Act for the effectual Suppression of Vice, and Restraint and Punishment of blasphemous, wicked, and dissolute Persons; and for preventing incestuous Marriages and Copulations," *The Acts of Assembly, Now in Force, in the Colony of Virginia* (Williamsburg, Va.: William Hunter, 1752), 118–20.

33. Randolph Ferguson Scully, *Religion and the Making of Nat Turner's Virginia* (Charlottesville: University of Virginia Press, 2008), 21–27.

34. On the gentry, marriage, and class formation, see Kathleen M. Brown, *Good Wives, Nasty Wenches, and Anxious Patriarchs: Gender, Race, and Power in Colonial Virginia* (Chapel Hill: University of North Carolina Press, 1996), 253–60.

35. "An Act Concerning Incestuous Marriages," *Acts Passed at General Assembly of the Commonwealth of Virginia* (Richmond: Dixon, Davis, and Nicolson, 1788), 16.

36. *The Perpetual Laws of the Commonwealth of Massachusetts* (Worcester, Mass.: Isaiah Thomas, 1788), 256.

37. "An Act for regulating and orderly celebrating of Marriages: and for preventing and punishing incestuous and other lawful Marriages," *The Public Statute Laws of the State of Connecticut, Book I* (Hartford, Conn.: Hudson and Goodwin, 1808), 478. The act was a capacious regulation of marriage and did include one perfunctory reference to God. "And whereas the violation of the marriage-covenant is contrary to the command of God, and destructive to the peace of families." This was quite different than earlier references to God, Leviticus, or the Table.

38. Carroll D. Wright, *A Report on Marriage and Divorce in the United States, 1867–1866* (Washington, D.C.: Government Printing Office, 1889), 31–35.

39. George Elliott Howard, *A History of Matrimonial Institutions*, vol. 2 (Chicago: University of Chicago Press, 1904).

40. Hendrik Hartog, *Man and Wife in America: A History* (Cambridge, Mass.: Harvard University Press, 2000), 19.

41. My choice of states is admittedly somewhat arbitrary—it is beyond the scope, and indeed, beside the point of this chapter to catalog every state incest law of the nineteenth century. These three states offer both geographic and temporal variety. Taken together, they exemplify the volatility of the incest law in a liberal democracy.

42. Salmon P. Chase, ed. *The Statutes of Ohio and of the Northwestern Territory, Adopted or Enacted from 1788 to 1833 Inclusive . . .* (Cincinnati: Corey and Fairbank, 1833), 354.

43. *Acts of a General Nature, Enacted, revised and ordered to be reprinted, at the first session of the Twenty-Second General Assembly of the State of Ohio*, vol. 22 (Columbus, Ohio: R. H. Olmsted, 1824), 159–60.

44. Ibid.

45. Ibid., 160.

46. As we will see later in the chapter, Ohio served as something of a testing ground for many variations in incest law. The 1881 statute is useful here because it tracks many of the changes between 1823 and 1881.

47. Moses F. Wilson, *The Criminal Code of Ohio, with forms and precedents for indictments, informations, and affidavits, forms for writs, docket and journal entries and Digest of Decisions*, 2nd ed., revised (Cincinnati: Robert Clarke, 1881), 209.

48. Ibid.

49. The distinction between acts and identities in the history of sexuality is well-covered ground. For one influential account, see Richard Godbeer, " 'The Cry of Sodom': Discourse, Intercourse, and Desire in Colonial New England," *William and Mary Quarterly* 52, no. 2 (April 1995), 259–86.

50. *General Laws of the State of Colorado* (Denver, Colo.: Tribune Steam Printing House, 1877), 296.

51. Ibid., 612.

52. On miscegenation law and incest, see Peggy Pascoe, *What Comes Naturally: Miscegenation Law and the Making of Race in America* (New York: Oxford University Press, 2009), 72; Eva Saks, "Representing Miscegenation Law," *Raritan* 8, no. 2 (Fall 1988), 39–69.

53. *General Laws of the State of Colorado*, 612.

54. Friedman, *American Law*, 71.

55. On the demographics of Colorado and the Mexican/Chicano population in the area, see Oscar Martinez, "On the Size of the Chicano Population: New Estimates, 1850–1900," *Aztlán: A Journal of Chicano Studies* 6, no. 1 (Spring 1975), 43–67.

56. *General Laws of the State of Colorado*, 612.

57. Consent, of course, was no simple matter and will be dealt with below. On the tension between consent and force in the law, with special attention paid to sexual crimes like rape and seduction within a liberal frame, see Pamela Haag, *Consent: Sexual Rights and the Transformation of American Liberalism* (Ithaca, N.Y.: Cornell University Press, 1999), 3–60. On the tension between consent and force in contemporary incest

law, see "Note: Inbred Obscurity: Improving Incest Laws in the Shadow of the 'Sexual Family,'" *Harvard Law Review* 119, no. 8 (June 2006), 2464–85.

58. James Schouler, *A Treatise on the Law of Domestic Relations* (Boston: Little, Brown), 26.

59. "Horrid Depravity," *New Hampshire Sentinel*,13 July 1837.

60. I am aware that there are relatively few extant examples in human history in which these kin relations were not prohibited from marriage and sex. However, to note that simply obscures, with a false universalism, the more salient feature— nineteenth-century legal writers found it incumbent on themselves to devise a new rationale for this seemingly universal prohibition. The problematic, it seems to me, is to negotiate the historical variability of the prohibition under specific social and political regimes while paying close attention to that kernel of the prohibition that seems to resist historicization. On the possibility of a society without an incest prohibition, and thus not subject to this universalism, see Cai Hua, *A Society Without Fathers or Husbands: The Na of China*, trans. Asti Hustvedt (New York: Zone Books, 2008).

61. Joseph Story, *Commentaries on the Conflict of Laws* (Boston: Hilliard, Gray, and Company, 1834), 103–4.

62. *Wightman v. Wightman*, 4 Johns. Ch. 344 (1821). Lunatic was a legal category at this point, derived from English common law. In his opinion Kent elided the distinction between civil and canonical impediment, placing the marriage of a lunatic on common legal ground with incestuous marriage. On this distinction, see Blackstone, *Commentaries*, 422–27.

63. *Wightman v. Wightman*, 4 Johns. Ch. 347 (1821).

64. *Wightman v. Wightman*, 4 Johns. Ch. 344 (1821).

65. *Wightman v. Wightman*, 4 Johns. Ch. 350 (1821).

66. Ibid.

67. Zephaniah Swift, *System of the Laws of the State of Connecticut*, vol. 1 (Windham, Conn., 1795), 186–87.

68. Ibid., 187.

69. Ibid., 186. By 1795, Swift's Levitical reference was inaccurate, suggesting again the nearly unconscious process of liberal secularization of the law. In 1702, Connecticut adopted the Massachusetts law of 1695, which was not a copy of the Levitical law; in 1750, revisions to the list of prohibitions were made, and again in 1793. By 1808, references to Leviticus or the Table of Kindred and Affinity had disappeared. See "An Act for regulating and orderly celebrating Marriages: and for preventing and punishing incestuous and other unlawful Marriages," in *The Public Statute Laws of the State of Connecticut, Book I*, 478–79.

70. *Wightman v. Wightman*, 4 Johns. Ch. 348.

71. Jay Fliegelman, *Declaring Independence: Jefferson, Natural Language and the Culture of Performance* (Stanford, Calif.: Stanford University Press, 1993), 119. Nature, in this telling, can be understood as a kind of deep reality.

72. *Wightman v. Wightman*, 4 Johns. Ch. 348, 349.

73. Jacques Derrida, *Of Grammatology*, trans. Gayatri Chakravorty Spivak (Baltimore: Johns Hopkins University Press, 1974), 267.

74. The phrase "status to contract" was coined by the British legal theorist and historian Henry Sumner Maine to describe the shift from a patriarchal society in which status signified a society in which people were born into fixed, ascriptive positions in a hierarchical order to a modern liberal society where social relations were organized by voluntaristic notions of contract. Such a historical narrative can be and has been reduced to the movement from subjection (status) to freedom (contract). My aim, in the following pages, is to trace the way in which status was a central part of the nuclear family produced by the new universal incest prohibition. See Maine, *Ancient Law* ([1861]; repr., London: J. M. Dent and Sons, 1917); Carole Pateman, *The Sexual Contract* (Stanford, Calif.: Stanford University Press, 1988), 9–10, 165–68; Amy Dru Stanley, *From Bondage to Contract: Wage Labor, Marriage, and the Market in the Age of Slave Emancipation* (New York: Cambridge University Press, 1998).

75. Janet Halley, "What Is Family Law? A Genealogy Part I," *Yale Journal of Law and the Humanities* 23, no. 1 (Winter 2011), 1–110. On marriage as a contract in the early republic and antebellum period, see Nancy Cott, *Public Vows: A History of Marriage and the Nation* (Cambridge, Mass.: Harvard University Press, 2000), 10–11.

76. *Wightman v. Wightman* 4 Johns. Ch. 350–51.

77. In the first edition of *Conflict of Laws*, Story simply cited Kent's opinion in *Wightman v. Wightman*. In subsequent editions Story included a portion of the text of Kent's opinion. In doing so, Story claimed he was reproducing Kent's opinion in full, but this tended not to be the case. Compare the first edition of *Commentaries on the Conflict of Laws* (1834) with the fourth edition (Boston: Little, Brown, and Company, 1852).

78. Joel Prentiss Bishop, *Commentaries on the Law of Marriage and Divorce* (Boston: Little, Brown, 1852), 101.

79. On the marriage of lunatics, see, for example, Jacob D. Wheeler, *The American Chancery Digest; Being a Digested Index of all the Reported Decisions in Equity, in the United States Courts and in the Courts of Several States*, vol. 2, 2nd ed. (New York: Gould, Banks, 1841), 158–59. On the expansion of the chancery's power, see, for example, "Olley Mattison v. Mary Mattison," in James A. Strothbart, *Reports of Cases in Equity, Argued and Determined in the Court of Appeals, and in the Court of Errors of South Carolina*, vol. 1(Columbia, S.C.: A. S. Johnston, 1848), 390–93. Indeed, the reasoning was hardly applicable in New York. As Hendrik Hartog notes, Kent's successors as chancellor ruled that the court of equity had no such authority precisely because its authority derived from legislative action, not the reception of English common law. Hartog, *Man and Wife*, 344 n. 68.

80. Asa Kinne, *Questions and Answers on Law, Alphabetically Arranged*, vol. 2 (New York: Collins, Keese), 148–49.

81. Story, *Conflict of Laws* (1834), 104.

82. *Sutton v. Warren*, 10 Metcalf 451 (1852).

83. The kin prohibition on marriage in England was confusing, to say the least, and as a number of scholars have noted, this occasioned much commentary and polemic. See Ellen Pollak, *Incest and the English Novel, 1684–1814* (Baltimore: Johns Hopkins University Press, 2003), 31, 35–36.

84. Sutton and Hills moved at an auspicious time. In June 1835, Lord Lyndhurst's Act was passed in Parliament. An attempt to clarify the ambiguities in the Henrician statutes, it declared all marriages within the prohibited degrees of affinity contracted prior to 31 August 1835 to be absolutely valid. However, all marriages within the prohibited degrees, both consanguineous and affinal, contracted after this date were absolutely void. Sutton and Hills's marriage, contracted prior to this date, continued to be voidable by the ecclesiastical court, but not absolutely void, in England, since it was expressly prohibited in the Levitical prohibition and was consanguineous. See Nancy F. Anderson, "The 'Marriage with a Deceased Wife's Bill' Controversy: Incest Anxiety and the Defense of Family Purity in Victorian England," *Journal of British Studies* 21, no. 2 (Spring 1982), 67.

85. Coverture still being in place in Massachusetts, technically Samuel Sutton was suing on his own behalf, his wife having no legal personality. See Hartog, *Man and Wife in America*, 115–16. On coverture, see also Norma Basch, *In the Eyes of the Law: Women, Marriage, and Property in Nineteenth-Century New York* (Ithaca, N.Y.: Cornell University Press, 1982).

86. *Sutton v. Warren*, 10 Metcalf 452 (1852).

87. Ibid.

88. Ibid., 453.

89. Ibid.

90. Ibid.

91. Tapping Reeve, *The Law of Baron and Femme; of Parent and Child; of Guardian and Ward; of Master and Servant; and of the Powers of Courts of Chancery* (New Haven, Conn.: Oliver Steele, 1816). Holly Brewer, "The Transformation of Domestic Law," in *The Cambridge History of Law in America*, vol. 1, *Early America (1580–1815)*, ed. Michael Grossberg and Christopher Tomlins (New York: Cambridge University Press, 2008), 289. Moreover, as Janet Halley argues, it is difficult to speak of family law before the mid-nineteenth century, noting that "the law of husband and wife and the law of parent and child were separate, parallel, and closely related legal topics, but they were equally proximate to the law of guardian and ward and . . . the law of master and servant. This pattern corresponded with a social order in which cohabitation, legitimate sexual relations, reproduction, and productive labor were assumed to belong in one place: the *household*." Halley, "What Is Family Law?," 2. Halley is certainly correct, but when we shift our attention to the delimitation of incest in the law, it is perhaps more useful to think of this configuration and the later one of family law as residual and emergent in the manner in which Raymond Williams has suggested. Williams, *Marxism and Literature* (Oxford: Oxford University Press, 1977), 121–27.

92. Tapping Reeve, *The Law of Baron and Femme*, 2nd ed., ed. Lucius Chittenden (Burlington, Vt.: Chauncey Goodrich, 1846), 202.

93. Chittenden, "Preface," *The Law of Baron and Femme*, iii.

94. Chittenden, Ibid., 204.

95. Ibid.

96. Ruth Bloch, "The American Revolution, Wife Beating, and the Emergent Value of Privacy," *Early American Studies* 5, no. 2 (Fall 2007), 227.

97. Lynn Sacco has found over five hundred individual cases of father-daughter incest in newspapers across the nineteenth century. Lynn Sacco, *Unspeakable: Father-Daughter Incest in American History* (Baltimore: Johns Hopkins University Press, 2009), 23.

98. *New-Hampshire Gazette*, 16 July 1844.

99. Ibid. As with Kent, Story, and others writing of the duties and obligations secured by the incest prohibition, this author links the transgression of incest to nominal confusion—the father is the grandfather of the same child. As Roland Barthes notes of incest, "the crime consists in transgressing the semantic rule, in creating homonymy: the act *contra naturam* is exhausted in an utterance of counter-language, the family is no more than a lexical area. . . . Incest . . . is only a surprise of vocabulary." Barthes, *Sade: Fourier: Loyola*, trans. Richard Miller (Berkeley: University of California Press, 1989), 137–38.

100. In 1844, New Hampshire had no incest law to address force. The incest law referred to marriage or carnal knowledge, both of which presumed consent. While the father could have been charged with rape, he was not, and the rape law did not include a provision for rape of a daughter. Nonetheless, the newspaper account did not imply that this was consensual. *Revised Statutes of the State of New Hampshire* (Concord, N.H.: Carroll and Baker, 1843), 291, 293, 434.

101. *Barre Patriot*, 10 June 1853.

102. *New York Herald*, 20 September 1860.

103. *Barre Gazette*, 9 July 1858.

104. "Mark the Villain!" *Rhode Island Republican*, 17 July 1833.

105. Ibid.

106. Timothy Walker, *An Introduction to American Law* (Cincinnati, 1837), 468–70.

107. Ibid., 469. As Leigh Bienen has noted, this knowledge requirement was a question of intent. "If the intent requirement is a knowledge of the relationship requirement, then is there a defense of mistake of fact? A mistake of fact defense makes sense in terms of doctrine if the 'crime' is unknowingly marrying or having sexual relations with a person unknown to be within a prohibited degree of relationship." Bienen, "Defining Incest," 1533.

108. On the association of women with the intimate sphere as a position inside, rather than outside, liberalism, see Elizabeth Maddock Dillon, *The Gender of Freedom:*

Fictions of Liberalism and the Literary Public Sphere (Stanford, Calif.: Stanford University Press, 2004).

109. *Investigation of the Wonderful Charge made against Daniel Burtnett, (the wealthy butcher), of Incest on his Daughters* ([New York], 1846), 1. The pamphlet itself is quite sensationalistic, but it does consist mostly of transcripts from the trial. In many instances throughout the trial, there is little legal logic. Rather, both sides play on the sexual and moral character of the participants in the trial.

110. On the National Police Gazette, see Donna Dennis, *Licentious Gotham: Erotic Publishing and Its Prosecution in Nineteenth-Century New York* (Cambridge, Mass.: Harvard University Press, 2009), 89–92.

111. "Incest by a Clergyman Upon three Daughters," *National Police Gazette*, 12 December 1846, 106; "Horrible Case of Incest and Child Murder; Shocking Immorality," *National Police Gazette*, 10 August 1867, 4; "Shocking Case of Incest," *National Police Gazette*, 4 May 1878, 7; "Investigation of the Charge of Incest, Made by Lavinia Brown, against her Father, John J. Brown," *National Police Gazette*, 13 February 1847, 178.

112. *Barre Gazette*, 9 October 1846.

113. On the restraint of women's sexuality in the nineteenth century, see Clare A. Lyons, *Sex Among the Rabble: An Intimate History of Gender and Power in the Age of Revolution, Philadelphia, 1730–1830* (Chapel Hill: University of North Carolina Press, 2006), part 3; Nancy Isenberg, *Sex and Citizenship in Antebellum America* (Chapel Hill: University of North Carolina Press, 1998), 172–86.

114. *Investigation of the Wonderful charge* 2.

115. Ibid., 3.

116. "Incest by a Clergyman,", 106.

117. Ibid.

118. *Haverhill Gazette*, 5 December 1850.

119. *New Hampshire Sentinel*, 9 December 1840.

120. *Pittsfield Sun*, 10 December 1840.

121. Wilson, *The Criminal Code of Ohio, with forms and precedents for indictments, informations, and affidavits, forms for writs, docket and journal entries and Digest of Decisions, Second Edition, Revised* (Cincinnati: Robert Clarke & Co, 1881), 209.

122. Robert Desty, *The Penal Code of California, Enacted in 1872; As Amended in 1889* (San Francisco: Bancroft-Whitney, 1889), 129.

123. Ibid.

124. Matthew Hale, *Historia Placitorum Coronae*, 2 vols. (London, 1736), 2:730. Lynn Sacco has shown how Hale's comment was expanded into legal doctrine in the United States. Sacco, *Unspeakable*, 53–55. See also Sharon Block, *Rape and Sexual Power in Early America* (Chapel Hill: University of North Carolina Press, 2006), 129–36.

125. Block, *Rape and Sexual Power*, 135.

126. *Noble v. Ohio*, 22 Ohio St. Rep. 542 (1873).

127. Ibid., 543

128. Ibid., 544.

129. Ibid., 545.

130. Ibid.

131. The historian of religion Ann Taves edited an edition of Bailey's memoir, which was published in 1989. Ann Taves, ed., *Religion and Domestic Violence in Early New England: The Memoirs of Abigail Abbot Bailey* (Bloomington: Indiana University Press, 1989). Despite being the only extant memoir of incestuous abuse in the early republic, Bailey's text has received relatively little critical attention. For exceptions to this, see Taves's introduction, 1–49; Hendrik Hartog, *Man and Wife in America*, 40–62; Jon Pahl, *Empire of Sacrifice: The Religious Origins of American Violence* (New York: New York University Press, 2009), 103–40. On Ephraim Wheeler, see Irene Quenzler Brown and Richard D. Brown, *The Hanging of Ephraim Wheeler: A Story of Rape, Incest, and Justice in Early America* (Cambridge, Mass.: Harvard University Press, 2005).

132. As John Lardas Modern puts it, "secularism conjured a natural presence. The categories and sensibilities that it generated were aggressively self-evident." Modern, *Secularism*, 9.

Chapter 4. Reproduction

1. Benjamin Trumbull, *An Appeal to the Public Relative to the Unlawfulness of Marrying a Wife's Sister, Part II* ([New Haven, Conn.]: E. Hudson, 1810), 13.

2. Both Claude Lévi-Strauss and Georges Bataille understood the relationship between sexuality and prohibition in a similar manner. The prohibition of incest was what made sexuality transcend the natural world and take on distinctly human characteristics. For Bataille, this was the difference between sexuality, which humans shared with all animals, and eroticism, which was distinctly human. As we will see at the end of this chapter, it was the erotic family that made for one component of human sexuality.

3. For readings of phrenologists as advocates of incest, see Bryan Strong, "Toward a History of the Experiential Family: Sex and Incest in the Nineteenth-Century Family," *Journal of Marriage and the Family* 35, no. 3 (August 1973), 457–66; G. M. Goshgarian, *To Kiss the Chastening Rod: Domestic Fiction and Sexual Ideology in the American Renaissance* (Ithaca, N.Y.: Cornell University Press, 1992). Karen Sánchez-Eppler reads the phrenological work as an obfuscation of incestuous violence between fathers and daughters. On this point I do not disagree with Sánchez-Eppler, but my aim is different. What is at stake in the language of incest deployed by phrenologists? What is at stake, in other words, in the absence of the word incest from discussions of familial eroticism and amativeness, even as they openly discuss incest elsewhere? See Sánchez-Eppler, "Temperance in the Bed of a Child: Incest and Social Order in Nineteenth-Century America," *American Quarterly* 47, no.1 (March 1995), 9.

4. I borrow the term "anthropological minimum" from the political theorist Uday Singh Mehta, who writes, "the universal claims [of liberalism] can be made because they derive from certain characteristics that are common to all human beings. Central among these anthropological characteristics are the claims that everyone is naturally free, that they are, in the relevant moral respects, equal, and finally that they are rational." Mehta, *Liberalism and Empire: A Study in Nineteenth-Century British Liberal Thought* (Princeton, N.J.: Princeton University Press, 1999), 52. On reproduction, citizenship, the state, and the political, see Jacqueline Stevens, *Reproducing the State* (Princeton, N.J.: Princeton University Press, 1999); Siobahn Sommerville, "Notes Toward a Queer History of Naturalization," *American Quarterly* 57, no. 3 (September 2005), 659–76.

5. The standard works on the history of phrenology are John D. Davies, *Phrenology, Fad and Science: A Nineteenth-Century American Crusade* (New Haven, Conn.: Yale University Press, 1955); Madeleine B. Stern, *Heads and Headlines: The Phrenological Fowlers* (Norman: University of Oklahoma Press, 1971); Roger Cooter, *The Cultural Meaning of Popular Science: Phrenology and the Organization of Consent in Nineteenth-Century Britain* (Cambridge, UK: Cambridge University Press, 1984). The history of phrenology in the United States remains without a recent comprehensive history on the order of Cooter's work on Britain. Two more recent studies begin to rectify this, although they approach phrenology with very particular concerns; see Charles Colbert, *A Measure of Perfection: Phrenology and the Fine Arts in America* (Chapel Hill: University of North Carolina Press, 1997) and Stephen Tomlinson, *Head Masters: Phrenology, Secular Education, and Nineteenth-Century Social Thought* (Tuscaloosa: University of Alabama Press, 2005). By far, the most critically engaging studies of phrenology have situated it in the context of other nineteenth-century problematics. See especially Christopher Castiglia, *Interior States: Institutional Consciousness and the Inner Life of Democracy in Antebellum America* (Durham, N.C.: Duke University Press, 2008), 168–89; John Lardas Modern, *Secularism in Antebellum America* (Chicago: University of Chicago Press, 2011), 147–71; Pierre Schlag, "Law and Phrenology," *Harvard Law Review* 110, no. 4 (February 1997), 877–921.

6. Davies, *Phrenology*, 7.

7. Spurzheim introduced the taxonomical organization of the faculties and was explicit in his deviation from Gall in this matter. J. G. Spurzheim, *Phrenology; or the Doctrine of the Mental Phenomena* (Boston: Marsh, Capen, and Lyon, 1832), 120.

8. J. G. Spurzheim, *Phrenology; or, the Doctrine of the Mental Phenomena* (Boston: Marsh, Capen, and Lyon, 1838), frontispiece.

9. Ibid., 121.

10. The nervous body imagined by physicians like Benjamin Rush made similar analogical claims between the ordering of the body and mind and the ordering of society. See Sarah Knott, *Sensibility and the American Revolution* (Chapel Hill: University of North Carolina Press, 2009), 69–107; Jason Frank, *Constituent Moments: Enacting the People in Postrevolutionary America* (Durham, N.C.: Duke University Press, 2010), 101–27.

11. George Combe, *The Constitution of Man, Considered in Relation to External Objects* (Boston: Marsh, Capen, Lyon, and Webb, 1841), vii–viii.

12. Horace Mann, "Letter to a Young Lawyer," *American Phrenological Journal*, May 1853, 98.

13. Justine Murison, *The Politics of Anxiety in Nineteenth-Century American Literature* (New York: Cambridge University Press, 2011), 4.

14. On interiority in antebellum America, see Castiglia, *Interior States*.

15. As Murison puts it in regard to the nineteenth-century nervous body, "the basic assumption . . . was of an embodied mind and a thoughtful body." Murison, *Politics of Anxiety*, 2.

16. Mark C. Taylor, *Hiding* (Chicago: University of Chicago Press, 1997), 15, 17. Taylor also usefully notes the centrality of phrenology to Hegel's *Phenomenology of Spirit*. Because phrenology has been discredited and treated as a pseudoscience, and an absurd one at that, there has been a tendency, until recently, not to treat phrenology as a central discourse of nineteenth-century transatlantic thought. Taylor's highlighting of the place of phrenology contributes, in its own way, to a repositioning.

17. Castiglia, *Interior States*, 172.

18. Rodney Hessinger, *Seduced, Abandoned and Reborn: Visions of Youth in Middle-Class America, 1780–1850* (Philadelphia: University of Pennsylvania Press, 2005).

19. John Adams to William Cunningham, 15 March 1804, *Correspondence between the Hon. John Adams, Late President of the United States, and the Late William Cunningham, Esq.* (Boston: E. M. Cunningham, 1823), 19.

20. On the saturation of late eighteenth-century America by sexuality, see Richard Godbeer, *Sexual Revolution in Early America* (Baltimore: Johns Hopkins University Press, 2003), part 3; Clare Lyons, *Sex Among the Rabble: An Intimate History of Gender and Power in the Age of Revolution, Philadelphia, 1730–1830* (Chapel Hill: University of North Carolina Press, 2006).

21. Spurzheim, *Phrenology*, 148.

22. Ibid.

23. Ibid., 149.

24. Ibid.

25. Ibid., 153.

26. Ibid.

27. Ibid., 152.

28. "On the Application of Phrenology in the Formation of Marriages," *American Phrenological Journal*, 1 April 1840, 298.

29. Helen Lefkowitz Horowitz, *Rereading Sex: Battles over Sexual Knowledge and Suppression in Nineteenth-Century America* (New York: Vintage, 2002), 328.

30. Walt Whitman, *Notes and Fragments*, ed. Richard Maurice Bucke (Ontario: A. Talbot, n.d.), 40.

31. B.D., "Amativeness vs. Phrenology" *Boston Medical and Surgical Journal*, 11 October 1837, 155.

32. Michel Foucault, *The History of Sexuality*, vol. 1, *An Introduction*, trans. Robert Hurley (New York: Vintage, 1978); Thomas Laqueur, *Solitary Sex: A Cultural History of Masturbation* (New York: Zone Books, 2004); Helen Lefkowitz Horowitz, *Rereading Sex*, 86–122; G. J. Barker Benfield, *Horrors of the Half-Known Life: Male Attitudes Toward Women and Sexuality in Nineteenth-Century America* (New York: Harper and Row, 1976); John S. Haller and Robin M. Haller, *The Physician and Sexuality in Victorian America* (New York: W. W. Norton, 1974), 195–211. G. M. Goshgarian, *To Kiss the Chastening Rod*, 46–53. This was by no means confined to the United States. Indeed, an antimasturbation panic focused on youth and pedagogy spread through Germany in the 1780s and Russia in the later nineteenth century. See Isabel V. Hull, *Sexuality, State, and Civil Society in Germany, 1700–1815* (Ithaca, N.Y.: Cornell University Press, 1996), 258–80; Laura Engelstein, *The Keys to Happiness: Sex and the Search for Modernity in fi-de-siecle Russia* (Ithaca, N.Y.: Cornell University Press, 1994), 226–28.

33. Orson Fowler, *Amativeness, or, Evils and Remedies of Excessive and Perverted Sexuality* (New York: Fowler and Wells, 1846).

34. On suicide as a symptom of individualism, see Richard Bell, *We Shall Be No More: Suicide and Self-Government in the Newly United States* (Cambridge, Mass.: Harvard University Press, 2012).

35. Russ Castronovo, *Necro Citizenship: Death, Eroticism, and the Public Sphere in the Nineteenth-Century United States* (Durham, N.C.: Duke University Press, 2001), 63.

36. Sylvester Graham, *A Lecture to Young Men on Chastity* (Boston: George W. Light, 1838), 96.

37. Holly Brewer, *By Birth or Consent: Children, Law, and the Anglo-American Revolution in Authority* (Chapel Hill: University of North Carolina Press, 2007); Caroline Levander, *Cradle of Liberty: Race, the Child, and National Belonging from Thomas Jefferson to W. E. B. DuBois* (Durham, N.C.: Duke University Press, 2006), 6–12.

38. Graham, *Lecture*, 89.

39. Goshgarian, *To Kiss the Chastening Rod*, 49–50.

40. Graham, *Lecture*, 91–92. The figure of the nurse or servant as one who introduces sexuality to children in the home was a common one in the nineteenth century. It was of course central to Freud's earliest articulations of psychoanalysis.

41. Thomas Low Nichols, *Esoteric Anthropology (The Mysteries of Man): A Comprehensive and Confidential Treatise on the Structure, Functions, Passional Attractions, and Perversions, True and False Physical and Social Conditions, and the Most Intimate Relations of Men and Women* (New York, 1854; repr. London: Nichols, n.d.), 83. .

42. Nicole Eustace, *1812: War and the Passions of Patriotism* (Philadelphia: University of Pennsylvania Press, 2012), 32.

43. Noah Webster, "Explanation of the Reezons, why Marriage iz Prohibited between Natural Relations," in *A Collection of Essays and Fugitiv Writings; on Moral,*

Historical, Political and Literary Subjects (Boston: I. Thomas and E. T. Andrews, 1790), 324. I have left the spelling as it was in the original.

44. Ibid.

45. Indeed, one might turn to what was the most widely distributed moral and political philosophical text of the period, William Paley's *Principles of Moral and Political Philosophy*. In it Paley devoted an entire chapter to incest. "In order to preserve chastity in families, and between persons of different sexes, brought up and living together in state of unreserved intimacy" Paley wrote, "it is necessary by every method possible to inculcate an abhorrence of incestuous conjunctions; which abhorrence can only be upheld by the absolute reprobation of *all* commerce of the sexes between near relations." Despite this, there was no reference to reproduction. See *The Works of William Paley, D.D.*, vol. 3 (Newport, R.I.: Rousmaniere and Barber, 1811), 219–20. On the popularity of Paley's text, see Mary Kelley, *Learning to Stand and Speak: Women, Education, and Public Life in America's Republic* (Chapel Hill: University of North Carolina Press, 2006), 90.

46. Webster, "Explanation of the Reezons," 324.

47. "Impartial Review of Late American Publications," *The Universal Asylum and Columbian Magazine*, October 1790, 257.

48. Ibid.

49. Cooter, *The Cultural Meaning*, 262.

50. Spurzheim, *Phrenology*, 195.

51. Combe, *Constitution of Man*, 114.

52. Ibid., 198.

53. Practical phrenology, as opposed to the more theoretical variant, was what took the U.S. by storm in the mid-nineteenth century. Practical phrenology was practiced mostly by itinerants, who, by midcentury had spread across most of the United States. Their concerns were primarily the practice of phrenology; that is, measuring the heads and headlines, the bumps on customers' heads, and offering practical diagnoses. This was, primarily, a commercial enterprise. As such, it was distinguished from the theoretical side associated with Gall, Spurzheim, and Combe. The Fowlers were, in some sense, suspended between the practical and the theoretical but in the end were more commercial than anything else. Their voluminous writings were oriented toward the enormous market created by the practical phrenologists.

54. Charles E. Rosenberg, "The Bitter Fruit: Heredity, Disease, and Social Thought in Nineteenth-Century America," *Perspectives in American History*, 7 (1974), 190–91.

55. Ibid., 191.

56. Ibid., 214–15.

57. Orson Fowler, *Hereditary Descent: Its Laws and Facts Applied to Human Improvement* (New York: Fowlers and Wells, 1847), 227.

58. On the arithmetic imperative of the nineteenth century, see Patricia Cline Cohen, *A Calculating People: The Spread of Numeracy in Early America* (Chicago: University of Chicago Press, 1982).

59. Fowler, *Hereditary Descent*, 227.

60. Anonymous, "Effects of Marrying Blood Relations," *American Phrenological Journal*, December 1843, 625.

61. Ibid.

62. William Blackstone, *An Essay on Collateral Consanguinity* (London: W. Owen, 1750), 7.

63. Marc Shell, "The Want of Incest in the Human Family; or, Kin and Kind in Christian Thought," *Journal of the American Academy of Religion* 62, no. 3 (August 1994), 625–50.

64. John Lee, *A Letter to the Honorable Joseph Story, LL. D., Discovering and Correcting the Errors of Blackstone and his Editors, on the Theory of Human Genealogy and Kindred . . .* (Cambridge, Mass.: Metcalf, Torry, and Ballou, 1840), 10.

65. Sereno E. Dwight, *The Hebrew Wife: or The Law of Marriage Examined in Relation to the Lawfulness of Polygamy and to the Extent of the Law of Incest* (New York: Leavitt, Lord, 1836), 102.

66. William Marshall, "Review of Dwight's Hebrew Wife," *Literary and Theological Review*, June 1837, 182.

67. On the reduction of kinship to blood relations, see David M. Schneider, *American Kinship: A Cultural Account* (Chicago: University of Chicago Press, 1980); and Schneider, *A Critique of the Study of Kinship* (Ann Arbor: University of Michigan Press, 1984).

68. Fowler, *Hereditary Descent*, 227.

69. Julius Steinau, *A Pathological and Philosophical Essay on Hereditary Diseases* (London: Simpkin, 1843), 39.

70. Joshua Coffin, quoted in Fowler, *Hereditary Descent*, 227.

71. These descriptions are taken from Fowler, *Hereditary Descent*, 228–30.

72. Hale, quoted in Fowler, *Hereditary Descent*, 230.

73. Fowler, *Hereditary Descent*, 230.

74. "Amativeness and the Social Faculties Hereditary," *American Phrenological Journal*, November 1843, 521.

75. Ibid.

76. On the political effects of "reproductive futurity," which is organized around "the Child," see Lee Edelman, *No Future: Queer Theory and the Death Drive* (Durham, N.C.: Duke University Press, 2004). As Edelman writes, "The Child remains the perpetual horizon of every acknowledged politics, the fantasmatic beneficiary of every political intervention" (3).

77. Claude Lévi-Strauss, *The Elementary Structures of Kinship* (Boston: Beacon Press, 1969), 13.

78. On monstrous births and "lustful sins," see Arnold Davidson, "The Horror of Monsters," in *The Emergence of Sexuality: Historical Epistemology and the Formation of Concepts* (Cambridge, Mass.: Harvard University Press, 2001), 98–100.

79. Combe, *Constitution*, 124.

80. Ibid. References to incestuous European royalty were not unusual in antebellum America. For instance, in 1817 *Niles' Weekly Register* reported on an insurrection in Pernambuco, Brazil, that, when discovered resulted in the king of Portugal putting all wealthy participants to death and confiscating their property. This story, which was, in total, one sentence, opened as follows: "The 'incestuous beast,' as the King of Portugal is, probably with truth but not very courteously called." "Foreign Articles," *Niles' Weekly Register*, 18 October 1817, 121.

81. Combe, *Constitution*, 124.

82. Georges Bataille, "The History of Eroticism," in *The Accursed Share*, vols. 2 and 3, trans. Robert Hurley (New York: Zone Books, 1993), 27.

83. S. M. Bemiss, "On the Evil Effects of Marriages of Consanguinity," *Ohio Medical and Surgical Journal* 10, no. 1 (1 September 1857), 27.

84. A Wool Grower, "Thoughts on Sheep," *Maine Farmer and Journal of the Useful Arts*, 4 March 1836, 34. This kind of writing may have reached its culmination in 1882, in John L. Hayes's pamphlet *Consanguinity in Breeding*. In it, Hayes, whose primary concern was the efficacious breeding of sheep, indulged in discussions of vice among sheep and the best types of sheep marriages. It is worth noting that Hayes was quite explicit about the connection between sheep breeding and humans in terms of incestuous reproduction: "High authority of the canons of the church and acts of legislatures forbidding consanguineous alliances, a discussion which will throw new light upon this vexed question can hardly fail to be of interest to those practically engaged in the creation of flocks and herds, while the broader aspects of the question will find their ready applications by the students of social science." Notably, unlike some others, Hayes saw this as a reciprocal relationship—animal breeders had as much to learn from the juridical realm as social scientists had to learn from animal husbandry. See Hayes, *Consanguinity in Breeding* (Cambridge, Mass.: John Wilson and Son, University Press, 1882), 4.

85. A Wool Grower, "Thoughts on Sheep," 34.

86. "Lottery's Get," *American Turf Register and Sporting Magazine*, November 1835, 115.

87. Ibid.

88. Another Virginia Breeder, "The Racehorse Again!" *American Turf Register and Sporting Magazine*, February 1836, 246.

89. Ibid.

90. In one of his more evocative passages, Lacan writes, "And the enigmas that desire seems to pose for a 'natural philosophy'—its frenzy mocking the abyss of the infinite, the secret collusion with which it envelops the pleasure of knowing and of dominating with *jouissance*, these amount to no other derangement of instinct than that of being caught in the rails—eternally stretching forth toward the *desire for something else*—of metonymy. Hence the 'perverse' fixation at the very suspension-point of the signifying chain where the memory-screen is immobilized and the fascinating image of the fetish is petrified." Jacques Lacan, "The Agency of the Letter in the

Unconscious, or Reason Since Freud," in *Écrits: A Selection*, trans, Alan Sheridan (New York: W. W. Norton,1977), 166–67. These prohibitions and their metonymic relation were more about the governance of the white liberal subject. See Werner Sollors, "Incest and Miscegenation," in *Neither Black Nor White, Yet Both: Thematic Explorations in Interracial Literature* (Cambridge, Mass.: Harvard University Press, 1997), 336–60; Elise Lemire, *"Miscegenation": Making Race in America* (Philadelphis: University of Pennsylvania Press, 2002).

91. Robert Newman, "Report of the Committee on the Result of Consanguineous Marriages," *Transactions of the New York State Medical Society*, 1869, 109–10.

92. Louis Agassiz was perhaps the most influential natural scientist in the mid-century America. He would become even better known, and ultimately marginalized, through his opposition to Darwin's theories of natural selection and evolution. In short, Agassiz believed in multiple, separate creations that made both flora and fauna specific to one geographic region, unable to adapt to another, a view he applied to race and found support for in polygenesis. See Louis Menand, *The Metaphysical Club: A Story of Ideas in America* (New York: Farrar, Strauss, and Giroux, 2001), 97–116; Louis Agassiz, *Contributions to the Natural History of the United States of America*, 4 vols. (Boston: Little, Brown, 1857–62).

93. Stern, *Heads and Headlines*.

94. Samuel R. Wells, *Wedlock; or, the Right Relations of the Sexes* (New York: S. R. Wells, 1871), 34. Note, too, that in the use of "congeners" Wells employed a term applicable to humans, plants, and animals. Even as he distinguished U.S. heterogeneity from European homogeneity, Wells elided the distinction between plant, animal, and human, or between the natural and the human.

95. Ibid.

96. Steinau, *A Pathological and Philosophical Essay*, 2. It is interesting that such a discourse seems to prefigure the rise of sociobiology by about one hundred years. Both seem to explain all social ills as the result of genetic, or biological, factors. See, for example, Joseph Shepher, *Incest: A Biosocial View* (London: Acadaemic Press, 1983).

97. Steinau, *A Pathological and Philosophical Essay*, 37.

98. Ibid., 38.

99. Ibid.

100. On amalgamation, see Lemire, *"Miscegenation,"* 4, 51. As Lemire notes, even though it was used in the late eighteenth century, the term took on specific political meaning in the 1830s. "The word 'amalgamation' was thus appropriated from the field of metallurgy, where since the seventeenth century, it has indicated a substance composed of two or more metals mixed together when molten" (51). "The term was most widely used in the North in the 1830s where the concept became a great concern for those opposed to the immediate abolitionists or, as they were so often called, the amalgamationists'" (4). Yet, like hybridity, amalgamation, precisely because of its etymological origins, may have signified a greater flexibility than the later miscegenation. See also Tavia Nyong'o, *The Amalgamation Waltz: Race, Performance, and the Ruses of Memory* (Minneapolis: University of Minnesota Press, 2009).

101. Anonymous, "The Black and White Races of Men," *DeBow's Review* 4, no. 4 (April 1861), 452.

102. S. M. Bemiss, "Report on the Influence of Marriages of Consanguinity upon Offspring," *Transactions of the American Medical Association* 11, no. 2 (1858), 320.

103. George B. Louis Arner, *Consanguineous Marriages in the American Population* (Ph.D. diss., Columbia University, 1908), 12.

104. Lynn Sacco, "Sanitized for Your Protection: Medical Discourse and the Denial of Incest in the United States, 1890–1940," *Journal of Women's History* 14, no. 3 (Autumn 2002), 80–104, has argued that in the late nineteenth and early twentieth centuries physicians began to develop obfuscatory explanations of the transmission of sexually transmitted diseases like gonorrhea in order to exculpate potentially incestuous white fathers. Bemiss certainly was not exposing such fathers—rather, his statistical positivism, at one level, eschewed the moral concerns of incestuous abuse.

105. Bemiss, "Marriages of Consanguinity," 321.

106. Ibid., 322.

107. Ibid., 323. It is relevant to note that the regnant interpretation of sterility in the eighteenth and nineteenth centuries, particularly in the varieties of racial science from Linnaeus, through Blumenbach, and on to American polygenicists like Charles Caldwell and Josiah Nott, was that sterile offspring was the key test of the legitimacy of a sexual union. In the racial science this was used to prove that the individual races were either of the same species, or according to Nott, of different species altogether. See Winthrop Jordan, *White over Black: American Attitudes Toward the Negro, 1550–1812* (New York: W. W. Norton, 1977), 234–37; George Fredrickson, *Black Image in the White Mind: The Debate on Afro-American Character and Destiny, 1817–1914* (New York: Harper Row, 1971), 79–80. For an example of this type of thinking, see Samuel George Morton, *Hybridity in Animals and Plants in Reference to the Question of the Human Species* (New Haven, Conn.: B. L. Hamlen, 1847).

108. Bemiss, "Marriages of Consanguinity," 325.

109. Ibid. Samuel Gridley Howe issued a number of reports in the late 1840s, all general studies of the population of idiots in Massachusetts. All of them had sections devoted to consanguineous reproduction. See *First Report to the Legislature of Massachusetts by the Commissioners appointed to inquire into the condition of Idiots within the Commonwealth*, House Document No. 152, 1849; *Second Report to the Legislature of Massachusetts by the Commissioners appointed to inquire into the condition of Idiots within the Commonwealth*, Senate Document, 1848; *Causes and Prevention of Idiocy* (Boston, 1848).

110. Bemiss, "Marriages of Consanguinity," 330.

111. Ibid., 332.

112. Anonymous, "Statistics," *Christian Register* 24, no. 26 (28 June 1845), 103. On the ideological uses of statistics, see Joan Wallach Scott, "A Statistical Representation of Work: *La Statistique de l'Industrie à Paris, 1847–1848*," in *Gender and the Politics of History* (New York: Columbia University Press, 1999). "Statistical reports exemplify

the process by which visions of reality, models of social structure, were elaborated and revised. If, in its final form, a statistical volume seems fixed and absolute—somehow true—its contents in fact suggest questioning and flexibility" (115).

113. S. M. Bemiss, "On the Evil Effects of Marriage of Consanguinity," 27.

114. Ibid.

115. I am of course reworking Agamben and Schmitt here. Bemiss did not speak in terms of the legality of the state, but in the affective language of the nation. Yet, he created a legal intervention, at both the level of natural law and statutory law. The United States, culturally and physiologically, both produced the law of incest, and in its sovereign virility, suspended it at will. See Giorgio Agamben, *Homo Sacer: Sovereign Power and Bare Life*, trans. Daniel Heller-Roazen (Stanford, Calif.: Stanford University Press, 1998); Carl Schmitt, *Political Theology: Four Chapters on the Concept of Sovereignty*, trans. George Schwab (Chicago: University of Chicgo Press, 2006).

116. Bemiss, "On the Evil Effects of Marriage of Consanguinity," 27

117. Ibid.

118. Ibid.

119. John D'Emilio, for example, has argued that specific developments internal to the history of capitalism in the United States, particularly the removal of production from the household, created the possibility of gay and lesbian identities, as economic survival was no longer inherently tied to one's association with a reproducing family. Michel Foucault's genealogical history of sexuality could also be forced into such a narrative and has been, however uncomfortable such a fit may be. John D'Emilio, "Capitalism and Gay Identity," in *The Gay and Lesbian Studies Reader*, ed. Henry Abelove, Michèle Aina Barale, and David M. Halperin (New York: Routledge, 1993), 467–78.

120. Nichols, *Esoteric Anthropology*,121.

121. Orson S. Fowler, *The Family: In Three Volumes: Volume I. Matrimony; Volume II. Parentage; Volume III. Children and Home* (New York: O. S. Fowler Publisher, 1859), 54.

122. Ibid.

123. Sigmund Freud, "Femininity," in *New Introductory Lectures on Psychoanalysis* (New York: W. W. Norton, 1965), 112–35.

124. Juliet Mitchell, *Psychoanalysis and Feminism: Freud, Reich, Laing and the Problem of Woman* (New York: Vintage, 1974); Gayle Rubin, "The Traffic in Women: Notes on the 'Political Economy' of sex," in Rayna Reiter, ed. *Toward and Anthropology of Women* (New York: Monthly Review Press, 1974), 157–209.

125. See Judith Butler, *Gender Trouble: Feminism and the Subversion of Identity* (New York: Routledge, 1990), chapter 2, for the melancholic structure of the heterosexual matrix.

126. See Goshgarian, *To Kiss the Chastening Rod*; Strong, "Toward a History of the Experiential Family," 457–66.

127. Fowler, *The Family*, 54.

128. Spurzheim, *Phrenology*, 175.

129. Fowler, *The Family*, 54–55.

130. Castiglia, *Interior States*, 106.

131. Fowler, *The Family*, 55.

132. For a compelling and persuasive reading of phrenology in a similar manner in relation to art in the nineteenth century, see Colbert, *A Measure of Perfection*.

133. Fowler, *The Family*, 60.

134. Nancy Cott, *Public Vows: A History of Marriage and the Nation* (Cambridge, Mass.: Harvard University Press, 2000), especially chapter 1.

135. Fowler, *The Family*, 62.

136. See Richard Brodhead, "Sparing the Rod: Discipline and Fiction in Antebellum America," *Representations* 21 (Winter 1988), 67–96; Sánchez-Eppler, "Temperance in the Bed of a Child."

137. Fowler, *The Family*, 65.

138. Similar to the father-daughter relationship, the mother-son relationship was perceived as a relatively unproblematic heterosexual relationship. While the accession to manhood through the resolution of the Oedipus and castration complexes was different for boys and girls, it was nonetheless a complex, ambivalent process. So again, while there are clear affinities between the phrenological and psychoanalytic accounts of intrafamilial desire and sexuality, phrenology is clearly pre-Freudian. Freud articulated the classic account of boys and the castration complex in the case history of "Little Hans"; see "Analysis of a Phobia in a Five-Year-Old Boy," in *The Sexual Enlightenment of Children* (New York: Collier Books, 1963), 47–189.

139. Fowler, *The Family*, 156.

140. Anonymous [Orson Fowler], "Progression: A Universal Law," *American Phrenological Journal*, August 1852, 39.

141. Ibid., 38.

142. Anonymous [Orson Fowler], "Progression: A Universal Law," *American Phrenological Journal*, April 1852, 81.

143. Ibid., 82.

144. Ibid.

145. Walter Benjamin, "Theses on the Philosophy of History," in *Illuminations*, ed. Hannah Arendt (New York: Schocken Books, 1968), 261.

146. On the relationship between domesticity and imperialism see Amy Kaplan, "Manifest Domesticity" *American Literature* 70, no. 3 (September 1998), 581–606; Laura Wexler, *Tender Violence: Domestic Visions in an Age of U.S. Imperialism* (Chapel Hill: University of North Carolina Press, 2000); Amy Greenberg, *Manifest Manhood and Antebellum American Empire* (New York: Cambridge University Press, 2005).

Chapter 5. Slavery

1. H. L. Hosmer, *Adela, the Octoroon* (Columbus: Follett, Foster 1860; repr., Freeport, N.Y.: Books for Libraries Press, 1972), 305. Subsequent references are cited in the text.

2. Karl Marx, *Capital*, vol. 1, trans, Ben Fowkes (New York: Penguin Books, in association with New Left Review, 1976), 168–69.

3. Walter Johnson, *Soul by Soul: Life Inside the Antebellum Slave Market* (Cambridge, Mass.: Harvard University Press, 1999), 58.

4. Stephanie Smallwood, "Commodified Freedom: Interrogating the Limits of Anti-Slavery Ideology in the Early Republic," *Journal of the Early Republic* 24, no. 2 (Summer 2004), 293. See also Ian Baucom, *Specters of the Atlantic: Finance Capital, Slavery, and the Philosophy of History* (Durham, N.C.: Duke University Press, 2005), who writes of a minute book, "a text which functions to convert history, for the most part, into a calculable matter of debits and credits, to reduce the vast business of empire to a column alternated labeled debt or misfortune and another labeled payment. . . . What haunts the record book, what haunts the accounting procedures and econometric logic of justice . . . is not only the specter of a modern principle of bookkeeping and a modern system of finance capital capable of converting anything it touches into a monetary equivalent . . . the specter of slavery, the slave auction block, the slave trader's ledger book; the specter, quite precisely, of another wounded, suffering human body incessantly attended by an equal sign and a monetary equivalent" (7). For a particularly astute reading of commodification, reproduction, and enslaved women, see Jennifer Morgan, *Laboring Women: Reproduction and Gender in New World Slavery* (Philadelphia: University of Pennsylvania Press, 2004).

5. This reading of the commodity fetish as both avowing and disavowing natality is informed by Freud's work on fetishism. See Sigmund Freud, "Fetishism," *The Standard Edition of the Complete Psychological Works of Sigmund Freud*, vol. 21, trans. James Strachey (London: Hogarth Press, 1986), 154.

6. See Morgan, *Laboring Women*.

7. Saidiya Hartman quoted in Judith Butler, "Is Kinship Always Already Heterosexual?" *differences: A Journal of Feminist Cultural Studies* 13, no. 1, 15; Orlando Patterson, *Slavery and Social Death: A Comparative Study* (Cambridge, Mass.: Harvard University Press, 1985), 5.

8. Patterson, *Slavery and Social Death*, 5.

9. On the uncertainty of kinship in slavery, see, in particular, Hortense J. Spillers, "Mama's Baby, Papa's Maybe: An American Grammar Book," *Diacritics* 17, no. 2 (Summer 1987), 64–81.

10. In treating the discourse of slavery fantasmatically, we can treat the northern, sentimental family and the southern, paternalist family as, in some ways, especially around issues of desire and affection, commensurate. With that said, I do not want to suggest that there are no differences. On the particularity of southern families, see Peter Bardaglio, *Reconstructing the Household: Families, Sex and the Law in the Nineteenth-Century South* (Chapel Hill: University of North Carolina Press, 1995) and Brenda Stevenson, *Life in Black and White: Family and Community in the Slave South* (New York: Oxford University Press, 1996).

11. On fantasy, see Jean Laplanche and Jean-Bertrand Pontalis, "Fantasy and the Origins of Sexuality," in *Formations of Fantasy*, ed. Victor Burgin, James Donald, and Cora Kaplan (London: Methuen, 1986), 8; Jacques Lacan, "The Direction of the Treatment and the Principles of Its Power," in *Écrits: A Selection*, trans. Alan Sheridan (New York: W. W. Norton, 1977), 272; Dylan Evans, *An Introductory Dictionary of Lacanian Psychoanalysis* (New York: Routledge, 1996), 59–61; Slavoj Žižek, *The Plague of Fantasies* (London: Verso, 1997); Jacqueline Rose, *States of Fantasy* (New York: Oxford University Press, 1996), 1–15. On the use of fantasy in the construction of social and historical narratives, see Joan W. Scott, "Fantasy Echo: History and the Construction of Identity," *Critical Inquiry* 27, no. 2 (Winter 2001), 285–304.

12. On the problem of incest for the southern patriarch, see Bardaglio, *Reconstructing the Household,* 39–48. Bardaglio traces the frequency with which southern patriarchs were put on trial for incest and what that says about southern patriarchy. Certainly, as Bardaglio notes, white men were frequently accused of incest; my point is less about these types of cases than it is the fantasy that sustained the link between incest and slavery in the production of race.

13. As both Eugene Genovese and Mark Tushnet have argued, proslavery ideology was more likely to lay bare the submerged logics of slave society precisely because proslavery ideologues were less likely to be encumbered with the actual responsibilities of slaveholding. See Eugene Genovese, *The World the Slaveholders Made* (New York: Pantheon, 1969), 125–26; Mark V. Tushnet, *The American Law of Slavery, 1800–1860: Considerations of Humanity and Interest* (Princeton, N.J.: Princeton University Press, 1981), 7, 33–35.

14. Joanne Pope Melish, *Disowning Slavery: Gradual Emancipation and "Race" in New England, 1780–1860* (Ithaca, N.Y.: Cornell University Press, 1998), 29.

15. Edward E. Baptist, " 'Cuffy,' 'Fancy Maids,' and 'One-Eyed Men': Rape, Commodification, and the Domestic Slave Trade in the United States," *American Historical Review* 106, no. 5 (2001), 1648.

16. Thomas Paine, "African Slavery in America," in *Common Sense and Related Writings*, ed. Thomas Slaughter (Boston: Bedford/St. Martin's, 2001), 60.

17. William Lloyd Garrison, preface to *Narrative of the Life of Frederick Douglass, An American Slave Written by Himself*, by Frederick Douglass (New Haven, Conn.: Yale University Press, 2001), 8.

18. Horace Mann, "Speech of Hon. Horace Mann of Massachusetts on the Institution of Slavery," *National Era*, 9 September 1842, 147.

19. Owen Lovejoy, "The Fanaticism of the Democratic Party," *National Era*, 17 March 1859, 44.

20. Anonymous, "Dr. Spring on the Relations of Slavery to the General Government," *National Era*, 12 June 1851, 94.

21. John G. Fee, "Slavery Sinful in Itself" *National Era*, 10 January 1850, 3. The tale of the incestuous man is at Corinthians 1 5:1.

22. Q, "Opinions," *Liberator*, 20 October 1848, 166.

23. Edmund Morgan, *American Slavery, American Freedom: The Ordeal of Colonial Virginia* (New York: Vintage, 1975), 333–37; Kathleen M. Brown, *Good Wives, Nasty Wenches, and Anxious Patriarchs: Gender, Race, and Power in Colonial Virginia* (Chapel Hill: University of North Carolina Press, 1996), 187–211.

24. Brown, *Good Wives*, 196.

25. Marilyn Strathern, "What Is a Parent?" *HAU: Journal of Ethnographic Theory* 1, no. 1 (2011), 245–78.

26. On the domestic slave trade, see Johnson, *Soul by Soul*; Walter Johnson, ed., *The Chattel Principle: Internal Slave Trades in the Americas* (New Haven, Conn.: Yale University Press, 2005); Steven Deyle, *Carry Me Back: The Domestic Slave Trade in American Life* (New York: Oxford University Press, 2005); on the sentiments of the slave market, see Phillip Troutman, "Correspondences in Black and White: Sentiment and the Slave Market Revolution," in *New Studies in the History of American Slavery*, ed. Edward E. Baptist and Stephanie M. H. Camp (Athens: University of Georgia Press, 2006), 211–42.

27. Baptist, " 'Cuffy,' 'Fancy Maids,' and 'One-Eyed Men,' " 1631.

28. Anonymous, "Internal Slave Trade," *Liberator*, 17 May 1834, 77.

29. On the uses of the family of northern domesticity in antislavery discourse, see Michael D. Pierson, *Free Hearts and Free Homes: Gender and American Antislavery Politics* (Chapel Hill: University of North Carolina Press, 2003), 14–15, 18, 71–96. On the rupture of enslaved families in antislavery writings, see Nicole Eustace, *1812: War and the Passions of Patriotism* (Philadelphia: University of Pennsylvania Press, 2012), 169–74.

30. Amos Phelps, *Lectures on Slavery and Its Remedy* (Boston: New-England Anti-Slavery Society, 1834), 50.

31. A B C, "Historical View of Slavery in the United States," *Evangelical Recorder*, 27 June 1818, 241.

32. William Mack, "Address, from the Moral Religious Manumisson Society of West Tennessee, to the Manumission Societies in America," *Genius of Universal Emancipation*, 4 July 1825, 2.

33. Jesse Hughes, "Clinton Co. Anti-Slavery Society," *Philanthropist*, 25 November 1836, 3.

34. On the breakup of the slave family through the internal slave trade, see Johnson, *Soul by Soul*, 19; Deyle, *Carry Me Back*, 32–35, 186–90.

35. I use the phrase "vernacular epistemology of kinship" advisedly and will return to it below. It seems a more useful designation than "fictive kinship," which has frequently been used to describe kinship in slavery. The problem with a term like *fictive kinship* is that the modifier *fictive* suggests that there is a legitimate form of kinship that does not rest on a series of useful fictions. To treat kinship as an epistemology, then, is to note that it is a structure of knowledge that subjects people differentially to its dictates. The vernacular epistemology of the enslaved, as we will see below, worked as a discourse counter to the legal and property-based forms of the

slaveholder and white society more generally. For a related account that deals with "kinlessness," see Nancy Bentley, "The Fourth Dimension: Kinlessness and African American Narrative," *Critical Inquiry* 35, no. 2 (Winter 2009), 270–92.

36. [Howard Meeks], *The Fanatic, or, the Perils of Peter Pliant, the Poor Pedagogue* (Philadelphia: Office of the Citizen, 1846), 6.

37. Ibid.

38. William Craft, *Running a Thousand Miles for Freedom: The Escape of William and Ellen Craft from Slavery* (Baton Rouge: Louisiana State University Press, 1999).

39. Lydia Maria Child, "The Stars and Stripes: A Melo-Drama," *Liberty Bell*, 1858, 141. Subsequent references are cited parenthetically in the text.

40. Harriet Martineau, *Society in America* (New York: Saunders and Otley, 1837), 2:117.

41. Lydia Maria Child quoted in Werner Sollors, *Neither Black nor White, yet Both: Thematic Explorations of Interracial Literature* (New York: Oxford University Press, 1997), 289.

42. Richard Hildreth, *The White Slave; or, Memoirs of a Fugitive* (Boston: Tappan and Whittemore, 1852; repr., New York: Arno Press, 1969), 9. Originally published in 1836 under the title *The Slave; or, Memoirs of Archy Moore*, the novel went through numerous editions under various titles, of which the above two were the most popular. The introduction to the 1856 edition claimed that the novel attained such a level of infamy that it was placed on the *Index Expurgatorius* by the pope. It is also worth noting that the initial publication was anonymous and most reviewers assumed it was written by an escaped slave, claiming that no one but a slave could have described such horrible cruelty. The narrative was generally praised in the northern press for its authenticity, lending credence to the assertion that this novel draws out the complicated meanings of incest in the wider culture. Subsequent references are cited parenthetically in the text.

43. Herman Melville, *Pierre; or, the Ambiguities* (Evanston, Ill.: Northwestern University Press, 1995). Melville's incestuous union, between Pierre and his half sister Isabella, also draws on the theme of hidden paternity and confused genealogies. However, the relation between Pierre and his mother carries the incestuous overtones common to much domestic rhetoric and sentimental fiction. Melville, like Hildreth, made this explicit by bringing out the incestuous relationships that are always just beneath the surface in sentimental fiction.

44. I use "seduction" here in the manner Saidiya Hartman has outlined. "Seduction erects a family romance—in this case, the elaboration of a racial and sexual fantasy in which domination is transposed into the bonds of mutual affection, subjection idealized as the pathway to equality, and perfect subordination declared the means of ensuring great happiness and harmony." This scene, as Hartman points out, denominates weakness as the source of agency, an agency that perpetuates subjection. Cassy, drawing on a vernacular epistemology of kinship, asserts her agency via the disruptions

and gaps in the slaveholder's fantasy of absolute mastery. Hartman, *Scenes of Subjection: Terror, Slavery, and Self-Making in Nineteenth-Century America* (New York: Oxford University Press, 1997), 89.

45. This scene follows the brutal whipping of Archy, which was also a staging of incestuous desire, as could be discerned from the illustration accompanying the text. Archy and Cassy, being punished for their marriage and attempted escape, suffered the reassertion of phallic authority by Colonel Moore. The whip, with its rather obvious phallic symbolism, served to reassert Moore's authority not only as a slave master, but also as a man. Yet Moore was also the father of both of them. In effect, he was wounding his son with his phallus and also forcing Cassy to whip him, whereby she would take hold of her father's whip/phallus. Cassy, however, resisted Colonel Moore, refusing to whip Archy through a refusal of the phallic authority of her father/master. This played on the ambivalence of paternity in the kinship of the plantation household.

46. Michael P. Johnson, "Planters and Patriarchy: Charleston, 1800–1860," *Journal of Southern History* 46, no. 1 (1980), 46–47.

47. Johnson, *Soul by Soul*, 114.

48. Russ Castronovo, *Fathering the Nation: American Genealogies of Slavery and Freedom* (Berkeley: University of California Press, 1995), 201.

49. While social death and natal alienation have proved compelling categories, the totalizing aspects of both, combined with Patterson's nomothetic project, make them problematic as well. For a useful critique, see Vincent Brown, "Social Death and Political Life in the study of Slavery," *American Historical Review* 114, no. 5 (December 2009), 1231–49.

50. *The Commonwealth v. Peggy, Patrick and Franky*, Governor's Office, John Floyd Executive Papers—Pardon Papers, May–September 1830. Box 316. Joshua Rothman also discusses this case in *Notorious in the Neighborhood: Sex and Families Across the Color Line in Virginia, 1787–1867* (Chapel Hill: University of North Carolina Press, 2003), 149–52.

51. *The Commonwealth v. Peggy, Patrick, and Franky*.

52. Ibid.

53. Ibid.

54. Petition for Transportation of Peggy, Patrick and Franky, Governor's Office, John Floyd Executive Papers—Pardon Papers, May–September 1830. Box 316.

55. Sollors, *Neither Black nor White*, 291.

56. On kinship as an epistemology that subjects populations to one dominant, Euro-American framework organized around blood relations, see David M. Schneider, *A Critique of the Study of Kinship* (Ann Arbor: University of Michigan Press, 1984).

57. J. C. Hathaway, preface to *Narrative of William W. Brown: A Fugitive Slave, Written by Himself*, by William Wells Brown, in *Four Fugitive Slave Narratives*, ed. Robin W. Winks (Reading, Mass.: Addison-Wesley , 1969), xxv.

58. William Wells Brown, *Narrative of William W. Brown, A Fugitive Slave, Written by Himself, in Four Fugitive Slave Narratives*, ed. Robin W. Winks (Reading, Mass.: Addison-Wesley, 1969), 1.

59. We might think of this vernacular epistemology of kinship along the line Joanna Brooks has articulated for the formation of a black counterpublic in the early republic. Brooks writes of "the emergence in this era of a distinctly black tradition of publication informed by black experiences of slavery and post-slavery, premised on principles of self-determination and structured by black criticisms of white political and economic dominance." Vernacular epistemologies of kinship challenged dominant discourses and fracture kinship itself. Brooks, "The Early American Public Sphere and the Emergence of a Black Print Counterpublic," *William and Mary Quarterly* 62, no. 1 (January 2005), 68.

60. The literature on slave families is voluminous. See, for example, Herbert Gutman, *The Black Family in Slavery and Freedom, 1750–1925* (New York: Pantheon Books, 1976); John Blassingame, *The Slave Community: Plantation Life in the Antebellum South* (New York: Oxford University Press, 1979), Deborah Gray White, *Ar'n't I a Woman?: Female Slaves in the Plantation South* (New York: W. W. Norton, 1999), 142–60; Stevenson, *Life in Black and White*.

61. Gutman, *Black Family*, 86–90.

62. Hortense Spillers, "Mama's Baby, Papa's Maybe," 74. On interracial sex and families, see also Martha Hodes, *White Women, Black Men: Illicit Sex in the Nineteenth-Century South* (New Haven, Conn.: Yale University Press, 1999); Joshua Rothman, *Notorious in the Neighborhood*.

63. On the intersection of vernacular practices and epistemologies of kinship in slave society, articulated through the practices of property ownership, see Dylan Penningroth, *The Claims of Kinfolk: African American Property and Community in the Nineteenth-Century South* (Chapel Hill: University of North Carolina Press, 2002).

64. James Curry, "Narrative of James Curry," in *Slave Testimony: Two Centuries of Letters, Speeches, Interviews, and Autobiographies*, ed. John W. Blassingame (Baton Rouge: Louisiana State University Press, 1977), 128.

65. "Thomas Hughes," in Blassingame, *Slave Testimony*, 211.

66. "Tabb Gross and Lewis Smith," in Blassingame, *Slave Testimony*, 347.

67. Benjamin Drew, *A North-Side View of Slavery*, in Winks, *Four Fugitive Slave Narratives*, 96.

68. Lewis Clarke, "Slave's Journal of Life," *National Anti-Slavery Standard*, 20 October 1842.

69. Yetman, *Life Under the "Peculiar Institution": Selections from the Slave Narrative Collection* (New York: Holt, Rinehart, and Winston, 1970), 46.

70. Josiah Henson, "An Autobiography of the Reverend Josiah Henson," in *Four Fugitive Slave Narratives*, ed. Robin W. Winks (Reading, Mass.: Addison-Wesley, 1969), 111.

71. Wendy Warren notes the language of slave breeding in colonial New England. Warren, "'The Cause of Her Grief': The Rape of a Slave in Early New England," *Journal of American History* 93, no. 4 (March 2007), 1031–49.

72. Theodore Dwight Weld, *Slavery and the Internal Slave Trade in the United States* (London: Thomas Ward, 1841; repr., New York: Arno Press, 1969), 24–25.

73. Ibid., 32.

74. Ibid., 33.

75. James Oakes, *The Ruling Race: A History of American Slaveholders* (New York: W. W. Norton, 1982), 172–73.

76. George Bourne, *Picture of Slavery in the Unites States of America* (Middletown, Conn.: Edwin Hunt, 1834; repr., Detroit: Negro History Press, 1972), 88. This extract was occasionally republished in antislavery publications throughout the antebellum period. See, for example, "Slavery," *Zion's Herald*, 25 March 1835, 46.

77. Bourne, *Picture*, 93.

78. Ibid., 94. On the racial transformations of hybridity and race, see Sollors, *Neither Black nor White*, chapter 4; Bruce Dain, *A Hideous Monster of the Mind: American Race Theory in the Early Republic* (Cambridge, Mass.: Harvard University Press, 2003)

79. Bourne, *Pictures*, 96.

80. Ibid., 94.

81. Anonymous, "What Have Abolitionists Done?" *Liberator*, 7 October 1853.

82. Anonymous, *The Adventures of Jonathan Corncob, Loyal American Refugee* (1787; repr., Boston: David R. Godine, 1976), 72.

83. Ibid.

84. Ibid.

85. Ibid., 73.

86. Kevin Berland, Jan Kirsten Gilliam, and Kenneth A. Lockridge, eds., *The Commonplace Book of William Byrd II of Westover* (Chapel Hill: University of North Carolina Press, 2001), 139–40.

87. Thomas Jefferson letter to Francis Gray, 4 March 1815, quoted in Sollors, *Neither Black nor White*, 113–14.

88. Ibid.

89. Ibid.

90. Orson Fowler, *Hereditary Descent: Its Laws and Facts Applied to Human Improvement* (New York: Fowlers and Wells, 1848), 230.

91. Lewis Henry Morgan, ethnography, and the construction of an incestuous Hawaii are discussed in the Epilogue.

92. This depiction of the Bahamas could be found in the *Christian Reflector* in 1838. "The Nassau Royal Gazette, Sept 4, speaks of a rumor having prevailed, of a refractory spirit, and indisposition to work, among the liberated people on Ragged Island." An investigator reported that such charges were untrue. "Not only were the Africans . . . brought to a contented mind, but the late apprentices, who also had been

said to be insubordinate, was [*sic*] found to have entered into voluntary and equitable arrangements for their former masters, and continued at their labors in the Ponds, with even greater industry and contentedness to what they had been previously manifesting." See "Slavery: West Indies. Bahamas. Trinidad," *Christian Reflector*, 2 November 1838, 4. This article, ostensibly a defense of emancipation, nonetheless depicts the "liberated people" as docile and willing to submit to their former masters. While devoid of the language of physical deformity, one can't but note the similarity to Pinckney's description of the population of the Bahamas as "employed in the meanest occupations" without the "capacity to take the lead in any pursuit." The investigator ends by informing his interlocutors that salt production was at an adequate level.

93. Douglas Ambrose, *Henry Hughes and Proslavery Thought in the Old South* (Baton Rouge: Louisiana State University Press, 1996). See also Jeffrey Sklansky, *The Soul's Economy: Market Society and Selfhood in American Thought, 1820–1920* (Chapel Hill: University of North Carolina Press, 2002), 93–103.

94. Henry Hughes, *Treatise on Sociology, Theoretical and Practical* (Philadelphia: Lippincott, Grambo, 1854), 239–40.

95. Eugene D. Genovese, *Roll, Jordan, Roll: The World the Slaves Made* (New York: Vintage, 1976), 418.

96. See Mary V. Dearborn, *Pocahontas's Daughters: Gender and Ethnicity in American Culture* (New York: Oxford University Press, 1986), 150; Eva Saks, "Representing Miscegenation Law," *Raritan* 8, no. 2, 53–54; Sollors, *Neither Black nor White*, 298–99; Baptist, " 'Cuffy,' 'Fancy Maids,' and 'One-Eyed Men',"1648.

97. *Laws of the State of Delaware*, rev. ed. (Wilminton, Del.: R. Porter and Son, 1829), 400.

98. Hughes, *Treatise*, 239–40.

99. Ibid., 66–67.

100. Ibid., 113.

101. Ibid., 155.

102. Ibid., 201.

103. Genovese, *Roll, Jordan, Roll*, 4–6; Gutman, *The Black Family*; Oakes, *The Ruling Race*, 193–94; Brown, *Good Wives*, 322; Johnson, *Soul by Soul*, 23.

104. Oakes, *Ruling Race*, 19.

105. Johnson, "Planters and Patriarchy," 45–46; Drew Gilpin Faust, *James Henry Hammond and the Old South: A Design for Mastery* (Baton Rouge: Louisiana State University Press, 1982); Dylan Penningroth, *The Claims of Kinfolk*, 43. An exception to this is Bertram Wyatt-Brown, *Southern Honor: Ethics and Behavior in the Old South* (New York: Oxford University Press, 1982), 19, who notes the incestuous overtones of paternalist discourse. In a manner similar to my own, but writing of Saint-Domingue, the literary critic Doris Garraway has argued that "evidence of white male desire for both black and mulatto women, whom they imagine as their symbolic daughters, raises the possibility of incest in the colonial family romance." Doris Garraway, *The*

Libertine Colony: Creolization in the Early French Caribbean (Durham, N.C.: Duke University Press, 2005), 277.

106. Susan M. Ryan, *The Grammar of Good Intentions: Race and the Antebellum Culture of Benevolence* (Ithaca, N.Y.: Cornell University Press, 2003), 151.

107. Anonymous, "The Creole Case" *Southern Quarterly Review*, July 1842, 70.

108. Anonymous, "Negro and White Slavery" *Southern Quarterly Review*, July 1851, 123.

109. Ibid.

110. George Fitzhugh, *Cannibals All! Or, Slaves without Masters,* ed. C. Vann Woodward (1857; repr. Cambridge, Mass.: Harvard University Press, 1960), 205.

111. Sklansky, *The Soul's Economy*, 101.

112. William Gilmore Simms, "The Morals of Slavery," in *The Pro-Slavery Argument* (Philadelphia: Lippincott, Grambo, 1853), 228–29.

113. Chancellor Harper, "Slavery in the Light of Social Ethics," in *Cotton Is King and Pro-Slavery Arguments*, ed. E. N. Elliott (Augusta, Ga.: Pritchard, Abbott, and Loomis, 1860), 580–81. Italics mine.

114. Ibid. Italics mine.

115. Ibid., 600.

116. J. H. Hammond, "Slavery in the Light of Political Science," in Elliott, *Cotton Is King*, 644.

117. Faust, *James Henry Hammond*, 241–45.

118. Ibid., 646–47.

119. Elizabeth Fox-Genovese, *Within the Plantation Household: Black and White Women of the Old South* (Chapel Hill: University of North Carolina Press, 1988), 31–32.

120. Fox-Genovese, *Within the Plantation Household*, 100.

Epilogue. The Geopolitics of Incest

1. The best biography of Morgan is Daniel Noah Moses, *The Promise of Progress: The Life and Work of Lewis Henry Morgan* (Columbia: University of Missouri Press, 2009); see also Carl Resek, *Lewis Henry Morgan: American Scholar* (Chicago: University of Chicago Press, 1960).

2. Philip Deloria, *Playing Indian* (New Haven, Conn.: Yale University Press, 1998), especially chapter 3.

3. Ibid., 73.

4. Moses, *Promise of Progress*, 124–25.

5. John Lardas Modern, Secularism in Antebellum America (Chicago: University of Chicago Press, 2011), 185. Morgan's work also frequently probed the line that divided human from animal, and in particular the porosity of that border, in terms of kinship. See Gillian Feeley-Harnik, "'Communities of Blood': The Natural History of Kinship in Nineteenth-Century America," *Comparative Studies in Society and History* 41, no. 2 (April 1999): 215–62.

6. Lewis Henry Morgan, *Systems of Consanguinity and Affinity in the Human Family* ([1871]; repr. Lincoln: University of Nebraska Press, 1997).

7. David M. Schneider, *A Critique of the Study of Kinship* (Ann Arbor: University of Michigan Press, 1984), 3.

8. Gayatri Spivak has argued that the native informant, a term she borrowed from ethnography, "*is* a blank, though generative of a text of cultural identity that only the West (or a Western-model discipline) could inscribe." Spivak, *A Critique of Postcolonial Reason: Toward a History of the Vanishing Present* (Cambridge, Mass.: Harvard University Press, 1999), 6.

9. Lewis Henry Morgan, *Ancient Society; or, Researches in the Lines of Human Progress from Savagery Through Barbarism to Civilization*, ed. Eleanor Burke Leacock ([1877]; repr., Cleveland: Meridian Books, 1963).

10. The publication of *Systems* was a torturous process for Morgan. He first submitted it to Joseph Henry, director of the Smithsonian, in 1865. After much revising and wrangling with Henry, the final draft was submitted in 1867. Its expense (it was the most expensive publication by the Smithsonian to that date) and its density, combined with the fragile financial position of the Smithsonian, still trying to rebuild from a devastating 1865 fire, combined to delay publication until 1871. See Trautmann, *Lewis Henry Morgan and the Invention of Kinship* (Berkeley: University of California Press, 1987), 115–16, 149.

11. The mid- to late nineteenth century was particularly invested in delineating global systems. As Morgan was creating a global kinship, European theologians were creating comparative world religion. See Tomoko Matsuzawa, *The Invention of World Religions; or, How European Universalism was Preserved in the Language of Pluralism* (Chicago: University of Chicago Press, 2005).

12. Morgan, *Systems*, 480–93.

13. Ibid., 479.

14. Dipesh Chakrabarty, *Provincializing Europe: Postcolonial Thought and Historical Difference* (Princeton, N.J.: Princeton University Press, 2000), 7.

15. Morgan, "A Conjectural Solution of the Origin of the Classificatory System of Relationship," *Proceedings of the American Academy of Arts and Sciences* 7 (1865–1868), 436–77.

16. Morgan, *Systems*, 480.

17. Ibid.

18. Ibid., 481.

19. Morgan's informants were Lorrin Andrews, a former missionary and current justice on the Supreme Court of Hawaii; Artemous Bishop, a Christian missionary; and Thomas Miller, the U.S. consul at Hilo. See Morgan, *Systems*, 451–52; Alexander Spoehr, "Lewis Henry Morgan and His Pacific Collaborators: A Nineteenth-Century Chapter in the History of Anthropological Research," *Proceedings of the American Philosophical Society* 125, no. 6 (Winter 1981), 449–59.

20. Morgan, *Systems*, 453n.

21. Trautmann, *Lewis Henry Morgan* 159.

22. Morgan's Hawaiian turn was suggested by one of his primary interlocutors, J. H. McIlvaine, who proposed that the Hawaiian custom consisted of both pinalua and cross-cousin marriage. As Trautmann laments, Morgan's privileging of pinalua over cross-cousin marriage is one of the great intellectual missteps in the early history of anthropology, as cross-cousin marriage has become one of the lynchpins of modern theories of kinship.

23. Morgan, *Systems*, 489.

24. Ibid., 481.

25. Ibid., 487.

26. Deloria, *Playing Indian*, 80.

27. Lewis Henry Morgan, *The Indian Journals, 1859–1862*, ed. Leslie White (Ann Arbor: University of Michigan Press, 1959), 110.

28. On the use of Native Americans in the European imagination, see Steven Conn, *History's Shadow: Native American and Historical Consciousness in the Nineteenth-Century* (Chicago: University of Chicago Press, 2006).

29. W. H. Norris, "Mexico—Its Moral Prospects," *Zion's Herald and Wesleyan Journal*, 13 December 1848, 200.

30. On this use of intimacy in the colonial imaginary, see, in particular, Ann Laura Stoler, "Tense and Tender Ties: The Politics of Comparison in North American History and (Post) Colonial Studies," in *Haunted by Empire: Geographies of Intimacy in North American History*, ed. Stoler (Durham, N.C.: Duke University Press, 2006), 23–67.

31. Morgan, *Systems*, 448–49.

32. Hiram Bingham's account of his time in Hawaii was in Morgan's library, in which Morgan had added notes concerning Hawaiian social structure. Thomas R. Trautmann and Karl Sanford Kabelac, "The Library of Lewis Henry Morgan and Mary Elizabeth Morgan," *Transactions of the American Philosophical Society* 84, nos. 6–7 (1994), 37. Hiram Bingham, *A Residence of Twenty-One Years in the Sandwich Islands* (Hartford, Conn., 1847). Morgan, *Systems*, 480.

33. William Ellis, *Polynesian Researches: Hawaii* (Rutland, Vt.: Charles E. Tuttle, 1969). This was a part of the larger *Polynesian Researches*, originally published in 1829, which included, in addition to Hawaii, Tahiti, Raiatea, Borabora, Huahine, New Zealand, and other, smaller South Pacific islands. William Ellis, *Polynesian Researches*, 2 vols. (1829; repr., London: Dawsons of Pall Mall, 1967).

34. Ellis, *Polynesian Researches*, 435

35. Ibid.

36. Ibid., 435–36.

37. Ibid.

38. As did Morgan demonstrate this force of Christianity, writing in *The League of the Iroquois* that there were only "two means of rescuing the Indian . . . these are education and Christianity." Morgan, *League of the Iroquois*, ([1851]; repr. New York:

Corinth Books, 1962), 447. Robert Bieder discusses this in the context of Morgan's rejection of polygenism; see Bieder, *Science Encounters the Indian, 1820–1860: The Early Years of American Ethnology* (Norman, Okla.: University of Oklahoma Press, 2003), 216.

39. Ellis, *Polynesian Researches*, 436

40. Ibid.

41. Ibid.

42. Bolingbroke, *The Works of the Late Right Honourable Henry St. John, Lord Viscount Bolingbroke*, vol. 7 (London, 1809), 493–99.

43. Gilbert Stuart, "Of marriage and modesty among the ancient Germans," *American Museum; or, Universal Magazine*, March 1792, 99.

44. Morgan, *Systems*, 492–93.

45. On the relationship between the liberal subject and genealogical society, with attention paid to Morgan, see Elizabeth Povinelli, *Empire of Love: Toward a Theory of Intimacy, Genealogy, and Carnality* (Durham, N.C.: Duke University Press, 2006), 216–17.

Appendix: The Theoretical Life of the Incest Prohibition

1. This is not a comprehensive accounting, by any means. In fact, my aim here is to suggest the manner in which a genealogy of the incest prohibition that rests on a wide and diffuse archive forces a revision of theoretical accounts *and* the manner in which an archive of the incest prohibition is always already mediated by and informed by this theoretical apparatus. So this is neither an full accounting of theories of the incest prohibition (one could imagine a fuller account that addresses Durkheim, Engels, Malinowski, Deleuze and Guattari, Rubin, and sociobiology) nor a full accounting of those figures—Freud, Lévi-Strauss, Lacan, and Butler—who are addressed in the following pages.

2. David S. Schneider, *A Critique of the Study of Kinship* (Ann arbor: University of Michigan Press, 1984), 175. For work that attempts to come to terms with kinship studies in the wake of Schneider's critique and have influence my approach, see Sarah Franklin and Susan McKinnon, eds., *Relative Values: Reconfiguring Kinship Studies* (Durham, N.C.: Duke University Press, 2001); Michael G. Peletz, "Kinship Studies in Late Twentieth-Century Anthropology," *Annual Review of Anthropology* 24 (1995), 343–72.

3. Arthur P. Wolf and William H. Durham, *Inbreeding, Incest, and the Incest Taboo: The State of Knowledge at the Turn of the Century* (Stanford, Calif.: Stanford University Press, 2004).

4. Edward Westermarck, *The History of Human Marriage*, vol. 1([1891]; repr., New York: Allerton, 1922), 439.

5. See, for example, Wolf and Durham, *Inbreeding*; Joseph Shepher, *Incest: A Biosocial View* (New York: Academic Press, 1983).

6. Françoise Hérritier, *Two Sisters and Their Mother: The Anthropology of Incest*, trans. Jeanine Herman (New York: Zone Books, 1999), 11, 26. For an alternative and more persuasive reading of bodily fluids and incest, see Julia Kristeva, *Powers of Horror: An Essay on Abjection*, trans. Leon S. Roudiez (New York: Columbia University Press, 1982).

7. Hérritier, *Two Sisters*, 316.

8. This is not to say that there is a complete void on this subject. Gillian Harkins has argued for the means by which the conflation of incest and pedophilia in the late twentieth century facilitated the workings of the disciplinary state under neoliberalism. See Harkins, *Everybody's Family Romance: Reading Incest in Neoliberal America* (Minneapolis: University of Minnesota Press, 2009).

9. This has been the method of some historical work on incest. See, for instance, Linda Gordon, *Heroes of Their Own Lives: The Politics and History of Family Violence, Boston, 1880–1960* (New York: Penguin Books, 1988), 207–9; Keith Hopkins, "Brother-Sister Marriage in Roman Egypt," *Comparative Studies in Society and History* 22, no. 3 (July 1980), 303. Gordon's book should not, by any means, be dismissed on account of this. Its aim is not to engage with the incest prohibition—I simply mention it as an influential book that explicitly rejects anthropology and psychoanalysis in its accounts of the prohibition. Other work in American history on incest reifies the category by evading the prohibition. See, for example, Lynn Sacco, *Unspeakable: Father-Daughter Incest in American History* (Baltimore: Johns Hopkins University Press, 2009). Much of the history of incest in the nineteenth-century United States addresses it as inherently family violence. See, for instance, Elizabeth Pleck, *Domestic Tyranny: The Making of American Social Policy Against Family Violence from Colonial Times to the Present* (Urbana-Champaign: University of Illinois Press, 2004); Peter Bardaglio, "'An Outrage upon Nature': Incest and the Law in the Nineteenth-Century South," in *In Joy and In Sorrow: Women, Family, and Marriage in the Victorian South, 1830–1900* (New York: Oxford University Press, 1992), 32–51; Irene Quenzler Brown and Richard Brown, *The Hanging of Ephraim Wheeler: A Story of Rape, Incest, and Justice in Early America* (Cambridge, Mass.: Harvard University Press, 2005). The problem is not that they focus on incest as family violence, but that when this is done, the category of incest is reduced to family violence.

10. "John Borneman, "Incest, the Child, and the Despotic Father," *Current Anthropology* 53, no. 2 (April 2012), 181.

11. Claude Lévi-Strauss, *The Elementary Structures of Kinship*, trans. James Harle Bell, John Richard von Sturmer, and Rodney Needham (Boston: Beacon Press, 1969), 12.

12. Ibid., 24–25.

13. Gayle Rubin's indispensable critique of Lévi-Strauss, which undercuts much of the patriarchal assumptions of a universal kinship system organized around the exchange of women, remains the foremost example. One can see this problem throughout the text, but perhaps nowhere more forcefully than when he equates

women and words. "What does this mean, except that women themselves are treated as signs, which are *misused* when not put to the use reserved for signs, which is to be communicated? . . . In contrast to words, which have wholly become signs, woman has remained at once a sign and a value. This explains why the relations between the sexes have preserved that affective richness, ardour and mystery which doubtless originally permeated the entire universe of human communications." Lévi-Strauss, *Elementary Structures*, 496. For the critique, see Rubin, "The Traffic in Women: Notes on the 'Political Economy' of Sex," in Rayna R. Reiter, ed. *Toward an Anthropology of Women* (New York: Monthly Review Press, 1975), 157–210.

14. Sigmund Freud, *Three Essays on the Theory of Sexuality* (1905; repr., New York: Basic Books, 2000), 91.

15. Ibid.

16. Ibid. On the association of cannibalistic tendencies with incestuous family, see Chapter 1.

17. Sigmund Freud, *Totem and Taboo: Some Points of Agreement Between the Mental Lives of Savages and Neurotics* (New York: W. W. Norton, 1989), 4.

18. On the way in which race structures Freud's account of incest, sexuality, the "primitive" and the "civilized," see David L. Eng, *Racial Castration: Managing Masculinity in Asian America* (Durham, N.C.: Duke University Press, 2001), 6–10. In the Epilogue I deal with Lewis Henry Morgan's ethnographic account of incest.

19. Freud, *Totem and Taboo*, 24.

20. And as Freud suggests in his essay on fetishism, this is a desire for a lost object that never quite existed. The fetish "is not a substitute for any penis, but for a particular and quite special penis that had been extremely important in early childhood but had later been lost. . . . The fetish is a substitute for the woman's (the mother's) penis that the little boy once believed in and—for reasons familiar to us—does not want to give up." Sigmund Freud, "Fetishism," *The Standard Edition of the Complete Psychological Works of Sigmund Freud*, vol. 21, trans. James Strachey (London: Hogarth Press, 1986), 152–53.

21. Jacques Lacan, *The Seminar of Jacques Lacan, Book VII: The Ethics of Psychoanalysis, 1959–1960*, trans. Dennis Porter (New York: W. W. Norton, 1992), 67.

22. Ibid., 70.

23. Joan W. Scott, *The Fantasy of Feminist History* (Durham, N.C.: Duke University Press, 2011), 20–21; see also Charles Shepherdson, "History and the Real: Foucault with Lacan," in *Vital Signs: Nature, Culture, Psychoanalysis* (New York: Routledge, 2000), 153–86. Along with Scott (whose work is oriented more historically, or genealogically), Shepherdson provides a compelling argument for the critical compatibility of Lacanian psychoanalysis and Foucauldian genealogy.

24. Judith Butler, *Gender Trouble: Feminism and the Subversion of Identity* (New York: Routledge, 1990), 67.

25. As Camille Robcis notes, Lévi-Strauss was acutely aware of this structural condition and it is what underwrote his rejection of historical explanations of the

prohibition. See Robcis, *The Law of Kinship: Anthropology, Psychoanalysis, and the Family in France* (Ithaca, N.Y.: Cornell University Press, 2013), 78–85.

26. Butler, *Gender Trouble*, 64.

27. Ibid., 65.

28. Ibid., 67.

Index

Acknowledgments

More than once I thought this book would never be completed; now that it is I can offer thanks one more time to all those people who patiently tolerated my desire to talk about incest.

Thankfully, in this age of austerity in higher education, the research and writing of this book have been generously funded. For that I would like to thank the Barra Foundation; the University of South Florida College of Arts and Science, for support through a Creative Scholarship Grant; Department of History at the University of South Florida; the Center for Historical Analysis and Department of History at Rutgers University; and the School of Social Science at the Institute for Advanced Study.

Also important have been the various networks of people who have supported me through the example of their scholarship, their patience in reading the manuscript, and their willingness to discuss the various ideas that make up this book. This support started in graduate school, where the Department of History at Rutgers University provided a warm and intellectually challenging environment to develop the ideas here. There I especially thank Jim Livingston, whose example even when I was an undergraduate was what prompted me even to ponder graduate school at all. Nancy Hewitt supported me and this project from the beginning with sympathetic encouragement and the kind of insightful criticism that we all hope for. In addition I would like to thank Herman Bennett, Ann Fabian, and Temma Kaplan for the time they spent supporting me while at Rutgers. Having now been out in the wider world of academia for a while, I have come to appreciate even more just how intellectually generous and expansive the history department at Rutgers was, and I am truly grateful for it.

More than anyone else, Joan Scott has been at the center of my intellectual life since the very beginning of graduate school, when she saw something (or at least I think she saw something) in a relatively unread master's student and encouraged me to continue on for a doctorate. Since then she has read nearly every word I have written, always supportively pushing me to produce something better. She has been a model of critique and politically engaged scholarship, and I hope this book comes close to the example she has set for me.

Two groups in particular—the scholars at the McNeil Center for Early American Studies and the my coeditors at *History of the Present*—made this book much stronger than it would ever have been. When Dan Richter called informing me that I would be a postdoctoral fellow at the McNeil Center at the University of Pennsylvania, I was both elated and apprehensive. By the end of my tenure there, my book was immeasurably better as a result of the intellectual vibrancy of the center and the wider community at Penn. Being afforded the time to research and write with so many other scholars working on the same period is, I have realized, a rare treat. And Dan has created an environment in which one is always being challenged to produce better work, through both the more formal events and the informal conversations that are the life of the center. In that spirit I would like to thank Dan, Amy Baxter-Bellamy, Irene Cheng, Sean Harvey, Hunt Howell, Carrie Hyde, Dawn Peterson, Joe Rezek, Elena Schneider, Christina Snyder, and Megan Walsh.

At the same time that I was at the McNeil Center I started another project only tangentially related to my book and not related at all to early American studies. That project resulted in a journal devoted to critical history, *History of the Present*. Too often, I think, historians eschew the critical and theoretical in favor of an empirical fantasy. So I would like to thank my coeditors—Andrew Aisenberg, Ben Kafka, Sylvia Schafer, Joan Scott, and Mrinalini Sinha—for being so wonderful to work with and reminding me that there is a community of like-minded historians out there. Their critical and political commitments are models of historical practice, and it was always nice to have ideal readers in my head as I brought the book to completion.

The University of South Florida has proved a welcome place to begin my career. My department chair, Fraser Ottanelli, has been unflaggingly supportive of my career, bending over backward to make sure that I (and my colleagues) received as much support as possible in this age of limited funds. I am particularly grateful for conversations and friendship with Sari Altschuler, Giovanna Benadusi, Barbara Berglund, Andy Berish, Maria Cizmic, Scott Ferguson, Darcie Fontaine, Julia Irwin, Phil Levy, Fraser Ottanelli, Steve Prince, Darcie Fontaine, and Amy Rust.

Projects like this, which develop slowly over a long period of time, bene-fit as much from conversations as they do from incessant writing. For conversations that helped me refine the ideas here, even when the conversa-tions were not directly about the book, I want to thank Jordan Stein, Gillian Harkins, Nancy Bentley, Judith Surkis, Camille Robcis, Jen Manion, and Jim Downs, and Cathy Kelly. Jen Manion deserves extra thanks for coming up with the title of the book. Sandrine Sanos gets special mention—she has discussed this, politics, and academics and has indulged my love of gossip since we met a decade ago. Our conversations have been one of the great joys of my academic life.

Audiences and panelists at conferences also provided valuable feedback along the way, so I thank those at the meetings of the American Historical Association, the American Studies Association, the Organization of Ameri-can Historians, the Society for the History of the Early American Republic, Connecticut College, Temple University, the University of South Florida, and the McNeil Center. In addition, I would like to thank all the partici-pants at the "Family Ties" conference that Camille Robcis organized at Cornell University in 2010.

The University of Pennsylvania Press has been wonderful to work with and Bob Lockhart deserves an entire acknowledgments section. Bob took an interest in this project from the first time he heard me tell him about it after Tom Sugrue introduced us in 2007. I don't think I was aware of just how fortunate I was to be working with Bob until years later. Bob has consistently offered a sympathetic and critical voice that made the book better. Indeed, Bob taught me how to think of my writings on this topic as a unified book. He has been patient with my sometimes slow pace, and then, when I needed things to proceed quickly, he moved everything along. It has been a pleasure to work with him on this book. Kathy Brown read the manuscript as series editor for the press, and I couldn't have asked for a better reader. The book is better for her critically engaged reading. Two anonymous readers for the press offered timely and important critiques of the manuscript. Noreen O'Connor-Abel managed the final stages of publi-cation with expert attention and patience and Kathleen Kageff was a terrific copyeditor.

Two chapters appeared in earlier versions as articles. I would like to thank the University of Illinois Press for permission to reprint parts of Chapter 1, which were originally published as "Liberalism's Incestuous Sub-ject: Private and Public Sex in the Nineteenth-Century United States," *His-tory of the Present: A Journal of Critical History* 1, no. 1 (Summer 2011), 31–58.

I would like to thank the University of Pennsylvania Press for permission to reprint parts of Chapter 2, which appeared in " 'every family become a school of abominable impurity;" Incest and Theology in the Early Republic," *Journal of the Early Republic* 30, no. 3 (Fall 2010), 413–42.

Thanking one's family after having spent ten years thinking about the incestuous structure of the bourgeois family is a somewhat bizarre exercise. My love for them exceeds the capacities of language. Olivia and Miles did not contribute to the writing of this book; indeed, it would have been done years ago had they not been around. But their presence in my life has sustained me through this process. Finally, Gena, this book is for you. It is done now, and at least for a little while, you won't have to hear me say that I am almost done with the book. You have put up with this for so many years, I hope these words can begin to show my thanks and love.